# More Praise for *Lessons from the Light*

"If any one person can claim to be an authority on near-death experiences without having had one, that person must surely be Kenneth Ring. . . . And more importantly, no other researcher has been able to transmit to the rest of us the true meaning and impact of near-death phenomena for the planet."

> **Bruce Greyson, M.D.**, Past-President of the International
> Association for Near Death Studies (IANDS)

"Arguably, the best book yet on the near-death experience."

> **Michael Grosso, Ph.D.**, Author of *Experiencing the Next*
> *World Now* and *Soulmaking*

"A magnificent achievement! For while Ring is indeed one of the leading scholars in the field, he now brings in his heart and shows those of us who haven't had an NDE how to use the inspiration of NDEs to change our lives."

> **Charles T. Tart, Ph.D.**, Professor Emeritus of Psychology,
> University of California, Davis; Author of *Altered States*
> *of Consciousness and Waking Up*

"The capstone of Kenneth Ring's career, this book is the distillation of all that death can teach the living. Ring's loving voice turns harrowing and resplendent near-death stories never published before into a practical guide that motivates through its sheer heart-gripping beauty . . . No reader will ever be able to think of life in the same way again after reading this book!"

> **Jenny Wade, Ph.D.**, Author of *Changes of Mind: A Holonomic*
> *Theory of the Evolution of Consciousness*

"*Lessons from the Light* opens the last door each of us will face in our lifetime. With clarity, wit, and crisp prose, it brings us to the cutting edge of what promises to be the most important discovery ever made in psychobiology—what truly happens after death."

> **Fred Alan Wolf, Ph.D.**, Author of *The Spiritual Universe* and
> *Taking the Quantum Leap*

"Inspiring and moving! An important, easy-to-read summation of the life-altering impact of NDEs on those who have had or heard about them."

> **Marilyn Webb**, Former Editor-in-Chief of *Psychology Today*;
> Author of *The Good Death*

"An extraordinary book in many ways—it is profoundly wise, filled with insight into the deepest aspects of human nature and the cosmos, it is beautifully written, making it a pleasure to read, and it is eminently practical for people who seek personal growth by offering the benefits of a near-death experience to readers who have not had an NDE."

> **John White, M.A.T.**, Former Director of Education, The Institute of
> Noetic Science; Editor of *What Is Enlightenment?*

"Unquestionably the most important book on the subject of near-death experience since Moody's *Life After Life*."

> **Ian Wilson**, Author of *The After Death Experience*

# Lessons *from the* Light

# *Lessons* *from the* *Light*

## What we can learn from the near-death experience

## Kenneth Ring, Ph.D.
### and Evelyn Elsaesser Valarino

Moment Point Press
Needham, Massachusetts

Moment Point Press, Inc.
P.O. Box 920287
Needham, MA 02492
www.momentpoint.com

Lessons from the Light: What We Can Learn
from the Near-Death Experience
Copyright © 1998, 2006 by Kenneth Ring
First Moment Point Press Paperback Edition, 2000
Published by arrangment with Perseus Books, a member of the
Perseus Books Group, Cambridge, Massachusetts.
Original hardcover edition published by Insight Books
(a division of Plenum Publishing Corporation).

Cover photography: DAJ / Getty Images
Cover design: Kathryn Sky-Peck
Printing: Maple-Vail
Distribution: Red Wheel Weiser

Library of Congress Cataloging-in-Publication Data

Ring, Kenneth.
    Lessons from the light : what we can learn from the near-death experience /
  Kenneth Ring and Evelyn Elsaesser Valarino.
      p. cm.
    Originally published: New York : Insight Books, c1998.
    Includes bibliographical references and index.
    ISBN 1-930491-11-5  (alk. paper)
    1. Near-death experiences--Case studies. 2. Spiritual life.  I. Elsaesser Valarino,
  Evelyn. II. Title.


BF1045.N4 R556 2000
133.9'01'3--dc21                                                    99-059665

ISBN 10: 1-930491-11-5
ISBN 13: 978-1-930491-11-3

Printed in the United States of America

10 9 8 7 6 5 4 3 2

Printed on partially recycled acid-free paper

To the dozens of near-death experiencers who have contributed to this book and the many hundreds who have contributed, immeasurably, to my life.

# Contents

# Foreword 2006
## Caroline Myss, Ph.D.

I consider it a pleasure for several reasons to write the foreword to Ken Ring's brilliant work on near-death experiences. First, Ken and I have been friends since 1983, and he introduced me to the field of near-death studies. Through him, I had the first of what would become years of encounters with individuals who had near-death experiences, not only in this country, but eventually all over the world as I began to lecture abroad in numerous countries. I learned that people everywhere were eager to share their NDEs, not just because of the phenomenon itself, but because of the transformation of the spirit that inevitably followed the profound act of dying, encountering the light of the Divine, reviewing the quality of one's life, and then being directly told to return to your life because your "work" in this lifetime is not yet complete.

After years of working with people in the field of human consciousness and spirituality, I know all too well that there is a fundamental yearning within people for an intimate relationship with the Sacred. There is also a fundamental fear of such intimacy, a fear that is rooted in a combination of an inability to surrender to the unknown and an inability to relinquish control over the illusion that we are in charge of the events of our life. One near-death experience and those two roadblocks are shattered in an instant, bypassing the armed guard called "reason" that stands at the gates of the mind that tells us, "Maybe there is a God but maybe there isn't. But if there is a God, let us approach this Being with due caution and intellectual prowess. Let us approach the 'mind of God' through the rational mind because in that way, we stand half a chance of maintaining control over our small piece of real estate here on earth." People have long believed that it is best to approach this God of ours with caution lest the winds of chaos begin blowing in the direction of our lives. Truth be told, we have far more faith in our superstitions about God than in any benevolent Divine Being.

"Near-deathers," as I have heard Ken lovingly refer to individuals who have had near-death experiences, long to share their experiences in part because they are indeed phenomenal, but also because as a result of their experiences, they are liberated from the near-schizophrenic fear that burdens so many on the spiritual path: find God—fear God, find God—fear God. As a result of their experience, they burst through that spiritual pathology and they found God. Indeed, they "experienced" God, past the intellectual babble about what God is and isn't and what God "thinks" and "doesn't think." They literally went right to the source, only to discover, as they all report, that God apparently doesn't "think" at all. Reports from near-deathers seem to indicate that upon death we are met with an indescribable sensation of unconditional love.

In every way, the near-death experience is a new brand of mystical encounter with the Divine. Unlike the classic mystical experience that descends upon the individual devoted to contemplation and silence, the NDE occurs as a result of a trauma, an accident, or an illness. It is trans-religion, trans-vegetarian, trans-everything. I know one man personally who was a mercenary who was "on his way to work one day," meaning he was off to shoot three people, when he had an accident and had a near-death experience. Suddenly he was out of his body and surrounded by the individuals he had murdered, all of whom told him he had to stop immediately. Needless to say, he did. But let me add, the message was delivered with compassion and not the fires of hell. Today he obviously leads a very different life.

As a mystical experience, the near-death experience is yet another expression of how we have arrived at a point in our spiritual evolution at which we are "mystics without monasteries." We are no longer choosing spiritual paths as such but rather we are "being called." No one "chooses" a near-death experience. From a mystical perspective, it can be considered a "calling," a directive from the Divine giving an individual a profound experience of illumination that results in a complete transformation of the senses and an awakening of the soul's authority within one's consciousness. Such a transformation reorders a person's life compass, shifting it from an externally focused instrument to an internally focused one in which values such as service to others is recognized as a true command from God.

The stories and wisdom contained in Lessons from the Light are, for me, a combination of hope and contemporary mystical wisdom. I know these stories are authentic and that the experiences of what comes after this life are real. But perhaps more importantly than waiting until we die to appreciate this wisdom, the true richness of the experiences of these individuals and Ken's research provide spiritual reasons to believe your life has meaning now. Everything you do, say, think, feel, and every action you initiate matters. Every relationship is significant and every choice you make, no matter how small, has enormous consequences. No matter how your day begins, by nightfall, you can be sure you have made at least 100 choices and each one has significantly changed your life, your body, your blood pressure, your friendships, your weight, your work, your finances, and the quality of your life—and the lives of countless individuals, most of whom you will never meet. Not only that, you have no idea how you have influenced your next day, next week, and next month. And each choice—each one—is noted by heaven, as is every prayer. That truth is as soft in the soul as knowing we never lose our loved ones and that the Divine is truly a Being of compassionate love.

This book is a treasure that validates all that is good about living a blessed, grateful, and conscious life. And while it is true that living a conscious life is difficult, knowing that every choice we make genuinely matters to others and ourselves makes the higher choice worth the effort. It is comforting to know, as NDEs suggest, how closely guided we are every moment of our lives. That may seem incomprehensible and even doubtful during times of despair, but such is the nature of mystical truth. It is incomprehensible and ultimately can only be appreciated through faith.

# Foreword 1998
## Bruce Greyson, M.D.

If any one person can claim to be an authority on near-death experiences (NDEs) without having had one, that person must surely be Kenneth Ring. After Raymond Moody sowed the seeds of modern near-death research by coining the term "NDE" in his 1975 *Life after Life*, it was Ken who watered and nurtured them till they grew into a self-sustaining phenomenon. It was Ken who was the first president of that band of scattered researchers who formed the International Association for Near-Death Studies (IANDS), 20 years ago. It was Ken's office at the University of Connecticut that housed the organization's volunteers, phones, and growing archives for its precarious first decade. And it was Ken who founded the only scholarly journal for near-death studies and organized symposia on NDEs at annual meetings of mainstream academic societies.

If anyone has interviewed more NDErs than Ken—and I don't know that anyone has—then surely no one has done it with as much depth, open-mindedness, and insight as he. For many years, Ken's home was known to experiencers across the country as "The Near-Death Hotel," where itinerant NDErs trying to rediscover their place in this world could, and did, "drop by" and end up staying, however long it took. And each one to whom Ken opened his home in return opened his or her heart and added to Ken's growing comprehension of the true essence of the NDE. No other researcher has been able to meld the large scale controlled study with the passionate friendships, the philosophical theories with the intuitive understandings, the command of the scholarly literature with the personal stories. And more importantly, no other researcher has been able to transmit to the rest of us the true meaning and impact of near-death phenomena for our planet.

In 1980, when America was beginning to question the validity of five years of near-death anecdotes, Ken came to our rescue with the first legitimate scientific study of NDEs in his *Life at Death*. Then after four more years of debates as to whether there might be no more to these remarkable phenomena than just a fleeting, if beautiful, hallucination, it was Ken again who, in his *Heading toward Omega*, produced the first comprehensive study of its aftereffects, the profound and long-lasting changes it wreaks on the lives of experiencers. Now, after a quarter century of Amazing Stories From the Brink of Death, after so many talk-show panels and sitcom parodies and neurochemical "explanations" that even Hollywood studios and paperback publishers are getting sated, we find ourselves asking about NDEs, "So what?" And once again it is Ken Ring who guides us toward the answer. And the answer this social scientist has come up with is a message of meaning, of purpose, and of love—what one might expect more from a theologian than from a scientist.

Ken dares to write frankly in these pages about the meaning of NDEs, inferring teleological conclusions from his empirical studies. In violating the scientistic taboo against mentioning such concepts as meaning and purpose, Ken honestly confronts a topic most scientists pretend plays no role in their thinking. As the biologist Ernest William von Brück put it more than a hundred years ago, "Teleology is a lady without whom no biologist can live. Yet he is ashamed to show himself with her in public." In raising these issues, Ken also makes us question the proper role of science and scientists in the exploration of the universe—and of the proper role of romance in the practice of science. Do scientists ply their trade just to enhance our ability to mold or control our environment, or is it to help us unravel the questions of meaning and purpose in the universe? The autobiographical writings of our greatest scientists make it clear that what motivates them to do science is in fact the quest for meaning.

While Ken's previous books focused on NDErs, this one speaks to the nonexperiencer, to those of us who feel our lives and our society could be enhanced by sharing in the fruits of the NDE. Ken presents practical lessons he has learned from NDErs and guides the reader through experiential exercises in straightforward language, with ample support both from evidence from NDErs' lives and from the scholarly literature. The consistent psychological changes that he had previously documented in

NDErs, he argues here, are achievable by all of us. Indeed, he argues, the true test of the value of whatever wisdom NDErs acquire is in its translation into everyday life. Most of us are familiar with the truisms of the NDE, and many of us give lip service to them: that death is not fearsome, that life continues beyond, that love is more important than material possessions, that everything happens for a reason. But what would we be like, what would the world be like, if we all really lived according to these precepts, if they were not mere bromides for us but living truths?

Can reading this book possibly help? Can readers really acquire the fruits of the NDE without actually experiencing one? Ken argues persuasively that they can, and he supports that belief with evidence from the classes he taught on NDEs at the University of Connecticut, and from the late Charles Flynn's "Love Project" for his students at Miami University of Ohio. As Ken has documented, learning about NDEs and their effects can indeed inspire similar changes in others. He writes of these effects as a "benign virus" that one can catch from NDErs—or from others similarly infected. I have met some of his students, and can attest to the fact they had indeed caught the NDE virus and were profoundly and permanently changed by it. But for you, the reader, this book is proof in itself that one can be transformed by learning about NDEs. This book is a testament to Ken's own transformation, his selfless gift to humanity. Since catching the benign virus of the NDE, Ken has become one of those scientists who are no longer ashamed to show themselves in public with their mistress. He argues here that the lessons from the light are not meant for NDErs alone, but are given to experiencers so that they can come back and infect others with this virus.

Ken's thesis has not been as warmly received as one might expect, even from theologians for whom it should be a familiar one. Some of his critics have warned that the allure of NDEs is that they compete with Biblical religion, that they point the way toward a moral code and spirituality more consistent than our Judeo-Christian tradition is with America's New Age mentality. But a funny thing happened on the way to the New Age: The road took a subtle turn that led us back home to our roots, to the Golden Rule that "all things whatsoever ye would that men should do unto you, do ye even so unto them" (Matthew 7:12), and to Jesus' admonition that "inasmuch as ye have done it unto to least of these my brethren, ye have done it unto me" (Matthew 25:40).

Some theologians have argued that because NDEs tend to replace the Grim Reaper with the Being of Light as the embodiment of death—a

Being of Light that seems to love born-again Christians, practicing Buddhists, and atheistic sinners unconditionally—their alluring visions must be Satanic rather than divine. How can we discern whether NDErs are truly blessed by divine light or deceived by the Prince of Darkness? No less an authority than Jesus gave us the methodology when he said, "By their fruits ye shall know them" (Matthew 7:20). As Ken shows us so eloquently in this book, the fruits of the NDE are compassion, humility, honesty, altruism, and love even for those who appear unlovable.

But if NDEs merely reinforce Biblical precepts, why do we need them? What do they—and this book—add to the message of the Gospels? Quite simply, it is the difference between hearing the word and experiencing it firsthand. For NDErs, the Golden Rule is no longer just a commandment one is taught to obey, but rather an indisputable law of nature, as inevitable as gravity. They know it is the way the universe works because they have experienced it firsthand in suffering directly the effects of their actions on others. Though they do not feel punished or judged for their prior misdeeds, they do receive back as part of their life review everything they have ever given out, measure for measure.

Theologians of a different stripe have decried NDEs for holding out the false promise of what Dietrich Bonhoeffer called "cheap grace," the unconditional foregiveness of sins without any required contrition. "Cheap grace," wrote Bonhoeffer in *The Cost of Discipleship*, "is the deadly enemy of the Church." But is that in fact what NDEs promise, or is that a misreading of its message? The promise of "cheap grace" may well be part of what has attracted to the NDE much of the public fascination with the phenomenon, but in reality the grace that is bestowed upon NDErs comes hand in hand with a very costly discipleship. The unconditional love NDErs report in their experiences does not by any means gloss over their sins or excuse their future behavior. Quite to the contrary, NDErs experience firsthand in their NDEs the painful consequences of their sinful behavior, and return to earthly life as confirmed disciples, who understand from their own experience that their behavior does indeed matter, far more than they could have imagined. NDErs do not come back with a sense that they are perfect beings as they are now, but rather with the firsthand knowledge of how they must act to work toward perfection. They return not to bask in the reflected glory of amazing grace, but committed to living the Golden Rule and carrying out the work of a higher power, often at great emotional, as well as material, sacrifice. There is nothing cheap about this grace. It is, indeed, the costly grace that Bonhoeffer wrote is inseparable from discipleship. Far from encouraging indiscriminate behavior, the unconditional love NDErs experience confers on them the self-esteem, courage, and self-knowledge to bring about the kind of life changes demanded of disciples.

But if NDEs do not sell cheap grace, then does this book? Reading this book may be less hazardous than coming close to death or inducing a cardiac arrest, as the medical students did in the movie "Flatliners," but is not without danger. Its purpose is to change you, and to inspire you to change your world; and those are neither easy nor safe endeavors. Bonhoeffer was right that true grace cannot come cheaply. What Ken offers in this book is not an easy road to grace but rather a map of discipleship, a plot of the course we must follow to work toward grace. Whether you choose to take that course is up to you, and it is not by any means an easy one. But as Ken shows in these pages, it comes highly recommended.

Ken might have stopped after his three descriptive books on NDEs, and still be acknowledged as our foremost scientific authority on the subject. But he did not stop there, because he would have failed to fulfill his responsibility. The purpose of his scientific explorations of NDEs—indeed, the purpose of all scientific exploration—is to lay the groundwork for plausible speculation about meaning and purpose. Ken, having been infected by his benign virus and having become what he calls a "near-death experiencer, once removed," was driven to discipleship. As surely as his NDEr friends and research subjects were given a great gift in their experiences, and as surely as they in turn gave a great gift to Ken, so too does Ken now give to you what he has received. This book is his contribution to the work of a higher power. It is Ken's hope, and mine, that every reader of this book will become similarly infected.

# *Acknowledgments*

Just as a film is always more than a director's vision, so a book inevitably has multiple authors, despite what the title page suggests. Here is where I introduce them to you and thank them for what they have contributed to the book you are about to read.

During the first stage of its composition, when I was still a professor at the University of Connecticut, I was particularly indebted to two good friends of mine, Lucienne Levy and Sharon Cooper, both of whom spent a great deal of time discussing the book's contents with me as well as doing superb editorial work to clarify the expression of my ideas. In a way, that part of the book, effectively Chapters One through Three and Five through Eight, really represents a joint partnership among the three of us and very much reflects something of a collective effort. Also helpful to me at this time were conversations I had about the book with two other friends, Gary Greenberg and Susan Powers.

After I moved to California, where I eventually resumed work on the book, other persons came along with me, so to speak, to provide assistance with the writing of this book. Foremost among them was my longtime friend and colleague, Evelyn Elsaesser Valarino, who helped me in innumerable ways, including providing me with a crucial entrée to my original publisher. Evelyn also assisted me by sifting through and selecting many documents I drew on for this book. Even though the writing in this book is my own, this book, especially in its final chapters, was a fully collaborative effort between Evelyn and me, and there is absolutely no way I could ever have written it without Evelyn's support, both logistical and emotional. In short, without her, you would not be holding this book in your hands right now. My debt to her is immense.

In addition, I would like to express my appreciation here for the assistance of my friend, Steve Tomsik, who makes more than one appearance in this book himself, in providing me with certain case material and for helping Evelyn and me compile information for the appendix. Other California friends and colleagues were important in other ways, particularly through either reading portions of the text or in discussing the book with me as it was progressing toward completion. In this regard, I would like to acknowledge the contributions of Jenny Wade, Seymour Boorstein, Sukie Miller, and Carolyn Talmadge.

Lastly, thanks must go to my original editor, Joanna Lawrence, always a fast E-mail near, however far away she was in London. Joanna was a delight to work with as much for her unfailing good humor as for her expertise in rooting out my gaucheries and other infelicities from the text, and in attending to all the details necessary to turn this manuscript into a presentable book.

# Introduction:
# Living and Dying in the Light
# of the Near-Death Experience

In the years since the 1975 publication of Raymond Moody's ground-breaking book, *Life After Life*, much of the world has become familiar, at least superficially, with the phenomenon Moody labeled the near-death experience (NDE). Because of the enormous public interest that was generated by his book, the media were quick to capitalize on its success, and a veritable barrage of talk shows, documentaries, and magazine and newspaper articles on the subject followed in short order. As a result, virtually everyone, it seems, is now generally familiar with the common testimony of near-death experiencers (NDErs) and their assurance that there is indeed "light at the end of the tunnel." The widespread acceptance of these accounts of what it is like to die has certainly brought a great deal of hope and comfort to uncounted millions. And can anyone doubt that, because of all we have learned from these near-death survivors as their stories have been fanned through the media and over the Internet to all corners of the globe, we have come to look at the hitherto frightening face of death anew, only to recognize it now as the image of the Beloved?

Of course, it isn't just the media that have fastened onto these inspiring NDE narratives. Researchers like myself have been doing the same thing for years as we have chronicled these accounts, published our statistics and our charts, and striven to understand and explain these extraordinary events. Starting out in this field in 1977, in the immediate aftermath of reading Raymond Moody's book, I was mainly curious to determine for myself whether these astonishing reports were on the level. But when I started hearing exactly the same kind of stories from my interviewees that Moody had related in *Life After Life*, I became charged with a different desire—I wanted to make it evident to other scientists and scholars that there was indeed a phenomenon here that merited their study and to urge them to investigate it themselves. Of course, others were already on the same track, and by the time my first NDE book, *Life at Death*, was published in 1980, research to authenticate the NDE was well underway. As scores of researchers from the United States and many other countries published their findings over the next decade, it became abundantly clear that the NDE, as Moody had originally delineated it, was a commonly reported experience and one that had profound and largely very consistent effects on the lives of those who survived it. What was controversial about the NDE was *what to make of it* and how, if at all, to explain it. That controversy continues to this day, but one thing about the NDE is incontrovertible: It happens. Many thousands of persons who have had NDEs have now been interviewed or otherwise studied by researchers, and polls indicate that millions of individuals have probably had NDEs.[1]

After the basic configuration of the NDE had been established, a great deal of the research that was then conducted had to do with documenting the aftereffects of NDEs, and there have now been many studies in several countries dealing with the changes that follow in the wake of these experiences.[2] There were also books, such as Phyllis Atwater's *Coming Back to Life* and Barbara Harris's *Spiritual Awakenings*, that concentrated on the problems that near-death experiencers (NDErs) may have in readjusting to life following their physical recovery. In any case, whether this research was concerned with the nature of the NDE itself or the difficulties besetting NDErs afterward, the focus was usually and often exclusively on the lives and experiences of the NDErs themselves. That emphasis was understandable enough, but it gradually became clear that whereas millions of persons may have had NDEs, many millions more who have become interested in the subject have not. Were such persons to remain simply an audience for the luminous NDErs? Where was the literature that would speak to the hunger of the *non-experiencer* to learn and profit from the experiences of the NDEr?

This book is an effort to place exactly this kind of information at the disposal of its readers by presenting in clear language the practical lessons for living and dying that are to be found from the study of NDEs. For example, we now know that the NDE tends to bring about lasting changes in personal values and beliefs—NDErs appreciate life more fully, experience increased feelings of self-worth, have a more compassionate regard for others and indeed for all life, develop a heightened ecological sensitivity, and report a decrease in purely materialistic and self-seeking values. Their religious orientation tends to change, too, and becomes more universalistic, inclusive and spiritual in its expression. In most instances, moreover, the fear of death is completely extinguished and a deep-rooted conviction, based on their direct experience, that some form of life after death awaits us becomes unshakable and a source of enormous comfort. In addition, many NDErs say they come to develop powers of higher sense perception, increased psychic ability and intuitive awareness and even the gift of healing. In short, the NDE seems to unleash normally dormant aspects of the human potential for higher consciousness and to increase one's capacity to relate more sensitively to other persons and the world at large.

The NDE, then, appears to promote the emergence of a type of functioning suggestive of the full human potential that is presumably the birthright of all of us. In a phrase, whenever the blessings of the NDE are fused properly into one's life, the individual comes to exemplify what a highly developed person would be and act like. Indeed, as I have tried to suggest in my earlier books, especially *Heading Toward Omega* and *The Omega Project*, NDErs—and others who have undergone similar awakenings by other means—may be the harbingers of humanity's evolution toward higher consciousness. However, even if this is true, it is clearly not enough to wait passively for this evolution to occur. The phenomenon of the NDE, in my view, is not merely an evolutionary catalyst but a *teaching* about life, love and the human potential that all interested persons could draw upon actively now in order to enrich their lives and to hasten their own progress toward enlightenment. This book, therefore, is oriented toward all those who would like to avail themselves of this knowledge, to use it in practical ways in order to live their lives more fully and with a greater awareness of the transcendental possibilities that the moment of death holds for us all.

Most NDErs say that they feel it is their mission to serve others by in some way drawing upon or sharing their experience and its lessons with those who are open to it. In like fashion, this is what this book will attempt to do. In fact, as I will show, there is indeed evidence that merely learning about the NDE has effects similar to those reported by NDErs. This means that the NDE may act like a benign virus. By exposing ourselves to it, we can catch it—that is, we can experience some of the same benefits as do those who actually have the NDE themselves. Therefore, as we hear from those who have had NDEs and understand more clearly just what they have gained from their encounter with the Light, you, too, will have the opportunity to learn and grow as the NDEr has. The aim of this book, then, is simply to help you make these connections for yourself in order to reap the seeds of transformation of the NDE without having nearly to die first to do so.

## PLAN OF THE BOOK

To begin the process of assimilating these NDEs and their implications into your own life, we must begin, of course, with the experience itself. Accordingly, in Chapter One, I want to offer you a sampling of a few selected instances of NDEs so that, if necessary, you can be reminded afresh of their incredible and compelling revelations as well as their power to bring about radical and radically positive changes in the individual's life. These examples, all of which will be drawn from previously unpublished research and represent some of the most exceptional cases I have recently encountered, are meant to furnish you with more than merely inspirational testimony, however. They should also begin to suggest to you the kind of life-changing possibilities that may be in store for you simply by reading and reflecting on the contents of this book.

Next, in Chapter Two, I want to begin to make the case for the authenticity of NDEs based on the latest research in the field so that you can be sure that these experiences are the real thing, and not just some kind of elaborate dream, fantasy or hallucination. In this chapter, I review some of the most persuasive evidence for this proposition, having mainly to do with reports of NDErs in which they appear to see or hear things that they could not possibly perceive through normal means. This body of research leads us naturally in Chapter Three to my own most recent work on NDEs in the blind in which we have been able to show that blind people, *even the congenitally blind,* have visual experiences during their NDEs, some of which pertain to verifiable things of this world (and not just "otherworldly" perceptions).

In Chapter Four, I continue to make the case for the authenticity of the NDE by drawing on a different line of work altogether in the field of near-death studies by presenting some of the evidence dealing with childhood NDEs, concentrating on instances where NDEs have apparently been experienced by exceptionally young children. Finally, in Chapter Five, the last of the chapters concerned with the authenticity issue, we begin to examine the aftereffects of NDEs. Whatever the nature of NDEs may be, there is no doubt that they are real in their effects on people's lives. In this chapter, then, I show that there is a consistent psychological profile that typifies the NDEr afterward. The point of this chapter, however, is to suggest that this common and attractive prototype may be possible for all of us, regardless of whether we have had an NDE or not. What NDErs have become through their encounter with death, we too may be by letting its power work through us vicariously, as well as by *actively* applying the lessons of the NDE to our daily lives.

This brings us to Chapters Six and Seven in which we begin in earnest to make the kind of connections necessary to absorb the implications of the NDE so that this knowledge can be of direct practical value to us. Toward this end, these two chapters consider one of the most remarkable features of the NDE, the life review—that panoramic playback of virtually everything that has ever happened in one's life—together with a number of illustrations of this still under-appreciated aspect of NDEs from interviews with those who have witnessed this astonishing phenomenon themselves. In my experience as a teacher and workshop leader, the lessons to be derived from this facet of the NDE can be dramatic and permanently life-altering for those who take the trouble to reflect on them, and this chapter provides exercises for you to do just that.

Chapter Eight deals with another important lesson of the NDE, that pertaining to self-acceptance, and again I have collected a mass of impressive testimony on the subject whose personal relevance for your own life I will make clear.

Chapter Nine highlights the shift in certain values and beliefs that come about in the wake of the NDE—for example, on the importance (and indeed primacy) of love, service, reverence for life, and on life after death. To make the connections for you personally here, this chapter also presents some of the evidence I alluded to earlier on the impact of information about NDEs on those who haven't had one. I do this, of course, in order to show how pondering and actively using the material I describe in this chapter can be of direct benefit to you by helping to bring about the very same shifts in values, beliefs and behavior reported by NDErs.

At this point, in Chapter Ten, I move into issues having to do with the higher human potentials that seem to be evoked by NDEs, particularly those having to do with the emergence of healing gifts. I give some examples and cite some of the research that suggests that the NDE stimulates the development of healing abilities and also confers a state of expanded mental awareness on the individual. I also discuss the Light as a healing force in its own right and offer some cases in which the NDE seems to have mended broken lives and set them on a course so as to fulfill an individual's initial promise. Because these effects need not be limited to those who have undergone NDEs, a key feature of this chapter is a discussion of how you may use this information to help in understanding the dynamics of illness and promote both physical and spiritual healing in your own life.

Having considered the lessons of the NDE for everyday life and the realization of one's human potential, I next delve into the still deeply unsettling matter of death itself. In fact, however, I mean to argue in

Chapter Eleven that three decades of research on the NDE have helped to bring about an undeniable revisioning of our understanding of the moment of death and, by implication, what may follow it. Images of light, and indeed the oft-mentioned being of light itself, have come increasingly to eclipse the traditional figure of death, the grim reaper, whose forbidding specter has haunted the Western psyche for hundreds of years. Now, the hooded man of the scythe is in full retreat, and those facing their imminent death have instead much more comforting and hopeful notions of death to contemplate—thanks largely to the publicity that NDE research has received ever since its inception in the mid-1970s.

In this chapter, I take a look at how this information has already begun to affect care and preparation of the dying—in nursing homes, hospices, hospitals and chaplains' offices. I also describe new studies dealing with the impact of information about NDEs on senior citizens, the bereaved and those who have received some kind of a terminal diagnosis. In this connection, I draw on a great deal of testimony that has been sent to me by bereaved persons (particularly by mothers who have suffered the loss of a child) and by patients dying of AIDS that demonstrate how incredibly helpful the provision of information about NDEs has been to those who have had an immediate concern with the emotional consequences or threat of death. This chapter also assists you to prepare for your own death by enabling you to eliminate unnecessary fears about what happens at death—just as NDErs themselves have lost their fear of death forever through their own NDEs.

Discussing the preparation for and the event of death itself naturally raises the prospect of what happens following the cessation of all biological function, which is the subject of Chapter Twelve. Although no living person, however wise, can speak with certainty on this question, many NDErs nevertheless speak with great certitude on this point and, as a group, are convinced, almost absolutely, that some kind of post-mortem existence awaits us all. Furthermore, studies have shown that their opinions are contagious and also inspire a greater belief in life after death in those persons who have a chance to listen to the views of NDErs.

From these considerations, it is but a small leap to the issue of the core spiritual and metaphysical teachings that derive from an immersion in the Light of the NDE since, according to NDErs, *all* knowledge is encoded in that Light. Therefore, being in the Light and becoming one with it makes this total knowledge accessible to these experiencers, and through them, to us. A highlight of Chapter Thirteen is a set of previously unpublished cases that represent *full* or *complete* NDEs. Of course, most NDEs in the literature are fragments, however complex, of the experience of dying and don't reveal the whole story. Some cases I have gathered in recent years, on the other hand, suggest that the complete NDE always involves an encounter with a *second* light. These examples are among the most profound and startling of any NDEs that have come my way since beginning my research, and if you can absorb their implications fully, your own faith in the unutterable radiant Love that seems to permeate our universe will be strengthened immeasurably. This chapter, then, represents the pinnacle of knowledge available to the NDEr—the ultimate lessons of the Light.

But this culmination will not represent the conclusion of the book itself. Instead, in Chapter Fourteen, we descend from the sublime splendors of the NDE empyrean to the world of everyday reality where the real test of this NDE-based knowledge is to be found. The theme of this short final chapter, therefore, is that all of us may and must learn from an experience that of necessity can occur only for a minority of persons (however large). Rather than reviewing the insights already provided in this book, this chapter encourages you to make use of specific resources for deepening and internalizing the lessons that were meant to be gleaned in the previous chapters. In a special Appendix to follow, then, further readings, audio cassettes and video tapes, NDE support groups, organizations oriented to NDEs and their implications, conferences, and the names and addresses of NDErs willing to be contacted are all provided toward this end, including all available Internet resources. In all these ways, it is my hope that you will continue to be able to draw on the near-death experience so as to enrich your own life, and that, through your own effort, its benefits will be spread to many others. It is in this manner that humanity's unquenchable yearning for a fully enlightened consciousness and ultimately the reclamation of our endangered planet will be hastened.


## 2006 UPDATE

Judging from the correspondence I have received from readers since the original publication of *Lessons from the Light*, the hope I expressed in my introduction, written ten years ago, has been gratifyingly fulfilled. Many people have written to me to say that they have indeed been "infected" by the benign virus of the NDE simply by reading and absorbing the information contained in this book and then applying it to their lives. In some cases, they have been led to do more than that and have sought out additional literature in this field and first-hand contact with near-death experiencers themselves. Of course, it would be preposterous to claim that this has been true for most readers—of that, I have no way of knowing—but there seems to be little doubt that the seeds I had hoped to implant in others have decidedly taken root in at least some of those who have exposed themselves to the teachings in this book. These people, too, according to what they have told me, have also begun to experience the same kind of personal and spiritual transformations that are typically reported by those who have actually had a physically induced near-death encounter. Therefore, we now know that if this has been true for them, it is certainly possible for you. The NDE virus is definitely proving to be contagious.

Perhaps it would be helpful to illustrate this by reference to a specific example, and for this purpose I will draw on a twelve-page letter sent to me by a sixty-two-year-old man who lives in the Northwest. Obviously, in this short update I cannot take the time to recount much of Jim's life before his discovery of the world of near-death experiences, including his reading *Lessons from the Light*, so let it suffice to say that his life had been difficult and among other things had involved his serving as an officer during the Viet Nam war where he had not only to witness many deaths but had been forced to kill enemy troops as well.

Jim writes that when he first came across the literature on near-death experiences about ten years ago, it initiated a series of profound personal changes that turned his life around. "When I look at the changes in my life that have occurred over the past decade or so since I first became acquainted with NDEs, I can't think of any other incident that has wrought such a powerful transformation or has even come close to it."

He recalls the day he stumbled upon a couple of books on NDEs, including one of mine. He first read Raymond Moody's book, *Life After Life*, and that, he says, sparked a flame inside him. Then he read one of my earlier books, and that one caused the flame to burst into radiant inner light. I will quote the following passage, not to draw attention to my book as such, but simply to indicate the incredible power this kind of literature can have on someone who finds himself drawn to it.

> The light [that Moody's book had kindled] then exploded into a glorious brilliance and warmth that traversed the entire length of my body. It was without question the most glorious high that I ever experienced in my life. I read your book a second time and profusely wept with tears of joy and gratitude. I don't think I slept for two days, yet I was fully awake. I was in a state of awe and wonderment.... Even when I think about it now as I'm typing this letter, I still get misty-eyed and cherish that warmth inside of me.... There are times when human language fails to express the depth of a person's feelings. This is one of those times. I can only say over and over again, thank you, thank you, thank you, ten to the hundredth power.

Jim says that this opening brought about a total metamorphosis in his life, which transformed his values, his behavior, his view of himself and his outlook on life and death. Speaking specifically of the impact of *Lessons from the Light*, Jim writes:

> Your most recent book seems to have planted a seed within me. Possibly it was already there but dormant. If that was the case, then exposure to this benign virus, as you so aptly call it, brought this seed into germination. And after all these years of gestation, I have experienced untold multiple bouts of joy and have developed a sense of calm that assures me that, despite all the challenges of my life and those undoubtedly to come, all will be well and will continue to remain well after I set foot into the hereafter. The additional gift that you have given me through this book is precious beyond words.

Most of the rest of Jim's letter is taken up with a very moving description of many of the changes he alluded to, which completely mirror those characteristic of most of near-death experiencers: an increased sense of self-worth, the loss of the fear of death, an unshakable awareness of the unity of all life, a commitment to environmental activism on behalf of the earth, a thirst for knowledge, and of course the *sine qua non* of the NDE, the importance of helping others. On this point, Jim writes in the vein of so many near-death experiencers I have known:

> I love being with people and trying to help them in what little ways I can. Invariably the discussion of NDEs always enters the conversation and I do believe that I have probably passed that infectious virus on to at least some people with whom I have associated.

One of those is his son, Aaron, who is in his late twenties. According to Jim:

> There is no doubt he's caught the NDE virus. Even his girlfriend has commented that he has changed in being a more giving person, notwithstanding his stealing off my bookshelf my copy of *Lessons from the Light!*...He has become...far more attentive to and caring for other people and his friends. He seems to exude a real benevolence that was not particularly characteristic of him before.... He is an environmental engineer but his second love is doing volunteer work with high-school students.

It goes without saying that I do not wish to claim that Jim is typical of the readers of my book, much less that there is anything in my book that can't be found in others on the same subject—apart from the fact that *Lessons from the Light* makes a deliberate attempt to instill the teachings of the NDE into those who are receptive to them and would like to make active use of them in their lives. But what testimonies like Jim's do demonstrate is that it is indeed possible that the effects of the NDE can be directly transmitted to readers who have never had an NDE themselves, and as Jim's letter implies, that these effects can in turn be spread to others by direct contact with those who have already been struck by the benign virus of the NDE. In short, there can be ripple effects from books like this, too, that could ultimately affect many people who may never even read books of this sort.

So, while not everyone will respond the way Jim has to this material, there certainly are other "Jims" out there. I know there are because of the many letters I've received. Maybe you're one, too. If so, I would love to hear from you someday.

## Chapter One

# *Journeys to the Light*

For the past ten years, I have been teaching a course on the near-death experience (NDE) at my university. Every semester, thirty-five to forty young undergraduates arrive at my classroom on the first day of the new term, usually somewhat nervous about taking such an offbeat course but generally enthusiastic and curious about the topic that has already excited their interest.

Normally, there is one person—and ordinarily no more than one—among these students who comes to the class with a markedly different orientation, and an advantage over his or her peers. This is the student, though I will only learn this later, who has already had an NDE. He or she is there for quite different reasons, and several weeks or even most of the semester may pass before the other students and I learn that there has been an experiencer all along in our midst. By the time the semester is over, however, we have usually been made privy to the story of the NDE of that student, who becomes for that day the real teacher in the class.

## *Craig*

I still remember quite vividly the first time one of these invisible NDEr students made himself known to me and my class. Craig, as I will call him, was a trifle older than most undergraduates, being in his late twenties, but he still had a definite boyish quality to his manner that made him seem like their exact contemporary. I had already noticed that

Craig seemed especially interested in our discussions and, perhaps abetted by the fact that he was comely in an athletic way, with broad shoulders and a powerful build, he had a very lively and attractive presence in the class. Perhaps I am guilty of a degree of idealization when I recall him now, but I feel quite certain I had even noticed that there was a kind of sparkle in his eyes that set him apart from most of the other students. At the time, I'm sure that I attributed this to his obvious involvement with the course, but eventually my students and I were to learn that there were decidedly more personal reasons that explained Craig's almost luminous presence and his infectious cheerfulness.

That was the day, of course, when he, with some shyness, confessed that he had had one of these experiences himself about ten years ago. Naturally, I drew him out and before the class was over that day, we had heard the gist of his story which, once he got into it, Craig told in a very natural, straightforward manner. Afterward, I asked him if he would be kind enough to write out a version of it for me in his course journal, and what follows are some excerpts from this written account, preceded and interspersed with some comments of my own to help place his remarks in context. In reading it, however, I would invite you not merely to peruse his words, but to *enter* into his experience as empathically as you can by imagining that it was your own. To the extent you are able to do so, his experience will become yours and its power will ramify through you.

Craig's NDE had occurred one summer as a result of a rafting accident in which he had nearly drowned. He had only been on his inner tube for about 30 seconds when he realized he was already in danger. In this moment of alarm, he became aware that

> the current was pulling me toward the middle of the river, where there was a small waterfall. There is a sharp drop of about 4 feet or so at this point, and the power of the river is extremely visible. The rocks below had eroded in such a manner that they created a sort of suction hole.... I tried to pull myself toward the route that [his friend and rafting companion] Don had followed as I paddled with my hands, but my attempts proved to be futile. The current was too strong, and paddling was only twisting me around so that now I was headed toward the waterfall backwards instead of forwards. As I looked over my shoulder, my heart began beating faster for I realized that there was no possible way of avoiding the falls. I tried to get a grip on the tube but it was too slippery to get a hold of. Over the falls I went, the inner tube sinking into the water backwards, and then throwing me back in a forward direction because of the air pressure in the tube. I was propelled headfirst into the falls where the force of the water tore me from the tube with sudden impact and brutal force and sent me crashing to the bottom. I was pinned there by its never ending supply of overwhelming force.

Craig now found himself seemingly inescapably trapped, face down in the sand and could move only his hands, but there was nothing for him to grasp to get any leverage. Quickly, he realized that there was no hope and that, with his air supply already dwindling, he would surely die. Meanwhile, his mind speeded up tremendously, and many things and thoughts seemed to be happening simultaneously. Then, he began to lose his sense of time altogether as the reality of his fatal predicament impressed itself upon him.

> I could not believe that this is where my life would end.... I never thought it would be by drowning, and never thought it would happen at such a young age.... It struck me as funny that I had been to this area many times before, and never knew that this was where I would die later in life. Scenes from my life began to pass before my eyes at superhigh speeds. It seemed as if I was a passive observer in the process, and it was as if someone else was running the projector. I was looking at my life objectively for the first time ever. I saw the good as well as the bad. I realized that these images were sort of a final chapter in my life, and that when the images stopped, I would lose consciousness forever. I thought of how a light bulb sometimes burns the brightest just before it goes out for the last time.

Craig is beginning to have what many people report on nearly dying, a kind of panoramic life review, and went on to describe various scenes from his childhood, beginning when he was a baby.

> I was astonished when I saw myself sitting in a baby's high chair and picking up some food with my right hand and throwing it onto the floor. And there was my mom, years younger, telling me that good boys do not throw their food on the floor. I also saw myself at a lake on a summer vacation when I was about three or four years old. My older brother and I had to swim with an air bubble on our backs to help us float because neither of us were able to swim on our own yet. For some reason, I was mad at him, and to demonstrate my anger, I threw his air bubble into the lake. He was very upset and began to cry, and my father walked over and explained to me that it was not nice of me to do what I did, and that I would have to row the boat out with him to get it, and would have to apologize. I relived a boating accident when I was about seven that was very traumatic for me because I had run over my brother by accident and nearly killed him. I was amazed at how many scenes I was seeing but had long since been forgotten.... It seemed that all the scenes had to do with experiences I had either learned from or were traumatic for me in some way. The images continued at high speeds, and I knew that time was about to run out, for the images were getting closer and closer to the present.... Then the images ceased ... and there was only darkness.

At this point of seeming finality, Craig says he began to relax a little and to surrender to the inevitable. He is aware, however, of a tingling sensation, beginning in his feet and then spreading over his entire body, which has the effect of making him feel increasingly relaxed. His body becomes extremely quiet and his heart stops beating. He no longer feels the need for air and comments that, paradoxically, he now does not feel uncomfortable in the least. There is a pause, and then suddenly,

> I felt myself moving through a dark void. It was like a tunnel but it was so dark that it could have been 5 feet in diameter or thousands of miles. I seemed to be picking up speed and traveling in a perfectly straight line through the void. I felt as if wind was blowing across my face. There was no actual wind though; there were only sensations that would be present if there were wind. I felt as if I were moving at the speed of light through the blackness, and far away in the distance, I could see a small pinpoint of light that seemed to be growing larger. I somehow knew that this was my destination. I sped along until it became a huge mass of beautiful and brilliant white light. I stopped short right before reaching it, for I felt I was getting too far away from the earth to find my way back, and I guess I had a feeling that one could equate with homesickness.
>
> As I sat there motionless, it seemed as if the light began to float toward me as if to take up the slack I had left between us. It was not long before it engulfed me, and I felt as if I became one with the light. It seemed to have knowledge of everything there is to know, and it accepted me as part of it. I felt all-knowing for a few minutes. Suddenly, everything seemed to make perfect sense. The whole world seemed to be in total harmony. I remember thinking, "Ahhh, so that's it. Everything is so crystal clear and simple in so many ways." I had never been able to see it from this point of view.
>
> Looking back at this point, I cannot explain the questions that were answered, or the answers themselves. All I know was that they were on a much higher level of thought that cannot be approached when limited by the physical nature of the mind.... Within the light, I could still feel the boundaries of my form, but at the same time I felt as one with it. I felt myself expand through the light over an area that seemed like miles, and then contract to my former size, which at this point was like a two- or three-foot egg-shaped mass of energy. I felt better than I had ever felt in my life. It was as if I were bathing in total love and understanding, and basking in its radiance.... It gives me a sense of traveling a long distance and finally making it home. I sensed that I had been here before, perhaps before being born into the physical world.

At this moment of apparent apogee, which suggests the absolute culmination of the NDE in ineffable union with the light, Craig is astonished to perceive that there are still other revelations about to be disclosed to him.

> All of a sudden, I noticed a floating sensation, as if I were rising. I was shocked to find that I was floating upwards into the open air above the river.

I remember vividly the scene of the water level passing before my eyes. Suddenly I could see and hear as never before. The sound of the waterfall was so crisp and clear that it just cannot be explained by words. Earlier that year, my right ear had been injured when somebody threw an M-80 into a bar where I was listening to a band, and it exploded right next to my head. But now I could hear perfectly clearly, better than I ever had before. My sight was even more beautiful. Sights that were close in distance were as clear as those far away, and this was at the same moment, which astounded me. There was no blurriness in my vision whatsoever. I felt as if I had been limited by my physical senses all these years, and that I had been looking at a distorted picture of reality.

As I floated there about six feet above the water, I gazed downward toward the falls. I knew that my physical body was eight feet below the surface of the water, but it did not seem to bother me.... Now, separated from my physical body, I found that I could survive without all the pain and suffering of physical existence. I had never thought of it as pain and suffering when I was in my physical body, but now, after experiencing such total bliss and harmony, it seemed like everything prior to this was like being in some sort of cage.

I felt like I was an energy form that could never be destroyed. I thought of all the handicapped people in the world who could not see, could not hear, and those who had lost limbs or were paralyzed. I realized that when they die, these physical limitations would be cast aside, and they would feel whole again.... It was such a reassuring feeling to know that all of these people would be set free from their handicapped conditions someday.

Craig then becomes aware of his distraught companion, Don, and tries to communicate with him.

I gazed down the river and could see Don clutching a rock as he looked back at the falls with his mouth hanging open in shock. I yelled to him, "Don, I'm up here. I'm okay, look, up here." He did not respond. There seemed to be no way for me to communicate with him [and] I quickly gave up.

At this juncture in Craig's journey back from the light, he has some further curious experiences, although similar ones have also been occasionally reported by other NDErs. He finds that his bodiless essence now has the power to enter into and experience elements of nature, such as trees and rocks, and amuses himself with these strange sensations. He is, in short, having a ball, and sees limitless possibilities in this new state.

I felt better than I had ever felt in my life. I felt like I could go anywhere in the universe in an instant. I remember thinking about my family, and suddenly finding my energy at home in my backyard, floating above the back porch and looking into the house through the kitchen window. There was a bird sitting on the window ledge, and I was so amazed that I could move so close to it without its flying away. I saw a shadow of someone walking through the kitchen, but I cannot be sure of who it was. Next I found myself floating on a street corner of a busy city. It was exactly like a scene I had seen while visiting San Francisco. After each of these excursions I found myself back once again, floating above the sand next to the river.

I was at the height of my euphoria and looking for something new to experiment with when a voice thundered through my head. It said, "What do you think you are doing? You're not supposed to die yet! You're being selfish. Sure you feel great and you love this new experience, but you must understand that it was not supposed to happen this way. You promised that you would never give up until every ounce of energy was used. You remember that wrestling match in high school when you were pinned, and afterward were disappointed in yourself because you felt you had given up? You just gave up. I am a little disappointed that you did not try harder to escape."

I thought about it, remembered the incident vividly, and the voice was absolutely right. I had given up rather quickly, and certainly had not used all of my energy to escape, but I explained that I saw no possible way out. I said, "And, besides, it's too late now anyway, my body must be filled with water by now." We seemed to be communicating not with words, but with direct thought.

At this point, I began to see a figure of a man, partially transparent, and old in appearance. When I realized that this is who I had been communicating with, I also noticed five other faces to his left. [Further exhortations come from these others and then] I realized that these spirits or souls seemed to know me very well, and seemed like some sort of blood relatives from my past, but I didn't recognize them.

The main voice then explained to me that it was not too late to return, and suddenly I saw a thin orange line appear across a black background. It was horizontal, and seemed to stretch to infinity on either side of a small area that was red and thicker than the rest of the band. The voice said, "This red area is your life." Then, a vertical black line cut through the red area about a quarter of the way of its length. It then said, "If you die today, this is where your life will end, but if you choose to live, you can see that you have the potential to live another three-quarters beyond what you have experienced so far."

The entity then showed me scenes of what would happen if I chose to die. I saw my family in tears, I saw images of police cars, an ambulance, scuba divers, and people from neighboring houses along the shore trying to get a view of what was happening. I also saw an image of Don explaining to the police what had happened. These images were rather unsettling, for I did not want to put my family and friends through that kind of torment. Then, the voice asked me what I liked about life. I told him I loved music. He asked if I had done everything with my music that I had wanted to. I answered that I hadn't, and told him that I had always dreamed of being an opening act for somebody famous. I then said that I would have liked to open up for someone from the Woodstock Festival, like Arlo Guthrie, for instance.

The voice saw how I gave Arlo Guthrie a sort of hero image and explained to me that he was no different from the rest of us on earth, and that if you want something bad enough it can be yours—as long as you realize that once you get it, you may find that it was not what you were looking for in the first place. It seemed to say if only people could see the importance of love and cooperation instead of competitiveness, the world could be a better place to live. It told me to use my senses to their maximum potential, and to gather as much knowledge as I could through them. I thought about the time line again, and how it continued past the point where my life would end, and how it stretched far before the beginning of my human existence. If there was nothing before and after my life, I wondered why I saw the orange line stretching to infinity in both directions, and not simply the red area that was designated as my life in this world. It seemed to be telling me that I existed in some form before this lifetime, and that I would continue to exist after it ended. The voice then said, "This place will always be here waiting for you, and if you want to stay now, I will accept you, but I will be sort of disappointed if you do not take this opportunity to go back—the choice is yours."

All of a sudden, I realized that it was almost going to be a personal insult to this figure if I did not choose to return to my present life. It was as if he was telling me that an earthly existence could be so wonderful if looked at through the right frame of mind. It did not take me long to realize that, deep inside, I really wanted to go back and live my life to the fullest. Even though this place made me feel so good, I felt that I could come back here someday, and that there was no rush. I said, "Okay," and before I could get out the words, "I'm ready," I shot back into my body like a lightning bolt.

In an instant, Craig becomes aware of the heaviness of his body and his physical pain, but at the same time feels a tremendous influx of energy that allows him almost to disregard the pain. Finding that he now was possessed of "the strength of three men," he fights resolutely to free himself from his underwater predicament and, of course, he prevails and manages to swim back to the shore, where he collapses on the beach, utterly exhausted. His mind, however, is still preoccupied with his experience, and while on the beach, he nevertheless remains in two worlds. "I tried to figure out what had just happened to me. I knew that I had a glimpse of a world on the other side of life as we know it, and it felt so good to be back. Even the pain in my lungs felt good."

Ten years later, reflecting on the lessons and impact of his experience, Craig wrote:

This experience changed my life in many ways. For one, I am no longer the least bit afraid to die. I know that I would not want to suffer, but I know that the actual dying process is nothing like what I thought it would be, and that it was probably the most beautiful and peaceful experience I have ever had. I realize now that our time here is relatively short, and it makes me want to live my life to the fullest. I found that among the few things that people can take with them when they die, love is probably the most important. The only things left after one leaves his or her body are energy, love, personality, and knowledge. It seems like such a waste of precious time to become caught up in materialistic modes of thinking. When I hear birds chirping, it sounds so beautiful and makes me feel so good inside. I notice trees and plants and other living things more than I ever had before. I guess I seem to get my happiness more from the little things in life than from things with great monetary value. Life in general seems more intricate and amazing than ever before. I feel that our bodies are the greatest gift of all, and I find that most people take them for granted. Most people do not stop to realize how lucky we are to be alive. I know that I have been given a second chance in life, and every day is so much more precious to me. Words cannot describe the feeling I get when I wake up in the morning and the sun is shining in through the window, and it is the beginning of a new day with all sorts of opportunities to experience new things, and to learn from them. I know now that an existence after this lifetime awaits all of us, and that death is not the end, but simply a new beginning.

In Craig's case, however, there was a surprise waiting for him and an eerie confirmation of something he had been told by the voice during his NDE. In a coda to his account, Craig relates this story:

One ironic occurrence after this experience: Three years after this experience, I decided I wanted to learn how to play the flute. After only a few months, I realized that I could touch people in the deepest parts of their souls with my playing—sometimes, they would even cry. I found that it was my way to reach out to many people at a time. Two years after first picking up the flute, I was playing in a bar, and a man came up to me and asked me if I would like to be the opening act for Arlo Guthrie at the Shaboo Inn [at the time, a local club]. I said, "Sure!," as a rush of excitement and the memory of what occurred during my near-death experience ran through my mind. I had my major dream in life come true. After performing, I had a tear in my eye as I looked back at the stage and said to myself, "Maybe the voice was right. Maybe this wasn't what I was looking for after all. Maybe what I really wanted deep down inside was to feel needed and loved, and to be able to touch the hearts of many."

I've quoted at length from Craig's narrative so that you could have here at the outset the opportunity to project yourself into a deep yet wholly typical NDE. What Craig saw, what he understood, and how he changed as a result of his experience constitute the common testimony and outcome of thousands of near-death survivors around the globe. In a way, it may be enough for you to read and ponder this experience for yourself, for truly it does speak, and speaks most eloquently, for itself. But perhaps, just to be sure we do not overlook anything of vital importance, it might be useful to linger a moment or two before considering our next account and take note of certain features of Craig's experience—especially those that are particularly relevant to us who have not had an NDE ourselves.

Of course, Craig's NDE has many of the familiar elements of these encounters—the feelings of peace and extreme well-being, the out-of-body perspective, a passage through a dark void toward a radiantly beautiful light, a sense of total acceptance, universal knowledge, a life review, meeting others, and being offered the choice whether to return to the physical body. And there were other features of his experience as well that are more unusual, but certainly not unique to Craig, such as his apparent ability to tune into distant scenes and places and to experience directly the creations of nature. For us, however, it is primarily the knowledge that Craig received during his NDE and how it affected his life afterward that are of particular moment. And if we are to begin to internalize these lessons for ourselves, it might be helpful to summarize some of the main ones here.

This, then, is what Craig—who, as we will see, speaks here for so many other NDErs—seems to have taken away from his experience:

1. There is nothing whatever to fear about death.
2. Dying is peaceful and beautiful.
3. Life does not begin with birth nor end with death.
4. Life is precious—live it to the fullest.
5. The body and its senses are tremendous gifts—appreciate them.
6. What matters most in life is love.
7. Living a life oriented toward materialistic acquisition is missing the point.
8. Cooperation rather than competition makes for a better world.
9. Being a big success in life is not all it is cracked up to be.
10. Seeking knowledge is important—you take that with you.

Many of these statements may seem self-evident, and you may wonder cynically, "Is it really necessary to nearly die to learn such bromides?" Of course it is not—that is the whole premise of this book—but what the NDE does for the individual who has one is to convert these propositions from lip-service truisms to *living truths*. The NDEr does not forget these things because they have been indelibly and permanently infused into his or her psyche, and they have an immediate and long-lasting effect on the NDEr's conduct. Therefore, if we are to learn from the same school that NDErs graduate from, we must be prepared to do the work ourselves—we have to strive to internalize what the NDEr is given directly. Reading and reflecting on these accounts—more than once if necessary—is a beginning toward that end, and so is considering the list of insights Craig received from his NDE. They are, after all, his gift to you. You could do worse than copying them down and posting them on your refrigerator door in order not to forget them—or him.

As for Craig himself, he went on to graduate from the university and, the last I heard from him, he was getting ready to move to a western state after having been hired by a major airline carrier. But while Craig was the first of the student NDErs I was to meet in my course, he was scarcely the last. And, in fact, it is the last—that is to say, the most recent—of these to whom I would like to introduce you next.

### Neev

This past year I made the acquaintance of a young man named Neevon (though everyone calls him Neev, he later told me). Unlike Craig, who was a very lively presence in my class, Neev was quiet and unobtrusive. In truth, I confess that this rather ordinary-looking but stocky fellow, with straight black hair, did not make much of an impression on me, though I did note that he was very faithful in attending the classes. Toward the end of the semester, I invited three persons who had had NDEs to my class in order to discuss the aftereffects of their experiences. As it happened, one of these persons was an undergraduate female who had taken the course the previous semester. As Neev later informed me, he was astonished to see this student there in that setting, for he had known her quite well and never knew that she had had an NDE (and for good reason—while an undergraduate, she had never informed any other students about her experience for fear of ridicule). As a result of hearing her speak in class about her experience, however, Neev was emboldened, finally, to share his with me privately. Naturally, I encouraged him to write out a version of his NDE for the course, and what you will be reading next are some excerpts from a term paper he wrote for that purpose. Again, I encourage you to allow yourself to experience Neev's NDE from the inside by putting yourself in his shoes—or rather his spikes, since his encounter with death took place on a baseball diamond.

In March 1988, when Neev was a high school sophomore, he was severely injured while playing first base for his team. A burly catcher slammed into him violently as Neev attempted to snare a low throw, and, as he put it, "The next thing I knew, the world as I knew it was gone." Neev soon discovered, however, that he was very much present after all—just that he was no longer in his body.

> I realized ... that I was not in my physical body. I felt no pain or discomfort. I felt totally at peace with myself. I was standing behind my coach and one of the other player's father. They were both kneeling over me in the infield, where I was lying on my back. The first thing I checked was if the ball stayed in my glove [it had].

Neev then watched—from his out-of-body vantage point, he says— his body being half-carried, half-dragged off the field, his face already grotesquely swollen, and loaded into the car of a teammate's father. He claims to have heard every word spoken, and when being driven to a nearby hospital, Neev writes that he actually felt himself to be following *behind* the car. He had clear vision of the interior of the car, however, as well as everything else his attention was drawn to during the ride to the hospital.

Once they arrived at the emergency room, Neev's body was placed onto a gurney—again, something Neev states he was aware of from the outside. In his words,

> I watched the interns place my body on a gurney and push it through the two big doors that led to the emergency room. The doctors immediately ran toward me in this long, well-lit corridor and checked for a pulse and took my blood pressure. Several doctors huddled around my body. My vital signs were steady but weak and an X ray for my head was ordered. I watched myself get rolled into the X-ray room, where a lead blanket was placed over the rest of my body, and then the lights went out.
>
> I was no longer able to see my body in the X-ray room. I was still out of my body, but now I had no sight. My world was utter darkness. I sensed myself but nothing was there.... There was an indescribable feeling of love and warmth. It could be like a child before birth in its mother's womb. I felt nothing but peace and tranquility. I never wanted to leave—it was as if I was searching for this place my whole life. This place was perfection in all its aspects except that I was alone. As soon as that thought came to mind, my feeling of stillness amid the darkness instantly changed to a movement of intense speed. It was at that moment that I knew I was not alone.
>
> It seemed to me as if everything that I needed to know or ever wanted to know was available to me. I felt an abrupt stop when I asked, "Why am I here?" I felt as if all this knowledge was coming from inside me, since I

did not have to speak to anyone—everything just happened. It was like having an epiphany every time I thought of something.

This time, my question led to my life review. It was like watching my life from start to finish on an editing machine stuck in fast forward. The review took me from my conception, which felt like the blackness I experienced after my out-of-body experience, through my childhood, to adolescence, into my teens, and through my near-death experience over again. I saw my life. I relived my life. I felt everything I ever felt before. When I say "everything," I mean every cut, pain, emotion and sense associated with that particular time in my life. At the same time, I saw the effects of my life on the people around me.... I felt all that they felt and, through this, I understood the repercussions of everything I did, be it good or bad. This life review was the most beautiful thing I had ever seen, and at the same time, the most horrifying thing I was ever to experience.

By the time my life review caught up to itself, I posed a thought of my younger sister with a desire to be with her. And at that very instant... I was returned to the world as I previously knew it, but not as I previously understood it!

At this point, Neev's NDE is apparently over, and he wakes up to find himself still on the gurney. Now, however, he is surrounded by his mother and father. He has sustained a severe concussion and has hemorrhaged internally, and, though he is told by his physician that he is lucky to be alive, he is assured that he will recover in time. In fact, he soon is released and driven home by his father. Upon arriving home, however, he loses feeling over the left side of his body, which soon becomes paralyzed, and experiences a total cessation of vision.

Within two days, his vision returns, but he remains paralyzed for a week and bedridden for eight weeks, his face still monstrously swollen. During the first two days of his recuperation, while he is still blind, Neev, drifting in and out of consciousness, enters into the near-death state again and extracts more information about his life. He says that he continued to see himself in his life review, "and hated what I saw. It was the life review that sparked my desire for change." He also became aware, just as Craig did, that he had a guide.

During these lapses back to the other side, I felt as if I had someone with me. This person was not there in a physical sense but was there more as a mental guide.... My guide during these ventures [into his life review] felt like a father figure to me. He seemed to ask me all the right questions at all the right times. I was able to pinpoint all the things necessary to change myself. Each time I slipped back into my other world of warmth and answers, it was as if my near-death experience was happening all over again.

As Neev continues to recover, the changes he has already made within himself, with the help of his guide, begin to stabilize—in his words, "They just began to happen." And the changes, occurring seemingly so naturally now, are enormous in their scope, as Neev explained in his paper.

The changes I have come to associate with my NDE seem to be so natural but, at the same time, unattainable without my experience. Before my NDE, my life was totally different. It seems like a lifetime ago [now], but in actuality, it has only been five years. As I stated earlier, I despised myself when I was younger. I grew up very different from everyone else around me. I was born a first-generation American in my family. My parents came over to this country from Israel and preferred to speak Hebrew at home. In doing this, I tended to speak Hebrew to everyone, even though they did not know it. This cultural difference made it very difficult for me to fit in, so I stopped trying. I was a very introverted child who had almost no friends. Getting picked on and teased was a daily occurrence that drove my self-esteem to the point where it did not exist. I was very inquisitive and smart as a child, but expressing my knowledge in school placed me in the spotlight, where I was subject to even more abuse. As a result of this, I became known as the world's greatest underachiever.

By the time I reached the age of ten, I realized I could express myself through sports. I became one of the top soccer players in my county, and the competition kept me going. The only problem I found with being so good was that the other kids were jealous and began to torture me even more. By this time I had reached junior high school. I had created such a thick shell to protect myself from all my social inadequacies that it only made things worse. I was one of the most antisocial people that ever existed. My life involved going to school to underachieve and get only fair grades, and spending every free minute either practicing soccer or staring blankly into the television, and sleeping. I was so scared of everything—especially rejection, public speaking, social events, girls, and so on—that I fell into a very rebellious state [that led to] vandalism and other troubles.

According to Neev, however, the NDE, and the extended reconsideration of his life it provided, changed everything, bringing about a total reversal of his previous tendencies and even ameliorated long-standing physical problems. The extent of his transformation is remarkable and his summary of it is worth quoting at length.

I instantly changed from a pessimist to an optimist. There always seemed to be a brighter side to everything. I knew that everything happened for a reason. Sometimes, that reason may not have been clear at first, but in the end, it would all make sense.

The NDE had a sort of physical healing with me. Physical problems that haunted me all my life disappeared afterward. These problems were chronic migraine headaches, for which I had to take pills for years, cramps, and a terribly anxious stomach, which would act up before school every day, soccer games, tests, and in just about all social situations. Before my experience I was the most klutzy, accident-prone fool you could have ever met. All these problems were solved through my NDE.

[But] it was not only a physical healer—my mental state was repaired as well. My outlook on life was no longer bleak and dismal. I felt like I now had a purpose, which was to help people and share my positive perspective. My dependence on time seemed to stop. I no longer felt pressured by the clock—there was always time to do something else or more. I tried to fit in as much as possible into every day. I experienced everything for what it was—not for what it could do or give to me. I was no longer interested in what "society" had to say about how I lived my life. I was no longer interested in what people thought or how they felt about me, or if I looked good or not. I learned that I am much more than my body.

In doing this, other people around me began to accept me for who I was. My feeling of warmth and love flew through from my body and brought me many new friends. I felt comfortable in groups of people to the point that I needed to be surrounded by them. I had no fears of rejection or embarrassment. These were trivial things that [had] no consequence in the larger scheme of things.

Pain—both physical and emotional—seemed to me to be only a state of mind. Physical pain was a very minor discomfort after my NDE. I realized my mortality, unlike most of my friends. The closeness I had with death kept me from foolishly toying with life, mine and others, like I had before. In learning of my mortality, I also learned to accept death, and in a weird way, I look forward to it. I do not fear many things anymore. Instead, I accept them for what they are and apply them to my life. I tend to try new things more readily, since I want to make the most of my new life without missing a thing.

From this large change in my personality, many of the things I valued previously seemed virtually unimportant to me. Money and material objects were not even a secondary thought to me. I became very generous with all of my time and material things. I joined several school philanthropy groups and spent time working in several soup kitchens. The most major change I noticed in myself was the loss of the desire to compete. Competition was the major driving force in my life before my NDE, but afterward, it seemed foolish and unimportant. Sports were still fun, but I lost that killer instinct that helped me get recruited by several universities.

From reading this extract, you can see that in essentially every department of Neev's life, he has become the opposite of what he had been before his NDE. Although we will review some of these specific changes shortly, it is enough to note for now that his NDE, by turning Neev inside-out as it were, peeled off his false protective mask and allowed a much more authentic and loving face to show itself to the world. And when it did, the world around him changed accordingly.

And there were other changes, too. Neev found that he had acquired the ability to reenter that otherworldly state during sleep, where he could, in effect, rehearse actions and test their effects before actually performing them in the physical world. Like many other NDErs, he also seemed to develop an extended range of intuitive and psychic perception that sometimes permitted him to know or sense the outcome of events before they took place. Perhaps his greatest gift, however, lay in his enhanced empathic ability. About this, Neev comments:

> These instincts also allow me to empathize with almost anyone. I feel that when I talk to people, I can physically and emotionally feel what they are going through at that time. It is as if I become them for an instant.... The gift of insight allows me to help many people with their problems, but sometimes [it] gets to the point where there are so many that I lose myself in other people.

In assessing the overall impact of his NDE on his life, Neev concludes:

> I look at it as ... a psychological healing process. All of these changes, as well as many little things that I cannot even describe, have moved me for the better. I feel that my NDE was the best thing that ever happened to me.... I see my experience as the most important event in my life. Without my NDE I would not be happy today.

In considering Neev's NDE, it is abundantly clear that it wrought a profound, life-changing transformation in his personality and behavior, and in his entire outlook on life, and that, indeed, he was "moved for the better." Perhaps it would not be going too far to claim, if only on the basis of Neev's own testimony, that his providentially timed NDE may have even saved his life by nearly ending it. By doing so, it seems, the very course of Neev's life was changed and his downward spiral into repeated failures in school, self-loathing, and even vandalism was thereby abruptly halted and reversed. Of course, it is certainly possible that had his NDE *not* supervened at this time in his life, he would nevertheless have found his way out of his travails by some other means. Possibly. But, as we have seen, Neev himself does not appear inclined to think so. For him, it was almost as though the NDE was purposively *designed* to rescue him from the personal nadir into whose abyss he was poised to fall.

However that may be, our task here is not so much to speculate about the possible meaning of Neev's experience as to learn from it so as to enhance our own lives. From that standpoint, what lessons are there to be derived from Neev's transformation that might be generally applicable to anyone? If you examine his account for such insights, for starters, you will come across the following:

1. There is a reason for everything that happens.
2. Find your own purpose in life.
3. Do not be a slave to time.
4. Appreciate things for what they are—not for what they can give you.
5. Do not allow yourself to be dominated by the thoughts or expectations of others.
6. Do not be concerned with what others think of you, either.
7. Remember, you are not your body.
8. Fear not—even pain and certainly not death.
9. Be open to life, and live it to its fullest.
10. Money and material things are not particularly important in the scheme of things.
11. Helping others is what counts in life.
12. Do not trouble yourself with competition—just enjoy the show.

Again, as with the list we extracted from Craig's experience, many of these statements have the ring of the familiar and, indeed, the obvious. But before dismissing them as mere platitudes, consider this angle: *What if you were really able to live life this way?* What kind of person would you be?

My answer is that you would be a truly free person. You would be forever liberated from the tyranny of others' opinions, from self-doubt, from the fear of life and the fear of death, and from the demands of time. Instead, you would be free to enjoy life as it is and to find fulfillment and joy in helping others.

This, ultimately, is the gift the NDE confers upon its recipient, though, to be sure, the individual must usually work hard to unwrap it. And, in the same way, this is the promise of the NDE to anyone who makes the effort to assimilate its teachings and make them applicable to his or her own life. Neev's story, remember, is yours if you identify with it. If you do and take it into you deeply, what happened to him should begin to happen to you. You will have taken a step toward your own liberation and finding your authentic self.

Unlike Craig, with whom I have lost contact, I have stayed in touch with Neev and have had a chance to spend a good deal of time with him. Immediately after taking my NDE course, he enrolled in a special advanced seminar on NDEs and carried out a project designed to determine the effects on undergraduate students of hearing about NDEs. In effect, Neev gave a number of talks on the subject, in which he, of course, recounted his own story to various student groups on campus and assessed the impact of his presentation by the use of specially designed questionnaires. During the semester, I had plenty of opportunity to see Neev in interaction with his fellow students, in conferences with me, and I even interviewed him informally at the end of the semester concerning his life review. From my observations of Neev in these contexts, I can certainly attest to the fact that he is very much the person he claims to be. I have found him to be unfailingly cheerful, even under stressful conditions, generous-hearted, wise yet humble, and with a lively sense of humor, too. When I last talked with him, at the end of the semester, he was about to leave for Israel to work as a counselor for teenagers touring the country— the sort of activity, he said, that he hopes will be a large part of his life following graduation.

Perhaps my most enduring memory of Neev, however, is based on the presentation I asked him to make in my introductory NDE course—the very course in which he himself had been a student the previous semester. Appearing with two other outside speakers, Neev spoke last about his own NDE to his fellow students. His account was poignant, funny—the class was frequently in stitches when Neev described his appearance following his injury—and spell-binding. When it was over, a number of students—men and women, both—came forward to embrace him warmly and many others gathered around. Some were in tears. Neev later told me that maybe sharing his NDE in this way was even better than the experience itself. For my part, it was the highlight of the semester in that class.

## Laurelynn

On the same day Neev shared his NDE with my students, another NDEr whom I had never previously met also came from a nearby town to tell her story. Her name was Laurelynn Glass Martin, and she turned out to be a tall, slender brunette, with a gentle, soft-spoken manner, who related easily to my students. Laurelynn, who is now in her thirties, began by explaining that when she was a senior in college, in the fall of 1982, she was on a tennis scholarship and was planning to go to the National Collegiate Tennis Tournament the following spring, and from there to join the professional tennis circuit that coming summer. But a simple surgical procedure that went awry on December 9 of that year changed everything.

She had gone into the hospital, she told us, to have what was supposed to be a routine twenty-minute laparoscopic surgical procedure. However, her physician, as she learned later, exerted undue force making the initial incision, puncturing her abdominal aorta, her right iliac artery, the inferior vena cava, and her bowel in two places, ultimately hitting her vertebral spine. As a result, Laurelynn lost almost 60 percent of her blood—and her pulse and, obviously, nearly her life. Before another physician intervened to save Laurelynn's life by performing an emergency laparotomy, she had already entered the near-death state and had the experience she was soon prepared to describe for us. There was no doubt, however, about her physical proximity to death. After five hours of reparative surgery, she was taken to the recovery room in critical condition. Afterward, according to Laurelynn, the physician who had saved her told her, "I snatched you from the jaws of death—your chances of living were slim to none."

In recounting Laurelynn's NDE here, I will be drawing on a written account that she had actually furnished me earlier.[1] In it, as she did for my class that day, Laurelynn indicated that without warning of any kind, she suddenly found herself floating above her physical body, off to the right side, observing with detachment, she says, the efforts of the medical team to revive her lifeless form below. As she narrates her story now, enter into it as before, and feel it as if it were happening to you.

> The surgical team was frantic. Red was everywhere, splattered on their gowns, splattered on the floor, and a bright pool of flowing red blood, in the now-wide-open abdominal cavity. I couldn't understand what was going on down there. I didn't even make the connection, at that moment, that the body being worked on was my own. It didn't matter anyway. I was in a state of freedom, having a great time. I just wanted to shout to the distressed people below, "Hey, I'm okay. It's great up here." But they were so intent, I felt like I didn't want to interrupt their efforts.
>
> I then traveled to another realm of total and absolute peace. There was no pain, but instead a sense of well-being, in a warm, dark, soft space. I was enveloped by total bliss in an atmosphere of unconditional love and acceptance. The darkness was beautiful, stretching on and on. The freedom of total peace was intensified beyond any ecstatic feeling ever felt here on earth. In the distance, I saw a horizon of whitish-yellowish light. I find it very difficult to describe where I was, because the words we know here in this plane just aren't adequate enough.
>
> I was admiring the beauty of the light but never got any closer because

next I felt a presence approaching from my right, upper side. I was feeling even more peaceful and happy, especially when I discovered it was my thirty-year-old brother-in-law who had died seven months earlier. Although I couldn't see with my eyes or hear with my ears, I instinctively knew that it was him. He didn't have a physical form, but a presence. I could feel, hear, and see his smile, laughter, and sense of humor. It was as if I had come home, and my brother-in-law was there to greet me. I instantly thought how glad I was to be with him because now I could make up for the last time I had seen him before his death. I felt bad about not taking the time out of my busy schedule to have a heart-to-heart talk with him when he had asked me to. I felt no remorse now, but total acceptance and love from him about my actions.

Reflecting on her behavior toward her brother-in-law seems to lead Laurelynn back further into her life and, before she knows it, events from her childhood begin to appear to her, all at once, yet in chronological order. She mentions two specific incidents. In one,

I had teased a little girl my own age (five years old) to the point of tears. I was now in a unique position to feel what that little girl had felt. Her frustration, her tears, and her feeling of separateness were now my feelings. I felt a tremendous amount of compassion for this child. This child, who was actually me, needed love, nurturing and forgiveness. I hadn't realized that by hurting another, I was really just hurting myself.

In the other incident that Laurelynn relived:

I had made fun of a boy my own age (twelve years old) for writing me a love letter. At that point again, I experienced his pain of rejection that became my pain and at the same time felt this tremendous amount of love for this boy and myself. He died a few years later from a cerebral aneurysm. I hadn't remembered these events and thought they were insignificant, until I reviewed them with objectivity and love. I now realized how important people were in life, how important it was to be accepting of them, and above all else, love them. I wasn't proud of those experiences, but they were part of my makeup and I was accepting of them.

Other thoughts were conveyed to me, and I remember thinking, "Wow, now I get it. Everything about our existence finally makes sense." I finally got around to questioning my brother-in-law (not with words but more [like] transference) about what was happening and asked him if I could stay. He told me it wasn't my time yet, that there had been a mistake, and that I had to go back. I remember thinking, "Okay, I'll go back, but I know how I can get back up here." At that same instant, his thoughts were mine, saying, "You can't take your own life (suicide).[2] That isn't the answer, that won't do it. You have to live your life's purpose." I understood, but I still remember thinking, I don't want to go back, and his thought came to me, saying, "It's okay, we're not going anywhere. We'll be here for you again." The last thought of his was "Tell your sister I'm fine."

With those final thoughts, I felt myself going back, dropping downward instantly through darkness. I didn't feel that I had a choice. I didn't feel afraid, but rather calm. Then, instantly, I felt myself slam into my body.... At that point, I felt the most incredible searing pain imaginable in my abdomen, all the way through to my backbone.... I couldn't believe I was returned to such a hellish environment, but then the beauty of the experience flooded back to me, giving me the most serene peace and calm I could hope for under the circumstances.

Laurelynn was back, but her physical ordeal, as she intimated, was hardly over. In fact, she had to go through additional surgery for a blood clot, and for several days, it was not clear that she would survive. Nevertheless, as is obvious now, she did make it, and afterward, she kept a journal about what had happened to her during this time. About it she says,

I ... left out the NDE because I didn't trust anyone. The initial reaction I got from my family was, "Be quiet, we don't want to talk about it. We just want you to get better." The health care professionals shrugged it off by saying, "You're highly medicated. You're taking shots of morphine every two–three hours."

Years later, in writing up this account, she remarks,

If I had only known that by talking about my NDE, and by acknowledging the event, my healing process would have been easier. However, I obviously had more lessons to learn because the next seven years were filled with rehabilitation (physical therapy), diagnostic tests and reparative surgery.

Laurelynn, however, was not bitter about her NDE, whatever the reactions it may have elicited from her family and those who treated her. Like most NDErs, she remains grateful for her experience, and her reflections on what she has learned from her experience, which concludes her statement, echo those we have heard before from Craig and Neev.

After the NDE, value changes came. I felt that the materialism and external stuff that was a big focus before just didn't matter anymore. My priorities in life took a complete turnaround. I felt there was a purpose for my life, even down to the smallest detail of being kind to others spontaneously and freely, loving more deeply, [and] being nonjudgmental and accepting of one's self and others. I also got a strong message about the importance of always seeking knowledge. I no longer fear death and, in fact, will welcome it when it is the right time—and that's only for the universal, supreme power to decide. Until then, though, I try to enjoy each day like it's my last and live more consciously in the moment. Now that I have acknowledged and am coming to terms with my NDE, I am seeing, feeling, and living through some magnificent changes. I'm finally feeling much healthier: physically, mentally, emotionally, and spiritually. I no longer take any medications, which was a monumental step, after at one time taking thirty-six pills per day. I have a love for life that is driven by the pure pleasure of appreciating each new day. I know my healing is a process and comes from within. I feel that I've been given a second chance in life and the more I share a part of myself, the more I feel at peace and at one with the universe.

Included as an appendix to the document describing her NDE, Laurelynn had written out a brief statement that itemized the principal after-effects of her experience. When I first read it over, I smiled to myself, for Laurelynn appeared to be a classic case as far as the effects of her NDE were concerned. In my research for my books, *Heading toward Omega* and *The Omega Project*, for example, I had found strong evidence for virtually all of the changes Laurelynn had specified for herself. However, when we went to lunch that day after her presentation, I was in for a surprise. Laurelynn, who had been referred to me by a colleague, confessed with some embarrassment that, actually, she had never read any of my books! So she could hardly be accused of trying to furnish me with merely a warmed-over version of my own findings to ingratiate herself (not that I would have imagined that for a moment, mind you!).

I would like to share this list of Laurelynn's with you now as a way of summing up both the lessons for life generally stemming from her NDE and its impact on her own life. Reading it, you will have a very good indication of what is true for many persons in their lives after an NDE. Indeed, it is as good and succinct a psychological portrait of the NDEr afterward as I have ever come across.

*Increased love for all people and all things*
*Increased sensitivity*
*Electromagnetic changes*
*Increased psychic ability*
*Seeing energy—auras, chakras*
*No fear of death*
*Lessened fear of many things*
*Decreased worry—surrendering to the divine plan*
*Reincarnation beliefs*
*Vegetarianism*
*Major relationship change—divorce*
*Career change*

*Less religious and more spiritual*
*Living each day like it is my last*
*Living more consciously in the moment*
*Increased concern for our planet—mother earth*
*Deepened appreciation of nature and the environment*
*Knowing that the greatest gift of all is giving love to self and others*
*Approaching all humanity and all creation with nonjudgment and complete acceptance*
*Less materialistic—seeing the "big picture"of life*
*Understanding we have a divine purpose in life*
*Understanding the challenges we face are simply lessons to learn here in earth school*
*Knowing with certainty always to follow my truth and to surrender to the flow of the universe*

Meeting and listening to Laurelynn was itself a spiritual experience of a kind. Like other NDErs I have known, she communicates directly what she lives and is. Perhaps even without meeting her, she has conveyed something of her essence to you through her words alone. In any case, I hope you will ponder with profit her story and the lessons for living that shine through it, and linger over it for a while before passing on to the next account.

As for Laurelynn herself, I have not seen her again, though I have kept in touch with her by letter and phone. She is now happily remarried and, until recently, when she had to take time off to have a baby (her conception was in itself almost a miracle, she told me), had been working as a physical therapist. In talking with her and her husband the day they both came to the university, I came away with the very strong impression that Laurelynn is deeply committed to living her life according to the spiritual principles and understanding she has glimpsed through her NDE. Even though her experience happened more than a dozen years ago, on the day we met, she seemed to me clearly to be living in the Light.

In reading these accounts I have so far presented, you might be tempted to assume that the beauty of the experience itself confers an unalloyed blessing on the NDEr's life afterward. If so, I must immediately disabuse you of such an idealized, if understandable, impression. Many, I dare say, most NDErs have a difficult time coming to terms with their experience, and the process of its integration into their lives may take a long time—and, certainly, in some cases, it does not occur at all. Long-standing relationships may be strained to and beyond the breaking point, marriages collapse, misunderstandings are common, and periods of painful introspection and even depression are not rare. The NDE, as we have seen, tends to turn a person's life topsy-turvy, and the radical reorientation and personal courage to live out the truth of one's NDE may be very taxing indeed, both to the NDEr and his or her family and friends.

## Sally

A case in point is a woman named Sally. Several years ago, she called me at my office, hoping to talk with someone about the problems she was having coping after her NDE, which had taken place many years before, in 1977. Sally, who lives in a small town in Colorado, shared with me some of her difficulties that day over the telephone, particularly in regard to her family, but, as it happened, I was able to meet with her personally not long afterward when I was vacationing in Colorado. At that time, I spent a good part of the day with Sally in her home and met several of her children. We have been friends ever since, and over the years, I have received many letters from her in which she has often spoken candidly of the difficulties living with her NDE has posed for her and her family.

To give you a sense of Sally, I should tell you that she is now forty-seven years old, and is of Mexican descent. A Catholic, she has a high school education, and she married young. With her husband, she has four children, ranging in age from seventeen to twenty-four, to whom she is very close. Though a recent illness has left her currently unemployed, she has mostly worked in various social service agencies and done a great deal of volunteer work. Physically, Sally is small, a little overweight, with dark, deeply compassionate eyes. When I met her, I had the impression that she was a very loving, if somewhat troubled, woman, and her letters have certainly reinforced that conviction.

Sally's NDE occurred as a result of a severe hemorrhage ten days after the birth of her youngest child. Relatives were summoned and an ambulance was called. Once Sally's body was placed in the ambulance, she, like Neev, found herself elsewhere during the ride to the hospital.

> You know what [she wrote to me in a letter]? I felt like I was above the ambulance en route to the hospital. I felt myself floating above it, although my body was still in it. Then, we arrived, and it took some time before ... I was taken into the emergency room. I felt I was going to die, but I don't recall being afraid.

Her physician tried to stem the bleeding but was unsuccessful, and surgery was deemed necessary. Sally remembers being aware of the doctors and nurses moving around her, but

> I felt so good. I didn't feel any pain.... Before the anaesthetic was given, the doctor said to me, "You might go in and come out okay, but you might not, due to severe bleeding." I was classified as a high risk. [I have copies of all of Sally's medical records, which confirm all the essential details of her condition, though, of course, they do not mention the words she says were spoken to her by her physician.] I didn't give it a second thought because I felt so good.
>
> The last [thing] I remember [was] my doctor's assistant standing by my bed and then I felt I left my body, and I could see it down below on the bed. I don't know how long I stayed above my body looking down at it, [but] suddenly, I was in the most beautiful Golden Light, and I stayed there. I felt so loved, calm, peaceful, happy. I can't find words to express what it was like. The Golden Light was all around me, all within me. I was in the Golden Light with no separation whatsoever. I didn't think of anyone or anything. Being there, I needed not a thing. Such powerful love, and so much love, so much beauty there. I felt love, compassion, understanding, knowledge. There is my true home, and here is my earthly home.
>
> Later, I saw beautiful flowers as I walked a beautiful path with someone on my right side dressed in a brown robe. We were walking up a mountain— beauty, beauty, beauty—flowers I had never seen before.
>
> I don't know how long I was in the Golden Light, but suddenly I found myself returning to my body … and then I opened my eyes, and a nurse said they were worried about me. I was so angry I felt like punching her! I was one angry Mexican! I wanted to be left alone.

Sally goes on to say that although she felt badly for insisting, she told her family please to leave her alone, that she didn't have anything to say to them. After she was discharged from the hospital, she continued to feel disturbed and "different." As she explains:

> I felt like [there were] two of me, angry, depressed, and I didn't want to be here. I wanted the beautiful Light, yet my children needed me. [After six months had passed] I continued to feel different, strange, weird, depressed, crying.... I stayed very busy and didn't have anyone to share my NDE with, and didn't know what I experienced. I did mention it to [my husband] at some time, but he had no interest.... I tried to talk with nurses, doctors, and so on, [but] they would [tell me] it was a dream, hallucination, medication, and so on, and said I should just forget it, [but] I can't forget it nor would I want to.

Fortunately, Sally eventually learned about NDEs, read some books on the subject, and then called me. In time, she met a number of people in her own community who could relate to her sensitively and with understanding, and this helped to ease her feeling of isolation. For Sally, it was very important to find persons who could appreciate what she had been through, as well as what she was continuing to experience in dealing with the ramifications of her NDE. Her life has not become easier after her experience, however, and partly because she has received no significant measure of support or understanding from her husband, she has often been on the point of leaving her marriage, but for her children's sake, she has not.

Nevertheless, in her many letters to me, Sally has often expressed the deepest gratitude for her NDE, for the continuing comfort its living memory brings to her, and for the lessons of love and compassion it has taught her. In one of her letters, for instance, she confided:

> I'm trying very hard here on earth, but I know where my *true* home is and how it feels. I remember it like it was today. I went directly to the Most Beautiful Golden Light. Real True Love. So much peace, protection, calmness. I didn't think or worry about anything. My beautiful Golden Light was around me, all through me, and I thank God for the Warmth of the Special Golden Light. I feel it so strong within me all the time.... I still feel the light in me and all around me. Ken, I also don't fear death. I feel like I would like to do so much for the family, for others, for myself. And I will continue to do what is honest and fair, with God's guidance.

We learn lessons from the NDE in Sally's experience, too, of course, but the ones I need to emphasize here are different and certainly more disquieting than those we have considered thus far. Most people, when they hear or read accounts of NDEs, feel a certain amount of envy, wishing that they too could have the experience (without, to be sure, having to go to the trouble of nearly dying for the privilege). But if they could really get under the skin and into the psyche of the NDEr, they would soon realize that the NDE is often a mixed blessing and may continue to extract a high cost in suffering from the individual's life, as it has for Sally.

I mention and, indeed, want to emphasize this in order to caution you that to the extent you begin to manifest these changes in your own life and try to live in accordance with the lessons and values of the NDE, you can also expect to confront difficulties and unexpected challenges. Do not think, for instance, that your family and friends will necessarily approve of or even understand your new behavior and attitudes. Do not suppose for a moment that you will not experience inner conflict, and even a significant degree of emotional turmoil, as these changes begin to take root in you.

Change is hard, and change without a significant degree of social support is even harder. If you want the benefits of the NDE, however, you will have to work for them and overcome the resistance you will encounter. Our society, after all, while it may accord nominal approval to many of the ideals of the NDE, often undermines them in practice. Even a moment's reflection on the behavioral implications of the NDE is sufficient to convince most people that the NDE is itself a subversive phenomenon in the sense that it undercuts the crasser forms of the American Dream. Swim in the current of the NDE for long and you will find yourself encountering powerful opposing forces. Be prepared for them and seek shelter when necessary. Like Sally, you may also find that you will have to seek new friends as well.

## Steve

Another person who has encountered much turbulence and inner conflict in his life following his NDE is my friend, Steve. He is the only NDEr to whom you are being introduced in this chapter that I have never met personally (though we plan to get together soon), but somehow I feel I have come to know him very well as a result of the many letters and E-mail communications Steve has sent me during the past year, in addition to a number of long telephone conversations we have had. In fact, I would estimate that I have received more than 300 pages of Steve's writings since he first got in touch with me in October 1993, as a result of which my file on him is already threatening to require a drawer of its own! He is, without question, one of the most brilliant, insightful, and deeply spiritual NDErs I have encountered in my nearly twenty years of research. And he is also one who has suffered much in his life, and suffers still more because of what he has learned from his NDE and other similar experiences.

Steve, who lives in southern California, is forty-three, married with three children, and works as a computer software engineer. He never completed college, but, as you will see, is something of an autodidact.

When he first wrote to me, he wanted to unburden himself of some of the conflicts he had been experiencing in trying to reconcile what he had learned from his NDE with the world of his everyday life. To begin with, however, Steve told me a bit about his NDE and how it had changed him.

In Steve's case, it is not clear to me that he was actually near death when he had his experience, which occurred during minor surgery, but the procedure did take much longer than expected, and he was told afterward that the surgeon did have "some trouble" performing the operation. Still, as has been well established, we know that one does not necessarily have to be close to physical death to have an NDE; there are many stressful but not life-threatening conditions that can precipitate an NDE or a functionally similar experience. And, in the end, it is, of course, the experience itself that counts, whatever may trigger it.

In 1975, when Steve was twenty-four, he underwent oral surgery in which some impacted wisdom teeth were to be removed. Before the procedure, Steve was injected with a sedative in his left arm and was later given sodium pentothal. That did not seem to take, and the surgeon, with some exasperation, then injected a total of four cartridges. After the surgery was completed—some two hours later!—Steve was taken to a dark, windowless, postoperative recovery room and, while there, had his experience.

> I awakened from the surgery, blinded by a river of white light. I thought it was an aftereffect of the general anesthesia. I thought it was odd that it pushed beyond my optic nerve and went through my entire body. I immediately rose to my feet and looked at the nurse who had helped me up.
>
> She wasn't a nurse. She was clothed in light, extraordinarily beautiful and loving. She was the most beautiful woman I had ever seen, and I almost cry when I think about it. She wore a loose-fitting white gown, and it gave off light of its own.... The light around her was flooding into me, and seemed to pour into everything.... The light that shone from the center of her was gloriously beautiful. This light, combined with her coloring, had an astonishing impact on me. The facial features were overpowered by this inner radiance. I could literally feel her love and care.... I had the impression that she knew me very well, and that I was very familiar to her, but she didn't say.
>
> I looked back and down at my body, still lying on the recovery couch under a blanket. Here I was, standing beside a being of light, looking at my body. Something seemed wrong.
>
> Before I reasoned it through, she intercepted my thoughts, and said, "Don't worry, you're not dead. You're quite alive. Your heart is still beating. Look!" I looked, I could see into it. I could see the chambers emptying and filling with blood. I could see the vascular system and the life-sustaining materials working their way through the entire body. I turned away, contented that things were all right.
>
> Just as I started to wonder why she was there, and what was wrong with my body, she intercepted my thought again, and said, "You're not breathing regularly. There is some concern that your respiration might stop. I'm here to stabilize it and make sure the problem doesn't go any further. You are very valuable, and no one is willing to take any chances with your life."
>
> She led me off to the side, and I [again] looked back at my body, lying

in the couch. Two walls separated us. She had a veil of energy to her back. It separated her world from mine.... I understood immediately that I wasn't allowed to go through there. "It's a one-way path. If you go through there, you can't come back here. Your life will be over, and you won't have done the things you need to do." Brilliant shards of light in all colors danced around the opening. They appeared and disappeared, as if the light energy was being fragmented and shattered at the contact point between two worlds at different energy levels.

I felt wonderful, and not too surprised—this was not the first time I had met someone like her. Her light was a signature that identified her, and I had seen that light before. To see her was to fall in love with her instantly. I never wanted to leave her. It may be that she felt the circumstances provided an unfair comparison to my wife. She showed me some details about my children [who were not yet born] and revealed a view of another woman even more lovely and desirable—the wife I was married to. She then said it was time to return, that my breathing had stabilized, and that my nervous system was able to work on its own.... I saw her light begin to withdraw from me as she retreated from my view. This light persisted for two or three seconds as I awakened, while my wife was holding my face in her hands.

Was what Steve experienced merely an effect of the drug he had been given? Steve himself considered that possibility—and rejected it.

People told me it was an hallucination caused by the drugs. I've had sodium pentothal before and never had such an experience. In fact, it wasn't pleasant the first time I had it.... [Years later] after reading Melvin Morse's[3] account of people who were drawn to NDE studies but didn't believe they had experienced an NDE, I came across an account very much like mine in the outline of events and began to realize that it may not have been a drug-induced hallucination.

Of course, drug-induced hallucinations do not ordinarily bring about dramatic changes in people's lives, and, as we will learn shortly, the effects of this and other similar experiences in Steve's life have been nothing short of astounding. But before we look into these aftereffects, it is necessary for me to clarify something that may have puzzled you when you were reading Steve's narrative of his NDE. At one point, he tells us that the light he glimpsed during his experience was already familiar to him—he had seen it before. When?

Well, the fact is that five years earlier Steve had had another NDE as a result of a severe liver infection and had had a few other "light experiences," as he calls them, as well around the same period of his life, though these were not associated with any life-threatening crisis. In the context of his life, then, the NDE Steve has just related for us might be best regarded as something of a culmination of a series of related transcendental experiences. In any event, they signified the beginning of some momentous shifts in Steve's life and seem also to be linked with the development of some extraordinary proclivities.

> My personality changed after those experiences, and I was never able to get along with my parents and family members after that. They said I was a flower child, a nonconformist without a purpose. People considered me a weak personality who couldn't accomplish anything.
>
> I suddenly felt tremendously ignorant. I started buying books. I filled up notebooks on histories of different nations, on archeology, and on philosophies.
>
> I found I could memorize and play a Bach prelude and fugue with only a few hours of preparation, whereas before I had to struggle for weeks to learn a piece of music.

After his NDE at age twenty-four, he says, many of the changes he had already noticed began to accelerate, and some of his conflicts and problems started becoming increasingly painful.

> [At that time] I worked in my family's business. My father was a very competitive businessman. He was an important man in the church. He knew the Bible backward and forward. He was a motivational speaker and sales trainer with a national reputation. He taught me that I could never succeed unless I developed an intense, burning desire for money and riches. I really tried, but I was never able to feel a burning desire for money. I was able to work effectively: I won some sales contests and later managed his business well enough to earn the respect of his clients and competitors. But they never accepted my "soft" personality. "Lowkey" was the nicest word they could put on it.
>
> They found my changed viewpoint unbearable. My ability to see the future, and my tendency to react and answer the private thoughts and intentions of my father's business associates, rather than their outward, polished manners, was very disturbing to everyone. I had to retrain myself to listen and think on two levels—face value and true feelings. Unless I was on guard, I would respond to questions by answering what was in the person's inner thoughts and motives, rather than to the face value of their words. My success was a nonconforming accident. I was never in a hurry. I was never competitive. The ones who were less generous told me I wasn't really a man.

Meanwhile, whenever Steve was free of the demands of his business life he threw himself into self-education projects, which eventually were to extricate him from the prison house of his family's firm.

> At twenty-six, I started buying books and learning languages. First French, then Spanish. After two semesters, I started on *Don Quixote* and read Vol-

taire's *Philosophical Letters*. Then, I returned to Portuguese [he had previously lived in Brazil]. At twenty-eight, I studied history and philosophy. At twenty-nine, I began excursions into particle physics and electronics. At thirty-two, I started designing oscillators and low-noise amplifiers. One of them is in an orbiting satellite. At thirty-six, I started designing microprocessors. I'm forty-two now. As a professional programmer, I write about 40,000 lines of C-language a year.

Steve still reads voraciously and widely:

I bought about 150 books last year. I went through most of them. They were on history, philosophy, other religions, astronomy, physics, and archeology. Excepting masterworks and classics, I don't read fiction anymore.

Now very successful in his work and an obvious bibliophile, Steve still has time to explore hobbies such as astronomy (he has two telescopes) and photography (he specializes in wild birds—I have one of his photographs of a pelican in my office—and flowers). Yet, like many other NDErs, he complains that he is too sensitive.

I can't watch TV cop shows. I think it's obscene to show a killing without remorse. My teenagers and I have a running battle about their TV selections. A TV show with a graphic murder is rated "X" in our home. If they watch a violent show, I can feel what they see even if I'm in another room, and it upsets me. They think I'm weird. Nothing causes me more pain than to have my family members quarreling.

I can't give up what I've seen. Nothing else really matters. Just driving on the freeway, sensing the anger other people have, is painful to me.

He has problems when he is in church, too.

I love God more than anything. But I almost can't go to church. I can't sit through a class.... I can't relate to the shame and guilt in the lessons. The discussions on guilt and sin don't hold any relevance for me, and don't make me happy. They don't fit into any of the experiences I've had.... I tried opening these subjects gently and cautiously with local church leaders, and they don't respond well. So I drop it.

When my life is not as it should be, I feel emotional pain, and I change as fast as I can. But the numerous rules and regulations don't hold any meaning for me. They don't move my heart at all. The laws seem like preparatory steps for something better. I know there's more.

These days, Steve says, he can find some comfort in literature, especially that in which "real religion" is taught. He is very fond of the writings of Antoine de Saint-Exupery, who is best known of course for his classic story, *The Little Prince*. In another of his books, *Terres des Hommes*, Steve tells me, there is another tale, apparently based on Saint-Exupery's own experience as a pilot.

> His plane crashed, and he had gone seven days with little or no water. He was past the pain of dying when a Bedouin picked him off the sand and gently lowered his face into a bowl of water. He looked up into the desert-dweller's wrinkled face and saw all of his friends, all of his enemies, all of mankind, and felt an eternal love. After that time, he said, he couldn't find any hatred for Arabs, Germans, Turks, or for any people. The only thing he hated was deliberate ignorance and insensitivity to other people's feelings.

It is easy to grasp why Steve would resonate so strongly with Saint-Exupery's epiphany in the desert, especially since Steve finds himself in a kind of spiritual desert of his own, looking for an oasis of understanding from someone among those to whom he is naturally drawn. To me, Steve is a sobering example of a man who has, perhaps, seen too much, experienced and absorbed too much of the Light, ever to be wholly comfortable in the ordinary world. He suffers for what he knows and for the pain of those who remain ignorant of what the Light teaches. Yet, at the same time, people like Steve are a bright beacon for others who are drawn to know what he does, and for them he is an incomparable teacher. To me, he is a being of light in his own right, a source of illumination, who instructs by his very being and through the medium of his plain-spoken language of the heart.

In another of his letters to me, Steve said, "There is no greater sermon than the lives we live (and no greater observers than our children)." It is aphoristic gems like these that make me look forward to hearing from Steve. He has been one of my teachers, too, and the lessons he imparts are, I hope you will now agree, the pure gold of the NDE.

## Peggy

Another, and our final, messenger from the Light is a woman named Peggy Holladay, who wrote me in 1989 about her NDE, sending me at the time a seventeen-page document describing her experience and the lessons it so forcibly impressed upon her. Had I space here, I would be tempted to quote her statement in full because of its power and profundity, but I will have to be content with sharing with you some excerpts from this and another account she later mailed to me, in order to give you a sense of Peggy's experience. They will be sufficient, I think, to make it obvious that her journey to the Light was taken, in effect, on behalf of all of us.

After hearing from Peggy, I naturally wrote her back to express my deep appreciation, and a year later, we were able to meet at a conference on NDEs in Washington. Peggy turned out to be a dark-haired, attractive woman who, at the time, appeared to be in her midthirties. She was married, had two children, and her joy in life was singing. She had been featured in some musicals (she later was to send me a video of one her performances, in Jerome Kern's *Showboat*), and, as I was to learn, is also a talented portraitist and inventor. In summary, she is a woman of obvious creative gifts, and in her personal manner, she is highly enthusiastic and very warm.

On Christmas morning, 1973, when Peggy was in her early twenties and living in Dallas, she was involved in a serious automobile accident, during which she suffered a potentially fatal compound skull fracture. She does not remember having an NDE as such at the time (of course, the term itself did not exist then), but afterward did recall having then puzzling images of seeing her body lying on the ground and later being placed into an ambulance. Nevertheless, this experience was a turning point in Peggy's life and brought about radical changes in her personality, worldview, and patterns of social interaction.

For one thing, she was possessed by a desire to return to college and took subjects in previously uncongenial areas, such as chemistry and biology, and discovered she excelled in them. She was learning in an entirely new way, and reminiscent of Steve, she comments:

> It was as if I was "seeing" things from a much greater depth of understanding!!! Needless to say, the absolute joy of learning was incredibly new to me and my mind felt like it was literally starving for new and interesting information. I couldn't pile it in fast enough.

For another, she found her friendships and lifestyle changing. Previously a frequent partier and something of a clown socially, she gradually realized these superficial roles no longer suited her: "After my head injury, I couldn't relate to my old life anymore. I was a different person, and everyone who had known me was starting to see that."

She began to have unusual mystical experiences in which she felt "the most profound joy I have ever known," and also to have conscious out-of-body experiences. Raised a Baptist, she felt a pull to return to her religion, but after a few months found that she could no longer relate to what she describes as "traditional Christian dogma." But perhaps the most soul-stretching change Peggy was undergoing at this time was in her experience of empathic love. In this connection, she relates the following illustrative incidents:

> I can remember many times I had the strong urge to hug total strangers with overpowering feelings of care and concern. I didn't understand where all this empathy was coming from, but I just knew it felt beautiful, even though I couldn't hug them.... A handful of times when this happened I was able to pick up on their thoughts. I actually read their minds and, at the same time, felt great love for them.
>
> However, the most memorable experience I had after my head injury was with two fellow students I had met in an English class. We had only talked briefly on a few occasions about the assignments, but I can remember feeling a strange bond, almost as if they were my younger brother and sister since they were eighteen and twenty-two. I was not prepared for the feeling that went through me one day as we talked. It only lasted for about 1½ to 2 minutes but was a LOVE so incredibly powerful and intensely deep that I was astounded and even in a state of shock as it went through me. I never knew such a LOVE existed. As I talked to them and looked into their eyes I loved them in a way human beings are not capable of loving (not yet, anyway). I not only knew what they both were thinking but, if you can imagine this, I became them!! There are no words or, for that matter, even human emotions at this point to describe how much I loved those two people in that 1½-minute span. I had never felt such a love for another human being before or since that experience, even my own children and I worship them!! Although I was never quite sure where that feeling came from, I knew it was not from this world.

Anyone familiar with the literature on the aftereffects of NDEs would by now have realized that the changes Peggy was undergoing after her head injury are all typical of persons who have themselves had NDEs. Could Peggy have had one, without fully being aware of it?

The answer is, most certainly. In the course of my own research, for instance, I have encountered quite a few persons, especially those who have been involved in vehicular crashes, who for sometime afterward, even years, have no conscious recall of an NDE. They suffer from what is called "retrograde amnesia." Then, eventually, something triggers a partial memory, and like a long-forgotten dream, the experience comes flooding back.

Something like this appears to have happened to Peggy, too, for thirteen years later, while riding in a van similar to the one in which her accident occurred, on her way to Dallas, where it took place, she seems to have had a *conscious* recollection of at least fragments of her earlier experience. Whatever the explanation, however, what came to her that day is the very essence of the ultimate teachings of the Light, as it is presented to the minds of NDErs, and for this alone, Peggy's statement is of enormous value and relevance to us.

On August 22, 1986, Peggy was in the van her husband was driving when she was emotionally overcome by some sorrowful lyrics of a song playing on the radio. She experienced a wave of all-consuming empathy for people and, overwhelmed by the suddeness and depth of her reaction, went to the back of the van to lie down. Trying to relax, she paradoxically found her heart to be racing, pounding, she says, "as if I had been doing some hard aerobic exercise for twenty-five minutes." Gradually, her breathing slowed down, however, and she found herself immersed in the "blackest blackness" but was not afraid. She felt totally peaceful and ecstatic and, at the same time, "locked into" the experience that was about to unfold.

> I can remember not knowing where I was while I was floating, but I seemed to be so caught up in feeling great I didn't really think about it. That is, until I saw over my left shoulder a small but bright light. I never felt like I was in a tunnel zooming to the light, but rather just serenely floating in blackness while the light came to me. The light was round and did get bigger and bigger VERY FAST, so I could have been zooming through a tunnel even though I didn't feel it. As everyone says who has ever seen this light, it looks like the brightest blue-white light in your imagination—multiplied by 10,000. I was a little scared when the light first zoomed to me (or me to it), even though it didn't hurt my eyes like I thought it would. In fact, the more I looked at it, the more mesmerized I became with peacefulness. The light was extremely soothing and joyful to "take in...." I clearly and instantly knew the light was not just a Light but was ALIVE! It had a personality and was intelligence beyond comprehension.... I knew the light was a being. I also knew that the light being was God and was genderless.
>
> Furthermore, I felt the light "talking" ... with a communication so sophisticated that my mind could not decipher what was being said.... I began to sense the light knew me VERY WELL right before it surrounded me completely.

Nevertheless, Peggy was able to understand what the Light was communicating to her, and also began to experience the energy of the light. "I KNEW completely without any shadow of a doubt that it was the strongest force in existence. It was the Energy of Pure Love. I thought, "I can't wait to tell people."

And the Light began to teach her in response to questions Peggy now thinks she must have asked:

The light showed me the world is an illusion. All I remember about this is looking down [at what she took to be the earth] … and thinking, "My God, it's not real, it's not real!" It was like all material things were just "props" for our souls, including our bodies. Heavier things we can see are of a lower reality and are real, but not like we think they are. There are invisible things to us now from higher levels that are far, far, far, more real. I thought, "I've GOT to remember this!"

In this state, Peggy soon noticed that her mind was functioning in an extraordinary manner, making many of the insights she was receiving self-evident:

In this place, whatever it is, I did not have the limited consciousness I have on earth. It felt like I had 125 senses to our normal five. You could do, think, comprehend, and so on, you name it, with no effort at all. It's as if the facts are right before you in plain sight with no risk of misinterpretation because the truth *just is!* Nothing is hidden. Communication is done by your thinking your question and answer. Well-formed thoughts would just pop into your mind and you would know it came from another source. You would project your own thoughts that way, too. In this other realm, things like truths were just there before you and all you had to do was just think of what you wanted to know and there it was. The mind was paramount, and one thing that astonished me was my ability to think as many things as I liked all at the same time. I can remember how stunned I was when I realized I was thinking many, many thoughts at the same time with complete comprehension and ease.

Other revelations poured into Peggy. Time also was an illusion, she learned. Horrific events on earth had an inner meaning that humans, with their limited and parochial understanding, could never hope to fathom. "I wanted to sob with pure joy," Peggy says, "at the perfection of all creation." But of all the things Peggy took in, in this state of tremendously expanded consciousness, the most meaningful to her, and perhaps to us, had to do with the all-pervading and primary nature of love in the universe.

I continued to see some other amazing truths.… One was when the light told me everything was Love, and I mean everything! I had always felt love was just a human emotion people felt from time to time, never in my wildest dreams thinking it was literally EVERYTHING!

I was shown how much all people are loved. It was overwhelmingly evident that the light loved everyone equally without *any* conditions! I really want to stress this, because it made me so happy to know we didn't have to believe or do certain things to be loved. WE ALREADY WERE AND ARE,

NO MATTER WHAT! The light was extremely concerned and loving toward all people. I can remember looking at the people together and the light asking me to "love the people." I wanted to cry, I felt so deeply for them.... I thought, "If they could only know how much they're loved, maybe they wouldn't feel so scared or lonely anymore."

Then, as if to drive home the incomprehensible immensity of this love so that she would never forget it, Peggy received an infusion of the light's energy:

I vividly recall the part where the light did what felt like switch on a current of pure, undiluted, concentrated unconditional LOVE. This love I experienced in the light was so powerful it can't be compared to earthly love, even though earthly love is a much milder version. It's like knowing that the very best love you feel on earth is diluted to about one part per million of the real thing. As this stream of pure love went through me, I felt as if the light was saying simultaneously, "I love you COMPLETELY and ENTIRELY *as you are*, BECAUSE YOU ARE.

Right at that moment, I began to sob deeply, feeling like I didn't deserve that much pure love and had done too many things wrong. All the while I was feeling this horrible sadness and wrenching unworthiness, I remember being loved by the light. It never once stopped loving me and I'll never forget the impression this made on me. I thought, "There is more love here than anything else...." It was like being bathed in energy particles of pure love. And while this radiant and energizing love was streaming through me, I KNEW, if only for a few seconds, I was totally one with the light. I knew there was nothing wrong with me in any way. NOTHING! Just for a few moments, I didn't think or feel perfection—I WAS PERFECTION. I wasn't just with the light. I became the light. I became everything at the same time!!

Perhaps we may now recall, with greater understanding of its source, that staggering outpouring of empathic love Peggy described in connection with the two students she befriended in college. ("I never knew such a LOVE existed.... I knew it was not from this world.") And in this connection, Peggy now feels she took home an important lesson about the healing power of unconditional love as a result of her receiving a direct transmission of it during her encounter with the light.

One of the many beliefs I have formed from this experience is that whenever unconditional love is bestowed upon an individual, no matter what the strength or from what source (a person or the light), it causes a purging of "unloving energy" or self-hating energy (which are all illusions) to come into the consciousness of the individual to be examined and discharged. Thus, the individual's level of consciousness is raised every time this is done.

Peggy herself, however, at this point in her journey, having absorbed these and other lessons from the Light, was about to begin her return to earth. While still bathed in the Light, she was asked if she "could do this forever?"

> I remember hesitating for a second, thinking about my family, I guess, but I definitely said YES.... Upon feeling even one moment of this pure energy, any human being alive would fall to his or her knees and deeply sob with unbridled and uninhibited joy at the perfection of the universe. I was willing to *give up everything* I had loved on earth to stay with that profound state of bliss.

But for reasons we will never know, Peggy's wish was not granted by the Light, and she found herself heading back, forced to enter her body, she says, as if it had in the meantime become a rock. On doing so, she found her eyes full of tears and "was in a state of shock, wondering *what the heck had happened to me!*"

Nevertheless, the insights from the Light continued to flow into her even after this experience, just as they did for Neev after his NDE, and, as we have seen before, at this point, rather than having the quality of ultimate revelation, they tend to have a more personal significance for the individual. It is almost as if the Light, having delivered itself of its universal truths, now seeks to inform the individual how all of this knowledge is to be used in his or her life. In Peggy's case, the implications were similar to those that were disclosed to Craig, and had to do with music.

First, however, Peggy states a lesson from the Light in more general terms:

> One thing I [learned] was that we are ALL here to do an "assignment of love." We don't have to do it at all, or we can do as many as we like. It's up to us. Our "assignment" is programmed in at birth and it is the very thing or things we *love* most. I was such a bozo. I always thought doing what you loved most was selfish. I can remember how amazed and happy I was when this information "came into my mind." This other source of energy, using my voice, said, "That is the most unselfish and constructive thing you can do for the world because that is your assigned energy and you will be happiest doing it, best at it, and most respected for it!"
>
> During my NDE, I did recall what it was like for me when I was around seven years old and singing all the time. I literally relived those moments and felt the joy I had known when I used to sing. I recalled the light telling me to try to go toward singing. It said nothing of fame, money, or even a nice singing voice.

I know what I am saying sounds absolutely nuts—believe me, I know.... But this was a BIG part of this incredible encounter, and to leave it out would make the whole story less true, or at least have less meaning for me. So even though I know in my heart the light told me singing was my "assignment," and even though I want desperately to sing and am working like crazy at it, I will try to be open to whatever comes my way.... I have had an enormous amount of fun just trying and I won't have to go to my grave knowing I never even tried.

Now that I have seen, been with, and experienced the source of this loving euphoric state of mind, I'll be chasing it for the rest of my life and doing whatever I feel deeply to do, knowing it is the *light* that is driving me. I used to think I was the artist when I was painting. I now see, since my NDE, that I am only the brush, my life experiences are the paint, my life is the painting, and the world is the studio with love as the subject.

Peggy concludes her commentary by expressing the gratitude that, as we now know, so many NDErs offer to the Light for their encounter with ultimate truth, despite the fact that it has launched her on an uncertain course:

It has become my whole life to pay that light back in some way for coming to me and loving me when I needed it most. I've got a feeling this is going to be a lifetime project. The "old me" is gone and every day I'm discovering the "new me." I don't know what the future will bring but I am going to do my best to stay open for change and growth. I know I'll probably spend the rest of my life adjusting, in one way or another, to what happened to me that day in August. But I wouldn't change it for the world! I will have it with me always and, I hope, find some way to share it.

Well, share it she certainly has! And I only wish I could present more of Peggy's experience and its lessons for you here, but perhaps you have read enough by now, in her account and in the others that preceded it in this chapter, to have formed a clear picture of what is encountered and learned in these journeys to the Light, and to understand how deep is the yearning of these travelers to share with others what they have seen there.

As for Peggy, we have kept in touch regularly over the years since we met in Washington. Although we saw each other only on that occasion, I did talk with her recently over the telephone to see how she was doing these days. She sounded bright and animated, as ever, and told me that she had indeed been pursuing her singing, which continues to give her great joy, and has been working on some new inventions as well. All in all, she gave me the impression that she was still happily following the course the Light had set her upon years ago and no doubt was continuing to spread that light to others she was meeting along the way. As she had to me when I first talked with her in Washington and as she has, I trust, to you, too, through her voice in this book.

## DRAWING THE GOLDEN THREADS TOGETHER

In considering these half-dozen journeys to the Light we have followed in this chapter, it is obvious that there are certain recurrent themes that run through them. To me, however, these themes represent three distinct *levels* of insight that must be made explicit if the full spectrum of lessons from the NDE is to be properly understood.

First, there is the level of what I would simply call here *the beatific vision*. This is the highest, most inclusive, and universal aspect of the NDE. When caught up in this beatific vision, the individual realizes the perfection of the universe and, because one is not separate from the universe but an indispensable and integral part of it, one's own perfection as well. This is the realm of pure, unconditional love and acceptance, a primordial womb of light blazing with beauty and glory beyond measure, where all knowledge is finally revealed, and where one becomes aware, with a sense of incontrovertible certitude, that this is our true and eternal home.

Next, there is the level of what I will call *earthly realizations*. At this level of the NDE, one comes to see with pristine eyes the importance of certain human values, beliefs, and strivings that ought to inform one's life in the world. Among these are the primacy of expressing empathic love and concern for others, the value of seeking knowledge for its own sake, the imperative to live life to the fullest with a never-failing awareness of the preciousness of life, the need to turn away from a competitive lifestyle or one based on material acquisition, the conviction that death is nothing to be feared but just a continuation of life, and so on.

And, finally, there is the level of what I think is best described as *personal revelation*. This is information that, as we have seen, normally comes to the individual toward the end of his or her NDE, where its lessons are particularized to the needs and circumstances of the NDEr by the Light itself, or by a presence or guide that is encountered within the realm of Light. Since, in later chapters, we will have ample time to consider more fully both the beatific vision and the earthly realizations stemming from the NDE, I would like to conclude this chapter by focusing on this last type of insight. One reason for doing so here is to make clear to you how these personal lessons can be made applicable to your own life, even though you may not have had an NDE yourself.

We begin by recalling certain salient features of the NDE that bear on the nature and significance of these personal revelations. To start with, please remember that in every case we have considered, the individual encounters some kind of a presence within the Light, someone or something that gives the impression of having an omniscient knowledge of the person and an infinite solicitude for his or her welfare and future well-being. When we nearly die, then, we find that we are not alone and presumably have never been alone. We have someone or something that appears to guide us benevolently, albeit invisibly, in our life on this earth, but that can intervene at critical moments and, even, as in the near-death state, manifest clearly into our awareness. This in itself is profoundly reassuring.

When we explore the function of this guiding agency further, however, we can see in virtually every case we have presented that it is almost as if it injects itself during the context of the NDE to help right the individual's life course and put him or her back on track again. This is particularly evident, for example, in Neev's life, where he was apparently enmeshed in a self-destructive downward spiral and trapped in a seemingly unbreakable cage of damaged self-esteem and pervasive feelings of failure. The self-insight he gained from his NDE, and particularly from his life review, with the aid of his guide, smashed that cage once and for all and freed him to live, I am tempted to say, as he was meant to. In Peggy's case as well, she was, according to her own account, living a largely vacuous and somewhat hedonistic life before her NDE, but having felt the influx of divine love from the Light and receiving her personal insights from the Light itself, she, too, found her way into a much more personally fulfilling way of being. Even with Steve, although he continues to suffer from his acute sensitivity, once he was free of a stifling family and business environment, his NDE helped to unleash his latent talents by spurring his desire for knowledge and enabled him to launch a much more satisfying career. And, indeed, Steve has told me, just recently in fact, that he continues to receive conscious guidance from his light beings, showing that this help is available in everyday life and not just in the extreme moments of near death.

In examining the lives of the NDErs we have met in this chapter, do you not feel that all of them, to various degrees, have been aided to live more authentic lives, much more in keeping with their previously dormant gifts and propensities, and emboldened to throw off the social shackles, where necessary, that previously constrained them? The Light told Peggy, in effect, that she should "follow her love," and that yielding herself to it was, in fact, to do the most unselfish and constructive thing in the world. The Light seems to be telling us, each of us, that we have a unique gift, an offering to make to the world, and that our happiness and the world's are both served when we live in such a way as to realize that gift, which is no less than our purpose in life. What the NDE does is to help crack the egg in which that gift has lain, neglected and even unsuspected, so that it can begin to emerge and grow to its fullest. It does this by showing each individual who he or she was, in essence, meant to be by enabling him or her to glimpse something of his or her true self and its vocation in the world. Thus, Craig is led to touch people with his flute and Peggy with her voice; Laurelynn helps to restore damaged bodies, while Neev works to guide children to discover and realize their own potentials; Steve has found his way by becoming a computer specialist and, lately, something of an NDE networker; Sally, though continuing to do good works, still struggles to realize her own true self.

I have talked about this authentic or true self as something that is the Light's function to disclose to the individual. How does it do that? The answer is, often by first showing the NDEr his or her *false* or socially conditioned self. In some cases, the mechanism by which this is effected is the life review. Do you remember, for example, in Neev's story, how he used the knowledge provided in the life review to refashion his life? At one point in his paper, he states emphatically,

> The most prominent thing [I] felt after the NDE was a need to correct and change all of the things I did not like about myself. This memory of the life review sickened me. I continually saw myself and hated what I saw. It was the life review that sparked my desire for change and also allowed this change.

In other instances, however, the NDEr is given a direct perception into the nature of the false self and is thereby allowed intuitively to understand that the person one has identified with and habitually thought of as one's essential self was nothing more than a fiction. This happened to Peggy, for example, and her recounting of this insight contains an important message for everyone:

> [At one point] my consciousness must have pulled away from my body because I suddenly observed it from a short distance as it sobbed. I was

completely unemotional as I observed my body. As I watched, I saw some shiny, clear object lift away from my body. It was obvious to me it was my ego. The moment my ego started lifting, my consciousness went back into my body and I felt distress, thinking, "It's my ego, it's my ego!," not wanting it to leave me. I felt like I had to have it or I wouldn't be alive. It pulled away from me anyway, and in it I saw all the things I had done wrong in my life. I was stunned because I thought all that was part of me and simply couldn't be separated from me. I can't tell you how happy I was when it dawned on me that "that was never me." That identity was never the real me.

I began to realize I was okay without it and was, in fact, better off. It was sort of like taking a dusty, old, clogged-up, used filter off an air -conditioner vent and letting the air go through unhindered. Only, in this case, it was that pure, undiluted love going through me. I decided to relax and let the light pour all this magnificent energy into me and, believe it or not, I began to feel like I actually deserved it! If there is such a thing as "restoring a soul," then that's exactly what happened to me.

The false self is socially constructed, but the true self is not so much given *by* the NDE as created and realized by the individual *after* the NDE. The knowledge provided by the Light, however, is enough to help the individual see the false self and how it came into being—and that knowledge itself is often sufficient to begin the task of its demolition. Once that happens, a space is cleared for the new, more authentic self to flower naturally, and, if there is an underlying personal aim of the NDE, it seems to be to encourage this very development in the individual. It is as if the Light wants everyone to become the self he or she was originally meant to be. Peggy expressed this thought when she said, "Our 'assignment' is programmed in at birth, and it is the very thing or things we *love* most." Acting from this love helps us to realize our true self, which is created anew every day of our lives through authentic behavior. This is what is meant by "following your love."

Now, it is as plain as the print on this page that these lessons from the Light are not just for the NDErs of this world. They are for everyone. The NDErs in this chapter, messengers of the Light, are simply our teachers here, whose job is to remind us of the truths we may have forgotten. Are you following your love? Or have you allowed it to be lost sight of as you go about your everyday life?

*Take a moment, please, to reflect on this*—don't just hurry on to the next chapter. This entire chapter has really been one long prologue to the questions I have just put to you, for they lie at the very heart of the personal significance *for you* of the NDEs I have recounted here. If you feel that your own life has somehow drifted off course, you do not have to have an NDE to put it right again. But you can learn from those who have and begin the job of steering it toward its proper direction again. If you sense my words may apply to you, perhaps you might try to consider your life afresh in the light of what the NDE teaches. And remember, the NDErs tell us that we are not and are never alone. We each have a source of inner guidance that, once we discover it, can serve us the same way it does the NDEr. And, remember, too, Peggy's words that the boundless Light that is the source of all love in the world also loves each one of us equally and infinitely. "I was shown how much all people are loved," Peggy said. "If they could only know how much they are loved." That love is there for all of us, and, once you open to it, it will inevitably lead you to yourself—your real self.

## Chapter Two

# The View from the Top:
# Dust Sightings
# and Misplaced Shoes

When one reflects on the contents of the NDE narratives I presented in the last chapter, it is hard to deny that something truly extraordinary has happened to these individuals. But perhaps it is also their tone of assurance and the obvious sincerity of their words that convince most listeners that what they have experienced while close to death constitutes a revelation containing some the essential truths about life and about how life is meant to be lived.

Certainly, virtually all NDErs are themselves persuaded that what they have seen and understood during their vision represents something as authentic as it is indubitable. And, by the same measure, typically, these individuals are equally sure that what they have experienced is no dream, fantasy, or hallucination. More than one such person has asseverated to me, and with great emphasis, that their NDE was "more real than life itself," or "more real than you and I sitting here talking about it," or similar avowals. In this connection, I particularly remember one middle-aged man asserting with vigor that his experience was "totally objective and utterly real."

Given both the consistent and *insistent* character of these avowals, it would be foolish and certainly cavalier to disregard this kind of testimony.

Yet, at the same time, since most of us have not had this experience, we are seemingly left in the somewhat uncomfortable position of having to take something merely on faith—faith in the accuracy of someone else's judgment. It is, of course, noteworthy that that judgment is essentially unanimous among NDErs, but clearly, from a strictly scientific point of view, that is no proof of anything. This collective body of opinion among NDErs, however impressive it may be in its passionate unity, is nevertheless unverifiable and rests entirely on subjective self-reports.

These doubts, however much some of us may wish to override them, must be acknowledged at the outset. After all, on a moment's reflection, everyone would concede that even earnest and patently sincere persons may be mistaken or even deluded about the nature of their own experience. And, in regard to NDEs in particular, there are certainly other books available, such as Susan Blackmore's *Dying to Live*, that take a rigorously skeptical view of these encounters and try to explain them away largely on neurological grounds. This kind of a challenge must surely be addressed, especially if you are considering basing some of your own thinking and actions on the teachings to be derived from these experiences. It would hardly do to find out, in the end, that you were being guided by nothing more than hallucinations produced by a neurologically disturbed brain deprived of oxygen!

The difficulty in resolving this issue, of course, lies in the very fact that NDEs are, at bottom, inherently subjective, deeply private, and often ineffable. As such, they would seem to be forever beyond the scrutiny of the scientific lens and have the status of undisconfirmable modern-day religious revelations. It does no good to argue, as many do in their behalf, that these experiences have a common pattern to them. That shows only that they are not idiosyncratic. It is still possible to regard this pattern, as Susan Blackmore and other skeptics do, for example, as nothing more than the predictable subjective detritus thrown up by a dying brain, signifying nothing.

We seem, then, to stand at an impasse. In principle, I would like to be able to show you that these experiences are indeed what NDErs claim, namely, that they are authentic, objective, and as real as they appear. But to demonstrate this, one would first have to establish that NDEs cannot plausibly be interpreted as complex hallucinations, fantasies, or dreams: in short, that the NDE is not merely a *psychological* phenomenon or simply the neurological artifact of a dying brain.

In fact, quite to the contrary, we now have good evidence, and from multiple sources, that the NDE is indeed an experience that has its own objective character and is, in a phrase, "on the level." In the next several chapters, I present some of this evidence for your own consideration and, by the time you finish this portion of the book, I hope you will be re-assured that the doubts about the validity of the NDE can be safely dis-patched on purely scientific grounds. *What follows, then, is in effect a brief of sorts for the defense that aims to establish the case for the authenticity of the NDE.*

## OUT-OF-BODY VISIONS

A hint of what is to come can be suggested by this anecdotal account of a twenty-year-old actor's experience one evening when he was in the midst of a very strenuous and frenzied dance on stage:

> Suddenly, without a moment's warning, I found myself in steel rafters near the ceiling of the room. I was aware of the gloom of the girders rising up through the shadows, and looking down on the spectacle below, I was startled to see that my vision had changed: I could see everything in the room— every hair on every head, it seemed—all at the same time. I took it all in, in a single omnipresent glance: hundreds of heads arranged in wavering rows of portable chairs, a half-dozen babies sleeping in laps, hairs of many different colors, shining from the light on stage. Then, my attention shifted to the stage, and there we were in multicolored leotards, whirling about in our dance, and there I was—*there I was*—face to face with [his dancing partner].[1]

Needless to say, this man was astonished at finding himself in two places at the same time—both in and out of his body, so to speak—and was utterly baffled by how such a thing could have happened to him. Later, however, he had cause to muse about his experience and its possible meaning, and he, too, considered the two obvious alternatives, just as we have in connection with NDEs:

> Was it a natural phenomenon or just a mental aberration? I naturally wanted to believe my eyes [but] … both the vividness of the experience and the omnipresent nature of my vision, which saw everything in the room at once with the eye of a hawk, could seemingly be argued either way. But when I think of things like the rivet pattern in the girders of the ceiling, or the balding spot on the man with the red checked coat in row five, or a hundred other details that filled my sight in the midst of the event, it seems more reasonable to call it a natural phenomenon than to call it an hallucination. No autoscopic ("self-seeing") hallucination, drawing only from the information my mind already possessed, could have been so full or accurate in detail.[2]

This narrative of an apparent out-of-body episode (OBE) is not only fascinating and suggestive in its own right, but it also contains an obvious clue for how researchers might go about gathering evidence for the validity of NDEs. Clearly, despite the admittedly subjective quality of these experiences, there is one component of the NDE that does, at least in principle, lend itself to the possibility of external corroboration. Although the man whose OBE I quoted was manifestly not close to death, his account of his experience is remarkably similar in content and detail to many reports that have been furnished by persons who have survived NDEs. They, too, tell of leaving their bodies for a moment and having a panoramic and detailed perception of the environment around their body. Suppose, then, these descriptions could be checked independently and verified. If one could show that these patients could not possibly have seen what they did naturally or acquired this information by other means, we would have some fairly impressive evidence to support the objectivity of NDEs. And, clearly, *if* these perceptions could be confirmed in this way, we might be justified in having greater confidence as well in those aspects of the NDE that must, by their nature, be altogether beyond the scope of science to verify directly.

To garner this kind of evidence has been, in fact, the aim of some serious research already conducted and currently underway in the field of near-death studies. To lead up to it, however, we need first to determine just what kind of perceptions NDErs report when they claim to leave their bodies while close to death.

To begin with, let me mention an investigation carried out by an NDE researcher named Janice Holden, who teaches at the University of North Texas.[3] Holden, who was especially interested in assessing the *quality* of visual perception during NDEs, sent questionnaires to a sample of persons that had indicated having had OBEs while close to death. Altogether, she received sixty-three usable questionnaires from her respondents, and what they told her demonstrated unequivocally that OBE perceptions are consistently described as clear and detailed.

For example, 79 percent of her sample reported having clear visual perceptions, and a comparable percentage also stated that it was distortion-free, in color, and involved (as noted by the actor cited earlier) a panoramic field of vision. Furthermore, 61 percent of her cases claimed they had a complete and accurate memory of the physical environment, and a like percentage even said they could read during their OBE!

Unfortunately, Holden does not seem to have inquired of her respondents whether their OBE-based visual perception was more fine-grained than in their ordinary state (as was implied, of course, in my earlier example), but other studies, as well as some specific examples to be presented shortly, make it evident that this is certainly sometimes the case.

In any event, Holden's findings strongly support the notion that, in principle, NDErs should be able to provide detailed accounts of the visual aspects of their environment that from a strictly physical point of view are impossible. That, at any rate, is the theory. What we need now to examine, of course, is whether there is any specific evidence, based on individual cases, that this is indeed so.

Fortunately, as a result of nearly twenty years of research on NDEs, such examples are not difficult to come by. Although no single instance may be absolutely conclusive in itself, the cumulative weight of these narratives is sufficient to convince most skeptics that these reports are something more than mere hallucinations on the patient's part.

Here, for instance, is a typical story, which I have excerpted from a letter sent to me by an Australian correspondent in 1989. The woman, in relating her own NDE, which took place during surgery, happened to comment on the reaction her physician had when she told him of her experience:

> I will never forget the look on the surgeon's face when I told him that I went through the OBE phenomenon during the operation. I then asked the surgeon whether he was sitting on a green stool with a white top on it. He replied yes. He then said, "But you could not have seen that from where you were lying on the operating table." I then said to him that I did not see that from where I was lying, but that I had seen it from where I was detached from my body looking down from above during this NDE phenomenon. This remark caused an even stranger look on his face.

I daresay that virtually all NDE investigators have encountered such stories in connection with their research; indeed, though puzzling, similar accounts are scattered in some profusion throughout the literature on NDEs.

In my own case, I think the genre of OBE I found particularly arresting when I was starting out in this field was that in which individuals claimed to be aware of the *dust or lint* on the top of a light fixture over which they seemed to be hovering while high above their physical body on the operating table below. I can assure you that, in those early days of

NDE research, to hear one such tale was amusing; to hear it a second time, in almost identical language, was distinctly intriguing; to hear it a third time was to be convinced that, whatever these episodes were, these persons could not possibly simply be making up these stories. They were just too eerily alike, yet precisely the sort of improbable perception one might actually have in that state, to be passed off as mere hallucinations.

By now, I have lost exact count of how many such reports of the "dust-on-the-light-fixture" variety I have come across in the course of my research, but a conservative estimate would be a half-dozen or so. Just to give you a feeling for them, however, and the way their peculiar details compel belief, I relate a few of them here.

One of them comes from a woman I interviewed in the early 1980s, who was forty-eight years old at the time. She had had her NDE in connection with a surgical procedure in 1974. What was especially noteworthy about her account at the outset, however, was her mention of her unusually garbed anesthesiologist. As she explained to me, he was a physician who often worked with children. And because he had found that his young patients often were confused by a team of similarly clad, green-garmented doctors, he had taken to wearing a yellow surgical hat with *magenta butterflies* on it so he, at least, could easily be recognized. All this will, of course, be highly relevant to this woman's account of her experience, which is now described in her own words. She had gone into shock when she heard her physician exclaim, "This woman's dying!" At that point,

> Bang, I left! The next thing, I was aware of was floating on the ceiling. And seeing him down there, with his hat on his head, I knew who he was because of the hat on his head [i.e., the anesthesiologist with the magenta butterfly cap] ... it was so vivid. I'm very nearsighted, too, by the way, which was another one of the startling things that happened to me when I left my body. I see at fifteen feet what most people see at four hundred.... They were hooking me up to a machine that was behind my head. And my very first thought was, "Jesus, I can see! I can't believe it, I can see!" I could read the numbers on the machine behind my head[4] and I was just so thrilled. And I thought, "They gave me back my glasses...."[5]

She goes on to describe further details of her operation, including how her body looked, the shaving of her belly, and various medical procedures that her surgical team were performing upon her, and then finds herself looking at another object from a position high above her physical body:

From where I was looking, I could look down on this enormous fluorescent light … and it was so dirty on top of the light. [Could you see the top of the light fixture?] Yes, and it was filthy. And I remember thinking, "Got to tell the nurses about that."[6]

One of the striking features of this case, of course, is this woman's observation that she was able to see so clearly during her NDE despite the fact that, as she avers, she was very nearsighted. In this respect, too, this woman's testimony is far from unique in my records. Another, very similar story is told, for example, in a letter to me from an audiologist who also, as it conveniently happens, reports seeing dust on the light fixtures of the operating room where his NDE took place. This incident occurred in a Japanese hospital during the Korean War. In addition, this same man, who became interested in NDEs as a result of his own experience, also learned of another case involving a nurse at the same hospital, which had a remarkable correspondence to his. On this point, he comments, by way of introduction:

The odd thing about both of our experiences is that we are both extremely myopic, that is, thick glasses and blind as bats six inches from our noses. And yet we were both able to describe accurately events, dials, details, expressions in OBE, without our glasses.

He then continues with a specific description of the circumstances surrounding his own NDE and what he was aware of as it unfolded:

I had had a spinal injury and was undergoing what was supposed to have been an uncomplicated cleansing and scraping procedure [when complications developed].… I sensed something turning sour in my system and literally yelled in my mind, "Hey, guys, you're losing me!" [Then] I just floated upward to the top of the canvas tent and looked down at the scene. (Here is where I emphasize the word *look* [he says].) In finite detail, I saw the dust on the supposedly clean and sterile OR lights, someone just outside smoking a cigarette, the near-panic of the medical staff, and the expression of the big, black Air Force corpsman who was called to come in to forklift me in his arms to get me on my back. He had a clearly discernible scar on the top of his closely cropped head, in the form of a small cross. He was the only one not wearing a face mask, having been summoned on the spur of the moment. He watched as the staff tried to pound life into me, pounding on my chest, pushing, seemingly forever.

Before concluding his letter, he returns once more to the curious parallel with the nurse and, though he is at pains not to speak beyond his knowledge of her NDE, adds this pregnant afterthought:

The nurse I mentioned above, very nearsighted, related similar details in vision in spite of her not wearing glasses at the time. I dare not try to recount her experiences for fear of inaccuracies creeping in, but the oddity of the visualization of these events by nearly blind people suggests room for some speculation in my mind.

Indeed! And, as you will see in the next chapter, I have recently pursued these speculations to their logical limit, resulting in new findings about visual perceptions during NDEs that are even more difficult to account for in conventional terms.

But before turning to this latest study, there are at least a few more cases of dust sightings and the like that we should consider, if only briefly.

A third instance comes from a young man who was nearly electro-cuted during an Industrial Arts course when he was a college undergradu-ate. As he felt the electricity surge through him,

> I rose six to ten feet above and three to five feet in front of my standing body. I could see the whole area, including dust, scrap paper and wood scraps on top of the cabinets behind my body. Another student, his back to me, was ripping twelve-foot boards of oak on a table saw about fifteen feet in front of my body.[7]

Then, there are the variants on this same theme. For example, some-times the tops of the light fixtures are seen *without* the dust. The following narrative is just a short passage from a twenty-eight-page letter written to me a few years ago by a Canadian anthropologist. The letter, which describes in great depth a number of extraordinary episodes in the writer's life, contains a vivid account of her NDE, which occurred as a result of pneumonia during her second pregnancy. As you will see, her experience has a startling resemblance to that of the actor whose spontaneous OBE began this section.

In this case, the woman was rushed to the hospital by her hus-band and, upon arrival, lost consciousness. Still, she was able to hear the nurses talking about her and to say, to use her exact phrase, that she was "Dead meat." Nevertheless, she herself was elsewhere at the time. As she relates it,

> I was hovering over a stretcher in one of the emergency rooms at the hospital. I glanced down at the stretcher, knew the body wrapped in blankets was mine, and really didn't care. The room was much more interesting than my body. And what a neat perspective. I could see *everything*. And I do mean everything! I could see the top of the light on the ceiling, and the underside

of the stretcher. I could see the tiles on the ceiling and the tiles on the floor, simultaneously: three hundred degree spherical vision. And not just spherical. Detailed! I could see every single hair and the follicle out of which it grew on the head of the nurse standing beside the stretcher. At the time, I knew exactly how many hairs there were to look at. But I shifted focus. She was wearing glittery white nylons. Every single shimmer and sheen stood out in glowing detail, and once again, I knew exactly how many sparkles there were.

Of course, it is precisely the clarity and exactitude of these details that make these narratives hard to discount even though we have, to this point, only the say-so of the experiencers themselves to rely upon. Even so, the general similarity among these independent cases is such that it must be reckoned with, especially when one realizes that only a small sampling of them can be presented here.

But just to examine one more variant at this point, consider that of a good NDEr friend of mine who, instead of spotting dust during her NDE caught sight, unmistakably, of a *cobweb*.

Nel, who is now in her early sixties, has long had a history of chronic ulcer problems. During one especially critical episode in 1972, while in the intensive care unit of a hospital in Boston, she became very seriously ill with a bleeding ulcer. While unconscious, she overheard a nurse and a doctor discussing her chances of surviving and learned that they were not good. Soon thereafter, Nel underwent a dramatic shift in her awareness:

> Very abruptly, I became aware that I was no longer in my physical body. I was up on the ceiling looking down at the bed, the IV bottles, the blood running; the beeps of the monitors were going, and the fluorescent light overhead was humming incessantly. I looked all around and thought, "Wow, this is really some kind of trip!" I felt no pain. I could see the pain and anguish on my face lying there in the bed, but I was up above. I was comfortable and pain-free, and I was amazed.
>
> I looked around, and I saw a beautiful, delicate cobweb, and there was some cracked plaster over the window. I thought to myself, "My God, for $325 a day, why don't they keep the room clean and fix that plaster?"

Perhaps we have now had enough specific examples to safely conclude that, somehow, persons close to death can indeed see minute and normally imperceptible optical "blemishes" from an apparent out-of-body vantage point. In fact, in some of these cases, it would be physically impossible for these individuals to see what they do from the visual field afforded by the position of their body (to say nothing of the fact that, of course, in these instances, their eyes are closed and they themselves are unconscious). Moreover, as we have found, in a number of these episodes (and I have further examples that might have been cited), poorly sighted patients claim to be able to see with astonishing acuity and even to be able to read something that would typically be out of the question for them.

In still other accounts I have come across involving accidents (usually motorcycle crashes), there is more evidence supporting Janice Holden's finding that many NDErs can read during their experience, even though the signs and numbers (e.g., on telephone poles or on the *tops* of buses) reported by these accident victims in their out-of-body state do not seem to be in the vicinity of where their physical bodies were hurled on impact. In other instances, NDErs have accurately recounted details of conversations they could not possibly have heard because they took place in settings completely removed from the location of their physical body, or volunteered information they could not have learned by normal means.

A striking case of this kind recently came to my attention in correspondence. A South African man, now residing in the United States, had an NDE in his native country in 1972, as a result of contracting double pneumonia. During his hospital stay, but before his NDE, he had become friendly with a nurse who worked there. As he then told me,

> While I was in a coma (and I believe clinically dead), my friend, the nurse, was killed in an automobile accident. I met her on the Other Side. She asked me to return, promised I would meet a loving wife, and asked that I tell her parents she still loved them and was sorry she wrecked her twenty-first birthday present (a red MGB). Needless to say, when I told the nursing staff upon my return that I knew Nurse van Wyk had been killed and the car she had been killed in was a red MGB (something only her parents knew) while I was "dead," people started to sit up and take notice.

Obviously, cases of the sort I have presented in this section provide a difficult challenge for anyone who would still wish to explain away these stories as nothing more than the curious hallucinations of apparently moribund persons. The perceptions described are too fine-grained in their details and too telling in their appropriateness—they are just the kind of thing one would expect to be reported if individuals really *were* able to see with extraordinary clarity from an elevated position near the ceiling—to be glibly written off on the grounds that they simply are not possible. Just because we cannot explain them does not mean they do not happen. On the contrary, plainly they *do* happen, which means we must now find a way to acknowledge and reckon with them, however much it may upset our theories of what is possible.

## VERIDICALITY STUDIES

> What if you slept, and what if in your sleep you dreamed,
> and what if in your dream you went to heaven
> and there plucked a strange and beautiful flower,
> and what if when you awoke you had the flower in your hand?
> Ah, what then?
> —Samuel Taylor Coleridge

Of course, any critical-minded person, to say nothing of an outright skeptic, could, as a last resort, always argue against these findings by pointing out (what we have in fact already conceded) that these are *unsupported* self-reports; that is, they are testimonies that rest solely on the word of the person who claims to have had such experiences. Therefore, since there is no outside corroboration of these reports and no way independently to verify them now, after the fact, they must remain inconclusive from a scientific point of view. Intriguing, yes, and suggestive, possibly, but, ultimately, they are proof of nothing.

Strictly speaking, this is a logical and defensible position. And when one takes into account the astonishing nature of these accounts and, if true, their momentous ontological implications, such an objection is even more cogent. Extraordinary claims, it is said, demand extraordinary evidence, and unsubstantiated personal testimony hardly constitutes it. Again, true enough—except for one consideration. Not all cases of this kind are based exclusively on the self-report of the NDEr. Some of them have, *in fact*, been corroborated by witnesses. In such instances, we speak of *veridicality studies*, and it is to a few of these that we must now turn in our search for stronger evidence of the authenticity of the NDE.

Perhaps the best known case of this kind is that of a woman named Maria, originally recounted by her critical care social worker, Kimberly Clark.[8] Maria was a migrant worker, who, while visiting friends for the first time in Seattle, had a severe heart attack. She was rushed to Harborview Hospital and placed in the coronary care unit. A few days later, she had a cardiac arrest but was quickly resuscitated.

The next day, Clark was asked to look in on her, and during their conversation, Maria began to tell Clark of her OBE during her arrest. Maria told the usual tale of being able to look down from the ceiling and watch the medical team at work on her body. Clark, who had heard about NDEs but was skeptical of them—and of Maria's story—listened with feigned but seemingly empathic respect to the patient's account of what was, for Clark, her bizarre-sounding narrative. Inwardly, as she now confesses, Clark found plausible explanations to dismiss it—until Maria mentioned something highly unusual.

At this point, she told Clark that she did not merely remain looking down from the ceiling; instead, she found herself *outside* the hospital. Specifically, she said, having been distracted by an object on the ledge of the third floor of the north wing of the building, she "thought herself up there." And when she "arrived," she found herself, as Clark put it, "eyeball to shoelace" with—of all things—a tennis shoe on the ledge of the building! Maria then proceeded to describe this shoe in minute detail, mentioning, among other things, that the little toe had a worn place in the shoe, and that one of its laces was tucked underneath the heel. Finally, and with some emotional urgency, Maria asked Clark to please try to locate that shoe: She desperately needed to know whether she had "really" seen it.

At this point, as Clark has mentioned to audiences in her personal recitation of this encounter, she had a moment of profound metaphysical misgiving of the sort suggested by the epigraph from Coleridge I quoted at the beginning of this section. Nevertheless, her curiosity now definitely piqued, she was prepared to do Maria's bidding.

I have been to Harborview Hospital myself and can tell you that the north face of the building is quite slender, with only five windows showing from the third floor. When Clark arrived there, she did not find any shoe—until she came to the middlemost window on the floor, and there, on the ledge, precisely as Maria had described it, was the tennis shoe.

Now, on hearing a case like this, one has to ask: What is the probability that a migrant worker visiting a large city for the first time, who suffers a heart attack and is rushed to a hospital at night would, while having a cardiac arrest, simply "hallucinate" seeing a tennis shoe—with very specific and unusual features—on the ledge of a floor *higher* than her physical location in the hospital? Only an archskeptic, I think, would say anything much other than "Not bloody likely!"

Certainly, for Clark herself, the discovery of that tennis shoe on the ledge dissolved her previous skepticism about NDEs on the spot. As she comments in this connection:

> The only way she could have had such a perspective was if she had been floating right outside and at very close range to the tennis shoe. I retrieved the shoe and brought it back to Maria; it was very concrete evidence for me.[9]

Not everyone, of course, would concur with Clark's interpretation, but assuming the authenticity of the account, which I have no reason to doubt, especially since I personally know Clark very well, the facts of the case seem incontestable. Maria's inexplicable detection of that inexplicably placed shoe is a strange and strangely beguiling sighting of the sort that has the power to arrest a skeptic's objection in midsentence. And yet, such a skeptic could still recover and contend that, after all, it is *only* one case, and however discomfiting it might temporarily be to one disinclined to believe such things, it can perhaps be filed away merely as a puzzling anomaly. In the end, it is quite possible that one day a prosaic explanation might be found to account for it satisfactorily.

Again, it is hard to take issue with such a stance—until one realizes that other cases of the "Maria's shoe" variety are known to have occurred in which at least one independent witness is available to verify a patient's out-of-body perception. My colleague, Madelaine Lawrence, and I have ourselves investigated three of these cases, two of which, quizzically enough, also involve shoes![10] I'll describe each of them briefly next.

In 1985, Cathy Milne was working as a nurse at Hartford Hospital in Connecticut. Ms. Milne had already been interested in NDEs and one day found herself talking to a woman who had recently been resuscitated, and who had had an NDE. Following an initial telephone interview with me about this case, Ms. Milne described the details in a letter:

> She told me how she floated up over her body, viewed the resuscitation effort for a short time, and then felt herself being pulled up through several floors of the hospital. She then found herself above the roof and realized she was looking at the skyline of Hartford. She marveled at how interesting this view was, and out of the corner of her eye, she saw a red object. It turned out to be a shoe.... [S]he thought about the shoe ... and suddenly, she felt "sucked up" a blackened hole. The rest of her NDE was fairly typical, as I remember.
>
> I was relating this to a [skeptical] resident, who, in a mocking manner, left. Apparently, he got a janitor to get him onto the roof. When I saw him later that day, he had a red shoe and became a believer, too.[11]

One further comment about this second white crow, again in the form of a single, improbably situated shoe, sighted in an external location of a hospital: After my initial interview with Ms. Milne, I made a point of inquiring whether she had ever heard of the case of Maria's shoe. Not only was she unfamiliar with it, but also she was, for reasons you will appreciate, utterly amazed to hear of another story so similar to the one she had just recounted for me.

The odd coincidence of these lone shoes in attracting the attention of NDErs who have temporarily vacated their hospital-based bodies has, I must admit, an almost irresistible charm and reminds me of a poem I once read by Muriel Spark with the title, "That Lonely Shoe Lying on the Road." Spark, also puzzled as to why *single* shoes seem to be left lying about ("Why only one?," she asks), concluded only "that there are always mysteries in life." Certainly, in the world of NDE research, it remains an unanswered question how these isolated shoes arrive at their unlikely perches for later viewing by astonished NDErs—and their baffled investigators! In any event, as you are about to learn, unusual shoes continue to figure in these veridical studies.

In the summer of 1982, Joyce Harmon, a surgical intensive-care-unit nurse at Hartford Hospital, returned from work after a vacation. On that vacation, she had purchased a new pair of plaid shoelaces, which she happened to be wearing on her first day back at the hospital. That day, she was involved in resuscitating a patient, a woman she did not know.

The resuscitation was successful, and the next day, Ms. Harmon chanced to see the patient, who volunteered, "Oh, you're the one with the plaid shoelaces!"

"What?," Joyce replied, astonished. She says she distinctly remembers feeling the hair on her neck rise.

"I saw them," the woman continued. "I was watching what was happening yesterday when I died. I was up above."[12]

A third case of this type occurred at Hartford Hospital a few years earlier. In the late 1970s, a clinical instructor named Sue Saunders was working there in the respiratory therapy program. One day, she was helping in the emergency room to resuscitate a sixtyish man who was flatlined. Medics were shocking him repeatedly, with no results. Ms. Saunders was trying to give him oxygen, using a "bag–valve–mask" apparatus. In the middle of the resuscitation, someone else took over for her and she left.

A couple of days later, she encountered this patient in the cardiac unit. He spontaneously commented, "You looked so much better in your yellow top."

She, like Joyce Harmon, was so shocked at this remark she got goose bumps, for she *had* been wearing a yellow smock that day (and had not worn it since).

"Yeah," the man continued, "I saw you. You had something over my face [correct—it was a mask], and you were pushing air into me [again, correct]. And I saw your yellow smock."

Ms. Saunders adds these final comments:

> This really gave me the chills! The only way he would have known that information was if he was there and alert/conscious/or "out of body!" He didn't say much more about his experience; he apparently had said something to his relatives, and they didn't believe him. I did not press for any more information because I was taken aback by what he had told me.... It's really uncanny to think that he remembered a color! I would never have believed it if I hadn't been a part of this.[13]

These four cases I have presented briefly all attest to three important observations: (1) Patients who claim to have OBEs while near death sometimes describe unusual objects that they could not have known about by normal means; (2) these objects can later be shown to have existed in the form and location indicated by the patient's testimony; (3) hearing this testimony has a strong emotional and cognitive effect on the investigators involved—either strengthening their preexisting belief in the authenticity of NDEs or occasioning a kind of on-the-spot conversion. Again, it is as difficult to suppose that these patients are simply imagining things as it is to understand just how they can see what they do. Perhaps all we can safely do at this point is to concur with Muriel Spark—"There are always mysteries in life."

And there are, to be sure, more such cases in the literature on NDEs, which only deepen this mystery while providing even stronger evidence for veridical perception. Perhaps the best known and earliest study of this kind was carried out by a cardiologist named Michael Sabom over a decade ago.[14] In his careful and systematic work, Sabom found a number of cardiac patients who described in detailed protocols extensive visual perceptions while undergoing surgery or in connection with cardiac arrests or heart attacks. Sabom then went on to consult with members of the medical team, when available, or other witnesses, and also examined the medical records of these patients, in order to determine to what extent these perceptions could be verified. In most instances, Sabom was able to provide compelling evidence that these patients were reporting precise details concerning their operation, the equipment used, or characteristics of the medical personnel involved, which they could not have known about by normal means.

Moreover, to further test his interpretation, Sabom devised an ingenious control group. He collected data from twenty-five chronic coronary care patients, none of whom, however, had ever been resuscitated. He asked these patients simply to *imagine* that they were resuscitated and to describe the procedure as though they were a spectator to it (i.e., from a similar perspective to that usually mentioned by NDErs). The results were very provocative and strengthened Sabom's case for the veracity of his NDErs' reports.

In short, twenty-two of his twenty-five control respondents gave descriptions of their hypothetical resuscitations that were riddled with errors. Furthermore, the accounts were often vague, diffuse, and general. The narratives of patients who had actually been resuscitated, however, according to Sabom, were *never* marred by such errors, and were far more detailed as well.

Overall, Sabom's data are, I think, very convincing evidence that veridical and conventionally inexplicable visual perceptions *do* occur during NDEs. And together with the specific cases I have already offered for your consideration in this section, we now have, I believe, enough information about these occurrences to conclude that henceforth, they must be acknowledged by NDE researcher and skeptic alike. Still, *how* they can be satisfactorily explained is a challenge that has so far stumped everyone.

## IN SEARCH OF AN EXPLANATION

Instances of apparently reliable but "impossible" perceptions, especially of the visual kind, that occur on the brink of death, such as those we have presented in this chapter, may strain conventional theories to the breaking point, but because their stubborn facticity persists, they must eventually be reckoned with. The problem, of course, is that, like NDEs as a whole, these wonders of perception would seem to force us to entertain notions that skirt dangerously close to the fringes of the paranormal and even to religion, and for that reason, these phenomena themselves tend to be relegated to the margins of science where, with time, the hope seems to be, these inconvenient facts will be conveniently forgotten.

Recently, however, there has been a new approach to these refractory observations that affords us at least a glimpse of how they and even more astonishing findings from the world of NDE research may be accommodated within an emerging scientific perspective stemming from the modern study of human consciousness. This is not to say that we can fully explain in scientific terms what we have related in this chapter. But when we combine what we have presented here with the results of the study to be reported in the chapter to follow, you will be able to see for yourself the way in which NDE research is helping to shape new explanatory models in science.

Intriguing as were all these cases of unsuspected dust particles, dangling spider webs, and mysteriously placed shoes on external hospital surfaces, we have still to consider some further visual perceptions of NDErs that, by definition, could not possibly have occurred—and yet they did. And that they did provides some of the strongest evidence yet for the authenticity of the NDE itself and even more mind-bending evidence of its transcendental nature.

## Chapter Three

# Eyeless Vision: Near-Death Experiences in the Blind

Perhaps the most stringent test of the hypothesis that persons are actually seeing what they purport during these OBEs would come, paradoxically enough, from a study of NDEs in the blind. After all, as you will recall, we have already learned that those persons who are very poorly sighted can sometimes describe with uncanny precision the visual features in the environment surrounding their physical body when there was apparently no natural means by which they could have obtained this information. If these reports are truly valid, then what is to stop us from taking the next logical step? And that is, of course, to wonder whether blind persons close to death can see too.

Preposterous though this may sound on the face of it, rumors of NDE-based perception in the blind have been circulating for years. Unfortunately, when investigators have tried to track these rumors to their sources, they do not seem to hold up.[1] And in at least one instance, we even know, thanks to the after-the-fact candor of one writer, that such stories have been entirely made up for heuristic purposes, precisely because these rumors have been so persistent![2]

Still, I have been intrigued by such possibilities, and since they would provide a kind of ultimate test for the validity of veridical perceptions during NDEs—as well as a keen challenge for skeptics—I recently decided to undertake a search for such cases. Together with my coresearcher,

Sharon Cooper, early in 1994, we first made contact with a number of national, regional, state, and local organizations for the blind and solicited their help in locating potential respondents. We were interested, we told them, in finding persons who were blind at the time of either an NDE or OBE, and who would be willing to talk with us about their experiences.

After three years of work, this investigation has recently been completed, and in this chapter, I present the first extensive nontechnical account of our findings.[3] I shortly give a brief synopsis of what we learned from this study concerning whether the blind do in fact ever claim to see during their NDEs. But, to begin with, I think you will find it more instructive simply to meet some of the persons whom we had a chance to interview during the course of our research project, and to read what they had to tell us about what they remember when they came close to death.

Our very first respondent, a woman named Vicki Umipeg, came to my attention thanks to the kindness of my friend, Kimberly Clark (now Kimberly Clark Sharp), whom you will remember as the social worker who inadvertently became interested in NDEs as a result of her unplanned encounter with the migrant worker, Maria, in a Seattle hospital. One day, in February 1994, just as Cooper and I were launching our study, I received a call from Clark, who has long been deeply involved in NDE work, and who leads a monthly support group in Seattle. She excitedly told me of another serendipitous discovery of hers: A blind woman had turned up, who had had not one but two NDEs, and she was soon to speak at Clark's support group. Needless to say, I was all ears, and by the time we finished our conversation, Clark promised to send me a tape of Vicki's presentation and to put me in touch with her.

I received the tape not long afterward and, a few days after that, I called Vicki myself. Since that initial contact, I have talked with Vicki many times over the phone and on two occasions had a chance to meet with Vicki and her husband while visiting Seattle. In addition, both Sharon Cooper and I have conducted extensive interviews with Vicki about her experiences and life history. With that as background, then, let me now introduce her to you and tell you a bit about her NDEs.

When we first talked with her, Vicki was forty-three years old, married, and the mother of three children. She was born several months premature, weighing only three pounds at birth. In those days, oxygen was often used to stabilize such babies in their incubators, but too much was given to Vicki, resulting in the destruction of her optic nerve. As a result of this miscalculation, she has been completely blind from birth.

Vicki earns her living as a singer and keyboard musician, though, of late, because of illness and family problems, she has not worked as much as in the past. She has had an enormously difficult life, full of hardship, abuse, and tragic loss, and it is a wonder to me, and, I know, to Clark and others who have heard her speak, that she has been able to endure it with such grace and courage. I do not think the details of her life, however, are appropriate for me to discuss here, nor are they immediately relevant to our interest in her NDEs. For now, we chiefly want to know, I think, what she experienced when she was close to death.

As I have indicated, Vicki has had two NDEs. One occurred when she was twenty, as a result of an appendicitis attack; the other, and the more vivid of the two, took place when she was involved in a car crash after she had finished performing at a local night club one evening. She was twenty-two at the time of her second NDE.

When I listened to the tape Clark had sent to me of Vicki's talk before the support group, I was immediately intrigued when she said, at the outset, about her two NDEs: "Those two experiences were the only time I could ever relate to seeing, and to what light was, because I experienced it. I was able to see."

A frisson of excitement passed through me when I first heard those words. She had said, unequivocally, that she had been able to see. Now, I felt sure we were on to something. Naturally, I had to find out more.

Listening to the rest of the tape gave me a better sense of the whole of Vicki's NDE, but I needed to talk with her directly to find out the details I was after for our study. Not long after hearing her tape, I was able to interview her specifically about the visual aspect of her experience.

At one point during her second NDE, she told me, she found herself out of her body at the hospital. I asked her to tell me more about that.

VU: The first thing I was really aware of is that I was up on the ceiling, and I heard this doctor talking—it was a male doctor—and I looked down and I saw this body, and at first, I wasn't sure that it was my own. But I recognized my hair. [In a later interview, she also told me that another sign that had helped her become certain she was looking down upon herself was the sight of a very distinctive wedding ring she was wearing.]

KR: What did it look like?

VU: It was very long … and it was down to my waist. And part of it had had to be shaved off, and I remember being upset about that. [At this point, she overhears a doctor saying to a nurse that it is a pity, but because of an injury to Vicki's ear, she could end up deaf as well as blind.] I knew, too, the feelings that they were having. From up there on the ceiling, I could tell they were very concerned, and I could see them working on this body. I could see that my head was cut open. I could see a lot of blood [though she could not tell its color—she still has no concept of color, she says]. She tries to communicate to the doctor and nurse but cannot, and feels very frustrated.

KR: After you failed to communicate to them, what's the next thing you remember?

VU: I went up through the roof then. And that was astounding!

KR: What was that like for you?

VU: Whew! It's like the roof didn't ... it just melted.

KR: Was there a sense of upward motion?

VU: Yes, um-hmm.

KR: Did you find yourself above the roof of the hospital?

VU: Yes.

KR: What were you aware of when you reached that point?

VU: Lights, and the streets down below, and everything. I was very confused about that. [This was happening very fast for her, and she found seeing to be disorientating and distracting. At one point, she even says that seeing was "frightening" to her.[4]]

KR: Could you see the roof of the hospital below you?

VU: Yes.

KR: What could you see around you?

VU: I saw lights.

KR: Lights of the city?

VU: Yes.

KR: Were you able to see buildings?

VU: Yeah, I saw other buildings, but that was real quick, too.

In fact, all of these events, once Vicki begins to ascend, happen with vertiginous speed. And as Vicki goes further into her experience, she begins to feel a tremendous sense of freedom (a feeling of "abandon," she called it) and increasing joy in this freedom from bodily constraint. This does not last long, however, because almost immediately, she is sucked into a tube and propelled toward a light. In this journey toward the light, she now becomes aware of an enchanting harmony of wood-chime-like music. Throughout all of this, of course, she reports being able to see.

Now finding herself in an illuminated field, covered with flowers, she sees two children, long deceased, whom she had befriended when they were all in a school for the blind together. Then, they were both profoundly retarded, but in this state, they appear vital, healthy, and without their earthly handicaps. She feels a welcoming love from them and tries to move toward them. She also sees other persons whom she had known in life, but who have since died (such as her caretakers and her grandmother), and is drawn toward them, too.

But before she can move to make closer contact with them, a radiantly brilliant figure—much brighter than the others, she says—interposes himself and gently blocks her way. This figure Vicki intuitively understands to be Jesus [and she was able to give a detailed description of his face, especially his eyes, and his clothing]. In his presence, she is enabled to have a total review of her life—and she sees this review, too, including of course images of her family members and friends—and then is told that she must return in order to bear her children. On hearing this, Vicki becomes tremendously excited because she had long cherished the dream of becoming a mother and now has the inner conviction that this will in fact be her fate when she returns. Before leaving this realm of light, though, she is also told by the figure that it will be very important for her to learn "the lessons of loving and forgiving" (and, as Vicki has told me, these did indeed prove to be prophetic words and a touchstone for her life following her NDE).

At that point, she found herself back in her body, which she entered almost as if slamming into it, she said, and experienced once more the heavy dullness and intense pain of her physical being.

Even from this brief description, you can appreciate that Vicki, though blind from birth, has had the same kind of classic NDE as do sighted persons. Furthermore, during it, she seems to be able to see both things of this world and the otherworldly domain, just as most NDErs report. In fact, apart from the feelings of visual disorientation Vicki felt at first (which disappeared as she found herself in the later stages of her NDE) and her inability to discern colors as such, there is nothing in Vicki's account of her NDE that would give an uninformed reader any hint that she is blind. As far as her NDE goes, in her own understanding, she was in fact not blind then.

Early in the last chapter, we briefly explored the possibility that NDEs might be some kind of a dream-like encounter with the numinous, and though we have not so far turned up any evidence that supports that view, still it is worth raising the point again in connection with NDEs in the blind. If the NDE is like a dream, blind persons, like Vicki, should notice at least some general similarity between the two. Wondering about this, I brought up this issue with Vicki toward the end of our interview.

KR:   How would you compare your dreams to your NDEs?

VU:   No similarity, no similarity at all.

KR:   Do you have any kind of visual perception in your dreams?

VU:   Nothing. No color, no sight of any sort, no shadows, no light, no nothing.

KR:   What kinds of perceptions are you aware of in your typical dreams?

VU:   Taste—I have a lot of eating dreams [she laughs]. And I have dreams when I'm playing the piano and singing, which I do for a living, anyway. I have dreams in which I touch things.... I taste things, touch things, hear things, and smell things—that's it.

KR:   And no visual perceptions?

VU:   No.

KR:   So that what you experienced during your NDE was quite different from your dreams?

VU:   Yeah, there's no visual impression at all in any dream I have.

KR:   Is it correct to say, then, that you don't think your NDE was dream-like in nature?

VU:   No, it was not at all dream-like in nature. It was nothing like that.

Vicki's story—both her life story and the story of her NDEs—is unusual. Her life itself, as I have intimated, has been so full of trauma, illness, and other ordeals that it is astonishing to me that Vicki has survived to tell of it. And perhaps because she is so articulate, her NDEs are remarkable for the clarity of their details. (I have more than 100 pages of transcripts of interviews with Vicki about them, in addition to the one I personally conducted.) Vicki, then, is in no sense your "average" person, not even your "average" blind person.

But the story of her NDE, nevertheless, is not unique, even among the blind. Other blind respondents we subsequently interviewed have independently related accounts of their NDEs that have many points of commonality with Vicki's, including assertions that they, too, can see during these episodes. By way of comparison, then, let me offer next a brief summary of the NDE of a blind man from Connecticut.

Brad Barrows, who was thirty-three when we first interviewed him, had his NDE when he was eight years old. It took place during the winter of 1968, when he was living at the Boston Center for Blind Children. At this time, Brad developed pneumonia and eventually had severe breathing difficulties. Afterward, he was told by nurses that his heart had stopped, apparently for at least four minutes, and that CPR had been necessary to bring him back.

Brad remembers that when he could not breathe any longer, he felt himself lifting up from the bed and floating through the room toward the ceiling. He saw his apparently lifeless body on the bed. He also saw his blind roommate get up from his bed and leave the room to get help. [His roommate later confirmed this.] Brad then found himself rapidly going upward through the ceilings of the building until he was above the roof. At this point, he found that he could see clearly.

He estimates that it was between 6:30 and 7:00 A.M. when this happened. He noticed that the sky was cloudy and dark. There had been a snowstorm the day before, and Brad could see snow everywhere except for the streets that had been plowed, though they were still slushy. [He was able to give a very detailed description of the way the snow looked.] Brad could also see the snowbanks that the plows had created. He saw a streetcar go by. Finally, he recognized a playground used by the children of his school and a particular hill he used to climb nearby.

When asked if he "knew or saw" these things, he said, "I clearly visualized them. I could suddenly notice them and see them.... I remember ... being able to see quite clearly."

After this segment of this experience was over [and it went very fast, he said], he found himself in a tunnel and emerged from it to find himself in an immense field illuminated by a tremendous, all-encompassing light. Everything was perfect.

Brad could clearly see in this domain, too, though he commented that he was puzzled by the sensation of sight. He found himself walking on a path surrounded by tall grass, and he also reports seeing tall trees with immense leaves. No shadows were visible, however.

While in this field, Brad became aware of beautiful music, like nothing he had ever heard on earth. Walking toward the sound, he came to and climbed a hill, eventually encountering a glittering stone structure so brilliant that he thought it might be burning hot. But it was not, and he entered it. The music continued here as well and, to Brad, seemed to be praising God. In this structure, Brad encountered a being whom he did not recognize, but from whom emanated an overwhelming love. This entity, without a word, gently nudged Brad backward, initiating a reversal of his experience, ending with his finding himself in bed gasping for air, attended by two nurses.

Brad, like Vicki, has been blind from birth.

In comparing this account with Vicki's, you can see immediately that it has a virtually identical structure. Like Vicki, Brad has an OBE in which he finds himself near the ceiling and reports seeing his body below. Then, again like Vicki (and also like the woman in Hartford Hospital who later espied the red shoe on the roof of that building), Brad finds himself rising through the floors of the school, and eventually he is raised above the roof and sees the morning scene spread out below him. He, too, comments that this stage of this experience went by very rapidly and, like Vicki, he is then drawn into a tunnel and emerges from it, like her, to discover himself in an illuminated field. And so on. There are still further commonalities, but we do not have to itemize each one in order to be certain that these two persons, both blind, are trying to describe a similar journey with the same features. What is even more extraordinary, of course, is that neither of these two persons had any previous experience with the world of sight, nor, of course, do they know of one another. And, both, it should further be noted, had their NDEs *before* the advent of modern NDE research, which was inaugurated by Moody's book, *Life after Life*, in 1975.

Moreover, Brad echoes Vicki's distinction between the obvious visual qualities of his NDE in contrast to their complete absence in his dream life. When asked about this, Brad said, "I've had the very same consciousness level in my dreams as I've had in my waking hours. And that would be that all my senses function ... except vision. In my dreams, I have no visual perceptions at all."

Vicki and Brad are certainly among our most impressive cases, but at the same time, they are entirely typical of our sample as a whole in that our blind respondents, as a rule, tend to describe NDEs that are no different from those reported by sighted persons. Altogether in our study, we interviewed thirty-one persons (fourteen of them blind from birth), of whom twenty-one had had an NDE (while the others had OBEs only but not in conjunction with an NDE). Among those narrating NDEs, not only did their experiences conform to the classic NDE pattern, but they did not even vary according to the specific sight status of our respondents; that is, whether an NDEr was born blind or had lost his or her sight in later life, or even (as in a few of our cases) had some minimal light perception only, the NDEs described were much the same.

Furthermore, 80 percent of our thirty-one blind respondents claimed to be able see during their NDEs or OBEs, and, like Vicki and Brad, often told us that they could see objects and persons in the physical world, as well as features of otherworldly settings. (A couple of others, besides Vicki, also mentioned that they were able to see during their life reviews.) However, I should note that even in some instances where a respondent did not indicate that vision was present, it is not always clear whether it was truly absent, or whether the individual simply failed to recognize what seeing was. Such uncertainties were particularly clear, of course, in the case of a few of our respondents who never had had any sight at all. As one man, whom we classified as a nonvisualizer, confessed, because "I don't know what you mean by seeing," he was at a loss to explain how he had the perceptions he was aware of during his NDE.

How well do our respondents find they can see during these episodes? We have, of course, already noted that the visual perceptions of Vicki and Brad were extremely clear and detailed, especially when they found themselves in the otherworldly portions of their near-death journeys. While not all of our blind NDErs had clear, articulated visual impressions, nevertheless enough of them did, so that we can conclude that cases like Vicki's and Brad's are quite representative in this regard.

For instance, one of our interviewees, whose sight was lost completely as a result of a stroke at age twenty-two and was nearsighted before that, told us in connection with seeing her body, her doctor, and the operating room during her NDE: "I know I could see and I was supposed to be blind.... And I know I could see everything.... It was very clear when I was out. I could see details and everything."

Another man, who lost his sight in a car accident at the age of nineteen, had a comforting vision of his deceased grandmother across a valley during his NDE. In commenting on its clarity, he said: "Of course I had no sight, because I had total destruction of my eyes in the accident, but [my vision] was very clear and distinct.... I had perfect vision in that experience."

Still another man, this one blind from birth, found himself in an enormous library during the transcendental phase of his NDE and saw "thousands and millions and billions of books, as far as you could see." Asked if he saw them visually, he said, "Oh, yes!" Did he see them clearly? "No problem." Was he surprised at being able to see thus? "Not in the least. I said, 'Hey, you can't see,' and I said, 'Well, of course, I can see. Look at those books. That's ample proof that I can see.'"

To conclude this section, let me bring all of these visual threads together in one specific illustrative case of still another of our blind respondents, a woman I will call Marsha. Marsha, who was forty years old when we interviewed her, is a married woman living in Connecticut, who had an NDE on January 16, 1986, when she was thirty-two, as a result of complications in her pregnancy.

Like Vicki, Marsha was premature, having been born after only a six-month pregnancy, and, as a result, had developed a condition of retinopathy of prematurity. Unlike Vicki, however, she has always had some limited vision. In this respect, Marsha told us, "I have some vision in my left eye, not a whole lot. I don't have any reading vision—I can't read print at all, but I can see, like, people and stuff, but they look ... blurry." Further inquiry established that Marsha's actual vision was extremely poor (e.g., she uses a guide dog), so for purposes of our study, she was classified as severely visually impaired rather than fully blind.

Marsha's case is mainly of interest here in showing how the visual perception of a severely visually impaired individual during an NDE is not only enhanced but also can become virtually perfect. In her interview with us, she made it plain that her heightened acuity pertained both to her out-of-body perception and to what she experienced in the otherworldly portion of her experience. As to the former, Marsha told us that when she was coming back, she was aware of seeing her body.

I: Could you describe it? Could you see it in detail?

M: Yeah, it just looked like me. I was, like, asleep.

I: And how was your vision, if I could put it that way, when you were looking down on yourself?

M: It was fine.... It was normal.

I: When you say normal, you mean clear?

M: Yeah, everything. There was no problem with it.

Concerning the quality of her otherworldly perception,

I: Were you able to see better than you could in the physical world?

M: Oh, yeah.

I: What was your visual perception like in this room [in the otherworldly portion of her NDE]?

M: Everything, I could see everything.... All the people, all the way back. Everything.

I: In what way? Could you be a little more specific?

M: It was perfect. It would not be like that here. There was no problem. It was, like, you know—everything, you could see everything. It was not like your eyes. I don't know what normal vision would feel like. It was not like your eyes see. It couldn't be my eyes, because my eyes were back over here. I could see gold in the room. Gold on the walls. There [were] white birds and angels and all these people.

I: When you saw birds and the people and the room, were you seeing it in detail or just like you see now?

M: No, no. It was detail. It was white light. Everything was white light in there. And there was gold on the walls.

Later on, in elaborating on her perception of colors during this part of her experience, Marsha was similarly definite about what she was aware of:

I: And could you see it [color] clearly in the experience?

M: Yes. Everything was the way it was supposed to be.

Finally, when the interviewer probed to get Marsha's further thoughts on her visual experience during her NDE, the following exchange occurred:

I:   If you had to say how much sight you actually had at the time of your experience, is there a way for you to describe it?

M:   It was, like, perfect. I don't see how it could not be perfect. I can't say I could see like I see now…. I could see everything [then].

I:   Do you have any thoughts on the fact that you had vision during this experience?

M:   Well, see, it was vision, but I don't think it was my eyes. I don't know how it works because my eyes were back here, and since they are not right and I could see everything right, there had to be more special vision somehow.

Although Marsha still has some residual physical vision, it is clear that her comments echo both those of Vicki and Brad concerning the quality of her visual perception, especially in the otherworldly realm. There, she sees perfectly and in detail that is astonishing to her, and for which she has no explanation. And like Vicki and Brad, who also noted the naturalness of their otherworldly vision in their interviews with us, Marsha uses a phrase almost identical to those we also heard from Vicki and Brad: "Everything was the way it was supposed to be." Likewise, her visual impression of her physical body seems clear and distinct, in contrast to her everyday vision. Overall, her testimony is as striking as it is consistent and shows that severely visually impaired persons, too, may find that coming close to death appears to restore their sight to normal, and perhaps even superior, acuity.

In summary, as a whole, our interviews with both NDErs and OBErs offer abundant testimony that reports of visual perception among the blind are common, that their impressions concern both things of this world and otherworldly domains, and that they are often clear and detailed, even in narratives furnished by those who have been blind from birth.

## CORROBORATIVE EVIDENCE FOR OBE AND NDE VISIONS

Obviously, in order to demonstrate that the perceptions described by our blind experiencers are something other than mere fantasies or even complex hallucinations, we need to provide some kind of confirming evidence for them, preferably from other independent witnesses or from reliable documentation. But just here, not surprisingly, is where it proves difficult to gather the type of indispensable corroboration that would help to cinch the argument that what they report seeing is indeed authentic. The reasons, of course, are apparent: In many cases (and here Vicki's and Brad's can stand as prototypes), the reported NDEs or OBEs took place so long ago that it was no longer possible for us to know precisely who the witnesses were or, even if their names were known, where to locate them. In other instances, potential informants have died or were not accessible to us for interviews. As a result, much of the testimony of our respondents is dependent on their own truthfulness and the reliability of their memories. As a rule, we did not have cause to question the sincerity of our respondents, but sincerity is not evidence, and one's own word is hardly the *last* word when it comes to evaluating the validity of these accounts.

Nevertheless, in at least some instances, we were able to gather some evidence, and in one case some very strong evidence, that these claims are in fact rooted in a direct and accurate, if baffling, perception of the situation. In this section, I present three new cases that provide some measure of evidentiality for the visual perceptions of the blind.

Our first example is one of apparently veridical perception during an OBE in which a respondent claims to have seen himself. What makes this case of special interest, however, is that he also saw something he could not have known about by normal means. Furthermore, he told us that a friend of his was in a position to confirm his testimony. Let us, then, examine this episode, as told to us by a man I'll call Frank.

Frank is sixty-six, but lost his sight completely in 1982. He cannot see anything now, including light or shadows. He has had several OBEs, however, since becoming totally blind. What follows is his recall of one of them.

Around 1992, a friend of Frank's was going to be driving him to the wake of a mutual friend. Frank remembered the incident as follows:

> And so I said to her that morning, "Gee, I haven't got a good tie to wear. Why don't you pick me up one?" She said, "Yeah, I'll pick you up one when I get down to Mel's [a clothing store]." So she picked it up and dropped it off and said, "I can't stay. I've got to get home and get ready to pick you up to go to the wake." So I got dressed and put the tie on. She didn't tell me the color of the tie or anything else. I was laying down on the couch and I could see myself coming out of my body. And I could see my tie. The tie that was on. And it had a circle on it—it was a red—and it had a gray circle, two gray circles on it. And I remember that.

The interviewer then probes for further details and clarification:

I: Now just for the chronology of it, you were lying down with this tie on, you saw yourself going out of the body, and then you saw the tie?

F: I saw the tie 'cause I told her the color.

I: You told your friend who was driving you?

F: Yeah, when she came back to pick me up.... And when she came down to pick me up, I said to her, "Are the circles gray in this tie?" And she said, "Yes."

I: Was she surprised that you knew?

F: Yes. She said, "How did you know? Did anyone come here?" I said, "No, nobody came here." You know, you can't tell 'em [laughs], 'cause they just don't accept, they don't believe in it.

I: And do you remember what the tie looked like even now?

F: Yeah. It's a rose-colored tie with circles on it and dots in the middle of the circle. Whitish–grayish circle around there. And it's a beautiful tie, 'cause every place I go, they remark on it. So she said to me, "Who told you?" And I said, "Nobody. I just guessed." I didn't want to tell because, like I said before … you can't say things to certain people.

Naturally, after hearing this story, we were eager to see if we could track down the woman involved in this incident. That proved difficult, since Frank had lost contact with her, but eventually, he was able to locate her and, without telling her exactly why we were interested in talking with her, put us in touch with her. At that point, Sharon Cooper was able to conduct an open-ended interview with this woman and later summarized it as follows in her notes:

> I independently called his friend, who said she did purchase a tie for Frank that day and did pick him up for the wake. However, she didn't have a clear recollection of the sequence of events that day to confirm the accuracy of Frank's story and didn't remember the exact design and colors of the tie. She added that Frank is a down-to-earth guy, who, in her experience, does not embellish stories. And even though she couldn't independently corroborate his account, she tended to think he was probably accurate in recounting the details.

So, here, although we lack the crucial confirming facts we need from the witness involved, we nevertheless have a highly suggestive instance that this man's recall of his experience is essentially accurate. However, the obvious weaknesses in and ultimate inconclusiveness of this case were partially overcome in my second example, and even more convincingly in a final case, where a direct and independent corroboration of the respondent's own testimony was obtained.

The second—and somewhat amusing—instance of possible veridical perception in a nearly blind person was actually described to me several years ago by another NDE researcher, Ingegard Bergström, in Sweden, following a lecture I gave in which I had described our own then-preliminary findings on NDEs in the blind. In a study she and a colleague had recently completed, Bergström had occasion to interview a woman who was virtually blind at the time of her NDE and had been so for at least ten years previously. While sitting in her kitchen, this woman had a cardiac arrest and during it claimed to have seen the sink and a stack of dirty dishes, something she said would not have been possible for her to see normally. She happened to make that statement in the presence of her husband, who then interrupted the interview to ask why his wife had not said anything to him about that at the time. "Because you didn't ask me," his wife replied, with some acerbity, according to Bergström. In a subsequent written account of this case that Bergström has kindly furnished for me, the husband was said to have appeared quite flustered and guilty upon hearing his wife's retort, since it had been his responsibility to clean the dishes and put them away[5] (Bergström, personal communication, November 3, 1994).

Our final case here focuses on a forty-one-year-old woman I will call Nancy, who underwent a biopsy in 1991 in connection with a possible cancerous chest tumor. During the procedure, the surgeon inadvertently cut her superior vena cava, then compounded his error by sewing it closed, causing a variety of medical catastrophes including blindness—a condition that was discovered only shortly after surgery when Nancy was examined in the recovery room. At that time, she remembers waking up and screaming, "I'm blind, I'm blind!"

Shortly afterward, she was rushed in a gurney down the corridor in order to have an angiogram. However, the attendants, in their haste, slammed her gurney into a closed elevator door, at which point the woman had an OBE.

Nancy told us she floated above the gurney and could see her body below. However, she also said she could see down the hall, where two men—the father of her son and her current lover—were both standing, looking shocked. She remembers being puzzled by the fact that they simply stood there agape and made no movement to approach her. Her memory of the scene stops at this point.

In trying to corroborate her claims, we interviewed the two men. The father could not recall the precise details of that particular incident, though his general account squares with Nancy's, but the second witness—her lover, Leon—did and independently confirmed all the essential facts of this event. Here is an excerpt from our interview with him, which bears on this crucial episode.

L: I was in the hallway by the surgery and she was coming out, and I could tell it was her. They were kind of rushing her out.

I: Rushing her out of where?

L: Of the surgery suite where she had been in the recovery area, I think. And I saw these people coming out. I saw people wheeling a gurney. I saw about four or five people with her, and I looked and I said, "God, it looks like Nancy," but her face and her upper torso were really swollen about twice the size they should have been. At that point I looked, and I said, "Nancy, Nancy," and they just—she didn't know, I mean. She was out of it. And they told me they were taking her down for an angiogram.

I: Who told you that?

L: I believe a nurse did. I'm not quite sure. I think I was still in a state of shock. I mean, it had been a long day for me. You're expecting an hour procedure and here it is, approximately ten hours later, and you don't have very many answers. I believe a nurse did. I know I asked. And I think Dick [the father of Nancy's child] was there at the same time. I think he and I were talking in the hallway.

I: Do you know how far you were from Nancy?

L: When I first saw her, she was probably, maybe about 100 feet, and then she went right by us. I was probably no more than three to five feet away from her. And I believe Dick was right next to me as well.

I: And do you know how they took her out? She was on the gurney?

L: She was on the gurney. There were IVs.... I'm not sure—I think she had some sort of a breathing apparatus. I'm not sure if it was an ambu bag or what it was.

I: And then where did they take her?

L: They took her downstairs to do an angiogram.

I: How?

L: They took her down in the gurney in the service elevator. They didn't take her in a regular elevator. They took her around the corner to the service elevator.

I: And did you see that whole process?

L: Yes, I did.

I: Did you see her go into the elevator?

L: Yes, I did because I walked around to watch her enter the elevator.

I: Was there any disturbance that you remember in getting her into the elevator?

L: I think there was a real sense of urgency on the staff. I've worked in hospital emergency rooms as well, and I can really relate to that. I think somebody was, like, trying to get into the elevator at the same time and there was some sort of a "Oh, I can't get in, let's move this over a little bit" kind of adjusting before they could get her into the elevator. But it was very swift.

I: Did you have a good look at her face?

L: Yeah, it really kind of shocked me. She was just really swollen. She was totally unrecognizable. I mean, I knew it was her but—you know, I was a Medic in Vietnam, and it was just like seeing a body after a day, after they get bloated. It was the same kind of look.

Here, as we have already indicated, it is obvious that Leon's account accords with Nancy's in virtually every significant respect, despite the fact that he was very worried about her condition and could scarcely recognize her because of her edema when he did see her. Yet despite his evident state of shock at the time, his interview appears to corroborate her story, as much as could be expected by any external witness. It should be noted, by the way, that this witness has been separated from our participant for several years, and they had not even communicated for at least a year before we interviewed him.

Furthermore, even if Nancy had *not* been totally blind at the time, the respirator on her face during this accident would have partially occluded her visual field and certainly would have prevented the kind of lateral vision necessary for her to view these men down the hall. But the fact is, according to indications in her medical records and other evidence we have garnered, she appears already to have been completely blind when this event occurred.

After a detailed investigation of this case and a review of all pertinent documentation, we concluded that in all probability, there was no possibility for Nancy to see what she did with her physical eyes, which, in any event, were almost surely sightless at that time. Yet the evidence suggests that she *did* see, and, as the corroborative testimony we have quoted shows, she apparently saw truly.

The question, of course, is *how?* And not only how did Nancy see, but also how do *any* of the blind persons in our study see what they certainly cannot possibly be seeing physically? While the evidence I marshaled in this section seems to establish a reasonable case that these visions are factually accurate, and not just some kind of fabrication, reconstruction, lucky guess, or fantasy, they leave unexplained the paradox of our discovery that, after all, the rumors some of us have been hearing all these years, that the blind can actually see during their NDEs, appear to be true. Whether and how this can be so is the mystery we must next be prepared to probe, and, if possible, to solve.

## BUT IS IT REALLY "SEEING"?

At this point, it seems justified to conclude that the findings from this study at the very least raise some very deep questions indeed, not only about the mechanisms of vision, but also about the ability of the human being to transcend the limitations of the senses altogether during NDEs. Certainly, if we can trust these reports, it is hard to avoid the implication that there is, under these conditions of extremity, some conscious aspect of ourselves that can separate itself from the physical body and no longer be bound by its physical handicaps.

Of course, there is a simpler way to say this: It sounds as if we are talking about what most ordinary persons would call "the soul." But that concept has no place in modern science, and these days, most philosophers and scientists would surely decry any attempt to sneak in through the back door any such remnant of dualistic thought. That is certainly understandable.

The dilemma we are left with, however, is not merely one that brings some discomfiture to modern thinkers. It is, rather, how else can we view these findings? What exactly is the alternative? That, to me, is the challenge for anyone who would grapple with these findings and their mind-stretching implications.

I myself do not make any claim to be able to furnish an answer to such perplexing questions, which should cause even the most facile of theorists to pause midsentence before leaping to the nearest convenient interpretative shore. I would, however, at least like to offer here some considerations for anyone who would like to try his or her luck at elucidating this mystery—and at the same time present some additional findings from this study that, I believe, furnish an important clue in the search for an ultimate explanation.

Let me begin by posing the basic question this study confronts us with: If the blind do indeed "see" during these NDEs, how is it possible for them, at least under these extreme conditions, apparently to transcend the sensory restrictions that have hitherto imprisoned them in a sightless world? Does seeing really depend on the eyes, after all? Or, alternatively, is there another form of awareness that comes into play when, *whether one is blind or not*, an individual is thrust into a state of consciousness in which one's sensory system is no longer functional?

In exploring such questions, Sharon Cooper and I were forced to consider a gamut of alternative interpretations for our findings. These ranged from conventional psychology (e.g., dream-based explanations of NDEs, or notions that these stories could have been retrospectively constructed on the basis of situational verbal or other cues) through little known studies of blindsight and skin-based vision, to perspectives based on esoteric and metaphysical systems, which postulate the existence of subtle bodies and spiritual senses. In the end, however, we found that none of these potential interpretations could provide an adequate explanation for the results of our study.

What ultimately proved more availing for us involved a reframing of our findings in the form of a new but particularly pointed question: Is what we discovered in our blind respondents *truly* a form of seeing? That is, is it in any sense something that might be conceived of as an analog to physical sight? We were led to ponder this question because a brace of telling considerations continued to draw us back to it ineluctably. For one thing, a close reading of our transcripts frequently revealed a multifaceted synesthetic aspect to the experiencer's perception that seems to transcend simple sight. Some of our interviewees, for example, were hesitant to assert that what they were able to describe was incontestably visual, either because they were blind from birth and did not know what vision was like or because, as Marsha just told us, they knew they could not possibly be *seeing* with their physical eyes. The following comments were typical of this vein:

> It wasn't visual. It's really hard to describe, because it wasn't visual. It was almost like a tactile thing, except that there was no way I could have touched from up there. But it really wasn't visual, because I just don't have vision any more.... It [was] sort of a tactile memory or something. It's not really like vision is. Vision is more clear.
>
> I think what it was that was happening here was a bunch of synesthesia, where all these perceptions were being blended into some image in my mind, you know, the visual, the tactile, all the input that I had. I can't literally say I really saw anything, but yet I was aware of what was going on, and perceiving all that in my mind.... But I don't remember detail. That's why I say I'm loath to describe it as a visual.
>
> What I'm saying is I was more aware. I don't know if it's through sight that I was aware ... I'm not sure. All I know is ... somehow I was aware of information or things that were going on that I wouldn't normally be able to pick up through seeing.... That's why I'm being very careful how I'm wording it, 'cause I'm not sure where it came from. I would say to you I have a feeling it didn't come from seeing, and yet I'm not sure.

Even Brad, whose initial testimony seemed so clear on this point, in a subsequent interview eventually qualified and clarified his earlier remarks about his memory of seeing snow on the streets outside his school:

> I was quite aware of all the things that were physically mentioned in there [i.e., his earlier description]. However, whether it was seen visually through the eyes, I could not say.... I mean, you have to remember, being born blind, I had no idea whether those images were visual.... It was something like a tactual sense, like I could literally feel with the fingers of my mind. But I did not remember actually touching the snow.... The only thing I can really state about those images was that they came to me in an awareness, and that I was aware of those images in a way I did not really understand. I could not really say that they were visual per se, because I had never known anything like that before. But I could say that all my senses seemed to be very active and very much aware. I was aware.

A second clue came from our gradual realization that the blind often use vision verbs far more casually and loosely than sighted persons do. Vicki, for example, says that she loves to "watch" television and uses phrases such as, "Look at this," which clearly cannot be taken literally.

Although this observation does not, of course, necessarily invalidate our reports, it does send up another amber flag of caution when it comes to the interpretation of the narratives of our blind respondents.

As this kind of testimony builds, it seems more and more difficult to claim that the blind simply *see* what they report. Rather, it is beginning to appear that it is more a matter of their *knowing*, through a still poorly understood mode of generalized awareness, based on a variety of sensory impressions, especially tactile ones, what is happening around them. The question that immediately confronts us now, however, is as unavoidable as it is crucial: *Why is it, then, that these reports, when casually perused, nevertheless often seem to imply that the blind do see in a way that is akin to physical sight?*

By this point, the answer, we believe, should be fairly obvious. However these experiences may have been encoded originally, by the time we encounter them, they have long come to be expressed in a particular linguistic form. And that form is a *language of vision*, since our ordinary language is rooted in the experiences of sighted persons and is therefore biased in favor of *visual* imagery.

Because the blind are members of the same linguistic community as sighted persons, we can certainly expect that they will tend—indeed, will be virtually compelled—to phrase their experiences in a language of vision, almost regardless of its appropriateness to the qualities of their own personal experience. Now, this is *not* to say that as part of this multifaceted synesthetic awareness there will not be some sort of pictorial imagery as well; it is only to assert that it must not be understood as anything like physical vision per se.

Even if we cannot assert that the blind see in these experiences in any straightforward way, however, we still have to deal with the fact—and it does seem to be a fact—that they nevertheless do have access to a kind of expanded supersensory awareness that may in itself not be explicable by normal means. Perhaps, as I have suggested, although these reports may not actually represent an analog to retinal vision as such, they clearly represent *something* that must be reckoned with. In my view, the blind—as well as others who experience an NDE or OBE—enter into a distinctive state of transcendental awareness that I would like to call *mindsight*. When sensory systems fail, mindsight becomes potentially available to us and affords direct access to a realm of transcendental knowledge to which our normal waking state is barred. Under these conditions, "with the doors of perception cleansed," things present themselves in true Blakean fashion, "as they are, infinite." Thus it is that the blind may perceive what they cannot literally see, and can know what was hitherto hidden to them. Clearly, this is not simple "vision" at all, as we commonly understand it, but almost a kind of omniscience that completely transcends what mere seeing could ever afford. In mindsight, it is not, of course, that the eyes see anything—how could they? Instead, it is the *inner* "I" that sees and suddenly beholds the world as it appears to eyeless vision.

## CONCLUSIONS

In the end, we can perhaps leave the resolution of these weighty ontological questions to the philosophers and to others who endeavor to unravel the arcane mysteries of the nature of consciousness itself. Our goal in this and the previous chapter, however, was far more modest. It was, as you may recall, only to begin to make the case for the authenticity of NDEs, that is to say, to try to show that this phenomenon was not merely some kind of psychological aberration or neurological artifact of a dying brain.

If you will now mentally review the various scraps of evidence I have assembled for your consideration in these two chapters, I think you will agree that they all fit together rather nicely on the assumption that what happens during an NDE is that it essentially affords another perspective from which to perceive reality. Furthermore, this perspective does not depend on the senses of the physical body or even upon an intact visual system. In fact, it occurs only when the senses are defunct. Under these circumstances, it seems, another kind of knowing, which I called *transcendental awareness* or, more simply, *mindsight*, is made possible and everyone— not just the blind—begins to see with eyeless vision.

Think about the data from these chapters: the fantastic detail in panoramic vision while out of body, the sightings, while elevated, of dust, cobwebs, and other normally disregarded minutiae of our everyday environments; the miraculously acute perceptions of the nearly blind, and the "impossible" vision of the fully blind. Does this not all hang together perfectly as long as one assumes that it is literally possible for an individual to transcend the body and see with one's mind? And if you are inclined to resist that interpretation, then how *would* you begin to explain the undeniable consistency of all the reports that I have just related to you?

And more—how does one otherwise explain the verified perception of those unlikely objects in improbable locations when no physical vision was possible at all, or, similarly, those overheard conversations that could not have been witnessed, or instances where NDErs have other information they could not conceivably have acquired through normal means?

Clearly, the evidence is overwhelming that these NDEs can no longer be regarded as dreams or fantasies, or things people merely imagine. And I cannot think of any neurological theory that can explain how Maria saw that tennis shoe on that ledge, can you?

Something real, indisputably real, is happening to these experiencers. When it begins with the OBE episode, they seem to be beholding things of this world, but with an enlarged understanding. They are at once elsewhere but still here, in some sense with us. Both we and they, albeit from different angles, are able to see the same things.

But, then, they are taken into an elsewhere to which we, the witnesses, can no longer have direct access. However, knowing that they have not been hallucinating even at the beginning of their journey gives us greater confidence that the visions they will soon encounter—those that we described at length in Chapter One as well as in the present chapter—also emanate from *another* reality and have their own self-existent truth. At this point, where they finally take leave of us, and we of them, these NDErs are seeing, without eyes but with mindsight, into the shining realms beyond this earth.

## Chapter Four

# *Children in the Light*

Several years ago, I received a letter from a mother who wanted to share with me a baffling conversation she had had with her young son. At the time it occurred, she told me, by way of introduction, that she had had only a passing familiarity with NDEs, but what happened to her that day was to lead her to want to know much more about the subject. Eventually, she read *Heading toward Omega*, and, that, in turn, prompted her to write me. As she explains:

> The incident concerning Steven occurred when he was two years and two months old. (He is now two years and ten months old.) I was framing a picture of my grandmother and grandfather, who have been dead since before Steven was born. Steven was sitting nearby playing with a toy, and asked me what I was doing. I told him and explained that it was a picture of his grandma and grandpa, who were now dead. No one had ever discussed death with Steven before, and all of a sudden I found myself faced with doing just that, with no prior preparation. I knew he would not drop the subject because he is a talkative, verbally precocious, and very curious child.
>
> I began by saying that they were no longer here with us and that they had gone to be with God. I was trying to think what to say next to elaborate while Steven continued playing. Before I could say more, he said in a very matter-of-fact way: "When you die, it's a tunnel."
>
> This caught me totally off guard. I asked him to repeat it, and he did. I asked him a couple of more questions in a half-interested way (although I was intensely interested). I asked if there was anything in the tunnel. He replied that there was light in the tunnel. I asked what color the Light was, and he replied, "White." I asked if, when you die, you go through the tunnel. He answered affirmatively. I asked what you do when you come to the

end of the tunnel. He said, "You go to the Light." He also volunteered that grandpa (pointing to the picture) was there with "a light on his head."

[He repeated the same information the next day in his father's presence, but eight months later, he had no recall of it.]

The mother adds this comment:

I don't work outside the home, and Steven spent his entire life exposed only to me and my husband, except for one very occasional baby-sitter who never discussed the subject. I know that his reply did not come from a source outside himself.

What are the chances that of all the things he could have made up regarding a subject with which he had no experience, he could have come up with "going through a tunnel and going to the Light?" I thought it was significant that several of your NDErs mentioned a feeling of homecoming, a familiarity, a feeling that they had always known everything they experienced. Is it possible that very young children retain some memory of having been there? Is it possible that by the time most of them have adequate verbal skills to express it, the memory is gone?

The questions that Steven's mother raises about the possible origin of his comments are, to be sure, provocative, but perhaps a more likely alternative is that the statements Steven made with such a knowing air were based on his own experiences *after* he was born. It is just barely possible, after all, that Steven is recalling fragments of his own childhood NDE.

In Steven's case, we cannot be sure of this, of course, but the possibility that children, especially very young children, might have NDEs is one that has excited the imagination of several researchers, in this country and elsewhere, and for obvious reasons. Consider, for example, still another argument that a critic, bent on explaining away the apparent authenticity of the NDE, might make about these narratives that now abound in our modern world.

Concerning their similarity of content, such a critic could easily point to the fact that all of us growing up under the influence of the Western tradition have absorbed from our Judeo–Christian heritage a body of teachings and assumptions about what happens at and after death. Although there is, of course, some variation in these religious doctrines, by and large, they are consistent with the reports that NDErs have furnished us by the thousands—reports that, furthermore, are often filled with stereotypical Christian imagery. Is it not perfectly obvious, the critic might well contend, that these pervasive religious ideas, whether we consciously accept them or not, *structure* these NDEs and, indeed, probably give rise to them in the first place?

"And furthermore," he or she might say, "just think about the sheer availability of information about the NDE in today's popular culture. It's pandemic. Everywhere you look, someone's describing one of these episodes on *Oprah*, *Geraldo*, or the *Larry King Show*. The tabloids trumpet them regularly in their headlines and sensationalize them in their stories. Many Hollywood films have depicted them or incorporated obvious NDE motifs into their stories. Popular magazines feature them all the time, and even *The New Yorker* has cartoons about them! And, for that matter, think about the best-selling books on the subject, from Moody's *Life after Life* to Betty Eadie's *Embraced by the Light*, that people have bought by the millions. You'd have had to be living in a Himalayan cave for the last ten years not to be familiar with these experiences—they simply saturate the popular culture as a whole these days. No wonder these accounts are so similar— everyone knows what to expect now! And these expectations, drummed into us first by our religious traditions and then reinforced on all sides by the retelling of these stories *ad nauseam* through the media, clearly dictate the form and content of these narratives. In short, these NDEs are purely derivative—nothing more than reflections in our cultural mirror, religion in new clothes."

Even for persons sympathetic to NDEs, the force of these arguments is difficult to deny—until one begins to think about children. If it could be shown that children, especially the very young, report essentially similar experiences to those of adult NDErs, the argument of our critic would, at a stroke, be vitiated. Clearly, if these potential influences could be plausibly ruled out, one would have to look elsewhere for the explanation for the NDE. So you can now better understand why some NDE researchers would be eager to seize the opportunity to talk with children who are known to have come close to death. Their stories, if consistent with the overall NDE pattern, would plainly be another very important type of evidence in the brief for the authenticity of the NDE.

## NDEs IN CHILDREN

Of a number of investigators who have pioneered studies of NDEs in children, by far the most preeminent is a pediatrician named Melvin

Morse, who is the author of the very popular book, *Closer to the Light*, on the subject, as well as other substantial works in this domain.[1] Morse's involvement with this particular segment of the field of near-death studies was, however, purely adventitious, not deliberate, and occurred because of a conversation he had with a seven-year-old patient of his named Kristle. The story has become one of the most celebrated in the whole area of NDE research and Kristle herself is now probably one of the best-known children NDErs, having also been featured, not only in Morse's first book, but on the popular television program, *20/20*, as well.

Put yourself in Morse's shoes, and you will be able easily to understand why Kristle's story hooked him just as immediately as seeing that shoe on a hospital ledge converted Kimberly Clark to instant belief in the authenticity of NDEs.

When Morse was a young intern working in Idaho, he found himself having to try to resuscitate a seven-year-old girl who had nearly drowned in a YMCA pool. This girl, Kristle, was hooked up to an artificial lung machine, a CAT scan showed that she had massive brain swelling, and Morse felt her chances of recovery were near zero.

He was wrong. Three days later, she had made a full recovery.

Later on, Morse saw her for a follow-up examination. As a physician, he was interested in such matters as brain tumors and childhood leukemia, and had no interest whatever in NDEs (I am not even sure that he had heard of them at the time). Kristle was to change all that.

After Morse introduced himself, but before starting his examination, Kristle turned to her mother and said, "That's the one with the beard. First, there was this tall doctor who didn't have a beard, and then he came in." [Correct, thought Morse.]

She then went on spontaneously to describe several other procedures that were performed on her, including a nasal intubation—all of which statements were again accurate. Morse, who had been there during all this time, knew that her eyes had been closed and that she had been profoundly comatose during this entire period. He confessed that Kristle's telling him all this in a matter-of-fact way amazed him.

Intrigued, he asked, "What do you remember about being in the swimming pool?"

"You mean when I visited the Heavenly Father," Kristle replied.

Nonplussed, Morse encouraged her to say more, but all Kristle would say that day was "I met Jesus and the Heavenly Father." Then, she got very shy or embarrassed and said no more.

However, when Morse returned the next week, he tried again, and this time he succeeded in prying out Kristle's full story. Here it is.

She remembered nothing of the drowning. However, in her words: "I was dead. Then I was in a tunnel. It was dark and I was scared. I couldn't walk."

She then told Morse that a woman named Elizabeth appeared, and that the tunnel then became bright. Kristle described Elizabeth as being tall, with bright yellow hair. Then, according to Kristle, they entered heaven. "Heaven was fun," she said. "It was bright and there were lots of flowers." She said there was a border around heaven that she could not see past.

Kristle reported to Morse that she met many people there, including her dead grandparents, her maternal aunt, and "Heather and Melissa," two souls waiting to be reborn. She also met the "Heavenly Father and Jesus," who asked her if she wanted to return to Earth. She said she wanted to stay with Him.

Elizabeth asked her if she wanted to see her mother, and, apparently at this time, Kristle then found herself able to see home and observed her mother cooking and her father, who was sitting on the couch, as well as her brothers and sisters playing. [According to Morse, when Kristle later described this scene to her parents, they were astonished that she accurately described their clothing, their positions in the house, and even the food her mother had been cooking.]

Kristle now felt that she did, after all, want to be with her mother, so she said "yes," to Elizabeth's question, and the next thing she knew, she awoke in the hospital.

About heaven, Kristle later commented, "I'd like to go back there. It was nice." She also continued to ask about "Heather and Melissa."

According to Morse, it took Kristle about an hour to tell her story that day, and he adds this comment: "She was extremely shy, but told the tale in such a powerful and compelling way that I believed her implicitly."[2]

It is obvious that this child has recounted, in a simple, straightforward manner, the same kind of story we have heard so often from the lips of adult NDErs. The elements of Kristle's narrative, related with such a guileless naiveté that Morse could not fail to be impressed with her sincerity, though a surprise to him, are by now familiar to us. And, as Morse attests, he himself was to hear many similar stories from kids he interviewed subsequently, during the course of his own further investigations of childhood NDEs, as have, of course, other researchers who have probed the same territory. One such is the man who, inadvertently with his book, *Life after Life*, established the entire field of near-death studies itself. Raymond Moody has also come across many cases of childhood NDEs during his nearly thirty years of research and has written about a number of them in his book, *The Light Beyond*.[3] Here, I just cite one representative example which, incidentally, has so many rather remarkable parallels to Kristle's story that one might almost think it is the same child. But, of course, it is not—it is a little girl named Nina.

Nina, who was nine years old when she had her experience, was undergoing an appendectomy when her heart stopped beating. Her surgeons immediately began to resuscitate her, but meanwhile, Nina herself had seemingly ejected from her body and was viewing the attempt to revive it from the usual elevated position. As Moody quotes Nina:

> I heard them say my heart had stopped but I was up at the ceiling watching. I could see everything from up there. I was floating close to the ceiling, so when I saw my body I didn't know it was me. Then I knew because I recognized it. I went out in the hall and I saw my mother crying. I asked her why she was crying but she could not hear me. The doctors thought I was dead.
>
> Then a pretty lady came up and helped me because she knew I was scared. We went through a tunnel and went into heaven. There are beautiful flowers there. I was with God and Jesus. They said I had to go back to be with my mother because she was upset. They said I had to finish my life. So I went back and woke up.
>
> The tunnel I went through was long and very dark. I went through it real fast. There was light at the end. When we saw the light I was very happy.... The light was very bright.[4]

Although, in my own work, I have concentrated on adult NDErs, I, too, have heard many accounts of childhood experiences. Some of them have come to my attention with no effort on my part to seek them out. My correspondence, for instance, offers a number of such examples, although the experiences described are normally from adults who are recounting them retrospectively. (We already know, by the way, that there are no substantial structural differences between NDE descriptions provided by children and those furnished years afterward by adults.[5]) Some are quite brief, others more elaborate, but all of them seem cut from the same cloth that other children have already displayed for us.

Here, for purposes of illustration, is an account of the briefer kind.

> When I was ten [a woman writes] I had an experience. Being extremely ill with mumps, high fever, and so on, I recall being somewhere above "me." A

dark, spiral-shaped funnel came to its smallest point far below me. There, I saw myself, my mother weeping on the shoulder of my stepfather, and another man, whom I didn't know, shaking his head. Then, I recall—"Guess I'll go back." All this in absolute silence, impersonal, totally peaceful.

A second example, more elaborate this time, comes from a correspondent who first introduced herself to me as the author of a then forthcoming book that was to be based on her own two NDEs, both having occurred when she was young. In her letter, she gave a partial description of each, and in further correspondence, I prevailed on her to furnish me with more details. What follows is the fuller version of her first NDE. The writer, by the way, is Roxanne Sumners and her book, *The Wave of Light*,[6] now published, is a luminous fictional rendering of her NDEs.

My first experience happened just after I turned eleven. It was December 23, 1958. My mother had just gotten home from work and she, my little brother, and I were excited to begin preparing for Christmas. Mom gave me the money to pay our baby-sitter, who lived across the street. Money in hand, I ran out of the house and into the street.

I don't remember the impact of the car that hit me, but what I do remember was that I was suddenly sitting in a tree, watching the scene below. I was very nonchalant about what I was seeing. I was interested, but I wasn't really concerned about the "little girl" lying in the street or the woman who got out of her car, screaming hysterically.

I looked up and saw my grandfather [who had died when Roxanne was three]. He was reaching his hand out toward me, and when I reached for him, we began moving. There was a sensation of moving very fast, and then we came to an incredibly beautiful place where everything around us was made of pastel colored clouds. There were flowers, but they were fluffy and made of tiny, soft colorful lights. And there were hills with castles on them in the distance. And everything, even the castles, was made of these soft, fluffy, beautifully colored clouds.

I asked my grandfather if he lived in this place, and he said he did. I asked him if I could stay with him and he said that I couldn't—that I needed to go back to help my mom and little brother. I was suddenly aware of my body again, and I was in tremendous pain. My arm hurt terribly and someone was carrying me. Then I was back in this beautiful place with my grandfather and I started crying. I said I didn't want to go back, that I wanted to stay with him.... There was so much love, so much understanding. I remember talking with him and feeling completely protected and understood.

And then I woke up in the hospital, with a broken arm and a concussion.

The four cases of childhood NDEs I have related to you could easily be multiplied many times over, since research in this subspecialty of near-death studies has become quite active in recent years. And the great preponderance of these encounters would continue to show, as the foregoing examples have, strong evidence of the prototypical NDE pattern. Nevertheless, all such accounts suffer from a crucial failing, and our critic certainly would not be slow to spot it.

"These stories are quite lovely, as far as they go, " the critic would first concede, "but intriguing as they are, they are entirely irrelevant to the argument under review. The children here range from seven to eleven years old. Clearly, children of this age are hardly immune from religious influences; on the contrary, they are probably fairly indoctrinated by this time. And, just as plainly, such children are likely to be avidly glued to television and would have had ample opportunity to learn about NDEs in this way. Children may have NDEs, but there is no indication here that they are not shaped by cultural and religious factors."

And, of course, the critic is right. But the critic has, conveniently, forgotten an important qualifier of the argument for authenticity here. We also said that the evidence for childhood NDEs would be especially impressive were it to be found in the *very young*, and the very young have yet to be heard from. At this point, therefore, we must turn our attention specifically to those whom this chapter promised at the outset—children who are mere babes in NDEland.

## NDEs IN THE VERY YOUNG

One of the earliest reports of NDEs in very young children was provided by two psychiatrists, Glen O. Gabbard and Stuart W. Twemlow, in a chapter of a book concerned, in part, with NDEs.[7] Of the three cases they describe, that involving a boy named Todd, is most relevant to our present concerns:

> Todd was two years, five months old when he bit into the electrical cord from a vacuum cleaner while playing with his siblings. His mother came upon him some two or three minutes after the accident occurred. He was lying motionless.... She noted a slightly bluish quality to his skin and instantly became alarmed.... [S]he realized he was not breathing and called an ambulance." [The paramedics instituted CPR and rushed Todd to the emergency room.]
>
> Medical records from the hospital emergency room indicate that there was a period of approximately twenty-five minutes when the child had no heartbeat or respiration. These records also indicate that Todd's pupils were

dilated and that he was completely unresponsive. [Todd remained unresponsive for several days; in fact, and it took four to six months before he gradually regained much of his cortical and neurological functioning again. Remarkably, there was no evidence of any permanent brain damage.]

About three months before his third birthday, he was playing in the living room when his mother asked him, "Could you tell Mommy what you remember when you bit the cord of the vacuum cleaner?" Without even looking up, he told her, "I went in a room with a very nice man and sat with him." His mother asked him what the room looked like. Todd replied, "It had a big bright light in the ceiling," which his mother took to mean some kind of chandelier. Todd's mother then asked him what the man said to him. Todd responded, "He asked me if I wanted to stay there or come back to you." Looking up at his mother he said, "I wanted to be with you and come home." Then he smiled, and went back to his toys.[8]

And lest you think that little Todd had in the meantime been stealing peeks at Oprah talking to NDErs, you should know that this incident took place in 1972, several years *before* the publication of Moody's *Life after Life*, and, of course, Todd's mother herself was completely unfamiliar with NDEs at that time.

A similar case, also made available through the testimony of the child's mother, again comes from my own archives. In this instance, the mother is describing the NDE of her son, José, which occurred when he was three years and eight months old.

The circumstances of this case are dramatic and are vividly narrated in the mother's letter. A family outing to a lake, attended by various signs of uneasiness and foreboding, was undertaken one summer day. José himself resisted going and announced upon arrival that he was still angry about having to be there. Nevertheless, when his mother's attention was elsewhere, José elected to go into the water. When the mother notices that her son has been gone an unaccountably long time, she lets out

> ... a scream of death. "Fay [her sister], I can't find José." Within seconds, everyone is looking. Neighbors on the beach. Ten minutes went by. No José. I ran up on a hill. Miguel [her husband] followed. He embraced me. I felt totally helpless as I screamed in his arms and he cried in mine. I just knew he was dead.

A few minutes later, lifeguards find José in ten feet of water by the dock. Miraculously, his heart is still beating. He is rushed to a hospital in a deep coma. The mother and father, of course, are by now nearly overcome with anxiety. And they have a further scare at the hospital two weeks later, as they continue to keep vigil over José.

Two weeks, no change. One day I went into his room. His bed was stripped. No sheets, no José. I dug my fingers into Miguel. A housekeeper came into his room and said, "He's down the hall." We walked down the hall completely numb. I thought he was dead. As we slowly walked into his room, José was laughing at a clown passing out balloons.

José eventually recovers, the only sign of his ordeal a minor ear problem that soon clears up.

Years later, when he is eleven, he takes his mother aside and begins to talk with her about a white light. The mother doesn't understand. José offers to explain, but begs his mother not to laugh at him. When he is assured, he begins to tell her about the Light he was in when he nearly drowned.

He said, "A long time ago I was awake. Not asleep! I was going up in the air and saw you and papa crying. Something came to me and said you have to go back. I felt good but I liked all the people I saw."

I asked José who he saw and he said, "They were too bright, but one man held me and I felt so good I wanted to stay, but he said no."

Typically, in these cases of very young children, we do not find anything like a full narrative of an NDE, of course. Instead, we have fragments, bits and pieces of memories of light and wonder that have to be filtered through the thin reed of the child's still rudimentary verbal skills. Nevertheless, what comes through is unmistakably reminiscent of the larger experience we know. Partial though it is, it connects with the whole.

And young as Todd and José were when they had their NDEs, there are yet other instances involving NDEs at even earlier ages. One of these comes from a remarkable NDEr named Bonnie Long, whom I know very well, and who now lives in the Seattle area. As a child, she had two such episodes, the first of which occurred when she was scarcely two years old. An unusually precocious youngster, she claims to have a clear recall of this incident. What brought it about, she told me, was "pulling a large, old-fashioned floor-model radio down on top of myself, knocking myself out." She went on to give me further particulars about the event, based partly on what she herself remembers and partly on what she was later told:

I was hit hardest in the middle of the forehead, and I still have the scar.... Anyway, my mother told me later that they were quite worried about losing me. The glass over the dial had shattered all over my face, and a large sliver had gone up inside my nose. But I found myself across the room, watching a man in a dark uniform with a dark matching hat, who was bandaging me. I felt fine from where I was. The thing that was getting bandaged was all limp.

I still remember the clarity I felt, and the brightness all around me—colors, light, calmness.... It was as if that moment was in color while the rest of my life was drab and grey. I didn't seem to be connected with what was going on in the room at all.

In a recent letter to me, Bonnie mentioned a tantalizing tidbit of cor-roborative detail about this incident that I had not previously known about:

An interesting postscript is that when I finally got around to telling my mother all about the experience when I was two, I wrote out a floor plan of the rooms in our little, tiny house in Indiana where it took place. She was flabbergasted that I knew where everything was.... My mother says there is no way I could remember the details. You should have seen her face when I told her about the man in the uniform. She said he was from a fire/rescue unit.

And I have other cases in my files, quite as astonishing as Bonnie's, from persons who say they remember clearly an NDE at even earlier, and therefore seemingly more improbable, ages. Some of these individuals claim, for instance, to recall such episodes when they were no more than 18 months old, or even younger, and occasionally indicate, as did Bonnie, that they have since received confirming evidence from parents or siblings that they were indeed very ill at the time. As one example of this kind of testimony, consider that from someone we have already met. In the last chapter, you may recall a woman, Nel, who, during an NDE in a Boston hospital, was taken by surprise when she noticed a cobweb near the ceiling. As I was later to learn, however, this was not Nel's first NDE. Her first one took place, she tells me, when she was only thirteen *months* old. And, furthermore, she has a vivid recall of this incident and direct knowl-edge from her mother that she had been hospitalized at that time for pneumonia. She first gives the following bit of background information about her circumstances:

I was very ill with bilateral pneumonia plus bilateral mastoiditis. In 1935, the world had not been blessed with antibiotics. The treatment for mastoiditis was generally radical and involved surgical removal of the mastoid bone located behind the ear. The serious condition of my lungs precluded the use of any general anesthetic.... The process was invasive and painful at the very least. For an infant, it was traumatic and quite similar to rape.

Nel next describes what she remembers about perceptions of the world around her:

My body was strapped to the bed while large, steel-like hands held my head. My mother was not permitted into the room, as I had been placed in isolation. Through the bars of the iron crib, with its drab and chipped white paint, I could see her on the other side of a window. Her face was twisted with anguish. Tears stained her cheeks.

Then, when the surgical procedure was finally undertaken, Nel suddenly found herself somewhere else:

> The familiar sense of overwhelmedness was replaced by a warmth and peace as a soothing, but radiant, light engulfed my body. I looked over to the window, looking for my mother. I wanted her to know that I was just fine. She was not there. The stark barrenness of the hospital room was gone. I was safe; I was secure; I was healed. The Light bathed my body in love; it strengthened my soul; it told me to fight—and I did!

As remarkable as these cases are in suggesting that children can remember NDEs as early as barely a year or two old, they are far from the most impressive examples of NDEs in the very young. Perhaps the most extraordinary, indeed mind-boggling, example of this kind, and one, furthermore, that has been documented, concerns a young man named Mark Botts, now twenty-two, who claims to recall an NDE that took place when he was only nine months old! Before you begin to think that to believe such an apparently far-fetched assertion would be to sacrifice one's critical senses altogether, listen to the facts and then make up your own mind.

I first encountered and heard Mark at an International Association for Near-Death Studies (IANDS) conference in June, 1991, in Seattle, where I had gone to speak about my own research on NDEs. During the conference, there was a panel comprised of several NDErs, and Mark, then nineteen, was on of its participants, along with his mother, Carol. Before Matt recounted his own story, Carol gave the audience some necessary background information about Mark.

Mark had been born, she told us, with a condition called tracheomalacia, which means, in effect, a floppy windpipe. This condition causes breathing problems. When Mark was nine months old, he was hospitalized because he could not breathe, and an emergency tracheotomy was performed. During it, Mark had a cardiac arrest and was without heartbeat for forty minutes! Finally, however, he was resuscitated but was now in a coma (which was to last three months). After his recovery (without brain damage, by the way) he was outfitted with a trachea tube, which remained in him until he was three and prevented him from speaking. Two years later, when he was five, he was having lunch one day with his father and spontaneously brought up the time "when he had died."

As the mother observed before she related this event to us, neither parent had ever heard this story before. She went on to say, "He had never, ever, been told that he had died. He was never told the things that had happened to him."

In any case, as the mother recalled the conversation, it went like this:

He sat down besides his dad, and he said, "Dad, do you know what?" And his dad said, "What?" "You know I died." "Oh, you did?" And he said, "Yeah." His dad said, "Well, what happened?" And he said, "It was really, really dark, daddy, and then it was really, really bright. And I ran and ran, and it didn't hurt anymore." And his dad said, "Where were you running, Mark?" And he said, "Oh, daddy, I was running up there [pointing upward].... And he said he didn't hurt anymore, and the man talked to him. And his dad said, "What kind of words did he say?" And Mark said, "He didn't talk like this [pointing to his mouth], he talked like this [pointing to his head]. Because he couldn't tell you with his little vocabulary that it was through the mind. And he said, "I didn't want to come back, Daddy, but I had to."

Both parents were completely flummoxed by Mark's tale. This was, of course, in the days before the term *near-death experience* had been coined by Moody, and neither parent had ever heard of such a thing. Yet, somehow, they believed Mark was telling the truth. But nobody they consulted, including Mark's doctors, could provide them with any useful guidance, much less confirmation of Mark's story. The mother says that when Mark tried to talk about it to his friends, he was ridiculed, so he quickly learned to keep quiet about it. And his understandable reticence to discuss it continued, she told us, until just a few years before, when Mark had a chance to share his memories with Melvin Morse. Morse helped to validate Mark's story and enabled his parents to understand what had happened to him. Carol Botts's gratitude to Morse, who was also a speaker at the conference, was obvious.

By now, all of us in the audience were eager to hear from Mark directly, who had been sitting, mostly with his head down, while his mother had been telling us about him. When his turn came, he raised his head and began to speak, almost shyly but with a steady, quiet voice, about what he remembered when he was nine months old. Of course, he is speaking now with the vocabulary of a young adult, but, as you will see, his narrative only fleshes out the account given by his mother when Mark was five: It does not depart from it.

After describing the circumstances that precipitated his cardiac arrest, Mark said,

I floated out of my body, and I could see the doctors and nurses working on me, trying to bring me back to life. And I could see my grandma trying to find my mother way down at the other end of the hall. And it was kinda strange. There was no way I should have been able to see my mom or my grandma, or anything, because my mom was way down at the other end of the waiting room, which was at least 100 yards [away], through many corridors, rooms and doors.

And I just kept floating on up. I seen [sic] doctors and nurses still working on me.... All of a sudden, I got to the top of the hospital room and I was through the roof and into another dimension at the bottom of a tunnel. This tunnel was very, very dark, and you could see absolutely nothing at all. I crawled up the tunnel. [It might seem odd that Mark says he "crawled" up the tunnel, but remember he is only nine months old at the time of his near-death incident!]

It was difficult, Mark explained, for him to make his way up the tunnel, but he found himself making slow headway all the same. Then:

Halfway up the tunnel, I saw just a tiny, tiny bit of light. Like daybreak, pretty much was what it was like. When I got three-quarters of the way to the top, I could see a lot of light. "Wow, I'm gonna go and see what this is." At about two feet from the top, all of a sudden there were these big, beautiful orange-yellow lights, just all over. It's like sunlight in a way, but it's just so bright—but it doesn't hurt your eyes....

When I got out of the tunnel ... I never hit the ground. I was gliding!... I didn't crawl, and I couldn't walk because I was just nine months old.... So I was just gliding and then, all of a sudden, about 50 yards in front of me, there were these white clouded figures.... They kinda gave me a warmth and love that I was welcome there... [For a moment, Mark turns around, but when he turns back, he finds these figures have gone.] But when I turned around, everything was golden.... [He now finds himself gliding down a road.] The road was this beautiful golden—it was gold as far as I could see. So it was, like, "Wow, where am I now?"

So I was gliding down this golden road, and, all of a sudden, this guy appeared in front of me. [A telepathic conversation ensues at this point, and Mark understands that this being is "God."] He asked me how I was doing, and I told him I felt great and wonderful. "I can breathe, I feel free up here. It's wonderful." [Shortly after this, they stop gliding down the golden road together and more conversation takes place, mind-to-mind.] And he asked me if I want to go back. And I said, "No." And he goes, "Why?" " 'Cause it's great and wonderful and peaceful up here. I don't want to go back to the hurt and the suffering." And he goes, "You have a purpose in life, and when you fulfill it, you can come back and visit me again someday."

And then I was back in my body, but in a coma.[9]

Hearing this account in person, it was difficult to doubt Mark's story, and his sincerity was, I think, obvious to all. But for anyone who was not there to hear him directly, it may be far more difficult to believe that this young man is actually recalling, and recalling accurately, events that allegedly took place when he was only nine months old. Therefore, we must ask: What additional evidence do we have that will allow us to credit Mark's story as a matter of fact, not fantasy?

Shortly, I review some research findings now available on infants that show quite convincingly, I believe, that children as young as Mark or younger can indeed remember incidents from this age, but for the moment I will concentrate on what we know about Mark himself and the account he gives about his purported experience.

First, we know that it is a matter of record that Mark did indeed suffer from severe bronchiolitis as a child because of his faulty windpipe, and that he was treated for his condition in the way he and his mother describe. We know this not only from their testimony, but also because Melvin Morse investigated this case thoroughly in connection with his research.[10]

Second, Mark's story tallies in many respects with details of other cases of childhood NDEs with which we are already familiar. For example, you will remember the story of the blind boy, Brad Barrows, I related in the previous chapter. Brad was eight when he had his NDE, but he, too, reported floating out of his body, going up toward the ceiling and eventually through the roof, just as Mark claims to have done. Furthermore, Brad, like Mark, then found himself sucked into a tunnel, which, he, too, negotiated with difficulty, and then emerged into a radiantly illuminated environment. Like Mark, he eventually encountered a being who restrained him and required him to return to his body, against his will. The commonalities between these two cases (and others I could cite) are so obvious as not to require comment. How likely is it that mere fantasies would be so coincident?

Third, we have further information from Mark's mother that when he was a young child, he led a very restricted life and was not subject to the usual influences that are typical for children of that age. In this connection, his mother happened to remark during the panel discussion,

> He had not been out in public. He had never been to church or Sunday school. He had never been to a grocery store. He could have no people into the house. He had lived a very isolated life. There could have been no way he could have known about these things.

Again, these words have a ring of familiarity. We have heard them before. Do you remember the comments that the mother of little Steven, the boy whose near-death tale began this chapter, made concerning possible external sources of his apparent knowledge of NDEs? She, too, averred that because her son had led a very sheltered life up to the age of two, she was certain that he did not learn what he did from something outside himself.

Finally, Mark's mother made it clear that she, too, has had to face the doubts and skepticism of persons to whom she had chosen to divulge Mark's story. And on this point, she spoke quite candidly of how she dealt with these challenges:

> People would say to us, "How can you believe a child telling you something that had happened to him at nine months old?" And I'd say, "How can you *not* believe when he can tell you where you stood, and when it's impossible to see you? How can you not believe him when the things he said happened, when there was no way he could have known it?"

Mark's story, while it may stretch our notions of what children may remember when very young, quite obviously cannot be easily set aside as mere fantasy. There are just too much data that support it, and, besides, Mark is by no means the youngest case on record of children who apparently recall an NDE. To demonstrate just how far back such memories can go, let me mention a couple of further cases more briefly, if only to suggest that these limits may well exceed all our cherished ideas about such possibilities.

In 1985, for example, a pediatrician named David B. Herzog reported a case in a medical journal that involved a little girl who was only *six* months of age when she may have had an NDE.[11] You can judge the evidence for yourself and draw your own inferences.

Herzog says that the girl in question was rushed to a hospital suffering from severe renal and circulatory failure, and was not expected to live. But against all expectation, she did survive, and was successfully treated and released. However, as Herzog notes, there were eventually to be some suggestive indications that when she was close to death she had an NDE.

> Some months after her discharge, she had a panic reaction when encouraged by some siblings to crawl through a tunnel at a local store. The cause of this reaction was not obvious but the "tunnel panic" was seen again on a number of occasions. According to her mother, during these episodes the patient would talk very fast, be unduly frightened and overwhelmed, and would seem as if she knew the tunnel quite well. At the age of 3½, when her mother was explaining the impending death of her grandmother, the child replied, "Will Grandma have to go through the tunnel to get to see God?"[12]

Finally, I will cite one last instance from still another correspondent of mine who, like a number of others who have written to me, claims to have recall of early childhood events. In this case, however, her letter contains a hint that her experience may indeed be based on an actual near-death incident. As she explains,

> At some point, I assume, it comes to all of us to recall our earliest concrete memory of this life. For me there were two. The second one was in 1950, when I was about two years old. I remember vividly lying on my back on a table crying, and seeing the table surrounded by people in gowns and masks, and seeing the ether cup coming down toward my face and smelling the awful odor, then blackness.
>
> The first concrete memory I have took place before this. I was in a dark tunnel with a bright light at the end of it. I looked down and slightly to my right and saw a baby. For years, I believed that somehow I remembered my own birth. Then, as I pondered this, I realized that that was absurd. Then, I wondered if I had been a twin. Genealogical research ruled out this possibility. I did, however, learn that at six weeks of age, I had had whooping cough and was very ill.

Her conclusion?

> I believe I had a real, albeit brief, near-death experience. I have peace and contentment believing that I've found the true explanation for this very early memory that has stayed in my conscious mind.... And I've never had a real fear of death, always believing with complete assurance in a continuation of life.

At this point, you may well be beginning to wonder if we have finally reached the edge of apparent conscious recall of early childhood NDEs. Certainly, for most people, the idea that a six-week-old infant could remember an NDE is hard to credit. And yet, as you will soon learn, we now have good empirical evidence that memorial processes in children can indeed be accurate at such a young age and even earlier. In fact, I myself have even been told by several persons that they are sure they can remember an NDE they had at birth! Some of these individuals have not only written up such recollections for me, but also have informed me that they were apparently stillborn, cyanotic, or otherwise imperiled upon delivery, which they feel supports their NDE memories.

Of course, I do not expect you to believe these claims on the basis of such flimsy evidence, but before you dismiss them altogether as fantasy, perhaps you should take a look at recent research dealing with memory in newborns.

## PERINATAL MEMORY

Modern research into the basis of human memory has clearly established that memory is not a unitary process. Instead, it is what today's neuroscientists call "modular," meaning that various components of the brain are involved in highly specific coding of different types of experience. Visual memory is represented differently in the brain than auditory memory, for example. And even within a particular memorial domain, such as vision, certain regions of the prefrontal cortex respond to shape and color, others register location, other areas are involved in pattern analysis, and so on.[13]

One implication of this modular understanding of brain function is that there are different *types* of memory as well. Most people are now familiar, for example, with the distinction between short-term and long-term memory. Another distinction in common usage within neuroscience is between *declarative* memory (remembering that something has happened) and *procedural* memory (remembering how to do something). There is autobiographical memory, semantic memory, cellular memory, and a variety of other kinds of memory that have been singled out for special study.

One of these, which is of special relevance to us here, is *perinatal* memory. The term *perinatal* means "at or around the time of birth," and was originally suggested by one of the pioneers of research into possible birth-related memories, Stanislav Grof.[14] The idea that adults can remember their birth and other experiences in their neonatal life has had a long and controversial history, but recent investigations into this seemingly ludicrous possibility have turned up evidence that is very difficult to counter. In fact, an Association for Pre- and Perinatal Psychology and Health has come into being in the last fifteen years to further this line of research and to spur its therapeutic applications. Hundreds of physicians and nurses, academics and scholars, and therapists and educators from around the world now make up its ranks and gather to share their findings and insights at international conferences.

One of their number, and a recent president of this organization, is David B. Chamberlain, a psychologist and perinatal researcher from San Diego. Dr. Chamberlain has for many years been one of the leading advocates for the existence of perinatal memory and has produced an abundance of research to support his contentions. His work is representative, I think, of the findings in this field, and because of its obvious relevance to the reports of childhood NDEs, it is useful to take a few moments here to describe some of his discoveries.

Chamberlain's interest in this area was originally piqued by stories he heard about very young children who appeared to remember their own birth. What made Chamberlain hesitant to dismiss these seemingly preposterous claims out of hand was that often the children turned out to be reporting factually correct events they had never been told about. A couple of examples will allow you to place yourself inside Chamberlain's bemused mind as he tried to puzzle out how these children could know what they did.

In a popular book Chamberlain wrote on the subject,[15] he recounts one such story, which came from a 3½-year-old boy named Jason. Riding home one night, Jason spontaneously piped up that he remembered being born.

> He told his mother that he heard her crying and was doing everything he could to get out. It was "tight," he felt "wet," and he felt something around his neck and throat. In addition something hurt his head and he remembered his face had been "scratched up."
> Jason's mother said she had "never talked to him about the birth, *never*," but the facts were correct. The umbilical cord was wrapped around his neck, he was monitored via an electrode in his scalp, and was pulled out by forceps. The photo taken by the hospital shows scratches on his face.[16]

Another girl, not quite four, in speaking of her own birth, knew a "family secret" that had never been divulged to her. In this case, a friend of the mother and later an occasional baby-sitter named Cathy was present at the birth, assisting the midwife. After the birth, the midwife was busy and the mother had by then been helped into a bath, leaving Cathy temporarily alone with the baby. As the baby began to whimper, Cathy reflexively gave her to suck from her own breast. By the time the mother returned, the baby was already asleep, and Cathy, feeling somewhat guilty about being the first person to nurse the child, elected to say nothing to the mother about it.

Nearly four years later, Cathy was baby-sitting this same child, and, just out of curiosity, happened to ask the child if she remembered being born. As Chamberlain relates, Cathy later told him,

> She answered, "Yes!," and proceeded to give an accurate account of who was present and their roles during labor and delivery. She described the dim light of the womb and the pressures felt during birth. Then the child leaned up close and whispered in a confidential tone, "You held me and gave me titty when I cried and Mommy wasn't there." At that, she hopped up and went off

to play. Says Cathy, "Nobody can tell me babies don't remember their birth!"[17]

Hearing such suggestive anecdotes as these, Chamberlain felt obliged to see whether he could confirm such reports through systematic research into the question. For this purpose, he eventually studied a paired set of ten mothers and children and independently hypnotized them, asking them for details about the birth from their separate perspectives. Of course, only mothers who could assure Chamberlain that they never shared details about the birth with their child were eligible for the study. For the purposes of evaluation, Chamberlain assumed that the report given by the mother would be at least an approximately accurate description of the circumstances of the birth, against which the child's testimony could then be measured.

When comparing these independent accounts, Chamberlain found that, in general, the respective stories of mother and child agreed impressively, dovetailing on specific points of detail in an almost uncanny fashion. Here is how he summarizes his overall findings:

> Children accurately reported many details such as time of day, locale, persons present, instruments used, position of delivery, behavior of nurses and doctors, first feedings of water or formula, room layouts and details of discharge and homecoming. Sequences were usually adequate: moving in and out of cars, rooms, on and off certain beds or equipment, nursing from the bottle and/or breast in correct order, and the appearance or disappearance of doctors and fathers.[18]

When I read the actual reports Chamberlain provides of children's recollections of their birth and the circumstances, I get a distinctively eerie feeling of *déjà vu*, because their accounts seem so much like the reports we have already encountered from adults who relate detailed out-of-body perceptions. Indeed, it is hard to resist the inference that the newly born and the once nearly dead are seeing what they do from a similar vantage point. Chamberlain, too, has elsewhere commented on the connection between perinatal perceptions and OBEs.[19]

And the details mentioned by these children also have the same kind of precision we have seen before in our review of NDE veridicality studies. In these instances, of course, the validation is provided by the correspondence with the mother's recollection. The following is a case in point:

> After the baby was brought from the nursery, one woman reported: "I pick her up and smell her. I smell her head. I look at her toes and say, "Oh, God!

She has deformed toes!' " She then called the nurse and asked about the toes and was reassured they were normal.

The child [independently] made this report: "She's holding me up, looking at me.... She's smelling me! And she asked the nurse why my toes were so funny.... The nurse said that's just the way my toes are and that they weren't deformed."[20]

From his review of the evidence, not only from his own work but from that of other studies of perinatal memory as well, Chamberlain states that he was led ineluctably to the conclusion that birth memories, gathered in a disciplined and systematic fashion, are often genuine recollections of actual experience. He further points out that modern research in developmental psychology and neuroscience is helping to eradicate previous beliefs about the impossibility of such memories. Objections based on the assumption that babies do not have enough neuronal myelination, for example, or that their brains are insufficiently developed at birth to permit these memorial processes have been shown to be unfounded. As Chamberlain, summing up the evidence, puts it, "For most of a century, birth memories have been called 'fantasies' and prenatal memories 'impossible.' Actually, it was the false boundaries of science set by psychology and neuroscience that were fantasies."[21]

And here, of course, we immediately discern another parallel between what nearly dying teaches us and the lessons found from studies of birth memories: Science itself is going to have to make room for facts formerly derided as fantasies.

> The maturity of mental processes evident at and before birth raises fundamental questions about the relationship of the mind to physical structures of the brain and nervous system, questions that probably cannot be answered within the current paradigm of developmental psychology.[22]

You will recall that this conclusion of Chamberlain's is virtually identical to that we reached in the last chapter after surveying the evidence for veridical perceptions during OBEs. In each case, experiences at the extremities of life, birth, and death force us to confront the possibility that our consciousness ultimately transcends its apparent bodily home.

## CONCLUSIONS

Findings such as Chamberlain's and the discoveries of contemporary neuroscience concerning early memory give us added confidence that events dating from our very first days, including, of course, NDEs, can be accurately recalled in later life. If that is so, then the reports you have read in this chapter of childhood NDEs, especially those that have occurred at *very young ages*, would indeed constitute a very important link in the argument pointing to the authenticity of these experiences. Rather than being derived from religious teachings or from a popular culture saturated with stories of NDEs, these children's stories seem to be describing something that is *intrinsic* to the human personality once it is caused to enter the state of consciousness that ensues on coming close to death. Religious teachings may in time color the experience and influence its interpretation, and television talk shows may sensationalize and even trivialize them through their relentless exploitation of our hunger to know more about these transcendent journeys, but neither of these influences *gives rise* to these experiences in the first place. Their structure and content derive from something outside of our own cultural framework.

About their ultimate origins, we can only wonder, and no amount of NDE research in itself will be able to answer that question. What the study of childhood NDEs *does* demonstrate, in my opinion, is that our critics' objections, though seemingly plausible to begin with, are not tenable and certainly do not in the end lead us any closer to unraveling the mystery of the NDE. But though the critics may now be silent (at least for a time!), it is not as though we have had the last word. We may perhaps have greater reason now to believe that the NDE is an authentic phenomenon, but just *what it is* remains refractory to all attempts to understand it from without.

## AND A FINAL WORD FROM A BOY NAMED MARC

I was reminded of this not long ago when I attended a large and tony conference in Montreal dealing with death and dying. The chief purpose of this conference was to bring together Western intellectuals and scholars with representatives of Tibetan Buddhism, headed by the Dalai Lama himself, to dialogue about such subjects as suffering, healing, and death. For three days, the audience listened to many polished academic presentations, workshops, and discussions featuring the assembled dignitaries from West and East.

On the last afternoon of a conference, a very impressive panel of speakers was chosen to conclude the gathering. Stanislav Grof was among them, in addition to various French Canadian scholars. And the Dalai

Lama was again present, as he had been on the opening day, in a special commentator's role. Each panelist was, in effect, asked to give a speech of perhaps a half-hour's duration, and then, at the end, to conclude by asking His Holiness to respond to a particular question the speaker wanted addressed.

As it happened, I was sitting in the third row of the audience, right in front of the speakers' table, and I could not help noticing a little boy who had come at the last minute to sit in the front row, alongside a woman who seemed to be his mother, and another woman. As the panelists were coming on stage to take their seats, I found myself gazing intently at this child, because he had such a remarkable bearing and appearance. There was a visible, quiet calmness about him, a decided dignity even, that made him seem almost like an island of silence amid an audience that was already noisily buzzing with anticipation of this gala concluding event. But apart from his striking presence, he was also a very unusual looking child. For me, it was almost as if I were in the presence of an apparition, because there was also something undeniably ghost-like about him. He was short but slender, exceedingly pale, and his hair was thin and sparse. I remember when I first caught sight of him, I thought immediately of the photos I had seen of the victims of the Holocaust—skeletal, wraith-like, and already smelling of death. This was no ordinary child, and I'm sure others near me were also guilty of staring at him.

There was now some commotion, some of the conference organizers having gathered around him, conferring with him and the woman I took to be his mother. Shortly afterward, he was led up to the stage and took his seat, this pallid little child, among the august personages who were now already seated on the dais. The audience was, of course, puzzled and intrigued about the identity of this young latecomer and the reasons he had been seated in such an attention-getting and unexpected manner with the other panelists.

The moderator soon explained that the boy had been asked to appear as a last minute addition to the program. He was introduced as Marc Beaulieu, and his age given (I do not recall it exactly, but I think he may have been nine years old). Marc, it turned out, was suffering from incurable leukemia, and, for reasons that were not fully made clear to us, had very badly wanted to meet the Dalai Lama. Everyone, I am sure, was very touched at learning these facts about Marc, who shortly thereafter read (in French) in a sing-song voice a short speech that he (or someone ) had written out for the occasion. Mainly, it was concerned with the fact that dying children, like him, just wanted to be treated like everyone else, and not to be isolated as though they were lepers. The audience applauded Marc politely, but with feeling, and then little Marc drew back into himself, placed his earphones on (for purposes of following the simultaneous translation, when necessary, into French) and seemingly retired from the proceedings.

For more than two hours, he sat there while the scheduled speakers pontificated and in one case (not Grof, by the way, who gave a very respectful and thoughtful address) strutted around the stage flamboyantly gesticulating toward erotic slides that most of the audience, I suspect, found in very bad taste, given the occasion. Meanwhile, punctuating each of these speeches, the Dalai Lama, assisted by his ever-present personal translator, made his wise and often humorous observations in response to each of them. By now, Marc had almost been forgotten, a nearly invisible presence up on the stage.

But as the afternoon was wearing on, the panel was dragging and had become, at least in my opinion, somewhat tedious. We seemed to be drowning in a sea of verbiage, French and English, as the final speaker droned on.

Finally, it was time for questions from the audience and, after about fifteen minutes of this, someone thought to ask *Marc* a question. He seemed taken aback to be addressed but came to attention quickly as he was asked, in effect, what he made of all of this, and, particularly, to give his own views about death.

One could feel, at this moment, a certain tension in the audience, as Marc removed his earphones and began to speak. His voice was quiet, and the audience was nearly hushed. In my earphones, listening to the English translation, I heard these words:

> I think that when you die, it's not over. It *can't be over*, because in my mind, it's just impossible. It continues—we just go back home. We go back home where we were before we were in this life. And that life is only something that we have to learn something. And when we learn that thing, then we go back home. We go back where we were before. And that life, of course, is limited to a certain time period. That is, exterior life. But the life that's inside is infinite, it never ends.

With that comment, the panelists seemed to be at a loss as to how to react. Hearing such a spontaneous and straightforward utterance, so obviously based on the boy's own direct experience, and delivered with such purity of heart, appeared to stun them, as it did, I think, most of us in the audience. After nearly three hours of talk, it took a child to silence us into a recognition of this simple but profound truth about life and death.

Stan Grof, sitting next to Marc, was the first to stand, and for a long moment he hovered over Marc, clapping. The other panelists, some seemingly a bit abashed, were almost forced to do likewise. The Dalai Lama then rose and in a tender gesture blessed the boy and placed a garland of flowers around his neck. Meanwhile, the audience had risen to its feet, applauding Marc. I was standing, too, my eyes filled with tears, as, doubtless, were those of many around me.

In this unexpected moment, a kind of chaos broke loose. A number of people in the audience began to rush up toward the stage, many taking photographs, flashes popping. The Dalai Lama was quickly escorted off the stage, joined and protected by his retinue, while people clustered around it. The other speakers stood around for a moment, not knowing quite what to do. Confusion suddenly was everywhere, the rigid structure of the conference completely broken up by a few words from a nine-year-old child dying of leukemia.

In fact, the conference was never properly brought to a close. Marc's words did that by bringing about a mass, convulsive realization in the audience. As I remember, they were, fittingly enough it seemed, the final words spoken at the conference, and shortly afterward, we all filed out, humbled and dazed, into the sunlit Montreal afternoon, Marc's words still echoing in our ears—and souls.

Another lesson from a light-filled boy, helping us to remember what death has to teach us.

And reading Marc's words here, do *you* remember what Steven's astonished mother wondered when she was reflecting on her own two-year-old son's spontaneous remarks about what happens when you die? What she wrote to me was,

> I thought it was significant that several of your NDErs mentioned a feeling of homecoming, a familiarity, a feeling that they had always known everything they experienced. Is it possible that very young children retain some memory of having been there?

Maybe, in view of Marc's testimony, she was right after all.

## Chapter Five

# Living in the Light: Afterward

In 1984, I brought out my book, *Heading toward Omega*, which was the first major study of the long-term aftereffects of the NDE. What my research showed was that just as the NDE itself comprises a distinctive pattern of elements, so, too, were the changes that tended to develop in an NDEr's life afterward. In the realm of beliefs, values, behavior, and outlook on life generally, NDErs, however different they may have been before their experience, showed astonishing similarities. From a psychological standpoint, it was almost as if they had all undergone much the same initiatory ordeal—triggered by the trauma of nearly dying which then, unexpectedly, gave rise to similar, life-transforming insights—and then emerged from it to speak in a single voice and act from the secret knowledge of a shared vision. The result was that the NDErs I studied, though still diverse in their personalities, tended to share a common *psychological profile* afterward. In short, most of them appeared not only to be transformed by their experience, but also transformed in much the same way.

In the fourteen years that have elapsed since the publication of *Heading toward Omega*, many other studies have confirmed my basic findings.[1] In fact, at least eight additional major investigations of NDE aftereffects in the United States, England, Australia, and Italy—indeed in every country so far where such studies have been undertaken—have afforded further evidence of the stability of this pattern. In beliefs, behavior, values, and worldview, NDErs, at least in the West, seem to be much the same following their encounter with near death.

The fact of this general consistency of aftereffects may be noteworthy and impressive, but you may be wondering just why I am introducing it here. The reason is straightforward: These studies show that whatever the nature of the NDE, *it is real in its effects*. Furthermore, when we come to examine these effects specifically and in detail, you will quickly see, if you are not already convinced, that they are decidedly not the kind of changes one would expect if the NDE were merely an elaborate hallucination or some other kind of purely psychological phenomenon. Thus, both the commonality of these changes among NDErs and their specific and abiding character constitute still another argument in the brief for their authenticity.

While I have indicated that the aftereffects pattern is widespread, I still have said nothing specifically about the elements that constitute the pattern itself. If NDErs afterward can be delineated in terms of a common psychological profile, then what precisely makes it up?

Actually, we *have* had intimations of this profile earlier. You will, for example, remember meeting a woman named Laurelynn Martin in our opening chapter. But, here, I must remind you that when Laurelynn originally wrote to me, she included a specific list of features to exemplify how her own NDE had affected her life (see pp. 31–32). At the time, I was struck by how well it typified most of the changes I had already witnessed so often in NDErs and had described in my previous books, but, you may recall, I was later to learn that Laurelynn herself had never read any of them. Hers, then, was a particularly refreshing confirmation to me of that familiar profile.

Before we begin to explore the anatomy of this profile, you may want to take a few minutes to review not only Laurelynn's list, but also the general statement she offered about the value changes that occurred for her afterward, presented on pages 30–31. Doing so will serve as a good overview of the territory we cover next.

## PSYCHOLOGICAL AND BEHAVIORAL CHANGES FOLLOWING NDEs

In several of the chapters to come, we explore some of the specific effects of the NDE in some detail, so what I will do here is simply introduce them to you in a brief but systematized way. And rather than taking the time here to illustrate each of the components I enumerate, instead I present some rich case-history material toward the end of this chapter, so that you will be able to see better how these facets of the NDE jewel tend to array themselves so as to shine harmoniously in the daily lives of NDErs.

## Appreciation for Life

Most NDErs come back into life with a much-enhanced appreciation for everyday life—for the beauty of an old woman's face, for the joys and majestic power of nature, for everyday pleasantries in conversation. They see, and see with greater delight, what to many of us has simply become habituation. Their sense of wonder and gratitude for life itself also tends to increase.

## Self-Acceptance

Afterward, NDErs come to have greater feelings of self-worth and self-acceptance. Feelings of personal insecurity, shyness, and exaggerated needs to please or defer to others are often replaced by a self-confidence and outgoingness that may astonish those who knew them before their NDE.

## Concern for Others

One of the most striking and consistent changes following an NDE is an increased and compassionate concern for other persons. To be of service to others is, as one man put it, "more real than this world." To express love for one's fellow humans is to give out a little of what one received in the Light, and the urge to do so is, in some cases, almost unquenchable.

## Reverence for Life

Most NDErs find that their concern for others cannot be limited to human beings, but must unhesitatingly extend to all life. So reverence for animal life, for nature, and a heightened sensitivity to the ecological health of the planet as a whole tend to characterize the values of many NDErs afterward.

## Antimaterialism

Following an NDE, a life centered on materialistic values and acquisition for its own sake tends to be seen as empty and pointless.

## Anticompetitiveness

Many NDErs comment that afterward, they can no longer follow the common, socially approved pathways that require one to compete with others for material rewards or success in life. Being somebody important or impressing others ceases to be important. Caring, rather than achieving, is what really matters.

## Spirituality

Interestingly, many NDErs will say that following their experience, they did not become more religious, but more spiritual. By this, they seem to mean that the formal aspects of religion—in the sense of organized religion—become less important to them and a more universal and inclusive spirituality that embraces everyone comes to exert a deeper hold on their allegiance.

## Quest for Knowledge

Many NDErs are imbued with a tremendous thirst for knowledge, which is often put in the service of their own spiritual search. To live in accordance with what they learned in the Light, and, toward that end, to somehow recapture some of the knowledge they believe was implanted in them during their experience, become prime motivations for many NDErs.

## Sense of Purpose

That life *is* meaningful and that there is a sacred purpose to everyone's life become deep-rooted convictions for NDErs. Many come to feel that the task of their post-NDE life is to discover their own spiritual *raison d'être* and thus fulfill their mission in life.

## Fear of Death

The NDE tends to vanquish one's fear of death, completely and forever. While one retains the normal fears associated with the process of dying, the moment of death itself is regarded positively as a liberating transition into a sublime state that NDErs know they have already encountered briefly.

## Life after Death

As a rule, NDErs become convinced that some form of sustained conscious existence awaits them following the death of the body. Quite a few of them become more open to or believers in some form of reincarnation.

## Belief in God

By whatever term they feel comfortable with, and almost regardless of what they had believed before, NDErs tend to aver that now they know, with deep inner certitude, that God exists. Some of them, however, simply prefer to use the expression "the Light" in this context.

These, then, are some of the chief defining attributes of the psychological profile of NDErs—a set of consistent and mutually reinforcing beliefs and values that tend to shape both their everyday behavior and view of the cosmos. *But the aftereffects of the NDE are hardly limited to such changes alone.* Recent research has also disclosed a whole series of other effects of the NDE that point even more strongly to the conclusion that this phenomenon brings about definite alterations in human functioning that can in no way be accounted for by purely psychological mechanisms. Naturally, it is to these further and often extraordinary manifestations that we must turn our attention next.

## CHANGES IN CONSCIOUSNESS AND PARANORMAL FUNCTIONING

In addition to changing the individual's beliefs and values, the NDE also appears to alter in a profound way the experiencer's consciousness itself. In a phrase, what seems to happen is that the NDE unleashes normally dormant potentials for *higher consciousness* and extraordinary human functioning. At least three major but clearly interrelated aspects of this kind of transformation can be distinguished here.

## Expanded Mental Awareness

Many NDErs report that afterward, they experience states of expanded mental awareness in which they are flooded with information, often at such a rate that they cannot begin to absorb it all. But information of various kinds does appear "to come through" from sources they usually feel quite certain are external to their egoic selves. The amount of information can be overwhelming, but its content can be quite varied—abstract and theoretical, deeply personal and meaningful, spiritual or practical— and is usually greatly valued by the individual.[2]

## Paranormal Sensitivities

Although a number of recent investigations have confirmed this,[3] it has been known for some time that having an NDE seems to accelerate the development of a whole range of psychic sensitivities. It has been found, for example, that following an NDE, there is a marked increase in reports of the incidence of such paranormal phenomena as telepathy, clairvoyance, and precognition. In addition, NDErs claim to have more instances of spontaneous OBEs and unusual perceptions, such as seeing energy fields (or "auras") around the bodies of others.

## Healing Gifts

Despite the lack of careful, systematic work on the subject, there seems to be little doubt there is a strong connection between having had an NDE and the development of healing gifts afterward. This relationship will in fact be explored at length in Chapter 11 of this book. For the moment, however, let me merely point out that the NDE literature as a whole is replete with accounts of persons who claim to have come into such abilities afterward, and statistical studies have confirmed that reputed examples are not rare. For example, in my own work, I found that 42 percent of my NDErs claimed healing gifts afterward (compared to only 11 percent of my control group).[4] Similarly, Cherie Sutherland found that whereas only 8 percent of her sample of Australian NDErs testified that they felt they had healing powers *before* their NDE, fully 65 percent did so afterward.[5]

Thus, we see that the changes NDEs bring about are not limited to the psychological and behavioral, but that higher order potentials of human consciousness also seem to be activated by this experience. Such developments again imply that the NDE must be more than a simple vision. On the contrary, it appears to *do something to* the individual that affects more than his or her psyche. In what follows, we will begin to see, for the first time in this book, that in fact the NDE actually appears to modify a person's nervous system and brain.

## PHYSIOLOGICAL AND NEUROLOGICAL CHANGES

Recent research by a number of independent investigators has provided impressive, if preliminary, evidence that the NDE also tends to trigger an array of consistent physiological and neurological changes that themselves serve to define a distinct *psychophysical* syndrome.[6] There are four major categories here that have emerged so far to help us identify the components of this NDE syndrome.

### Hyperesthesia

Many NDErs afterward tell us that they find they have become unusually sensitive to light, sound, humidity, and a variety of other environmental stimuli or conditions. Taste sensitivity increases, and one's tolerance for alcohol and pharmaceutical drugs diminishes. Not surprisingly, NDErs report more allergies afterward, too. And particularly noteworthy here is a marked increase in electrical sensitivity—NDErs begin to have many "strange encounters of the electrical kind." A surprisingly large proportion of these persons discover, for instance, that digital wrist watches will no longer work properly for them, or they "short out" electrical systems in their cars, or computers and appliances malfunction for no apparent reason, and so on.[7]

This entire pattern defines a syndrome of *hyperesthesia*, which is an unusual sensitivity to environmental stimuli, and is known often to include electrical sensitivity as a component. This syndrome has been previously identified and studied, though it is still poorly understood.[8] The point here, however, is simply this: Many NDErs appear to "catch it" as a result of their NDE.

The obvious question is: How could a "mere hallucination" or other purely psychological phenomenon trigger such an effect?

## States of Physiological Hypoarousal

There is some evidence that there is a characteristic physiological change for a significant number of NDErs afterward that consists of reductions in body temperature, blood pressure, and metabolic rate—in other words, a state of physiological hypoarousal.[9] This state also seems to coexist with another condition, to be described next, that would appear in some ways to be its paradoxical opposite.

## Energetic Shifts and Kundalini Activation

In general, NDErs tend to report that they have more energy afterward, that they sleep less and get along well on less sleep, too.[10] And, as a whole, the energetic shifts they report seem to coordinate very well to a concept that has its origins in Eastern spiritual traditions but which has come increasingly to be recognized and accepted in the West by psychotherapists trained to deal with spiritual awakenings. This concept is called *kundalini*, which is held to be a specific mechanism that mediates the release of *prana* (or life energy) throughout the body. Theoretically, when this mechanism is activated, it causes this energy to flow through the body along certain predetermined channels and has the effect of stimulating the development of higher consciousness and what is called "higher sense perception." However this may be, it cannot be overlooked that three independent studies have now shown that NDErs tend to report a huge increase in symptoms that have long been associated with *kundalini* activation.[11] Whether this interpretation is correct or not, there seems to be little doubt that a tremendous energetic force of some kind has begun to manifest bodily in many NDErs.

## Neurological and Brain Changes

Unfortunately, very little work has so far been done to investigate the effects of NDEs on neurological functioning, though there has been considerable theoretical speculation about this matter in the NDE literature. Nevertheless, *subjective reports* of such changes are widespread in samples of NDErs. For example, in my Omega Project study, I found that over 50 percent of my NDErs indicated that their nervous systems were functioning differently than they had previously and, more intriguing still, more than one-third of my NDE respondents felt their brains were actually *physically* altered by their experience.[12] Of course, our brains, as dynamic systems, are in Heraclitian flux all the time, but unless we are afflicted with something potentially disastrous, such as a tumor or a lesion, we remain unaware of these changes. What, then, would cause a significant percentage of NDErs to assert (and in conversations with me, sometimes to insist) that they know that their brain has been "rewired" by their experience?

In the absence of rigorous research, we can only be left to wonder, but when we take into account all the findings referred to in this section, it no longer seems preposterous to hypothesize that the NDE may actually have a pronounced effect on an experiencer's nervous system and that the tremendous and radical changes following in the wake of the NDE, which we have briefly surveyed in this chapter, may be mediated precisely by such a powerful structural alteration.

The research mentioned in this section is only in its infancy, and it goes without saying that its preliminary findings, based almost exclusively on self-reports, await confirmation from rigorous laboratory studies grounded in careful, objective measurement. Nevertheless, the data we have gathered so far are very consistent in suggesting that the NDE affects *soma* as well as *psyche*, and that far from being a psychological phenomenon, the conscious experience of nearly dying is one that tends to reprogram the individual at a deep *psychobiological* level. Obviously, if this turns out to be supported by future research, we would have still another firm reason to conclude that the NDE cannot be explained away on purely subjective grounds.

In any event, whatever the ultimate explanation for the NDE itself, and whatever it may "truly" be, we are still left with one incontestable fact: *The experience leaves its mark, deep and lasting, on the individual who survives it.* These effects withstand *any* explanation of the NDE and must certainly now be acknowledged, since they are the personal, tangible legacy for every experiencer. As such, they are the NDEr's harvest and, if we are to share in this bounty and eventually make it our own, we must begin to taste these fruits, if only vicariously at first, for ourselves.

## LIFE AFTER AN NDE: SOME SELF-PORTRAITS

Now that we have completed our review of the evidence that points to the authenticity of the NDE, we are ready to return our full attention to the main theme of this book: How to make practical use of the information about NDEs in our own lives. In Chapter One, we began this quest simply by listening to some of the stories NDErs had to tell about their experiences and trying to draw out their essential lessons for everyday life. Here, we continue that inquiry, not by focusing on NDEs as such, but on how life is lived after the experience has begun to exert its characteristic effects. In this way, you will be able to see how, in specific individual cases, the typical aftereffects of the NDE come to weave a completely new design into the tapestry of a person's life.

After I published *Heading toward Omega*, I received many letters from readers, quite a few of whom, not surprisingly, were NDErs themselves. These persons often wrote to tell me, in effect, that they could really identify with the pattern of changes I had found to follow NDEs, and not infrequently they would say something like, "It was as if you were describing *my* life in your book." Sometimes, the "fit" would seem so gratifyingly close that the writers would feel moved to send me not just a letter, but something more like a long autobiographical document, so that I could be aware of the whole context of their life and see exactly how their NDE had been a crucial turning point for them. In most instances of this type, the writer would also respond, at least in part and sometimes fully, to the items in various questionnaires I had used in my research and had listed in an Appendix of my book. In this way, then, I came to acquire a number of unsolicited but very full case histories that helped to confirm and fill out the portrait of the NDEr I had tried to paint in *Heading toward Omega*.

Here, I would like to introduce you to a few of these persons, but before meeting them, I need to advise you of two considerations you should take into account when listening to these accounts of their post-NDE life. First, please be aware that the narratives I have chosen emphasize the shifts in beliefs, values, and behavior, rather than the psychophysical changes that are also a part of the aftereffects syndrome. The reason for this selectivity is that while the psychophysical changes constitute an important piece of evidence for the *authenticity* of the NDE, they are less relevant for a discussion of how the rest of us can grow from our study of NDE materials. Here, how a person comes to see with new eyes as a result of a profound transformation in values, for example, will be far more helpful to us.

Second, you may wonder about my use of such obviously selected cases drawn exclusively from persons who had read and responded favorably to my book. Is there not a great possibility of bias here? Perhaps, but I do not think so, and for this reason: Remember that the pattern I first described in my book has now been independently confirmed by various researchers in at least four different countries. Thus, what you will be reading in a moment is a common story in many thousands of lives—and of this number, surely, only a tiny fraction of persons have heard of, much less read, my book! And for a particular instance of this, recall Laurelynn Martin, who is a virtually perfect exemplar of the NDE aftereffects pattern, but who was completely unfamiliar with my books. So I think we can safely rule out the notion that the persons you will now meet were "contaminated" by their reading *Heading toward Omega*. Instead, they seem only to be particularly good specimens of the type of NDEr who is already depicted there.

## Robert

In June, 1987, a slender, casually dressed man in his mid-fifties, with a burnished face and disarmingly radiant smile, greeted me in the local cafe near the university that was then my usual lunchtime hangout. Robert, in from Hawaii, where he now made his home, had been visiting his eldest daughter in New York and had driven up to Connecticut just for this meeting. We had actually "met" the year before, however, as a result of his writing me a series of letters about his NDE and his subsequent life, but when an opportunity to meet in the flesh unexpectedly presented itself, I was delighted to invite him up to learn more of his story in person. What follows is based in part on my own recollection of our conversation at lunch that day, but mainly draws on one of the documents Robert had sent me the year before, from which I will quote extensively.

Before his NDE at the age of forty-four, Robert had been a successful lawyer living in Los Angeles. Though divorced, he was the father of three daughters and on the whole reports that he was quite content with his life, which was going well. On June 10, 1974, he was set upon by a robber late at night who viciously slashed him on his head and body with a roofer's hatchet in the course of his attack. Despite a serious compound skull fracture and the loss of a great deal of blood, Robert escaped and was later taken to a hospital where he had his NDE. After recovering from his wounds, however, Robert found that he was a changed man. For one thing, he no longer had any interest in practicing law. For another, he left Los Angeles and went to live on a farm in Idaho with a friend.

> I felt no interest in competing and felt myself opening to the problems of others—that was sort of hard to understand. I heard about T.M. [Transcendental Meditation] and became a meditator. I made new friends and left the business community and lawyers.... I felt prestige and status needs dropping away and liked the simple life in a farm house on the Snake River in Idaho.

Like so many other NDErs I have known and heard from, Robert soon found himself launched into his own spiritual journey and, in the words of the poet, Mary Oliver, began to stride "deeper and deeper into the world." By 1977, he was in India, where he intensively pursued his developing interests in meditation and spirituality, and eventually he settled in Hilo, Hawaii, to ground his life in a natural setting that seemed to fit the man he had now become.

> In the last several years, my focus has been on nature and interpersonal relationships and personal growth. Much has happened in all of these areas. My judgmentalness of others has diminished. I feel everyone is doing the very best he or she can at any given moment of their life.... I found all the points you made [in my book] about heightened appreciation of life, greater feeling of self-worth, increased concern for the welfare of others, decline in importance of material things, a seeking of a deeper understanding of life, and a correlative search for more self-understanding all being true for me.

To demonstrate that this shift in values was more than just lip service in his case, Robert mentioned a few examples of how these changes had affected his lifeways:

> In the last five or six years, my focus has been on natural organic gardening and farming. I sometimes want to be a teacher but think my teaching role can best be by my example—not by a class or going to find students. I have also studied human nutrition on my own. I am a strict vegetarian, making my own soy milk, tofu, and dressings, and, of course, cooking from scratch. I seem to feel like sharing this with new friends but not putting on classes.... I have decided to take the training offered by a very well-respected hospice here in Hilo and will finish that in March.

Travel, particularly in countries with traditional cultures, as part of his continuing search for spiritual wisdom is, however, still an important facet of Robert's post-NDE life.

I am particularly anxious to respect all cultures of peoples worldwide. I have traveled very simply with a backpack in Mexico and Central America, including Guatemala, Honduras, and Costa Rica, and have learned Spanish from living with friends. I have a foster child in Guatemala, whom I visited in October 1986, and support the work of a cultural survival group.... I think I am becoming wiser and would be glad to give away all my formal education for more wisdom. I see it in Indians when I travel, in some native Hawaiians, and in indigenous peoples everywhere.

Robert and I passed a couple of hours in deep conversation during his visit and, like most NDErs I have met, was very forthcoming about his personal struggles, his life not having been easy since his NDE. He also impressed me by his humility and by his warmth, qualities that were obvious to me almost from the moment he sat down opposite me. The last time I heard from him, he was traveling again, but this time back to the mainland, having joined still another friend at an organic farm in Oregon. As with other NDErs I have known, Robert passed through and then out of my life again, but he left his mark on me and I have not forgotten him.

## Mia

In June 1991, an ominously thick envelope from Finland found its way into my mailbox at the university. Opening it, I found a document of thirty-eight single-spaced pages, which began,

Dear Mr. Ring,

I've just read your book, *Heading toward Omega*, which I enjoyed very much. I think that books concerning near-death experiences are very valuable for all people, but specially for people like myself, who have had similar experiences themselves. It is not very often you meet someone who has had a near-death experience, and there aren't many people who believe you and can understand what you are talking about. Therefore, it is refreshing to be able to read about others that have had the same kind of experience, and to know that you are not all alone in the world with these experiences.

That was my introduction to a woman I will call Mia, whose life story was about to be unfolded to me in the many pages that followed. No summary of it in just a few sentences can do her justice, of course, but I must try to provide at least some context for her experiences if you are to understand just how her NDE affected her life. At the time she wrote to me, Mia was a university-educated, thirty-three-year-old mother of three children, but in the midst of a difficult divorce from her husband. Presently unemployed, she was planning to begin training as a nurse, a childhood dream that, she implies, was reactivated by her NDE. Mia has had a life full of anomalous experiences, including, judging from her account, many paranormal ones, and although she does not remember the exact date of her NDE, it seems to have taken place around 1982, when she would have been twenty-four. Of all her experiences, however, she says that "I think that NDE was the most important experience in my life," and her document offers abundant evidence of its profound effects on her. For example, she goes on to write:

> The strongest impact to my life of [my] NDE was that I wasn't afraid of death or dying anymore. It is a very liberating feeling when you can throw your fear of death away. I am still afraid of the probable pain in connection with dying, but I am not afraid of the dying itself. I know how it feels, I know what happens after death, and I know that it is the best thing that could ever happen to anyone.... The other impact of this experience was that I started to take paranormal things seriously. I had had some *déjà vus* and dreams that have come through before my experiences, but this kind of thing has begun to happen more and more in my life.[13]

But there were, in fact, certainly many other ramifications of her NDE, which Mia went on to describe for me. One of the strongest was its effect on her religious and spiritual views. An atheist before her experience, now, she says, "I don't have to believe that there is a God and heaven. I *know* they are true. I have been there." Elaborating, she reflects on her Lutheran background and the role of its church in her life:

> I have never been a churchgoer.... I still don't believe in church although I understand and respect its meaning to many people. I don't feel nearer to God in church than somewhere else. I know that I can talk to God wherever I am. I don't need a specific building for that.
>
> I don't specially agree with my church's view of God. I know that God is a loving, not an angry, hard-to-satisfy old man. I know that everyone finally comes to heaven. There is no hell, or hell is here, where we live right now.... [This] hell is a necessity to go through [here] in our lives, [but] in heaven, there is nothing evil.

Mia also evinces a quality of religious universality and spiritual inclusiveness, so typical of many NDErs:

> I believe that all religions are of the same origin. It is the same God we are talking about, whatever we choose to name him. It is we, people, who have twisted the original knowledge or truth. People have described their experiences or messages from the basis of their own lives and cultures ... and at the end, your message can be quite different from what it was in the beginning.

Likewise, her view of life after death was also affected so as to incorporate a reincarnational perspective:

Being an atheist, I didn't believe in reincarnation before my experiences. I thought that there was nothing at all after death. It was the end. After my NDE, I understood that this life here is only one of many we have to go through. We are bound to be born here time after time [until] we are good enough to go to other dimensions permanently.

Another major area of change had to do with Mia's feelings about relationships with others. Now, she says:

I feel strongly that I want to help people. I've even thought that I would go to some poor country, for example, Africa, and try to help as much as I could. Then again, I have realized that I couldn't be of any help there with my chronically ill children and my own allergies. So I've begun to figure out a way to help people here, where I am.

These considerations, as I said earlier, have led Mia to the threshold of pursuing a new career as a nurse in Finland.

She also finds that she has become less judgmental of others:

Before my NDE, I was much more intolerant and impatient toward other people than I am now. I thought that I knew how you should live your life and how you shouldn't. I thought that if you face some great troubles in your life, you can blame only yourself. They are consequences of your own laziness or stupidity.

Now I try not to judge people by first sight. I try to think that there might be some greater tragedies that have caused the troubles in their lives.... I now have more tolerance. I felt in heaven God's and Jesus' love and compassion to me. I know that they don't judge you and that they love every one of us equally, whatever we are like. I know that they are happy when you treat other people well and show their "children" the same love and compassion that they show you.

The relevance of that last lesson of compassion has not been lost on Mia in relation to her own life difficulties, especially having to do with her impending divorce from her husband. Here, too, she learned to forgive herself and to practice the art of *self*-compassion as well. In reflecting on her situation, she speaks very straightforwardly of how her NDE helped her to come to terms with a problem that earlier would have seemed insoluble:

I feel sorry about my divorce, but it helped me when I read in your book that there had been many divorces in NDErs' lives. When I married, I thought that it was my duty to stay married with this man until the end of my life. (We had our son then already, and I thought that I owed that to my child.) I thought, "What God has joined together, let no man separate," and I felt bad that I even thought about divorcing. It took a long time for me to understand that even a divorce can be God's will in order to develop the person in question by admitting that he/she can fail in his/her very best attempts, and by understanding that there can be more to learn (e.g., compassion to other people in the same kind of situation) by going through these difficulties.... Anyway, I now feel free to live life (after the divorce) more according to my principles. I think that I will be a better mother and better person after that.

Unlike Robert, whose letters led up to our eventual meeting, Mia entered my life suddenly, without advance warning, wrote extensively about her life and what she was going through, thanked me, and then disappeared from view. I would like to believe that in the seven years that have elapsed since she wrote me that mammoth letter she has indeed become the nurse she aspired to be, but that, if true, is a part of her story I have yet to hear. Nevertheless, in my own mind, somehow I have little doubt that, following her divorce, she was a better person. That person was in view all along. "By their fruits...."

*Fler*

Down in Australia for a lecture tour in 1993, I found myself already famished one evening before a scheduled talk in Melbourne. Somehow, my host and I had talked away the afternoon, and by the time we realized we had to leave for the lecture hall, there was no opportunity even to grab a bite to eat. We arrived about twenty minutes before the appointed hour, and while he was attending to some last minute details, two women rushed up to me, one clutching a copy of my book, *Heading toward Omega*, and fairly overwhelmed me with the heartiness of their reception. In a moment, it was clear that they were mother and daughter, both NDErs, and such apparently devoted fans of mine that they told me proudly that they had purchased the very first tickets for my talk many weeks before. Their credentials having been established, I quickly blurted out a complete nonsequitur:

"Is there any place around here to get something to eat?"

They looked at each other doubtfully, but then the older of the two said, "I think there may be a cafeteria or some such next door."

"Let's go, " I said.

Without hesitation (everything somehow being understood), they led me through a gentle mist, trying to shield their poor starving speaker and themselves from the rain with a single umbrella, into a labyrinthine set of pathways that eventually led to a large building. The first doors we tried were locked, but undaunted, we persevered until we found some that were open. It turned out that we were at a nearby university dining hall, which, alas, had just shut down. But when my new friends explained the situation to the help, they immediately agreed to serve us some fish and chips, whereupon we rushed to the nearest table to gobble them down. Or, at least, I did. My friends—named Fler (mother) and Andrea (daughter)—were not interested in the food, but in talking with me. So while I wolfed down my meal, they chatted, forever interrupting each other, but gaily and with great good humor, and told me about themselves, their experiences, and their work. Rarely have I enjoyed a rapid-fire conversation more or heard one to rival their lightning-like speed of discourse. In a wink of time, it was over and we had to rush back to the lecture hall so I could be there to hear the introduction.

That is how I met Fler and Andrea Beaumont, who have since joined the ranks of my far-flung correspondents. As a result, it was only after I had met them that I learned in detail about their NDEs and, in particular, that Fler herself had had no fewer than three of them! This particular information came to me in an extensive document that Fler enclosed with one of her recent letters to me. And since she has given me permission to quote from it, I will do so shortly. First, however, allow me to give you a proper introduction to Fler.

She is now sixty-five years old, has had only an elementary school education (having quit school at the age of thirteen), but has long been active in various spiritual groups in Australia, has worked as a journalist, and is currently writing a book on the issue of life after death. She also is suffering from incurable leukemia and has been hospitalized several times since we met.

Her three NDEs took place in 1959 (when she was thirty), 1961, and, most recently, in 1988. They were all hospital- or illness-related events. In discussing them in the document she sent to me, she conveniently (for my purposes) summarizes the specific aftereffects for each incident separately, and I will simply follow her format here in quoting her.

> Prior to my first rather brief experience in 1959, I was a very insular, self-centered person, an atheist, almost totally unaware of the people and the world around me. After the experience ... I was more aware of the needs of people, more caring and loving. [Also] I developed a great interest in the

physical universe, and although I had left school at thirteen years of age, began to study astronomy, science and archeology. It was as though my eyes were suddenly opened to the world and its people for the first time.

Her second experience, two years later, was much deeper, in consequence of which, she says, its effects were more dramatic. To begin with,

atheism vanished. I knew there was life after death, that there was a spiritual dimension through which we all progress. Love and compassion increased greatly. Psychic abilities, such as OBEs, precognition, clairvoyance, and so on, manifested.

It was after her second NDE that her interests in spiritual and paranormal subjects developed and she became deeply involved in such organizations as the Theosophical Society, among others.

Her third NDE, in 1988, further enhanced her feelings of loving compassion toward others, and indeed all life. As Fler puts it,

I am much more tolerant and understanding, more spiritual than religious, take time to speak to help the lonely, destitute and elderly, comfort and counsel the bereaved and distressed, feed and aid animals and birds, and love and support the environment.

I feel an empathy with everyone and everything, and am aware of the interconnectedness and oneness of all.

Although I now have cancer, there is no fear of death.

Fler's summary of the aftereffects of her NDE are pithy, but, as you will have noticed, they nevertheless comprise most of the elements that make up the basic pattern I spelled out earlier in this chapter. Though Fler is in some ways an unusual person, the aftereffects of her NDEs are entirely typical. And in her case, I can testify that her letters to me have been all of a piece with her self-description here: She has shown herself to be an exceptionally kind and thoughtful person and has already done me many professional favors, despite an incredibly busy life, made even more difficult by recurrent hospitalizations for her illness.

Ever since meeting Fler and Andrea, I had hoped to return to Australia to see them, and in 1995, I got my wish—thanks largely to them. These two delightful ladies, despite the enormous effort involved, helped to organize another lecture tour for me, making sure this time I would have some extra days to spend with them in Melbourne. They had promised me, if I made it back down there, that they would be eager to demonstrate Australia's world-famous brand of hospitality. I was not disappointed. We had a ball together, and we remain in touch as deep and loving friends to this day.

## Marty

Marty Chandler, now in his early fifties, was a twenty-year-old college sophomore majoring in electrical engineering back in 1964, when he had his NDE. In those days, of course, nothing much was known about such experiences, and the very term *near-death experience* would not be coined before another decade had passed. In 1966, he did mention his NDE to the woman he later married, but since she initially had a negative reaction to it, as did his mother, Marty, in effect, put it away and kept it to himself.

This remained true even when he and his wife discovered Raymond Moody's work in 1977, but about ten years later, an event occurred that was to initiate a dramatic reversal in Marty's relationship to his NDE. Early in 1988, his wife happened to see a notice in their local newspaper that Moody would be speaking nearby at a conference on NDEs, and they decided to attend. There, Marty had a chance to share his NDE with Moody himself and with several other experiencers, and receiving validation from them had, he said, "a profound effect" on him. Within short order, he was speaking publicly about his experience at various IANDS meetings and at its 1988 national conference. Not long afterward, he came across *Heading toward Omega*, which, as he was to tell me, helped him to organize his thoughts, not only about his NDE, but also particularly about their aftereffects. An orderly and systematic man, he then followed my book's format in writing a twenty-three page paper in which he, in effect, comments on all the life changes and insights he believes derived from his experience, in addition to answering all my questionnaire items.

In justifying this somewhat unusual and time-consuming undertaking, Marty mentions (under the heading, Purpose in Life) that he was almost compelled to do so because of something that happened while he was in the Light:

> During the experience, I made a definite statement to the Light that I had to accomplish important things when I came back. This was, in fact, the reason that I did not choose to go on. I enjoy helping people very much. I feel that I must do the very best I can while I am here; this is a commitment between myself and the Light (God). I strongly feel that writing this account of my experience is part of my purpose in life.

How did Marty's experience change him? Let us count the ways, using his own categories as headings.

*Attitude about Self* I felt better about myself as a person and was able to become more socially involved. In general, my confidence increased.
*Feelings/Relationships Toward Others* Desire to help others, compassion for

others, empathy or understanding for others, patience/tolerance for others, ability to express love for others, acceptance of others as they are—all definitely increased, although I started to develop values along these lines as a child/teenager.

*Spiritual/Religious Beliefs/Values*   I was brought up Catholic. By the time I was a student in college, I had developed doubts about some aspects of the religion. The experience helped [me] to move away from organized orthodox religion and into liberal religion. In 1970, my wife and I joined the Unitarian Church.

The experience strengthened my feelings about the existence of God, but the concept was beyond the traditional Judeo–Christian one. I view God as the creator of all physical law and of the universe. God transcends the universe, and lies beyond time and space. While being infinite, God also has a very personal and caring nature. I see a God of love, compassion and forgiveness. The concept of a God of retribution and of infinite punishment, who casts souls into everlasting fire, gives me a problem.

*Quest for Spiritual Values/Higher Consciousness, and So On*   My quest increased and intensified, particularly in the area of trying to meet again with the Light through meditation. Thus far, I have not been able to replicate the experience. My quest for spiritual values became more personal and less based on any particular religion. In the last year or so, my quest for spiritual values has increased severalfold. This is related to becoming active in the local IANDS group.

*Fear of Death*   The fear of death diminished, but the fear of dying continued.

*Psychic Abilities*   Prior to my experience, I had no psychic abilities. After the NDE there was a major increase in precognition (advanced knowledge of future events). This has occurred through very vivid dreams.

(Like Mia, Marty then goes on to give a number of examples of his precognitive visions, and, again like Mia's, some of them are quite impressive.)

You can see that Marty, too, fits the now familiar pattern of NDE aftereffects to a "T." And, like so many others, he feels that there is an essential message (the term is his) for others that NDErs are meant to bring back and to share with the world. In Marty's case, he sums it up as follows:

Loving and caring for others are the most important things that we can do as human beings on this earth. An ultimate and loving God does exist [and] we must search for truth and deal with each other honestly.

These are unremarkable, almost banal sentiments to which most of us would already subscribe without having to be reminded of them by NDErs. But as we have already seen in Chapter One, as well as this one, NDErs are not inclined to preach but to *teach by example*. As a group, they are impressive precisely because they live out their experience in action and strive to honor it in the practice of their everyday life. What we have to learn from them, then, is not so much how we should live (because we already know this in our hearts), but how, if we so choose, we can actually make an example of our own lives so that they, as much as possible, reflect the teachings of the Light. It is, at any rate, to this vocation that we must now return our attention.

## CONNECTING TO THE NDE

People who are drawn to the NDE sometimes envy those who have had the experience (though NDErs themselves usually point out that there is a high price to be paid for the privilege, and they are not necessarily referring just to the physical trauma they have had to survive). "If only I could have such an experience" is a frequently felt yearning and sometimes explicit wish on the part of persons who listen to or read accounts on NDEs. This is an understandable and predictable reaction, but it entirely misses the point NDErs are at pains to get across.

I remember a vivid but instructive instance of this useless envy that took place in one of my classes many years ago. It was around 1978, just after I had got involved in NDE research, when one day I asked one of my newly discovered NDErs to come to class and share her story with my students. Virginia, who has since died, was a small, plump, middle-aged woman of Italian extraction who would, as I was later to learn, invariably describe herself as "just a housewife." But when she was narrating her story—and in those days they were far more exotic than they are now—she became a spellbinding speaker and undeniably magnetic personality. And when she began to describe the changes her NDE had brought about in her life—all the usual ones we now know so well—many of my students seemed even more agog.

Finally, it was time for questions, and one of my students, a fellow, piped up (as best I can now recall), "I would love to have an experience like that! But how can I?" With scarcely a pause, Virginia shot back: "Love others."

What a perfect answer! Virginia was telling us, of course, that her experience was wasted on us if we listeners did not get the message: You do not have to have an NDE in order to live by its teachings or to begin your own spiritual search. Its fruits are in its effects, and its effects are contagious to an open heart. Listen, absorb, and act, and everything of essence given to the NDEr can become yours.

Of course, it is easy to listen, but much harder to absorb, and so difficult to remember. But it is precisely to the mastery of these hard tasks that this book is dedicated. You have listened, and if you have listened with an open heart, you have already begun to absorb (if you do not trust your own experience, I will present evidence of this later on). The more you reflect on the stories in this book, the more they will become *your* story, so reread them, as necessary, to incorporate them more fully. And be assured: The fruits of the NDE you have begun to taste in this chapter will be offered to you again in ways that will make them even easier to assimilate into the particular circumstances of your own life. The important thing for you to realize now, if you are not already aware of it, is that the process of absorption has already begun, and it will become stronger as you progress through this book.

In these past few chapters, however, I have been mostly concerned to show you that the NDE is truly an authentic phenomenon and one that we can trust to have genuine spiritual import. Along the way, almost incidentally at times, you have been reading various accounts of NDEs and their aftereffects so as to gain something like a full picture of the phenomenon and what it engenders. My intention has been for you to be able to use this material to form something of a model of the typical NDEr, and to become aware of the main lessons for living that derive from the experience itself. All this helps to set the stage for your own personal and unique connection to the NDE.

But to develop further and deepen that connection, we have to move from mere passive absorption of this information to making *active* use of it. It is like learning a new language: Use it or lose it! To learn by doing, then, is the new course we will now be following, beginning with the next chapter.

## Chapter Six

# Living It All over Again:
# The Experience of the Life Review

Most people, even those who have no conscious familiarity with the phenomenon of the NDE as such, have heard of the life review. "Oh, yeah," they will say, "that's when your life flashes before your eyes, right?" And then, they might add that this sort of thing sometimes happens to drowning victims.

And, indeed, it really does, as I found out when I began to conduct my own research on NDEs in 1977. For instance, one young man who nearly drowned in a boating accident told me:

> It was amazing. I could see in the back of my head an array, just (an) innumerable array of thoughts, memories, things I had dreamt, just in general thoughts and recollections of the past, just raced in front of me, in less than thirty seconds. All these things about my mother and grandmother and my brothers and these dreams I've had. I felt like this frame, millions of frames, just flashed through. It was thoughts and images of people. And a lot of thoughts just raced [snaps his fingers several times] in split seconds. I had my eyes closed under water, but I could still see those images.... Just [pause] silly things—just nitpicking things I thought I had forgotten. Just [snaps his fingers] kept on racing through. It was like I was going through this memory, and, ah, ah, like my whole memory was retaping. I was in reverse. And everything was backtracking so I could go over it again like a tape recorder.[1]

Of course, you may remember that we have already encountered this kind of memory playback in connection with a near-drowning incident earlier in this book. Do you recall now the very first example of an NDE I described at the beginning of the first chapter—the case of Craig? (If not, you may wish to reread p. 13 for another illustration of this phenomenon.)

Not surprisingly, other investigators have often heard similar accounts from individuals who have nearly lost their lives through drowning, and, according to Russell Noyes and Roy Kletti, two researchers who have specialized in the study of NDEs caused by accidents, persons who survive the threat of sinking into a watery grave are particularly likely to attest to having had a life review as part of their NDE.[2]

So the common stereotype concerning the inner experiences of drowning victims is borne out by modern systematic NDE research. That research, however, has also shown that individuals who nearly perish in other kinds of accidents report exactly the same phenomenon. As an instance of this, compare this recollection by another of my respondents in *Life at Death*, who miraculously survived a plunge from an airplane flying at 3,500 feet when his parachute failed to open. As he told me,

> It's like a picture runs in front of your eyes, like from the time you can remember up to the time, you know, what was happening [that is, the present moment].... It seems like pictures of your life just flow in front of your eyes, the things you used to do when you were small and stuff: stupid things. Like, you see your parents' faces—it was everything. And things that I didn't remember that I did. Things that I couldn't remember now, but I remember two years ago or something. It all came back to me, like it refreshed my mind of everything I used to do when I was little. Like, I used to ask my friends, "Remember this, remember that?" And I say, "Wow, that was a long time ago, I don't even remember that." Everything refreshed my mind of everything.... It was like a picture, it was like a movie camera running across your eyes. In a matter of a second or two. Just boom, boom [snaps his fingers]. It was clear as day, clear as day. It was very fast and you can see everything.[3]

The number, rapidity, and clarity of these images are astonishing, to be sure, but the very familiarity of these episodes perhaps dulls their impact to an unfortunate degree for the modern reader. In order to begin to appreciate the significance of these experiences, however, it will be necessary for you to clear your mind of these habituated perceptions and free yourself from stereotypical thinking about the life review. I can assure you that to conceive of these episodes as merely "your life passing before your eyes" is equivalent to regarding the NDE as nothing more than "seeing a light at the end of a tunnel." Such banal phrases only serve to trivialize the NDE with a tabloid blandness suitable for the worst sort of sound-bite purposes. No feature of the NDE lends itself more easily to this kind of trite characterization than the life review. Accordingly, we need to take special pains to examine this phenomenon in depth with pristine eyes. What we have seen so far is only the superficial outline of an experience whose profundity and power to change lives at their root could not even be imagined at this point.

In my opinion, *no feature of the NDE is more important as a guide to daily life for those who have not had an NDE than the life review.* Careful examination and absorption of the material to be presented in this chapter and the next could alter your own life in the most far-reaching ways. So let us linger over the life review for a bit now and, as we begin to delve into its deep structure, see what it has to teach us.

To orient us to the critical dimensions of the life review, perhaps it would be best to start with a little survey of its principal features. Illustrating these will also serve to help you appreciate why this one aspect of the NDE tends to be so powerfully transformative for those persons who undergo it. And, as always, what they have learned from their NDE, you can learn from them.

## THE EXPERIENCE OF THE LIFE REVIEW

### Frequently, You Are Not Merely Reviewing Your Life but Actually Reliving It

While it is true that there is an aspect to the life review in which one watches the scenes of one's life like a spectator, many persons report that at the same time they are *in* these scenes and are living through them as if *they are actually experiencing them again.*

Just pause here for a moment to take in the implications of this statement. In the life review, you are more than a passive observer watching yourself in the movie of your life. You are back in it all over again, and you experience what happened to you just as if it were happening once more. In short, and to simplify, you are living your life afresh—your memories have somehow transformed themselves into vivid re-creations of the episodes of your life.

To illustrate this startling feature of the life review, let me return to one of the NDErs we met in the second chapter of this book. This is my former student, Neev, who had his NDE, you may recall, as a result of a bone-crushing baseball collision. At the end of the spring 1994 semester, after Neev had completed two courses with me, I asked him to my office in order to question him more closely about his life review. When he began by telling me he saw various incidents from his life, I asked him if they came in the form of pictures. Or I tried to, but Neev interrupted me and said, "It was like I was there again. I guess it was like reliving it…. It wasn't all visual. It was like me reliving it. It was like experiencing it all over again for the first time."

After giving me some specific examples of these experiences (and I will present one of them in the following chapter), I asked him if he could give me a metaphor that would capture the qualitative feel of his life review. Pausing a moment, he then replied, "I once said that it was like being in an editing room, and watching a film on my life in fast forward." But then he went on to qualify this statement, saying that the simile was misleading, since it might imply he was more detached than he actually felt. He then continued:

> I look at it now, and I see the life review as—life! Physically, I wasn't there, but it felt like I was reliving my entire life. It felt like I went through it all, and did it exactly the same way, but understood differently…. You know, it was just like living.

From Neev's comments, we now understand that the life review is an experience that often involves the individual in an incredibly gripping way by thrusting him or her back into what appears undeniably to be the actual events of one's life. No wonder, then, that this feature of the NDE has the power to cause those who undergo it to look at their life with new eyes of understanding—and, in the light of that understanding, to transform themselves, just as Neev did.

## You Reexperience Everything

You may have noticed that Neev said that he felt that he was reliving his *entire* life. Such statements are, in fact, fairly typical for persons who report this phenomenon. Here, for example, are a half-dozen brief but representative statements I've culled from my collection of such cases and others I've come across:

> The life review was absolutely, positively, everything for the first thirty-three years of my life … from the first breath of life right through the accident.

> It proceeded to show me every single event in my twenty-two years of life, in a kind of instant three-dimensional panoramic review…. The brightness

showed me every second of all those years, in exquisite detail, in what seemed only an instant of time.

My whole life was there, every instant of it.... Everyone and everything I had ever seen and everything that had ever happened was there.

Then I was seeing my whole life from beginning to end, even all those little things you forget along the way.

I had a total, complete clear knowledge of everything that had ever happened in my life—even little minute things that I had forgotten.

My life passed before me ... even things I had forgotten all about. Every single emotion, all the happy times, the sad times, the angry times, the love, the reconciliation—everything was there. Nothing was left out.

And when these persons aver that they reexperienced everything in their life review, they mean *everything*. One NDEr who has insisted on this point with great emphasis is the researcher and writer, P. M. H. Atwater, who in her first book on NDEs, *Coming Back to Life*, wrote, in part, "For me, it was a total reliving of *every* thought I had ever thought, every word I had ever spoken, and *every* deed I had ever done.... No detail was left out. No slip of the tongue or slur was missed."[4] Indeed, Atwater has contended that her experience involved even more than this, as we will shortly see, but her statement, serving as a kind of capstone to those that preceded it, gives us plenty to ponder as it is.

All the observations we have encountered in this section make it clear that the life review is, in many cases, a *reliving of one's entire life*, even those parts of it that occurred in one's earliest childhood, and a dredging up of countless events that had long been forgotten.

Again, it may be useful for you at this point, before moving on to the next section, to take a moment to try to project yourself imaginatively into this kind of total memorial experience. The effort will fail, of course—even a Nabokov would come a cropper—but the very attempt at this impossible task will make it evident to you what prodigious stores of self-knowledge lie latent in us, lacking only the requisite key to cause it all to come spilling out into our inner vision.

## You See It All at Once, and Yet Chronologically, Too

NDErs stress that their experience does not take place in time, but in a state of virtual simultaneity—all at once. When they return to their ordinary consciousness and recall the experience, however, they are forced to do so under the artificial but compelling constraints of clock time. Thus the *narrative* of the NDE tends to imply a sequence of sorts *through* time, but it is important not to confuse the experience itself with its description. Most stories depend upon a continuum of time—past, present, future— but the NDE is more like an encounter with a holographic domain in which all information is compacted into an omnipresent unity.

What is true for the NDE generally holds for the life review as well. This state of affairs is well brought out by another of the NDErs we have previously encountered, Nel, who had both a childhood NDE at thirteen months and a second one when she was thirty-eight. As she puts it,

> With regard to the question of time, everything happened instantaneously. The whole thing happened all at once but we are bound by the restraints of language.... It is like an explosion, it is all there. When my life went before my eyes, it was not from my earliest memory at thirteen months. There was an enormous TV screen in front of me.... Way over on the left was my memory at thirteen months, and way over on the right was July, 1972, age thirty-eight. Everything in between was right there and I could see the whole thing, all at the same instant.

This is a very helpful observation in another way, too, because it suggests that in the life review, *time is spatialized*; that is, events in time are deployed for the experiencer in a manner suggestive of their being arrayed across a spatial continuum.

Here, a simple analogy may be useful. Imagine yourself driving a car along a twisting mountain road. Necessarily, you take the curves one at a time, without knowing what will be found ahead of you and quickly forgetting what you have left behind. Now, imagine you are up in the air about 500 feet, so that you have a complete visual command of that car's track. From your aerial perspective, you can literally see the car's past and its future, as well as its present position. In other words, time has become spatialized for you, though, as the driver, of course, you were limited by the blinders of linear time.

I think something similar happens during the life review. It is as if NDErs are able to get outside of their life when they see it as a spectator and grasp something like its entire trajectory at a glance.

Noyes and Kletti, the researchers who have specialized in the study of panoramic memory, seem to have come to a similar conclusion, and some of their cases in fact even suggest that my analogy may be more literal than fanciful. In this connection, they note:

> Due to an expansion of space, memories were often viewed from a distance as though on a screen [remember Nel's image]. A drowning victim said he

saw his life "like a panorama far below." In the midst of an explosion one man said, "It was as if I were sitting on a cloud looking down upon the whole scene—past, present and future."[5]

If the kind of conception that Noyes and Kletti and I are proposing has any merit, something else ought to be found in these accounts of life reviews. There ought to be some evidence of what we can call life *previews*, too, since this formulation implies that NDErs *transcend* ordinary time barriers during their experience. Therefore, they ought, at least sometimes, not only to be able to remember their past but see into their future as well.

Can they?

Fortunately, the evidence on this point seems to be quite conclusive: Indeed, they can—or at least reports of such claims dot the literature on NDEs. Noyes and Kletti give some suggestive examples (at least of contingent future events), and a survey by psychiatrist Bruce Greyson revealed that about one-third of those recalling a life review had visions of personal future events. Likewise, I have already reported quite a few cases of this kind in my books, giving many specific details of apparent uncanny foreknowledge.[6] Here, I must content myself with just a single, previously unpublished illustration of this unusual aspect of the life review.

For this instance, I return once more to Nel. You will remember that at one point she found herself looking at a giant television screen in which were depicted all the events of her life, beginning when she was thirteen months old. Toward the end of her experience (at least, as she narrates it), she had made a conscious decision to return to her physical body.

> At that moment there was a second TV screen, which was just as big as the first. It showed me glimpses of what was to come. It showed me that I would have a prolonged period of physical pain for myself; it showed me that members of my family would suffer physical pain; it showed me that my sister-in-law would die prematurely, and she did. I saw a very rocky road. The presence [who was with her the whole time] said, "You will go back and hold your family together; you will be its cement."

I have known Nel personally for more than fifteen years now and have spent a good deal of time with her. From my contact with her, I am convinced that the events she foresaw during her NDE (not all of which are described in the passage I have just quoted) did indeed take place, just as she was shown.

The foregoing considerations, in any case, should help us to resolve the apparent paradox implied by the heading for this section—that the life review is simultaneous yet chronological. From the context of the experience itself, which takes place outside of time, all information is present in virtual simultaneity. But as one *describes* the experience, with the seconds of clock time ticking in the background, one has to take these events one after another in order to coordinate them to the known track and trajectory of one's life. It is an irony that the very act of making this experience more comprehensible to the listener cannot help but distort the nature of the life review itself.

## You Have to Describe It in Metaphors

In trying to convey the qualitative feel of the life review process to the listener, NDErs naturally resort to metaphors. And the metaphors may reflect either the simultaneous or successive aspect of the phenomenon. As examples of the former, I have heard individuals liken the experience of seeing their life to a display of innumerable bubbles in space, each of which contained a scene from their life. Another person said she beheld her life in an array of "tiny points of light and patterns of light." Still another said it was as if the arranger of her experience "took a toothpick for each scene of my life and stuck them one beside the other; it was like a picket fence with each picket representing a particular segment of my life."

More common, however, are images that reflect a feeling of a tremendous rapidity of informational exposure during the life review. To convey this quality of the experience, NDErs will sometimes say that it is like seeing a million frames of your life in a movie on superfast forward, or riffling through a deck of cards, or feeling yourself subjected to a computer-generated burst of images, yet each one clear and distinct as it passes. Typical of such comments is this statement from a woman: "I had a very— it seems as though it was fast—I had a span of my life, just everything that happened. [She mentions various memories] all fanned in front of me. Very rapidly. Just kind of went past like a million and one thoughts. Very fast movie."

In selecting metaphors for these processes, as this woman's case also illustrates, experiencers tend to invoke familiar, contemporary entertainment media—movies, television, tape recorders, and, especially these days, videos. Their understanding is that somehow their entire life has been *recorded* and, under the conditions of the NDE, is played back for them to see. But you should not think that this process is purely mechanical, with the images flashing by at an unvarying rate of incredible speed. On the contrary, what NDErs say is that they can, as a matter of will, slow down these images and even dilate them so as to reach a deeper understanding of their significance. If one uses the metaphor of the videotape, for example, one might say that NDErs claim that they can do the equivalent of editing, fast forwarding, freeze-framing, zooming, and even, under some circumstances, deleting certain frames completely.

Some examples here will help you to appreciate just how the experiencer may come to take an *active* role in the process of understanding what his or her life has been about. Taking advantage of this interactive mode of relating to the life review very much enhances, as we will come to see, the educative potential of this experience and offers the NDEr something far more instructive than merely being a passive witness to the story of his or her life.

One woman—one who had reviewed her life in an array of bubbles—told me: "Whenever I wanted to, I could sort of zoom in on different huge events in my life maybe I felt were good or bad—but there was no good or bad, just me reexperiencing stuff."

Neev, who, you will recall, once used a fast-forwarding analogy in connection with his own life review, said something similar to me in his interview about this point:

> When I stop to think of scenes, or things that I remember, it seems like I can stop and if I want to pick something out, I just kinda think about it, and then everything comes back to me, and I can remember the whole thing. I'm wanting to say that it ran through that way, the whole life.... And certain things that I had the most questions about, and I needed to understand the most, stuck out more.

A further elaboration of this process of scenic dilation comes from a Swedish physician, Göran Grip, who had an NDE at the age of five. In his case, a being of light was guiding him through his review, much of which had to do with his relationship with his younger brother. Occasionally, there would be a pause in the succession of images so that the being of light could focus the young boy's attention on a specific event.

> An entire episode—with its beginning, its middle and its end—stood out as an entity: It was possible to see simultaneously every little action or spoken word with its emotion (my brother's or mine) tacked to it. With an adult description, it was as if we were able to wander about, back and forth, in a static landscape, the features of which were not trees and hills, but actions, words, and emotions. His suggestions were there at the same "time"—as an alternative landscape superimposed on the original one.

Often, of course, what one sees in the life review is painful to witness. In some instances, however, it seems to be possible to fast forward over these images, to pause them, or even to erase some painful aspects of them afterward. In such cases, it is hard to avoid the impression that the agency responsible for orchestrating the life review does so with compassionate intent, a point we will have cause to return to in a moment.

One woman, for example, told me that when she got emotionally caught up in a scene that was distressing to her, "I stopped and I said, 'I don't want to be here anymore; I don't like that situation....' If that experience happened to me, I skipped some of the things, and I just went on from the beginning until I came to the end." When I sought to clarify this process, I made a point of asking her directly whether she felt she could skip over scenes of little emotional relevance, too. She confirmed this by telling me straight out: "Right, and go on to another part."

A man who found his life review an ordeal to watch was surrounded by a group of light beings. When he was emotionally overwhelmed, a strange but beautiful thing happened: "Every time I got a little upset, they turned it off for awhile, and they just loved me."

Another woman commented that *after* her life review was over, her light beings "spared me from suffering any great pain I was feeling during my life review by removing that experience from my memory." However, she made it clear that though the sense of suffering itself was taken away, the specific information she learned during her life review—and the lessons it had taught her—remained intact.

So we see that far from being a mechanical process in which the experiencer is just a passive spectator during his or her life review, this experience offers many opportunities to become involved in one's life, to see it with new eyes, to learn from it, and, potentially, to grow from it. In this sense, as we must now explore more fully, the life review can be understood to be both a self-witnessing *and* interactive event.

## You Experience It from a Dual Perspective

In the life review, the individual is alternatively, and sometimes simultaneously, player and viewer—a participant in one's own life, and yet also an observer of it. Sometimes you are in the movie, sometimes you are only watching it, sometimes it seems that both are occurring at the same time.

The woman I quoted earlier, who was able to skip over certain scenes in her life, also spoke of this dual aspect:

Some [images] I watched in a very detached way. Because I could see stuff going on was like opening up a door and just watching everything going on, and me stepping back away from it and leaving it there. But some of the things I got emotionally caught up in.

Neev was even more explicit on this point:

Like, if you were going to have a life review, and we were going to have a play of it, I would be in the play, but I'd also be watching the play from the audience. And I would feel all the emotions, pain and suffering of all of the characters around me in the play. And I'd feel it as an actor in the play, and I'd also experience it as the viewer of the play. So I'd have both perspectives.

Likewise, Göran Grip states:

The way we went through the episodes was much like the way you go through things in your own mind: in a wordless way, you simultaneously relive something as if it happened once again and watch it from above, seeing yourself as an actor among the others.

This dual perspective obviously allows for both detached observation and emotional involvement during the life review, so that the individual can learn in different but complementary ways over the course of the experience. But having now come to understand *the way* the process works, we need to push our inquiry forward to the essential lessons of the experience itself. Just what is learned through this experience, and how are these insights instilled?

## LESSONS OF THE LIFE REVIEW

When one studies life review narratives, one sees almost immediately that this experience, *in its essence*, is educative in nature. Life reviews teach and, despite the enormous diversity of the images they contain, each pertaining uniquely to the life of the NDEr under review, what they teach is astonishingly universal. They teach us, unmistakably in my judgment, how we are to live. It is as simple as that. There are certain values—universal values—we are meant to live by, and life review episodes contain vivid and incredibly powerful reminders of these values. No one who undergoes one of these encounters can avoid becoming aware of these teachings, because they are *shown* to be self-evident and, as we will see, it is impossible not to be affected by them. You see, you remember, and you change your life accordingly. Nothing compels like a life review, and, as we begin to get into them more deeply, you will come to understand why.

Here are some simple, even homey, examples of what I mean drawn from persons I interviewed for my book, *Heading toward Omega*:

You are shown your life—and you do the judging. Had you done what you should do? You think, "Oh, I gave six dollars to someone that didn't have much and that was great of me." That didn't mean a thing. It's the little things—maybe a hurt child that you helped or just to stop to say hello to a shut-in. Those are the things that are most important.[7]

Instantly, my entire life was laid bare and open to this wonderful presence, "GOD." I felt inside my being his forgiveness for the things in my life I was ashamed of, as though they were not of great importance. I was asked—but there were no words; it was a straight mental instantaneous communication— "What had I done to benefit or advance the human race?" At the same time all my life was presently instantly in front of me and I was shown or made to understand what counted. I am not going into this any further, but, believe me, what I had counted in life as unimportant was my salvation and what I thought was important was nil.[8]

I had a total, complete, clear knowledge of everything that had ever happened in my life ... just everything, which gave me a better understanding of everything at that moment. Everything was so clear.... I realized that there are things that every person is sent to earth to realize and to learn. For instance, to share more love, to be more loving toward one another. To discover that the most important thing is human relationships and love and not materialistic things. And to realize that every single thing that you do in your life is recorded and that even though you pass it by not thinking at the time, it always comes up later. For instance, you may be ... at a stoplight and you're in a hurry and the lady in front of you, when the light turns green, doesn't take right off, (she) doesn't notice the light, and you get upset and start honking your horn and telling them to hurry up. Those are the little kind of things that are really important.[9]

How does one come to grasp these things in the context of the life review? The answer appears to be that you are helped to *see* and intuitively understand them by the being or beings who often seem to regulate this process, whether they are visible or not. In a word, you are shown and *made* to understand. Let me give some examples now to make this clear.

Göran Grip gives us a particularly instructive instance of the kind of tutelage that is available in this state. Speaking of the being of light he encountered during his NDE, he writes:

His love encouraged me to go through my life up to that point. I saw, relived, remembered things that had happened in my life; not only what actually took place but also the emotions involved. Being five years old, you haven't had the opportunity to commit many bad things, but I had a two-year-old-brother of whom I was very jealous, and a lot of times I had been mean to him in the usual way between brothers, and had been punished in the usual (nonviolent) way between parents and children.

Going through what happened to us, my focus was not on what we actually did to each other (or "who started"). The emphasis was all the time on our exchange of emotions. And because of the love and understanding radiating from the being of light, I found the courage to see for myself, and with open eyes and without defenses, what in my actions had caused him pain. And for most of the episodes we went through, the being offered me an alternative way to act; not what I *should* have done, which would have been moralizing, but what I *could* have done—an open invitation that made me feel completely free to accept or not to accept his suggestions.

The lessons that come from the life review, however, are not always so gently and lovingly proffered. In some cases, they are administered quite differently but with an unforgettable impact. No story exemplifies this better than one I heard from a good friend of mine when he joined me for a lecture at the University of Connecticut in the mid-1980s.

Tom Sawyer—yes, that's his actual name—is someone I met shortly after the publication of my first book on NDEs in 1980. I came to know Tom and his family very well in the years following and present something of his story in my book, *Heading toward Omega*. But, unaccountably, I never heard about this particular incident from his NDE until the evening of the lecture at the university.

As a youth, Tom had an uncontrollable temper, and one day, as he explained to us, it really got him into trouble. He had been driving his hot-rod pickup truck through town when a pedestrian darted out and almost collided with Tom. Tom, rather than being relieved that no accident had occurred, found himself incensed that this man had almost damaged his beautiful truck, of which he was inordinately proud. Angry words were exchanged, soon followed by blows, and Tom eventually pummeled his victim into unconsciousness and left him lying in the middle of the street. Shortly afterward, however, overtaken a bit by remorse after his surge of anger had subsided, he reported the incident to the police but was let off with a warning.

Years later, during his NDE, Tom was forced to relive this scene, and like others we have already talked about, he found himself doing so from a dual perspective. One part of himself, he said, seemed to be high up in a building overlooking the street, from which perch he simply witnessed, like an elevated spectator, the fight taking place below. But another part of Tom was actually *involved in* the fight again. However, this time, in the life review, he found himself in the place *of the other party*, and experienced each distinct blow he had inflicted on this man—thirty-two in all, he said—before collapsing unconscious on the pavement.

This role reversal in the life review in which one finds himself *directly* experiencing the effects of one's actions on another is hardly unique to Tom. In fact, as you will see in a moment, it is found quite often in accounts of life reviews and seems to ram home their lessons for living with all the force of a psychic body blow to those who experience this surprising empathic turnabout.

So that you can get a better idea of just what this process entails, as well as its effects on the experiencer, I would like to invite you now to engage in a little exercise—an exercise in imaginative identification. Doing so will help you to incorporate the lessons of the life review into your life *now* and to make the insights gleaned by others from this experience your own.

## A LIFE REVIEW EXERCISE

In perusing some of the literature on the life review, I was able quite easily to locate a number of accounts in which NDErs not only mentioned this role-reversal effect but also reflected on how it made them feel and what it taught them. In what follows, I want simply to share these excerpts with you, without comment, but I would like to ask you to read them in a certain fashion and with a specific intent. *First, please read each of these reflections slowly and, after finishing it, pause for a moment or two in order to think about what the writer has just said. In doing so, try to take in what these persons have experienced by putting yourself in their place.*

Here is the first one, which I have taken from a newsletter of the Seattle IANDS group.

> FLASH! Brilliant colors came radiating from within me, to be displayed in front of us [she was with a group of persons whose faces radiated unconditional love], like a theater floating in air. It was a three-dimensional, panoramic view of my life, every aspect of my life. Everything I had ever said or done, or even thought, was right there, for all of us to experience. I rethought every thought, I reexperienced every feeling, as it happened, in an instant. And I also felt how my actions, or even just my *thoughts*, had affected others. When I had passed judgment on someone else, I would experience myself doing that. Then I would change places in perspective, and experience what that judgment had felt like for them to receive from me. Then I'd return to my own feelings, to be able to respond to the drama I'd just witnessed and

experienced, to react, for example, with shame or remorse because of that episode. Multitudinous actions or thoughts, derived from my own mean-ness, unkindness, or anger, caused me to feel the consequent pains of the other people. I experienced this even if at the time I had hurt someone, I had chosen to ignore how that would affect them. And I felt their pain for the full length of time they were affected by what I had done. Because I was in a different dimension where time can't be measured, as we know time to exist on earth, it was possible to know all of this and experience it all at once, in a moment, and with the ability to comprehend all of this information!

### From Raymond Moody, *Reflections on Life after Life*:

Then it seemed there was a display all around me, and everything in my life just went by for review.... When I would see something ... it was like I was seeing it through eyes with (I guess you would say) omnipotent knowledge, guiding me and helping me to see. That's the part that stuck with me, because it showed me not only what I had done, but *even how what I had done had affected other people* ... because I could feel those things.... I found out that not even your thoughts are lost.... Every thought was there. (p. 35)

### From Kenneth Ring, *Heading toward Omega*:

All of a sudden ... my life passed before me.... What occurred was every emotion I have felt in my life, I felt. And my eyes were showing me the basis of how that emotion had affected my life. What my life had done so far to affect other people's lives, using the feeling of pure love that was surround-ing me as the point of comparison. And I had done a terrible job. God, I mean it!... Lookin' at yourself from the point of how much love you have spread to other people is devastatin'. (p. 71)

### From Raymond Moody, *The Light Beyond*:

[During her life review], I remember one particular incident ... when, as a child, I yanked my little sister's Easter basket away from her, because there was a toy in it that I wanted. Yet in the review, I felt her feelings of disappoint-ment and loss and rejection. What we do to other people when we act unlovingly!... Everything you have done is there in the review for you to evaluate (and) when I was there in that review there was no covering up. I was the very people that I hurt, and I was the very people I helped to feel good.... It is a real challenge, every day of my life, to know that when I die I am going to have to witness every single action of mine again, only this time actually feeling the effects I've had on others. It sure makes me stop and think. (pp. 37–38)

### From another *Seattle IANDS Newsletter*:

It proceeded to show me every single event of my 22 years of life, in a kind of instant 3-D panoramic review.... The brightness showed me every second of all those years, in exquisite detail, in what seemed only an instant of time. Watching and reexperiencing all those events of my life changed everything.

It was an opportunity to see and feel all the love I had shared, and more importantly, all the pain I had caused. I was able to simultaneously reexperience not only my own feelings and thoughts, but those of all the other people I had ever interacted with. Seeing myself through their eyes was a humbling experience.

From P. M. H. Atwater, *Coming Back*:

Mine was not a review, but a reliving. For me, it was a total reliving of *every* thought I had ever thought, *every* word I had ever spoken, and *every* deed I had ever done; *plus*, the effect of each thought, word and deed on everyone and anyone who had ever come within my environment or sphere of influence, whether I knew them or not.... No detail was left out. No slip of the tongue or slur was missed. No mistake or accident went unaccounted for. If there is such a thing as hell, as far as I am concerned, this was hell. (p. 36)

From David Lorimer, *Whole in One*:

[A prisoner found that a scroll began to unroll before his vision and comments:] And the only pictures on it were the pictures of people I had injured. It seemed there would be no end to it. A vast number of those people I knew or had seen. Then there were hundreds I had never seen. These were people who had been indirectly injured by me. The minute history of my long criminal career was thus relived by me, plus all the small injuries I had inflicted unconsciously by my thoughtless words and looks and omissions. Apparently nothing was omitted in this nightmare of injuries, but the most terrifying thing about it was that every pang of suffering I had caused others was now felt by me as the scroll unwound itself. (p. 23)

These quotes are, I know, as a result of using them in my classes and workshops, quite a bit to take in at one sitting. In the groups I have presented them to, I have witnessed many persons becoming deeply pensive when contemplating these observations and later, when discussing them, some have even burst into tears. If you should feel this way, simply upon reading them, imagine what it's like for the NDEr!

But it is not enough merely to note that these comments tend to provoke some deep reflections and strong emotions in their readers. To get more of the full impact of these observations and, more importantly, to begin to make them relevant to your own life, we have to take this exercise one step further.

Please take a piece of blank paper or, if you keep a personal journal, pick it up now. Or, if you prefer, go to your typewriter or computer screen. In any event, here is what I want you to do for the next ten or fifteen minutes (or longer, if you wish). Begin with this sentence stem, and then continue to write:

*When I reflect on these commentaries in relation to my own life, I ...*

After you finish your writing, you may or may not feel like continuing with this chapter. No matter—it will wait patiently for your eyes to return to its remaining words.

## A COMMENTARY ON THE LIFE REVIEW EXERCISE

If you had been in one of my workshops where I use this exercise, I would have asked you, following your writing period, to break up into small groups of four or five in order to share your reactions to the life review commentaries themselves and, if you felt comfortable doing so, some of what you wrote about them in relation to your own life. Following that, you would have been asked to return to the group as a whole, and a general discussion would have ensued.

As I implied earlier, these subsequent portions of the exercise, augmented by the group context, can be very powerful and generative of important insights for those participating in it. Unfortunately, by doing the exercise on your own, you cannot reap these additional benefits here, but there are at least two things you can do to enhance its impact in ways comparable to what occurs in a group setting.

First, I know that some of my participants take home copies of the sheet I distribute that contains these excerpts, so that they can reproduce them and use them in small groups of their own devising—with fellow students, friends and family, for example. I encourage you to do likewise. Just copy the relevant pages of this book or type out these excerpts onto a couple of sheets of paper for later reproduction, and then conduct your own version of this exercise, ending with group discussion.

Second, in what follows in this section, I would like to try to bring out some of the main themes that usually emerge from the discussions I have with those groups that participate in this exercise with me.

Perhaps the most obvious—and important—insight that is voiced, in one way or another, is that this exercise forces one to think about the meaning of the Golden Rule in an entirely new way. Most of us are accustomed to regard it mainly as a precept for moral action: "Do unto others as you would be done to." But in the light of these life review commentaries, the Golden Rule is much more than that—*it is actually the way it works*. In short, if these accounts in fact reveal to us what we experience at the point of death, then what we have done unto others is *experienced* as done unto ourselves. Familiar exhortations, such as "Love your brother as yourself," from this point of view are understood to mean that in the life review, you yourself *are* the brother you have been urged to love. And this is no mere intellectual conviction or even a religious credo— it is *an undeniable fact of your lived experience*.

This insight becomes self-evident to NDErs who report a life review and it sometimes causes them to look at this universal religious injunction with much deeper appreciation for just *why* it must be true. A characteristic statement along these lines was provided in an article by a recently deceased correspondent of mine, Minette Crow, who had her NDE in 1954. She realized, she said, that

> no matter what I did to any person—no matter what that action might be, good or bad—that action would react not only upon me but also on others around me. I knew that every action was its own reaction. What we do for or against another, we do to ourselves. I fully understood what Jesus meant when He said, "As ye do it unto the least of these, you do it unto me."[10]

Another way of putting this would be to say that the life review demonstrates that, psychologically and spiritually, there is really only one person in the universe—and that person is, of course, yourself. Every act, every thought, every feeling, every emotion directed toward another— whether you know the person or not—will later be *experienced* by you. Everything you send out, returns—just as Tom Sawyer felt each of the thirty-two blows he had viciously rained down on his overmatched victim. Remember what one of the NDErs quoted earlier said to pithily encapsulate this lesson from the life review: "I was the very people that I hurt, and I was the very people I helped to feel good." Next time you are in the middle of a heated argument with someone, you might find yourself stopping in midsentence when you realize that your verbal assaults will one day inevitably be reflected back to you in the unsparing mirror of your life.

I do not know about you, but meditating on these implications of the life review makes me think about justice in a new way, too. It occurs to me, what could be a *more perfect* form of justice than this: Everything you do becomes yours. It is not that we are rewarded for our good deeds or punished by our cruel ones; it is simply that we receive back what we have given out, and *exactly* as we have done it. Unselfish love given to your child is love you experience as bestowed on you. And likewise, a careless word that wounds somebody's feelings cuts into you—measure for measure, perfectly, with no possibility of error. What Solon could devise anything fairer?

These reflections in turn suggest a revisioning of one aspect of the NDE that seems to give many people trouble. Very often, following a lecture on NDEs, a question is raised to the effect of whether *everybody* will eventually find him- or herself in the presence of the Light and receive the incomparable blessings that the Light seems to extend to anyone who comes within its embrace. Behind the question, there is usually the implication that some persons should be disqualified for this experience— rapists, for example, or others who have led morally reprehensible lives (or even, with some fundamentalists, persons who are "unsaved").

The answer I have heard several NDErs give to this question is unqualified: Everyone, they say, will come into this Light. The Light is unconditional and plays no favorites. This reply invariably stirs an agitated response in some members of the audience, and someone will then play the trump card. "Even Hitler?," someone will ask incredulously.

I remember an answer that was given to this query by an NDEr friend of mine who, as a child, had suffered severe sexual and physical abuse from her father. When she found herself in the Light, she asked it telepathically, "Does everyone come here?" She was told "Yes." Then, she herself asked the very question that represents the limit for most people: "Even Hitler?" "Yes." And, then, pushing the light even further, she found herself asking, "Even my father?" Again, "Yes."

But when she told of her encounter with the Light, she also happened to mention the other side of the coin—the life review. Remember what we have already been told by the NDErs I have quoted:

> Multitudinous actions or thoughts, derived from my own meanness, unkindness, or anger, caused me to feel the consequent pains of other people. I experienced this even if at the time I had hurt someone, I had chosen to ignore how that would affect them. And I felt their pain for the full length of time they were affected by what I had done.

P. M. H. Atwater, echoing comments I have heard from other NDErs, said that having to reexperience what she did to, thought, and felt about others, was hell itself for her. And the prisoner, who actually had a long criminal career, said, in a passage whose relevance to Hitler's atrocities cannot be overlooked, "Apparently nothing was omitted in this nightmare of injuries, but the most terrifying thing about it was that *every pang of suffering I had caused others was now felt by me as the scroll unwound itself.*"

Again, seemingly perfect justice. From this perspective, can you imagine what Hitler's life review must have been like? One may even wonder whether it is over with yet!

Such reflections, however much they serve our need to see justice done, especially to figures of world-historical moral depravity, are nevertheless very disquieting for most of us. None of us, obviously, has lived a blameless life; we have all done things of which we are deeply ashamed and now must live with the knowledge that the shadow of these deeds will haunt us like an unexorcised ghost. And then there are actions of whose consequences we may remain unaware, but whose effects, not always pleasant, we will be forced to experience for ourselves during the life review. Such thoughts—and maybe you had them when you were doing your writing—are likely to be disturbing, even deeply distressing, to many of us. Even to think about them now is a burden no one would wish to carry, and yet there seems to be no honest way to shake it off.

But there is, after all, a way to come to terms with this problem that threatens to weigh us down with gloomy and fearful anticipations of almost Dickensian proportions. And it is one that may come as a surprise almost too good to be believed. For the incontestable fact is, in these life reviews, justice is seemingly always tempered by a kind of mercy that allows most of us to reexperience our lives without teeth-gnashing anguish and remorse.

> *There is never any condemnation—you are not judged.*
> *You are in the presence of a being who loves you unconditionally.*
> *You are treated with total compassion.*
> *You are already forgiven.*
> *You are only asked to look at your life, and to understand.*

Although the life review may be the price you pay for entrance into the Light, the presence within the Light helps you through it with the greatest and most tender compassion and love and, even at times, humor. You are not being punished; *you are being shown*, so that you can learn.

Now you will understand that for my own pedagogical reasons, I have deliberately left out until now a crucial feature of the life review process that both completes it and makes it possible to absorb its lessons without self-condemnation or guilt. Therefore, to present the full picture of the life review now, we must return to some of the previous commentaries I have cited for you, only this time allowing their authors to tell you how they were gently assisted to assimilate into their own lives what they were shown. Again, what holds true for the NDEr here holds for everyone: In the life review, you need never fear being judged by a force outside yourself.

## THE LIFE REVIEW AS A NONJUDGMENTAL PROCESS

In the set of quotations I used for the life review exercise, there is one from a woman who ended her comments by observing that it was a humbling experience for her to see herself through the eyes of others. But it is most instructive to listen to what she adds immediately afterward by way of striking the balance to which I have alluded:

> And yet, as I relived in my life, there was no judgment being placed on it by anyone. No one pointed a finger at the horrors, or blamed me for any of my mistakes. There was only the overwhelming presence of complete acceptance, total openness, and deepest love.

Such statements are, in fact, fairly typical from persons reporting life reviews. Another woman, an Australian friend of mine, said much the same thing in a letter to me, but went on to add a significant point about the educative function of the life review: "I felt the pain, the joy, the shame of it all, including how others, whose lives I had touched, had felt. Yet never once did the Being condemn me. He just said, 'You were learning.' "

A man from California, also writing in a letter, voiced the same refrain in these words:

> The review of my life started and I knew that everything ever occurring in my life was already known by myself and Christ. The review was not so I could be punished, but so that I might have the opportunity to learn the lessons I had not learned from my life. As the review continued, I could see it was not a judgment at all but a wonderful life experience.

A man I had interviewed for *Life at Death* spoke in a similar vein:

It was like I got to see some good things I had done and some mistakes I had made, you know, and try to understand them. It was like, "Okay, here's why you had the accident. Here's why this happened. Because of so and so and so...." But there was no *feeling* of guilt. It was all *all right*.[11]

Earlier in this chapter, we heard from the Swedish physician, Göran Grip, who described the patient, nonmoralizing way in which the being of light who was guiding his life review attempted to instruct him. In this connection, a further comment from him helps us to appreciate how this kind of nonjudgmental teaching strikes the mind of a five-year-old child:

I knew for sure that if I would accept his suggestions he wouldn't become triumphant, saying: Goooooood boy," and if I turned down his suggestions, he wouldn't sulk or try to talk me into changing my mind. I felt totally free and respected. Needless to say, his suggestions were all for a more loving and understanding attitude.... And although I reexperienced envy, hate, humiliation, loneliness once again, this time it was flooded with his love and the strength it gave to me.

These elaborations on the nonjudgmental *context* of the life review enable us to construct a more accurate mental model concerning how its sometimes painful *content* can be handled without overwhelming stress or guilt. The being or beings who seem to regulate this process provide such a sense of compassionate, loving, and understanding concern that the individual can move through even the most difficult events of his or her life with relative equanimity. And even when a person's limits are temporarily exceeded, these wonderfully caring beings can still find ways to keep the flame of self-examination from scorching one's soul. A case in point comes from a man, a fragment of whose story I quoted earlier:

I feel strongly that the whole life review would have been emotionally destructive ... if it hadn't been for the fact that my friend [the being of light] and my friend's friends, while we watched the whole thing, were loving me. I could feel that love. Every time I got a little upset, they turned it off for awhile and they just loved me. Their love was tangible. You could feel it on your body, you could feel it inside of you; their love went right through you.

The therapy was their love, because my life review just kept tearing me down. It was pitiful to watch, just pitiful.... It was nauseating. But through it all was their love.[12]

In listening to the accounts I have presented in this section, it is hard not to feel that, whatever a person's transgressions, from the being of Light's seemingly omniscient perspective, there is already a sense of implicit forgiveness. And, indeed, sometimes this intimation of forgiveness is directly apprehended, as in one of the cases I cited earlier where a man said, in part, "I felt inside my being his forgiveness for the things in my life I was ashamed of, as though they were not of great importance."

Others, as I have implied, have made similar avowals. One NDEr friend of mine wrote me that in the midst of her encounter with the Light, she discovered that her being had been transformed, and that "my delusions, sins and guilt were forgiven and purged without asking." Another woman told me that in her life review, she, too, was aware that "you have been forgiven all your sins."

But, again, we must remind ourselves there is a balance here: There may be no blame, but there is certainly self-examination in the life review. The being of Light holds you, as it were, in arms of unconditional love in order to allow you to see yourself truly—without guilt, and objectively— so that you can become a *clear-eyed judge of yourself.* For make no mistake about it, you still have to face yourself and learn from your actions. The life review does not let you off the hook, but merely suspends you from it so that you can see and understand your life as a totality.

And NDErs, of course, understand this—and are plain to say that while the being of Light never judges, *they themselves do.*

For instance, the last woman I quoted about the forgiveness of sins actually made that comment in this context:

> You are judging yourself. You have been forgiven all your sins, but are you able to forgive yourself for not doing the things you should have done and some little cheaty things that maybe you've done in your life? This is the judgment.[13]

When I asked Neev about whether he felt judged during his NDE, he replied,

> I didn't see anyone as actually judging me. It was more like I was judging myself on what I did and how that affected everyone. I guess I was learning about myself and how I fit into the puzzle of all these people's lives.

Finally, a similar remark was made by an Australian man who recalled an NDE when he was fourteen years old:

> I told the Light that I thought there was a judgment on many people and that I expected him to judge me rather sternly. He said, "Oh, no, that doesn't happen at all." However, at my request, they then played back over the events that had occurred in my life ... and I was the judge.[14]

So there is a kind of judgment in the life review after all, but the only one making it in the end is you. It is another instance of the perfect justice meted out by the life review, but always carried out under the loving and wise aegis of beings whose only goal seems to be our own understanding and self-acceptance.

## CONCLUSIONS

In this chapter, we have examined, as it were, the general anatomy of the life review, explored its principal features, and begun the task of understanding what and how it attempts to teach the individual about his or her life, and, indeed, about how one is to live in this world. I have used the phrase "begun the task of understanding" quite deliberately, because however deeply you may feel we have probed into the nature of the life review, I can assure you that we must penetrate more deeply still if we are to extract all of its lessons for *our* lives, that is, for those of us who have not had NDEs ourselves. Of course, even here, we have made a beginning in this chapter, but there are further practical insights to be gained from a more searching exploration of the lineaments of the life review.

A limitation of this chapter, which you may have noticed, is that in illustrating various facets of the life review I have chosen to present snippets—fragments from many accounts—so that you could begin to form an overall picture of this complex phenomenon in your mind. But no exposition of the life review could be considered complete without giving examples of entire episodes, from start to finish, so that the full compass and manner of its extraordinary teachings can become evident. The next chapter, then, will change our focus on the life review from distance to zoom, permitting many of its heretofore general features to become visually accessible to us in what Blake would call its "minute particulars." And we, too, will see heaven in these grains of sand.

## Chapter Seven

# The Life Review as the Ultimate Teaching Tool

You are an eight-year-old boy. It is summer, and you are free to play and get into mischief. One day, though, your father gives you a task. You are to mow your Aunt Gay's lawn and cut down the weeds in her yard. You love your aunt, and she is very fond of you. Previously, she had taken you out to her backyard to tell you about her plans for some wildflowers that grew on little vines in the section your father wanted weeded.

"Leave them alone," your aunt had said, "and as soon as they blossom, we'll make tiaras for all the girls and flower necklaces for some of the guys."

But now your father has told you to cut down those very weeds. As a thoughtful little fellow, you consider your alternatives. You could tell your father of your aunt's wishes to allow the weeds to grow. If your father still insisted they be cut down, you could explain to your aunt that you were made to do it. Or you could ask your aunt to speak to your father. Or, of course, you could just go ahead and take the weeds down. Now, let us enter your head and hear what your eight-year-old mind is thinking.

"I decided to cut the weeds. Well, worse than that, I even came up with a name for the job. I called it 'Operation Chop-Chop.' I deliberately decided to be bad. And I went ahead, feeling the authority that my father gave me when he told me to cut the grass and the weeds. I thought, 'Wow, I got away with it. I did it. And if Aunt Gay ever says anything, I'll just tell her Father told me to do it. Or if Father asks me, I'll say, well, that's what you told me to do.' And I would be vindicated. It would be okay. End of story."

You do the job, and your Aunt Gay never says a word about it. You are relieved—you got away with it totally. And, in time, you forget all about this incident.

Now, it is a quarter of a century later. You are in your early thirties and one day, in May, while working underneath your truck in your driveway, the supports for the vehicle collapse and you are pinned underneath. Before you can be rescued, you have an NDE, and during it, you experience a life review. Afterward this is what you have to say:

"Guess what! I not only relived [this incident] in my life review, but I relived every exact thought and attitude—even the air temperature and things that I couldn't have possibly measured when I was eight years old. For example, I wasn't aware of how many mosquitoes were in the area. In the life review, I could have counted the mosquitoes. Everything was more accurate than could possibly be perceived in the reality of the original event.

"I not only reexperienced my eight-year-old attitude and the kind of excitement and joy of getting away with something, but I was also observing this event as a thirty-three-year-old adult. But it was more than that.

"I experienced it exactly as though I was my Aunt Gay, several days later, after the weeds were cut, when she walked out the back door. I knew the series of thoughts that bounced back and forth in her mind. 'Oh, my goodness, what has happened? Oh, well, he must have forgotten. But he couldn't have forgotten, everyone was looking forward to—Oh, no, knock it off. He's never done anything like that. I love him so. Oh, come on, cut it out.'

"Back and forth, back and forth, between thinking of the possibility, and saying to herself, 'Well, it is possible. No, he isn't like that. It doesn't matter, anyway. I love him. I'll never mention it. God forbid, if he did forget and I remind him, that will hurt his feelings. But I think he did, though. Should I confront him with it and just ask him?' Thought pattern after thought pattern. What I'm telling you is, I was in my Aunt Gay's body, I was in her eyes, I was in her emotions, I was in her unanswered questions. I experienced the disappointment, the humiliation. It was very devastating to me. It changed my attitude quite a bit as I experienced it.

"I experienced things that cannot be perceived. I watched me mowing the lawn from straight above, anywhere from several hundred to a couple of thousand feet, as though I were a camera. I watched all of that. I was able to perceive and feel and know everything about my Aunt Gay regarding our relationship and regarding Operation Chop-Chop.

"In addition to this, I was able to observe the scene, absolutely, positively, unconditionally. But not with the horrendous emotions and feelings that my Aunt Gay experienced about her uncertainty, conflict, hurt, and disappointment. And yet she did experience hurt in losing the flowering weeds, not being able to do the things for the children she had promised, and wondering whether I could have done this on purpose. But I experienced all this through the unconditional love of God's eyes.

"There was never anything like 'There, now do you feel bad enough?' Or, 'You sure were bad.' None of that. Only, in the eyes of God, simple, pure, complete, total nonattachment. No judgmental aspect whatsoever. This is simultaneous with the total emotional devastation of what I had created in my aunt's life. And the arrogance, the snide little thoughts, the bad feelings, and the excitement of what I created in my own life at that young age."[1]

Now, you are another little boy about the same age. This time you are Jewish, and it is the day of Yom Kippur, the holiest day of the year—the Day of Atonement. Your parents have taken you and your younger brother to the synagogue and left you alone for a moment while they take their seats and enter into prayer and inwardness. You and your brother sit obediently for a while, but then you begin to get bored and give your brother a look. He is only four, and clearly he is bored and restless, too. Without your parents' noticing, you both sneak outside. There, in the parking lot, you find a shopping cart. You put your brother in it and begin to push him around, just for fun.

Then, you go to the top of a hill, and, on an impulse, you give the cart a push and watch as it begins to careen down the hill. Horrified, you notice that your little brother is heading for a wall, and he is bound to crash into it—hard. But you stand frozen until after the accident has occurred. Only then do you run down to find your brother has hit his head in the collision and is bleeding heavily. Now, you have really done it!

Ten years later, during your NDE, you have a life review and you relive this whole scene. Here is how you experience it now:

"At first in the life review, there was joy and amusement and happiness. It was a really nice feeling. I could feel my brother and me, and I could feel the connection between us. Then, all of a sudden, it changed into something inside me that was more deviant, more corrupt—in a sense, more evil. Just on a whim, I decided to push him down a hill and let him go on his own.

"And I could feel in my brother, at first it was excitement. You know, 'I'm goin' so quick, I'm movin' real fast,' you know, a real thrill for him. And then, when he saw this upcoming wall he couldn't avoid, it turned into panic and fear and distress. And it's not like I watched him panic. I *felt* him panic. And I felt me, at the top of the hill, realizing what I did. And not until he actually hit the wall did I actually act and run down to see if he was okay.

"But in the review, I saw how I acted, and I felt everything I did. And it was shocking for me to see that, at first, I tried to cover it up. 'You're okay, nothing happened, don't worry about it.' And then I realized that I couldn't. It was like an inner conflict that I had all over again. I had it when I was seven or eight [at the time of this incident], and then I had it again during the life review. And during the life review, it seemed stupid. I mean, why cover it up, because it's not going to help you at all. Someone's going to find out, it's just hurting him.

"And not until my brother realized he was bleeding from his head did he become terrified inside. And I felt this intense fear and pain that he had. We went and took him back into the synagogue. I didn't know what else to do, and I was panicking. And this is the highest of the holidays and everyone there is praying—it's the one day you're not supposed to do something like this!

"And I run inside, and there was an elderly lady standing to the right of us, as we walked in through the glass doors. And she saw—and I felt from her, like a, 'Oh, my God, what just happened,' and like a fear. That is, in the *life review* I felt it. When it happened I barely paid attention to it.

"I just kinda ran in with him. And I started to yell, 'Is there a doctor, is there a doctor?' Of course, being that it's a synagogue, everyone there throws up his hand. 'I'm a doctor.' And that caused chaos also.

"And in the life review, it's like I felt all the chaos. And I felt everyone. It's like it was a bombardment of feelings, concerns, emotions, anger and—like everyone was running over. Like, if you're in a crowd, and everyone is running toward you, and you're feeling entrapped. Well, in the review, not only were they running toward me, they were throwing all these emotions at me, all these feelings. And they were all hitting me, and I was feeling them.

"But at the time this was actually happening, I only knew that I was causing a commotion, but I was blinded to what everyone was feeling. I was thinking, more or less, 'Take care of him, I'm sorry for doin' this.' But that was it. I didn't really see everything that was goin' on.

"I felt the first few people that were coming up—they were checking him, and my brother was panicking like all these people were saying something big had happened to him. He didn't know what was going on. The doctors were concerned because of the injury to his head. They were not panicking, but they were, like, working in a frenzy. And all these people were huddling around. And then there were people who were extremely angry because their prayer was disrupted on this day by some kid who should have been watched by his parents.

"And then when my mother came out, at first she was angry because her kids were causing this commotion—she was pissed. She was infuriated because she was religious, and this day was very important to her. And then when she saw what happened, she realized that my brother was injured, and the anger turned more into fear because she didn't know what happened, and she wanted to nurture my brother.

"During this time, in the life review, I remember I felt like something was stabbing me from what my mom was feeling. It felt like her emotions were all jumbled up, she didn't know what was going on. She was confused. And she needed to know, and she needed to hold him and take care of him and yet she felt bad for me. But she was also very angry at me.

"In the life review, I got to sense and feel, basically, what everyone around me felt at the same time. I was watching it, and I was doing it. And I got to experience both aspects of it at the same time. But I didn't see anyone as actually judging me. It was more like I was judging myself on what I did and how that affected everyone."[2]

These stories, as you will understand, do not describe imaginary incidents, though I have presented them in such a way as to invite you to imagine they had happened to you. They are instead taken from actual accounts from NDErs I know: the first is from Tom Sawyer—whose pugilistic encounter involving role reversal you will remember from the previous chapter—and the second comes from my interview with Neevon Spring. Obviously, both stories are similar in that they involve boys of roughly the same age doing naughty things that little boys are wont to do. Although there was the possibility of serious injury in the case of Neev's brother, both are examples of quite ordinary mischievous actions that virtually all of us have committed in the course of our own childhoods. And yet, in the life review, look at how they are magnified into events of the most soul-searching anguish and self-revelation!

By examining these complete life review episodes through our microscope (and remember, I have provided just one episode of many from the lives of each of these individuals), we are obviously able to see many more fine-grained details than before. And what does our closer scrutiny of these cases reveal?

Here, I will skip over those features we have discussed previously—such as the experience of a dual perspective or the lack of external judgment—in order to concentrate on what is largely new for us.

Of course, we have already learned that when you relive an incident within a life review, it is not merely that you go through it again in precisely the same way you originally perceived it. But with these cases, we can begin to glean a further and vitally important elaboration of this principle. In the life review, you will actually experience the episode as you *would have* been able to then, had you been totally present to the event—sensorily, psychologically, and telepathically!

Now, let me unpack this last sentence for you, since it contains a great deal that has only been implicit before.

First, the original event is reexperienced with all the sensory pathways open to it. Remember Tom saying that he was again aware of the air temperature and "things that I couldn't have possibly measured when I was eight years old." He even claims that had he wanted to, he could have counted the number of mosquitoes present (a fantastic assertion, you might say, though I have heard similar assured declarations from other NDErs). "Everything," he says, "was more accurate than could possibly be perceived in the reality of the original event."

When I asked Neev about this point, he told me much the same thing: "In the review," he stated emphatically, "it's like every blade of grass was obvious to me, and every kind of sensation or perception that I could have—feeling, touch, smell—was magnified. It wasn't just visual."

Second, one's degree of psychological self-insight is correspondingly heightened. You see into your motives, even if you were not fully conscious of them at the time or had forgotten them, and there is no possibility of self-deception. Neither are there any longer any excuses or lame self-justifications available for one's actions, such as those that may have arisen at the time of the event to put a self-serving gloss on one's behavior. As Neev later informed me,

> When I was me in my life all over again, I didn't feel as concerned with excuses for what I did. There were no excuses. I did these things already, I

couldn't change them and I couldn't justify them. Now I had to understand why they happened and what will happen because of them.

And, finally, and perhaps most remarkably of all, during the life review, you seem to have telepathic understanding of others' thoughts and emotions to such an extent that there is a virtually complete empathic identification possible. We saw this clearly in the case of Tom's ability to find himself inside the head of his aunt and apparently to know what she was thinking and feeling. Indeed, he explicitly states, "I experienced it exactly as though I was my Aunt Gay." Similarly, Neev was also able to do this throughout his life review, particularly with his brother, whose panic he felt as his own, and with his mother.

In commenting on another scene in his life review—the one concerning his fight with the pedestrian—Tom gives an exceedingly graphic rendering of just how complete this empathic identification can be:

> I also experienced seeing Tom Sawyer's fist come directly into my face. And I felt the indignation, the rage, the embarrassment, the frustration, the physical pain. I felt my teeth going through my lower lip—in other words, I was in that man's eyes. I was in that man's body. I experienced everything of that interrelationship between Tom Sawyer and that man that day. I experienced unbelievable things about that man that are of a very personal, confidential, and private nature.[3]

Even when the identification is with a mass of persons, as in Neev's case, the amount of information about their feelings and emotions that becomes available during the life review can be overwhelming and, as Neev indicated, felt as blows to one's psyche.

What does all this mean? If we can trust these accounts (and there are other similar ones in the literature), it suggests that when you undergo a life review, *all previous filters that may have screened you off from yourself and others are removed.* There are no longer any barriers to your understanding. There is no real separation between you and others, and your illusory isolation as an individual in this world is revealed to be a sham. It never was real. You see immediately that rather than having lived apart from others, you are always truly *a part of them,* and they are a part of you.

The implications of these now self-evident realizations (at least within the context of the life review) clearly need to be lingered over, and lead us directly to another theme that has been implicit throughout much of our previous discussion of the life review, especially in our consideration of the role-reversal effect in the last chapter. And that is the theme of interconnectedness.

## THE LESSON OF INTERCONNECTEDNESS

When we considered the role-reversal aspect of the life review in the last section, we saw unmistakably that ordinary boundaries dissolve during the NDE, permitting complete identification with the other. The vignettes from Tom and Neev we have just considered show us just how deep and specific this empathic connection can be. But this feature of the life review can be taken even further and, at a higher level of abstraction, can now be understood as a *basic principle of life* from which standpoint the Golden Rule is a logical derivative.

Just a few days ago, I received another letter from Roxanne Sumners, the NDEr to whom you were introduced in Chapter Four. She is, you may remember, a writer who has had two childhood NDEs, the first of which I have already related to you. But in her most recent letter, she is speaking of her second, which occurred when she was a teenager. And what she happened to say, in such a timely fashion, helps me to illustrate this basic insight of the life review:

> When I nearly drowned in the ocean at seventeen, my whole life was there within the light—but instead of a sequence of events, it came all at once. I learned that time as we think of it doesn't exist, nor does the separation between us.... In fact, it was almost as if there was no "other." I say almost because I had self-awareness, but knew my awareness lived within an intricate pattern that existed eternally, everywhere.

That eternal, omnipresent "intricate pattern" of which Roxanne speaks, in which her self was embedded is something many NDErs come to apprehend directly, has immediate implications and effects. Another NDEr friend of mine, Fler Beaumont, from Australia, whom I met while on a lecture tour there in 1993, also happened to write me recently about this same matter. She had had an NDE (and life review) in 1988, and from it, she told me with pithy directness: "I feel an empathy with everyone and everything and am aware of the interconnectedness and oneness of all."

Such sentiments, as I have implied, are not only common among NDErs in the wake of life reviews, but also are extended to all life, and not just to other human beings. Tom Sawyer himself was explicit on this point:

> You do have (an) effect on plants. You do have an effect on animals. You do have an effect on the universe. And in your life review, you'll be the universe and experience yourself and how ... (you) affect the universe.... The little bugs on your eyelids that some of you don't even know exist. That's an interrelationship, you with yourself and these little entities that are living

and surviving on your eyelids. When you waved a loving good-bye to a good friend the other day, did you affect the clouds up above? Did you actually affect them? Does a butterfly's wings in China affect the weather here? *You better believe it does!* You can learn all of that in a life review![4]

As Tom's last sentence makes clear, he is not just quoting from an abstruse treatise on chaos theory. His is not intellectual knowledge derived from books but, rather, as he indicates, it is a direct and incontestable realization from his life review itself.

P. M. H. Atwater saw the same thing in hers, which I cited for you in the last chapter. Here, what I need to note, however, is that when she said she was aware of the effect of every action, thought, and word on those her life touched, she also included "weather, plants, animals, soil, trees, water and air."[5] In short, she was connected to everything in an intricate pattern of wholeness.

Raymond Moody's respondents have proclaimed identical insights. One of them, for example, told him this:

One big thing I learned when I died was that we are all part of one big, living universe. If we think we can hurt another person or another living thing without hurting ourselves, we are sadly mistaken. I look at a forest or a flower or a bird now, and say, "That is me, part of me." We are connected with all things and if we send love along these connections, then we are happy.[6]

This kind of awareness, of course, is primordial and is found in many of the world's great spiritual and religious traditions, as is the Golden Rule itself. In America, we tend to associate such a perspective with our own indigenous peoples, the Native Americans. Probably everyone, in their core, recognizes immediately the truth of this understanding and yearns to act upon it in daily life. At the very least, we all have read John Donne and resonate to his "No man is an island" refrain. But the life review *shows* it to you, and once you see it for yourself, you can never forget it. That intricate web of wholeness of which you are indelibly a part then *becomes* your world and serves as the experiential basis of your ethics.[7] It is simply the way it is.

When Neev was summing up his comments to me in his interview about the lessons of the life review, he interrupted himself to blurt out:

I wish everyone could have one—it would change the world! Everyone would understand each other, and there wouldn't be conflict, and there wouldn't be chaos, and there wouldn't be greed and war…. The life review is the ultimate teaching tool.

Of course, not everyone *can* have such an experience, but everyone can learn from it and try to make its self-evident truths one's own. The agencies responsible for orchestrating the life review seem to imply that this experience is given not just to benefit NDErs but everyone, and NDErs themselves accordingly are not merely its recipients but its messengers.

It is up to the rest of us to hear the message, to act on it, and thereby to change the world.

## THE HEALING POWER OF THE LIFE REVIEW IN PERSONAL TRANSFORMATION

The world will not change, however, until *we* do, and change must therefore start from the ground zero of the self before it can begin to spread. Similarly, the lessons of the life review must be taken down from the high level of abstract principles and applied to one's behavior in everyday life if they are to serve as effective catalysts for change. In order to see how this might be done, we first need to examine one further aspect of the life review, and that is how it actually comes to change the life of the NDEr who undergoes one. What we will see by making this inquiry is that the life review may often be *the* crucial stimulus for the kind of personal transformations we have already discussed in Chapter Six and for the changes in self-acceptance we will be considering in the next chapter. Our task now, however, is to see not only how but also *why* the life review changes the NDEr's life so profoundly afterward.

The essential point to grasp here is that for the experiencer, the life review is not only a personal revelation or an insight into principles of cosmic relevance, but also a *healing*. Not just what you see about yourself, but *how* you come to see and understand it is what heals you of what may be long-standing feelings of inadequacy and patterns of self-defeating behavior. The result is a kind of forgiveness of oneself and others that returns you to your authentic self.

To see how this works, it will be useful once again to focus in some detail on particular cases. I present two illustrative instances, beginning with an NDEr I know very well, Barbara Harris Whitfield, who is now a well-known writer and researcher in the field of near-death studies.[8]

I first met Barbara in the early 1980s at a conference in Florida. Following that meeting, she began to write to me and later moved to Connecticut to work with a colleague of mine, the psychiatrist, Bruce Greyson, who works at the University of Connecticut Health Center. Before moving to Connecticut permanently, however, Barbara visited me so that I could interview her in detail about her experience, and her story is told at length in my book, *Heading toward Omega*. Here, however, I will confine myself to quoting some of Barbara's remarks during that interview that pertain chiefly to what she saw, learned, and came to understand through the life review itself.

> It was like I was there again.... I was that child again.... [Speaking of the physical abuse she received from her mother, which she was reliving] I was saying, "No wonder." No wonder you are the way you are, you know. Lookit what's being done to you at such a young age.... It was like I was understanding how insecure I was and how inferior I felt because nobody had put their arms around me and given me a sense of value. Then I was able to see my whole life unwinding from that perspective of this poor, neurotic little girl.... I was watching this whole childhood unfold and realizing that my head was in the wrong place and I was able to refocus so that I had a better understanding of all the rejection I had felt. All that rejection was in my own head.... It was like the most healing therapy there could be.
>
> I was forgiving myself for not always being good. I was forgiving myself for being as neurotic as I had been. And I felt a great deal of forgiveness and compassion for people I thought were being mean to me.... And I could understand their beauties and their qualities. And it was like the slates were all being wiped clean.... It was a kind of thing where I just wasn't the victim any more; we had all been victims.... And I was able to just understand everything that was going on.... It was like a healing.... The whole effect was that I had relived my life with a much healthier attitude that had healed me. And by the time I got to the end I had the first sense of wanting to live.[9]

As I pointed out in my book, the knowledge that came to Barbara in her life review was absolutely crucial to her transformation, and the dramatic changes that took place in her self-concept and her life afterward were not only apparent to me at the time I was working on *Heading toward Omega* but have persisted to this day, as anyone who knows her can attest.

Another person whose life review was responsible for a major upheaval and shift in self-evaluation and behavior was Neev. Indeed, you may recall that back in Chapter One, I presented a fair amount of information about this aspect of his case. If you remember or take the time to reread that section now (see pp. 20–27), you will be aware that the changes in Neev's life, as a result of his life review, were just as remarkable as those which occurred for Barbara. I will not repeat that discussion here, but just remind you, to begin with, that Neev also attributes these changes to the life review itself. Reliving his life had sickened him, he said, and it "was the life review that sparked my desire for and also allowed this change."

In his interview with me, Neev elaborated on just what and how the life review had taught him, and also commented specifically, as Barbara did, on its healing effect on his life. He told me, in part,

> I learned how to live. The life review was, I guess, like a healing process for me. It was actually what generated all the change in me, because it allowed me to put away things that I didn't understand, and that were a source of anger and frustration for me. Like the pains of not being understood and not being accepted. Why people did things that I thought were grotesquely cruel to me.

He then went on to say that because he could now see that they had acted out of ignorance, he could no longer hold their actions against them. They did not know any better. And having that insight was, Neev says, what allowed him to forgive them.

Summing up, Neev added this:

> The life review was, like, my healer. It's like, I could have gone to a psychiatrist, sat on a couch for twenty years, and not understood what I understood now because I got to relive it, and experience it, and understand it better and fully. Like when I lived it [in his actual life, he means], it was only a portion I understood and no one filled in the pieces. So, basically, I carried around that baggage with me until I found the pieces that helped me understand it. The life review was, like, finding the answer book to the test—it's like I got the *Cliff Notes* to the book in the life review. It explained everything to me.

This sense that the life review holds "all the answers" to one's life and that it effectively obviates the need for a certain kind of psychotherapy is not a claim (whatever its actual true value) that is unique to Neev. In fact, Barbara Harris Whitfield said something virtually identical to me about this in her interview with me. At one point, she asserted with some feeling, "Years and years of intense psychoanalysis of the most intense type of external therapy could not have brought me through what I was experiencing rapidly."[10] Tom Sawyer, too, joins the chorus: "As this [the life review] takes place, you have total knowledge. You have the ability to be a psychologist, a psychiatrist, a psychoanalyst, and much more. You are your own spiritual teacher."[11]

Rather than simply endorsing the suggestion that the life review is a superior substitute for psychotherapy, which hardly gives us non-NDErs anything to work with and offers even less comfort to conscientious psychotherapists, what comes to me is a decidedly different slant on these observations. Imagine a therapeutic technique that was *itself* based on an attempt to induce a life review type of experience. Indeed, we do not have simply to imagine such possibilities—they already exist in such approaches as psychosynthesis and holotropic breathwork, and doubtless in other therapeutic modalities as well. I would therefore encourage enterprising therapists interested in harvesting the healing power of the life review for their clients to innovate practical techniques to help induce this powerful, life-changing experience. In that way, many persons, and not just NDErs, would be enabled to reap the same fruits that NDErs are permitted to pluck directly from their own personal tree of knowledge.

This suggestion, though it may seem like a divagation from our subject, actually serves to prefigure our concluding concern in this chapter, namely, how to put all of this information to use in practical ways in our own daily lives. Now that we know the power that lies latent within the life review to enhance self-acceptance and to alter worldviews and lives in the most radical ways, how may we access it? Theoretical knowledge here is useless. To profit from this and the preceding chapter, you must now be prepared to apply what you have learned to your own life.


## THE USES OF THE LIFE REVIEW

Most of the practical lessons that derive from the study of the life review depend for their success on a fundamental human ability—empathic identification with others: to place yourself in someone else's shoes, and then to experience his or her thoughts and feelings as your own is the key. It is precisely this kind of empathic identification that seems to be enormously enhanced as an aftereffect of the life review, and it is what you can develop from putting its lessons to use.

You may remember that in Chapter One, Neev spoke of how his life review had instilled this gift in him. There, he said, in part, "These instincts also allow me to empathize with almost anyone. I feel that when I talk with people I can physically and emotionally feel what they are going through at that time. It is almost as if I become them for an instant."

Wishing to explore this point further in my interview, I asked him to expand a bit on this statement. He told me that he now uses these skills almost unconsciously to anticipate the consequences of his words and deeds *before* he acts—something anyone could do deliberately and volitionally—in order not to behave carelessly and insensitively to the feelings of others.

> Like now, afterwards, I'm much more attuned to what I'm going to say before I say it. And it's not like I think about it all the time. It's, like, I instinctively do it. And I'm kinda able to look before I leap, but in a mental way. That way I keep from causing these kinds of ripples—the negative ones. The ones that are positive, the ones that are necessary, I kinda do, anyway.... I wasn't able to see this beforehand, but in the life review, I guess that's where I learned how to do it.

What Neev learned from his life review, you can obviously learn from him. Let me give you now a specific example, courtesy of another of my correspondents, of exactly how this kind of anticipatory behavior, based on explicit knowledge of the life review, can be usefully employed to benefit everyone.

Recently, I heard from a good friend of mine named Judy who is very conversant with the literature on NDEs. In her letter, she described the following incident to me:

> One evening, a friend, two recently acquired acquaintances, and I met at a restaurant. The four of us found ourselves sitting at a table in such a way that no general conversation inclusive of all of us could be held—and the decibel level in the crowded room also precluded that. The physical arrangement was such that a woman named Michelle was seated to the far left; my friend, Jim, was immediately to her right; I was positioned next to Jim; and another woman, Kathleen, was on the far right-hand side of the table.
>
> Jim and I were eager to talk with Michelle because we were very interested in her work and knew we would not have a chance to see her again for a long time since she was soon to go to Europe for an extended period. However, a four-way conversation being impossible under the circumstances, I gradually gave up trying to chime in, especially since I had become aware that Kathleen seemed somewhat removed from the developing situation. It would have been difficult for her to participate, anyway, because Michelle, who is something of an "entertainer" and always "on," quickly dominated the conversation. And it had already become apparent by now that Michelle and Kathleen had something of an antipathy toward each other.
>
> Anyway, sure enough, Kathleen began to show signs of withdrawal, perhaps even resentment, and it was becoming increasingly obvious to me that she didn't feel included. Later, Jim told me that he was vaguely aware of this at the time, but felt that the circumstances prevented him from doing much about it.

Judy, however, who was already keenly aware of the implications of the life review from her knowledge of the NDE literature, suddenly had a thought flash through her mind that changed everything.

> I was feeling a bit frustrated about not being able to talk more with Michelle and having instead to make conversation with someone who didn't seem to want to make any effort to engage and remained very distant. It is not easy for me to choose to be superficially social, though, just out of obligation, so this was a difficult predicament for me. Suddenly, the thought came, "How would I like to see this scene in my life review?" *Immediately*, I felt Kathleen's pain, and the degree of that pain sent shudders through my body. I didn't see my own life review per se, but rather I felt Kathleen's life inside of me, almost as if I were experiencing it myself, particularly the immense amount of rejection she had felt most of her life (which she later confirmed for me) and how distancing herself had become a protective device for her against further pain.

After this insight had hit Judy like a thunderbolt, she says that

> feelings of empathy and compassion rose to the surface quite rapidly, accompanied by a genuine and strong sense of caring toward Kathleen. Without hesitation or hypocrisy, I turned—not just my head, but my entire body—toward her and gave her a very warm smile and began again to talk with her (although I knew within me that words wouldn't even be necessary). She responded as though she had just been given the most loving hug, and we soon became engrossed in a conversation of our own.
>
> As a result, not only was the evening a success after all, but there now developed between Kathleen and me a very tender and genuine mutual affection, which has since ripened into a friendship. And I have truly felt, ever since, an unchanged and unconditional empathy toward her, as if I had been allowed to peek for just a brief moment through all the deceiving veils into the heart of another, thus receiving the full force of complete understanding that comes from truly walking in someone else's shoes. "To truly know someone is to love them," I remember reading somewhere, "and I can tell you that was shown to me that evening, incontestably.

All this, it would seem, simply because Judy had *consciously* used her knowledge of the life review to behave as she would have wished to see herself in her own life review.

This device of imaginatively projecting yourself into your own life review in order to change your actions in the present has also been hit upon by others familiar with this subject. For instance, in a review of the book, *What Tom Sawyer Learned from Dying*, I read with considerable interest this passage from the writer:

Sawyer's revelations about the life review cause me to examine my own life, and each action, each motive, every word and thought directed toward others. Will I be pleased with myself, or ashamed, on the day that I experience how my life has affected others?

Learning about the life review has definitely improved my husband's demeanor! Now, whenever he begins to lose his temper, he wants me to head him off with the words, "Remember, movie time!" He is dreading the day when he will find out what it's like to be *me*, listening to his rantings and lectures on various topics. I remind him that both of our "movies" will include joyful scenes as well as sad ones. These days he is trying very hard to insure the second half of his movie will be applause-worthy![12]

The use of such a mnemonic as "remember your life review," said gayly or even with an edge, may help others to practice Neev's strategy, but it is probably best said to oneself, compassionately, as a gentle reminder that the present moment will not be lost somewhere in the huge archive of your life, but may well recur. All you need to do, in *this* moment, is to reflect, as my friend did, "How would I like to see this scene in my life review?," and then act accordingly.

There are still other methods to put this knowledge to work for you in practical ways. One, for instance, is suggested by a comment from Göran Grip. You may remember he told us that, when undergoing his life review under the guidance of his being of light, he was shown what he had done, and what he could have done (not, you will notice, what he *should* have done). You can do likewise by performing the following exercise.

At the end of your day, go to a quiet place or, if you prefer, simply do this exercise in bed before you retire. Allow yourself to relax by taking a few deep breaths or by some other procedure you are accustomed to use to become calm and inwardly centered. Once that state has been attained, begin to review the events of your day as they actually happened. When you come to a scene that jars you because of events or encounters that still rankle, consider it more closely and ask yourself this question: "From the perspective of the life review, how might I have acted or responded?" Let the new revised version of this scene now play out in your mind. Do not judge yourself—just watch it unfold. After taking it in, release the original actual version from your mind, and then continue to review your day. Every time you come to a problematic scene, go through this same procedure again.

If you are the type of person who can build this type of daily review into your life, and make it a habit, you will be sure to profit from it.

If that kind of exercise, however, is more than you think you can practice, then I have a substitute for you. Remember the exercise you did for the last chapter on role reversal? I suggest that you simply reread those quotes from time to time, with as much concentration and reflection as you can bring to them. I can assure you that as you continue to absorb them and make them your own, they, too, will begin to have an impact on both your thinking and actions.

Well, you get the idea, and doubtless you can think up further variations on these suggestions on your own as well as some entirely new techniques for practicing the lessons of the life review. (By the way, I would love to hear from you if you have some further ideas along these lines that you think might profit others.)

One final point I need to make is that, of course, you need not undergo an NDE in order to have a life review so as to gain its benefits directly. Such experiences are known to occur spontaneously on occasion, to result from stress, and, as I indicated earlier, may be induced, at least to a degree, deliberately by therapeutic techniques or other means. Here, for example, is an account I recently received from a previously unknown correspondent that shows how a full life review may occur without an obvious trigger, virtually "out of the blue," and yet with all of the same features and realizations as those that take place within the context of an NDE.

> Then there was the time I was just lying on the floor and thinking, and my whole life passed before my eyes. I knew everything that had happened in my own life was a result of my own actions. All was absolutely just. I saw the interconnection of all I had done. There was no feeling of guilt or self-blame or blame from "God." Just an absolute knowing that all was just in my life and that I had absolutely nothing to complain about.

Such spontaneous incidents help to remind us in still another way that we are not dependent on having an NDE itself in order to profit from its lessons. What often comes through an NDE may come to others in different ways, and without any near-death crisis ever being necessary. Blessings may reach us unbidden, or may be sought, or may simply stem from seemingly purely adventitious circumstances. But the lessons of the life review itself, as we have seen, are available to anyone, whether one has the direct experience or not. All that is necessary is not to forget what you have learned, and to act upon your knowledge.

## Chapter Eight

# In the Light of Love:
# The Lesson of Self-Acceptance

Of all the teachings in the world, the greatest is love. And of all the lessons of the NDE, none is greater than the importance, indeed the primacy, of love. And what the NDE teaches about love is that everything *is* love, and is made of love, and comes from love.

Do you remember, for example, Peggy Holladay's discovery of this truth while in the Light? What she said was, "[T]he Light told me everything was Love, and I mean everything! I had always felt love was just a human emotion people felt from time to time, never in my wildest dreams thinking it was literally EVERYTHING!"

Since we are part of everything, we, too, are conceived in and by love. Love, therefore, is our true nature. And, yet, why do so many of us fail to experience this love in our lives and even come to feel so unlovingly toward ourselves at times? Why do we have such difficulty connecting to this molten core of love or even believing that it exists within us? What keeps us so estranged from the essence of what we are?

If we accept the truth of the NDE's chief revelation, it can only be that we have lost touch with the Source. For us moderns, this is the Fall. Existentially, we have fallen out of Love, like babes thrust from the womb into the cold world, and have forgotten our true home. But the teachings of the NDE now come to remind us, to reconnect us to the Source, and to restore us into the arms of Love. And more than that: Since Love is the essential truth of the NDE, it can also set us free.

But, you may fairly ask, what is binding us? From what do we need to be freed? The answer, of course, has already been hinted at: It is simply how we tend to think of ourselves and especially the *judgments* we continually make about ourselves that wall us off from the love of the Light. We have created our own prison through self-judgment, and every judgment immures us ever more deeply. But remember, the Light *does not judge*. It loves. And, as we saw in the chapters on the life review, it also shows us, when necessary, *another* way in which we might have acted, which in turn fosters discrimination and self-insight. When we learn to see ourselves as the Light sees us, we will finally be free to experience ourselves as we really are and perhaps come to love ourselves truly for the first time.

What can help us to do this? First, just remember what the Light teaches about this. To quote Peggy again,

> I was shown how much all people are loved. It was overwhelmingly evident that the Light loved everyone equally without *any* conditions. I really want to stress this because it made me so happy to know we didn't have to believe or do certain things to be loved. WE ALREADY WERE AND ARE, NO MATTER WHAT. The Light was extremely concerned and loving toward all people. I can remember looking at the people together and the Light asking me to "love the people." I wanted to cry, I felt so deeply for them.... I thought, "If they could only know how much they're loved, maybe they wouldn't feel so scared or lonely anymore."

The aim of this chapter is to make use of this knowledge by focusing on the subject and crucial importance of *self-love*. Self-love, however, is an ambiguous and perhaps somewhat unfortunate term, as it may suggest to some the idea represented by the French expression, *amour-propre*. That phrase, implying a kind of egoistic regard for self, would be misleading here. What I mean by self-love in this context might be better conveyed by the term *self-compassion*. This concept is also very close to the more common psychological construct of *self-acceptance*, and I generally use this term to designate the view of oneself that seems to be facilitated by an encounter with the Light. This chapter, then, will explore the various ways self-acceptance is taught by the Light, how that teaching comes to affect the conduct of NDErs, and, most significantly of all, how you can incorporate these lessons into your own life by coming to appreciate yourself from this same perspective.

## THE FIRST GIFT OF THE LIGHT: SELF-ACCEPTANCE

When I was working on my book, *Heading toward Omega*, I received a letter from a woman in Ohio, Nancy Clark, who wished to share with me a profound experience she had had while in the Light. In her letter, she went on to describe a number of aftereffects we now know to be characteristic of NDEs, including the impact of this experience on her self-concept. In this connection, she wrote,

> Before my experience, I guess I was like most people struggling with a better self-image. But I really *experienced* how precious and how loved I am by God—the light—and I am constantly reminded of that in my daily life. I often think, "If He values me so much (as I experienced it that January day), then no matter what bad thoughts I may think about myself—I HAVE to be a worthwhile person." You see, with all my faults—and I have them—He still chose to give me this life-changing experience. Not because I deserved it in any way or initiated it on my own. But for some reason unknown to me, I am worthy in his eyes. Believing that, then in my own eyes, I AM!

Not long after receiving this letter from Nancy, I met Nel at a lecture in Boston, and a few months later, she shared an insight from her own NDE that was so similar to what Nancy had written me that it was as if she had had the identical experience: "After a difficult lifelong struggle, I have learned to accept myself as I am. If the Light and the presence could accept me with all my weaknesses and my faults, then I must be an okay person."

And when you read what Nel experienced while in the Light, it is easy to understand why this encounter had this profound effect on her. To gain this background, here is a brief summary of it:

> Suddenly, I became aware of a light. It was all around me, it enveloped me, it completely surrounded me. It was an unearthly kind of light. It had color that is unmatched here on earth. It was not a beam of sunlight; it was not the glow from a 100-watt bulb; it was not a roaring fire; it was not a host of candles; it was not a celestial explosion in the midnight sky.
>
> It was warm; it was radiant; it was peaceful; it was accepting; it was forgiving; it was completely nonjudgmental; and it gave me a sense of total security the likes of which I had never known. I loved it. It was perfection; it was total, unconditional love. It was anything and everything you would wish for on earth. It was all there, in the Light.

We have, of course, read similar accounts of the Light before in this book—many of them—but here we see specifically how this immersion in the Light leaves its mark on how the individual thinks about him- or herself. From Nancy and Nel's testimony (and it is typical for many NDErs), we understand that they do not lose sight of their shortcomings (indeed, they may become even more aware of them because of the insights of the life review), but *despite them*, they know that as *persons*, they are loved infinitely by the Light and therefore, in that sense, they are ultimately okay as they are, and always have been.

Try to take this in by projecting yourself into a realm where you are bathed in this all-accepting love and learn, with a sense of absolute and undeniable certainty, that whatever harsh judgments you may have imposed upon yourself for your perceived failings and inadequacies are not shared by the Light. What a liberation from the tyranny of your own judgmental self! You are not the person you thought you were: Your alleged "sins" and wrongdoings are already forgiven, and your compassion for yourself, stemming from that of the Light, begins to permeate every aspect of your being. No wonder you emerge from this encounter with the makings of an entirely new sense of self, fashioned in the image of the all-embracing love that now lives permanently within you.

And do not make the blithe assumption that such self-shattering revelations are the privileged lot only of NDErs. In fact, as some readers of *Heading toward Omega* may have recalled, Nancy Clark herself was in no way near death when she found herself surrounded by the Light. She was actually delivering a eulogy for a close friend at the time. As we will see later in this book, the Light often manifests to persons who, like Nancy, are not in a life-threatening situation, and tends to leave the same kind of impact on their lives as does a typical NDE. You do not have to be close to death, then, to experience this Light—it could happen to you at any time. And, as I have repeatedly insisted throughout this book, you do not even have to experience the Light directly to learn from it. Its lessons are free to anyone who is open to its teachings; all it takes is the gift of self-application.

I have said that the lesson of self-acceptance confers a tremendous liberation upon the individual in that he or she is now able to begin to shed the judgmental self that when stripped away also reveals one's underlying essential being. But there are other blessings that come at the same time as a result of this dismantling process that are almost equally important in a practical sense. One of the most impressive of these is the freedom from the opinions of others that may have previously affected one's self-concept in a limiting way, as well as one's conduct in the world.

Again, Nel's case well exemplifies these secondary effects. In a letter she wrote to me several months after we met, she spoke about these consequences and her newly discovered sense of personal freedom and empowerment:

> The most profound aftereffect of my NDE is that I now accept myself because of who I am. I am no longer bound by the preconceived restraints and conditions which others impose. I am no longer bound to do what others want; neither do I find the need to seek approval from others by measuring up to *their* standards. I have found a central core within me, a spirit, which knows what is best for me and which directs me in all that I do. I trust this inner spirit and I listen to what it says, and I act on its directions. While I respect the opinions of others, while I appreciate the concerns of others for my well-being, I am no longer compelled to follow the dictates of others. I am secure with the inner knowledge of what is best for me. I no longer fear rejection because I do not seem to measure up to the expectations of others. I am growing, daily, in the knowledge that I am an individual unto myself and, as such, I am a fully functioning human being with a mind, a body, and a spirit of my own.

These words were written over fifteen years ago, but they still hold true. I have known Nel all these years and, in my opinion, these words have decidedly come to inform her character and her way of being in the world. The document she sent me was, in a sense, her own personal emancipation proclamation, as her NDE was her deliverance from the bondage of others' opinions about and expectations for her. Now, after her NDE, she was finally free to be herself. But notice, she does not act out of her own selfish strivings. Instead, she seems to have become aware of her own voice—a spirit within her, she says, but hardly an interior spectral presence—and she now follows its guidance.

That does not mean she is indifferent to others; indeed, she cares greatly for her family and for other persons in her life and has demonstrated this concern abundantly. But she walks her own course as a result of having opened herself up to the internal guidance system she has learned to trust and knows is right for her.

Not all NDErs are as clear and unconflicted about this as Nel has become, but many have had similar realizations following their NDEs and have tried, sometimes struggled, to find their way to their authentic self and into a way of life that allows that self full expression. In previous chapters, we have, of course, been able to learn a great deal about the way in which NDErs tend either to seek a new lifestyle congruent with their emergent sense of self, or, occasionally, to return to earlier but abandoned interests around which to constellate their selfhood. These persons, too, have declared their independence from their conditioned selves and their programmed lives that had hitherto been dictated largely by others' or society's expectations for them, and have struck out on their own. Our task now, however, is to see just how that has been possible for them, and what secret resources the Light has made available to equip them with the strength they will need to begin the journey their inner voice has guided them to undertake.

## FURTHER GIFTS OF SELF-EXPRESSION FROM THE NDE

Once the old self begins to unravel the threads woven by a lifelong history of judgmental conditioning, the natural core self of the individual is free at last to emerge, rooted as it now is in an entirely new understanding of life. This process takes time, however, since the nascent self does not manifest ready formed, like a new discovery, but has to be *created* by the individual through a distinct and often radical change in attitude and behavior. Furthermore, the friends and family of the NDEr may resist these changes, fail to understand their basis, and fear their consequences. Thus, anyone who would use the gift of self-acceptance has to overcome both inertial tendencies within him- or herself and possibly external obstacles as well. Nevertheless, the NDEr is aided in this process of self-transformation by new allies that unexpectedly make their appearance in the psyche of the individual and provide the means by which the self can be refashioned in action.

Perhaps the most basic of these sources of support is a new faith in oneself that comes from having received, as it were, the imprimatur of the Light itself. We have, of course, already encountered this effect in the testimonies of Nancy and Nel, and other NDErs, not surprisingly, tend to echo a similar refrain in speaking of what has sustained them in making necessary changes in their own lives. To paraphrase one such NDEr, "Because someone has faith in me, I cannot fail to have faith in myself."

The most obvious practical expression of this faith is a marked increase in feelings of self-worth and in personal self-confidence. In my book, *Heading toward Omega*, for example, I give many instances of this kind of shift from the interviews I conducted for that research.[1] Here are just a few brief citations to illustrate the point:

> I was easily intimidated.... I'm not like that anymore.... I can talk with anyone now.... I have more confidence in myself.

[Before] I was insecure, always.... [Now] if somebody doesn't like me, I don't fret about it.... I [had] always been—believe it or not—shy and reserved and you could not get me up in front of any group of people to speak out. Well, I did a complete one-hundred-eighty-degree turn.

I have changed three-hundred-and-sixty degrees, from a very shy, introverted person to an extrovert. All the way out! I now talk in public.... I could never have made a speech in my life [before].[2]

Earlier, I mentioned that the changes in self-acceptance that were exemplified by Nancy and Nel are in fact characteristic of NDErs. So, too, are these increases in self-esteem. In *Heading toward Omega*, for instance, I found it true for about 85 percent of my sample of NDErs. And, recently, Cherie Sutherland, in her Australian study, reported virtually identical findings in this respect, 83 percent of her sample of NDEs having attested to increased feelings of self-worth.[3] Indeed, if you were to examine some of Sutherland's protocols, you would have a hard time distinguishing them from mine. Here are just a couple for the sake of comparison:

At the time of my experience, I believed I was a nothing, that everybody else was far better educated than I. I was a very shy person in those days. Hard to believe now! [laughs] I was very shy, very diffident about my own skills. I had no skills, really.... I felt as if I was a downtrodden and underneath sort of person in those days.... But since then, absolutely my whole life has changed. It's opened up and I've become more assertive and more aware of who I am. I now realize that I am a perfect being in my own right and I don't have to fear anybody else or anything else. I mean, I'm still the same old Moira making the same mistakes, but I'm much more aware of what's going on. I have much more self-confidence now.

Since the experience I've really grown in self-confidence and self-esteem. I couldn't enter a room with people at one stage, and I'd walk on the other side of the road rather than have to talk with someone. But now, I'm the first to speak if I'm in a queue. I always used to admire my grandfather—he'd go up and talk to anyone at a bus queue. I didn't dare, I had no self-confidence at all. But after [the NDE] I knew there was somebody or something looking after and directing me.[4]

What is happening here? Clearly, formerly latent, even unsuspected, potentialities of the self—strengths, abilities, and will—are beginning to grow and flourish in the suddenly fertile soil of individual's soul. The Light of one's own true nature, like the sun shining on the plants of the earth, brings forth what was primed to develop but only lacked the catalyzing stimulus. In short, the absolute and unconditional love of the Light reveals the essence of the individual's true self, and once alignment with that self begins to take place, the growth of natural self-confidence and feelings of self-worth come as a necessary by-product, as they were always meant to. When the old crippled self—a fear-based congeries of defenses and compromises—falls away, its crutches can be dispensed with also. The result is courage. One can finally stand on one's own.

And courage is still another ally that makes it possible not merely to hear the voice of the new self but to *follow* it. In Chapter Four, I mentioned that one of the common themes of an NDEr's life is a kind of spiritual journey, which is at bottom a quest to realize one's own authentic self in action, and illustrated it by the example of Robert. Here, from our present perspective, we can understand not only why this sort of journey is as prevalent as it is among NDErs, but also what impels it and makes it possible in the first place. The new self is not merely a matter of insight; it demands expression or it will be stillborn. And its demands can be ruthless.

Consider the case of another of my correspondents, Maria, from Peru, who had her NDE in Lima in 1975, in connection with the birth of her third child. When she came back from this experience and recovered, she found that her previous way of life could no longer provide the proper container for her energies. In her case, she had the courage to smash it.

> This originated a fundamental change in my attitudes toward life. I left aside all my activities as an executive and started searching for an answer moved by some energy—a little bit strange for me. I started picking from the Bible, met mystics, gurus, philosophers, esoteric groups, religions, and so on. My nine-year search was pretty intensive. Sometimes I felt anxious, but I could overcome all these states because every new discovery let me see with clarity that my searching and its result were pretty coherent with [my NDE] itself. This filled me with optimism and internal peace.
>
> No more could I identify myself with people in my familiar social surroundings. My values had suffered a shock and started changing [but] were reaffirmed when I increased my searching. I had to leave all my friends, which are now composed of artists and avant-garde intellectuals, many of them with a true vocation for social service. My husband was very comprehensive and open, but sometimes I couldn't explain what I felt and I just told him, "I am on the edge of profoundness—an abyss." And he heard me, tenderly and seriously, and this helped me a lot. "Go on," he said.

And she did. I have heard from Maria a couple of times since her first letter to me, most recently within the past year. She is now far from Lima, geographically and metaphorically. She is deeply involved with South American shamanism, which she regards as an alternate pathway into the same realm that was opened to her through her NDE, and is currently helping persons who wish to explore this traditional practice in her own native culture to learn its methods. She has become, in a word, a *shamanista* herself, and her last letter shows she feels she has indeed found her true calling.

Maria, however, was one of the lucky ones, for she had the support of her husband in pursuing her vocation in life and in allowing her new self to constellate around it. Many NDErs are not so fortunate, since the road they feel compelled to follow often forces them to become alienated from both friends *and* family, in consequence of which divorce or a ruptured primary relationship is another all-too-frequent casualty of surviving an NDE. Breaking away from one's spouse or lover, as we saw in the case of Mia, for example, in Chapter Five, also requires courage, but courage is precisely the ally that can now be called upon to sustain one in taking this drastic step. And the NDEr knows that sometimes it *must* be taken, not out of mere personal unhappiness with one's partner, but because the new self simply cannot come into being, much less thrive, in an environment hostile to its existence.

The deep struggle that so many NDErs must confront if they are to realize their true self and follow it wherever it leads obviously requires a plenitude of self-compassion. But the struggle to heed one's own voice amid the din of those that shout and admonish, and may even threaten can still be fraught with anguish for the NDEr. How often in my private consultations with such persons in the throes of trying to find their own path toward self-liberation and spiritual fulfillment have I had to listen to their plangent pleas for right guidance as they faced the hard choices that they could no longer avoid.

And yet, although this kind of *cri de coeur* is one that I have often heard from the lips of the NDErs I have worked with, we must remember that the way that beckons is by no means always one that entails such profound soul searching or requires a severe disruption in one's personal life. As an example of an easier transition to one's authentic self, you may remember from Chapter One when Peggy was given to understand the imperative of "following your love." Here, as we revisit in a new context some of the themes we first explored toward the end of that chapter, it will be helpful to return to some of Peggy's comments so as to round out this discussion and give it a balance it now requires.

In Peggy's case, you will recall, she was gently led by the Light to appreciate that her natural love had to do with music, specifically, the joy of singing, and in her post-NDE life, singing again became central to her. For Peggy, then, it was not necessary to divorce her husband, to trek all over the world seeking spiritual teachers, or to leave her old world behind like a heap of discarded garbage. All that was necessary in her life was simply to remember "to follow her love" *back* to where she herself had forsaken it, and to start anew from there. And all that was necessary for that was not so much courage as *insight* and *self-understanding*, another gift from the Light, of course, and one that for many NDErs may be sufficient to lead them onto the road, not far from home, where they must now walk, even if they cannot be certain of its ultimate destination. For Peggy, however, there was also a sense of gratitude that motivated her journey, and that was for the greatest gift of all.

> It has become my whole life to pay that Light back in some way for coming to me and loving me when I needed it most. I've got a feeling this is going to be a lifetime project. The "old me" is gone and every day I'm discovering the "new me." I don't know what the future will bring but I am going to do my best to stay open for change and growth. I know I'll probably spend the rest of my life adjusting, in one way or another, to what happened to me that day in August. But I wouldn't change it for the world! I will have it with me always, and, I hope, find some way to share it.

Obviously, everyone's path is different, and the ways to create or reconnect with one's authentic self are equal to the number of sojourners who seek to discover their true footing. Some, like Maria and Robert, will need to venture far from where their prior lives had taken them, find new companions along the way, and discover through their seeking an entirely different calling upon which to base their lives. Others, like Peggy and Craig, only need to return to their childhood garden, as it were. Some will divorce, while others will find their family life enhanced and renewed. Someone else's path could be your *cul-de-sac*.

And different gifts of the Light will be necessary for different kinds of journeys. But the Light also teaches this: If you need them, you will have them. The unceasing love of the Light will guide your way, unfailingly, and give you everything you require. The only thing necessary is to take the first decisive irreversible step into the world that leads to the path your own open heart has helped you to discern.

## THE SEARCH FOR SELF: USING THE GIFTS OF THE NDE

So far in this chapter, we have seen the power that the gift of self-acceptance confers on the NDEr to effect major changes in his or her self-concept and how the various facets of this gift—increased self-esteem, self-confidence, courage, and self-insight—then support the individual to make the kind of life changes that reflect and in turn strengthen the newly emergent self. What we are faced with now, however, is not merely a need to understand these phenomena more deeply, but a greater challenge still: We must again learn to apply what we have learned to our own lives.

But, first, an important caveat: *Of course*, many persons—and, doubtless many readers of this book—are already "on track" in their lives and largely act from their authentic selves. Such persons will have no need to apply these lessons, because they have already done so. While probably most persons could do with a "refresher course" of the sort this chapter offers, what follows is intended primarily for those readers who feel that this chapter has awakened some doubts about whether and to what extent they are in touch with their essential selves or are living as they were meant to live. If you feel that way, then read on: This is for you.

Let us look at this authenticity issue more closely by reflecting on your reactions to what has been presented here and, indeed, throughout this book, but especially the material in Chapters One and Four as well. There must have been certain cases in particular with which you identified or that made you pause for a moment to think about your own life. Take just a few minutes now to recall these cases, or, better yet, suspend reading when you get to the end of this paragraph and peruse them again. What do they bring up for you? Do they suggest certain blockages in your own life? Turning points where you took a *wrong* turn, in retrospect? Times when you acted merely to please others to the detriment of your own essential needs? Occasions—too many, perhaps—when you yielded to those voices pleading for you to "mend my life?" Are you reminded of your failures to "follow your love," thinking that by doing so you were only being selfish? But you can generate your own questions—the ones that only you know apply with special force to you. Take some time now to reflect and to write about these matters in a journal or on whatever paper you have handy, or on your personal computer. The form does not matter, only the process of self-inquiry that enables the necessary inner work to be done. Come back to this chapter only when you're finished and take as much time as you need.

You yourself will, of course, have to decide what, if anything, to do about your self-discoveries. Perhaps you will just have to sit with them a while, let them simmer in the background of your mind, or dream about them, if such is your inclination. Perhaps you will do nothing—or seem to do nothing. Some of you will talk to a close friend, while others may continue to think them through or write further about them on their own. You may, if you are so inclined, enter therapy to pursue these issues, seek out more radical means of self-exploration, find your own group of NDErs, look for a spiritual teacher or, like Robert and Maria, chart an entirely new course for your life. I have already observed that there are myriad ways to search for one's authentic self, and it is hardly necessary for me to do more than adumbrate a few of them, much less to prescribe any. This is your work, anyway, should you decide to engage in it. All I can do in this respect, and this will be in my final chapter, is to point the way to some specific resources and programs, and let you take it from there.

However, there are still a few general guidelines and reminders that can be extracted from this chapter of which *anyone* can make good use. And these all have to do with what is to be found when one encounters the Light, whether through nearly dying or in some other way. There is an essential teaching from the Light that, NDErs say, applies to everyone. And that teaching and this chapter might be summed up as follows:

Everyone is loved infinitely, and with incredible compassion. There is a plan or, one might say, a kind of blueprint for everyone's life, and, while we each are free to embrace or reject it, the Light is there to help us find it. If we can open ourselves to the Light, invoke it into our lives, we will, in time, be shown our own way—and we will recognize it as ours unmistakably because it will give us joy. Joy in living is the truest sign that we are living right.

What kills is judgment; what heals is love. The Light itself is only love, and it never judges; instead, it gently *nudges* you toward your essential self. It wants you to realize that your core being is this Light—it is not something external to you. When you become identified with this Light, you will have only love and compassion for yourself—and for everything— and you will be able to let go of all judgment. Self-condemnation, guilt, and other forms of self-laceration likewise are vanquished. When judgment— that ruthless sower of division—falls away, there is only acceptance—of everything. And that is called love.

"Of all the teachings in the world, the greatest is love. And of all the lessons of the NDE, none is greater than the importance, indeed the primacy, of love. And what the NDE teaches about love is that everything is love and is made of love and comes from love."

## Chapter Nine

# *Through a Glass Lightly: Seeing the World with NDE-Opened Eyes*

In the last chapter, our focus was on the sense of self that the near-death experience tends to foster. There, we came to understand that the effect of an NDE is to stimulate the growth of self-esteem and self-acceptance, and thereby further the individual's courage to pursue a way of life in keeping with his or her own authentic self. And of the several related lessons for us from that chapter, perhaps the most essential was that of the importance of self-compassion.

Here, our focus reverses direction so that we gaze, not at the self, but at the world as seen through the eyes of the NDEr. In doing so, we are in effect returning for a moment to some of the concerns of Chapter Five, where I tried to draw a portrait of NDErs in terms of a characteristic constellation of beliefs, attitudes, and values that tends to arise in the aftermath of an NDE. This pattern of psychological aftereffects is in its own way also a *worldview*, a distinctive filter that enables the NDEr to see and experience the ordinary world with heightened sensitivity and appreciation. As a result, self-compassion turned outward turns into compassion for others—and that, as we will see, is, in a nutshell, perhaps the essential lesson for us to absorb in *this* chapter.

I say "absorb" deliberately, because our task here is not merely to understand that the NDEr now sees the world through eyes brimming with compassion, but to learn to see the world this way ourselves. How we can begin to internalize this perspective—and indeed, how we may have already begun to do so even without our awareness—is the work of this chapter, but *that* it is possible is, of course, the whole premise of this book. And NDErs share this conviction, too. As my friend, Steve, whom we first met in Chapter One, said to me, "It is possible to gain all the knowledge persons learn when they die, without dying. You don't have to die to get there."

How, then, can we make a start to capture this knowledge and come to adopt an NDEr's way of experiencing the world? To begin with, there would seem to be two distinct modalities of learning available to us, which, although we can certainly isolate them for heuristic purposes, may often work together in synergistic ways. The first operates by a principle of contagion, whereas the second involves a deliberate effort to emulate the behavior of NDErs and thus put into practice what one has learned about their manner of being in the world. In this chapter, we consider both of these learning modalities, though we will begin by concentrating mostly on the former.

## THE NDE AS A BENIGN VIRUS

As you now know, information about the NDE has been available since the mid-1970s, ever since the groundbreaking work of Elisabeth Kübler-Ross and Raymond Moody appeared with such electrifying effect, and since that time, the Western World at least has grown very familiar with the stories near-death survivors tell of their journeys into the Light. Indeed, the level of popular fascination with these experiences, although it has certainly had some distinct peaks of particularly keen interest, has never really abated, and the NDE remains to this day almost a staple of our mass culture. It is curious, then, that for all the attention that has been given to this phenomenon, especially through the media and, these days, over the Internet, there has been virtually no research conducted to examine the *effects* of all this information about NDEs on those who have never had such an experience themselves—obviously, the great preponderance of persons on this planet! The fact that, after all this time, we still know so very little about how most of the world has actually responded to the tremendous volume of NDE-based material now available points to a striking lacuna in the field of near-death studies and the need to fill it through careful and systematic investigations.

Of course, it would be misleading to imply we do not have any data bearing on this issue. There have already been, for example, a number of surveys of various professional groups, such as physicians, nurses, psychologists, or members of the clergy, in the United States, and of selected communities elsewhere that have inquired into their knowledge and acceptance of NDEs. And there are naturally a scattering of published letters and many unpublished ones, some of which I cite in later chapters, that offer eloquent and moving testimony about the power of NDE literature to provide comfort, hope, and inspiration to individuals who have not themselves had these experiences. These surveys and personal accounts are certainly suggestive of the impact that information about NDEs may have on selected groups and individuals, but they are still a long way from careful studies directed to the question of how such information has been received by the population at large.

In fact, there are only two studies I am familiar with that have consciously attempted to explore this question, albeit with samples of non-experiencers that are still very far from being representative of people in general. The first of these was described a few years ago by the late sociologist Charles Flynn in his book *After the Beyond* and was called "The Love Project." This undertaking represented Flynn's attempt to drive home some of the moral lessons of the NDE by asking the students in his sociology classes at Miami University of Ohio to make a specific semester-long effort "to relate in a loving manner to someone they wouldn't otherwise relate to."[2] Obviously, here Flynn was employing a learning strategy based on a patently direct imitation of an NDEr's orientation toward others. Although his courses were not *primarily* concerned with NDEs, Flynn did lecture about them, emphasizing how such experiences tend to bring about a more loving and compassionate attitude toward other people, and also played videos featuring NDErs. Furthermore, as a guide for the kind of action he was seeking to encourage in his students, Flynn also required them to read a then popular book by Leo Buscaglia, *Love*,[3] and showed them videos of Buscaglia's lectures.

Altogether, more than 400 students took part in these "Love Projects." Flynn evaluated the results of his students' activities through a combination of questionnaires and personal journals. His findings showed strong evidence that these interactions resulted in an increased sense of compassionate concern for others in general (more than 80 percent of his students reported this effect) as well as greater feelings of their own self-worth (indicated by about 65 percent of these students). Furthermore, these effects tended to persist, though with some diminishment, as shown by a follow-up survey a year later.

Of course, this attempt to foster "the lessons of love stemming from the NDE," as Flynn unabashedly put it,[4] goes well beyond simply examining the effects of mere exposure to NDE information, which is what we will be chiefly concerned with shortly. Nevertheless, more recent research suggests it is by no means *necessary* to induce persons to become involved in an active way in order for them to begin to experience some of the benefits of NDEs for themselves. Apparently, at least for persons who are open to or become interested in NDEs, simple exposure may be sufficient to bring about the same kind of changes—and more—that Flynn found characteristic of his students.

Here, I am alluding to some recent work of my own, which was published as a book under the title of *The Omega Project*.[5] The relevant part of that study involved seventy-four NDErs and, especially pertinent here, a control group of fifty-four persons who were known to be interested in NDEs but had never had such an experience themselves. In examining the pattern of belief and values changes, I found that the control group showed many of the same effects as NDErs *since becoming interested in NDEs*, though, not surprisingly, the magnitude of these changes was usually somewhat less than for the NDErs themselves. Nevertheless, the results showed clearly that members of the control group felt they had also become more appreciative of life, more self-accepting, more compassionately concerned for others, more spiritual, less materialistic, and so on—in short, they reflected the same kind of values profile as actual NDErs, presumably just as a result of finding themselves drawn to the world of these experiences. Not only that, but further analysis revealed that the shifts in values and outlook reported by the control group tended to persist and did not fade with the passage of time. In some cases, these persons were describing changes that had already lasted almost two decades.

Moreover, I found that there were still other enduring shifts in beliefs and values for the control group that showed them to have moved to positions virtually indistinguishable from the views typically expressed by NDErs. For example, like NDErs, the great majority of the controls now also evinced an increased ecological sensitivity and a greater concern for the welfare of the planet following their exposure to NDE materials.

Furthermore, more than 80 percent of the controls indicated a diminished fear of death, and a like percentage affirmed that their belief in life after death had increased—effects that, again, are typical of those described by NDErs.

In general, then, the overall pattern of our data here gives us a strong suggestion that merely acquiring knowledge about NDEs can act rather like a "benign virus"; that is, by exposing yourself to NDE-related information, you can "catch it," because the NDE appears to be contagious. Therefore, it seems quite plausible to argue that in this way you can reap some of the benefits of an NDE—possibly for life—without having to go to the extremity of throwing yourself under the wheels of the nearest oncoming train, like a modern-day Anna Karenina, in order to induce the experience. Clearly, this book is based on that very premise, and if it is correct, you should already be showing some signs of having contracted the condition from which NDErs "suffer" and thus seeing the world with eyes not unlike theirs.

In any case, another possible indication of the way that exposure to information about NDEs may serve to bring about changes in personal values similar to those typical of NDErs themselves comes from a study by the psychiatrist Bruce Greyson, who for many years has been the editor of the *Journal of Near-Death Studies*.[6] In 1983, Greyson published the results of a survey of personal values that was based on a sample of 89 NDErs as well as 175 members of the International Association for Near-Death Studies (IANDS) who had *not* had NDEs but had, obviously, enough interest in them to join an organization devoted to their study.[7] In his research, Greyson was particularly concerned with four clusters of personal values: self-actualization, altruism, spirituality, and being successful in life. He had all of his respondents rate these factors in terms of their personal importance to them.

What is instructive about Greyson's findings is how *similar* his two groups—NDErs and those interested in NDEs—were in their values profiles. Both groups rated the values of self-actualization, altruism, and spirituality as quite important to them, and, statistically, there was no difference between them. Success in life, however, was downplayed by both groups, though here the NDEr group was statistically somewhat lower on this dimension. Overall, however, as with the findings from the Omega Project, we see that the value profiles of persons interested in NDEs tend to mimic those of persons who have actually had these experiences. Of course, there may be various reasons for this, but one possibility that seems likely to have played a strong contributory role is that the compelling testimonies of NDErs on what matters in life significantly influenced those persons who were sufficiently drawn to the NDE phenomenon to become members of an organization like IANDS in the first place. Here, at least, is another investigation whose findings are consistent with the benign virus hypothesis we have advanced.

The findings of the studies I have summarized for you here, and especially their implications, have come to intrigue me and, as I have already argued, warrant further attention on the part of NDE researchers. As a preliminary effort toward this end, a few years ago I conducted an informal survey of my own, which has since been replicated twice, that combines facets of Flynn's approach with something of the methodology of the Omega Project. Although it is hardly more than a bagatelle, it does provide some additional tantalizing clues as to how NDE-related information can affect a target population in some ways not so different from that for which this book has been written.

## A TEST OF THE BENIGN VIRUS HYPOTHESIS

As I mentioned at the very beginning of this book, from 1985 to 1994, I offered an undergraduate course on the NDE at the University of Connecticut. Eventually given every semester, it normally had an enrollment of about thirty-five to forty students, and over the years, I probably had close to 500 students in it. In this course, I required my students to maintain an extensive journal in which they recorded their reactions to and commentaries upon the classes, the assigned reading, and events in their lives or others' lives that bore on the topics we considered during the semester. In reading these journals and my students' term papers, as well as from discussions with them, I often had cause to be aware that the course, by and large, tended to have a pronounced and, in a number of cases, I would say, quite obviously personal, deep, impact on my students. Still, I was reluctant to attempt to assess these effects in any careful, rigorous way lest I be perceived as having some kind of blatant personal investment in how students responded to my teaching. Indeed, for this reason, I made it clear at the beginning of the semester that I welcomed and invited all points of view, including the rankest form of skepticism, and simply requested my students to consider the material I presented in a spirit of open-minded inquiry through which to reach their own conclusions about the NDE.

What was actually presented in the course? I began by giving an overview of the NDE itself and then spent a couple of class periods showing some videos of persons narrating their NDEs. This was followed by three NDErs coming to class to share their own experiences directly with the students. Occasionally, throughout the semester, I would break up the students into small groups to discuss among themselves issues we were dealing with in the course, and I always did this first in the class following the visit from the NDErs. Eventually, we went on to review what we now know about the NDE and various interpretative models that have been offered to explain the experience, along the way considering such topics as veridicality studies (of the sort I presented in Chapter Two), NDEs in children, frightening NDEs, suicide and NDEs, cross-cultural research, and so on.

In the second half of the course, I presented material on other phenomena related to NDEs, such as deathbed visions, out-of-body experiences, and mystical experiences, and then devoted a portion of the course to an examination of the aftereffects of NDEs. Toward the end of the course, there was some but not a lot of consideration given to larger, speculative questions suggested by NDEs and their possible evolutionary implications. During the semester, I would bring to class at least three more NDErs, usually to discuss aftereffects, and other guest speakers, including researchers. I also conducted a limited number—usually two—of experiential classes for which, for example, I had designed exercises that asked students to confront their own death or ponder the implications of the life review for their own lives (as you did in Chapter Six). Altogether, we met twenty-eight times over a period of fourteen weeks, with each class lasting approximately seventy-five minutes.

For reading, I assigned Raymond Moody's *Life after Life*, my own *Heading toward Omega*, one of Scott Rogo's books, *Life after Death*, mainly for its discussion of various parapsychological phenomena related to NDEs (the subject of life after death itself was only discussed in passing and was not at all a major theme of the course), and, finally, a work by Michael Talbot, called *The Holographic Universe*, which provided a unifying theoretical perspective in terms of which anomalies such as NDEs could be understood within a "New Paradigm" scientific approach.

What kind of student was it that ended up in this course? I conducted an informal survey at the beginning to find out, just to see what these students might already know about NDEs, and what their view of them was. Generally speaking, these students, almost always juniors or seniors, did not know a great deal about NDEs, and most of what they did know seemed to be based on the expected unreliable or sensationalistic sources, such as talk shows, tabloids, magazine articles, and films. Thus, as a rule, they tended to enter the course with a fairly shallow, usually superficial, acquaintance with the NDE. Most of these students were open to it, however, and expressed curiosity to learn more. Strong skeptics or outright debunkers were relatively rare (though I had them), but a fair number of students did express some degree of skepticism or other forms of reservation about NDEs at the beginning of the semester.

In short, these students, while obviously self-selected and generally talented, were to start with by no means "true believers," nor were they particularly knowledgeable about NDEs. As a group, they could be characterized at the outset of the course, then, as intrigued with the subject matter but full of questions about it.

What we want to know, of course, is how did their exposure to a semester-long course on NDEs affect them?

I have already said that I had been reluctant to inquire into this matter for fear of appearing invested in the outcome. Accordingly, for years I had simply noted for myself that many students gave clear indications that the course had had a strong and positive effect on them. In the spring semester of 1993, however, as I was pondering the issue of the impact of NDEs based on the findings of the Omega Project, I decided, on the spur of the moment, to ask my students to fill out a little questionnaire for me at the very end of the course (that I had concocted just the day before). Thus, they did not know this self-assessment was coming, and I certainly had not planned it.

Twenty-eight students happened to be in class the day I administered the survey. The survey itself consisted of eight sets of multiple-choice statements, all of which began with the stem, "As a result of taking this course ...," and two open-ended questions. Students were asked in written instructions to answer anonymously and as truthfully as possible.

I present findings from this study in several different chapters of this book, but here, I simply highlight those that are especially pertinent to us in this context. These have mainly to do with how students came to view the NDE itself, and with their reported changes in values and worldviews.

The first statement dealt with the authenticity of NDEs. Twenty-seven of the twenty-eight students (96 percent) said they were now *more* convinced of the authenticity of NDEs, while one person's opinion was unchanged. When one recalls that most of these students were already open to NDEs in the first place, the fact that their sense of the authenticity of the NDE increased almost universally is even more noteworthy. Even the skeptics tended to melt away faced with the evidence bearing on NDEs.

Responding to another item, seventeen students (61 percent) felt as a result of taking the course that they were now more spiritually oriented individuals, with the rest of the students reporting no change.

With regard to a sense of purpose, nineteen students (68 percent) were more convinced that their own lives had a purpose, while all but one of the remainder were unchanged.

Finally, twenty students (71 percent) said that their ideas about God had altered as a result of the course, including eight students (29 percent) who specifically stated that their belief in God had been strengthened. No one reported that his or her belief in God had been weakened, though another eight students (29 percent) indicated that their ideas about God were unchanged.

Though the number of cases here is small, the results are quite consistent in speaking to the effects on the course on the issues I inquired into. But, let's face it, statistics alone make for a dull dish, so to liven up the fare, let me pluck a passel of brief quotations typical of these students to spread before you. That way, you can see for yourself how much these bare statistics conceal the nature and depth of the changes they reported.

I feel I have become more spiritual, and it also has reinforced my beliefs about the unimportance of wealth and material objects.

I feel that the most important thing I gained from my study of the NDE is a higher spiritual sense and a greater belief in God.

I have less fear of death ... [and] am more spiritual.

[What] I have gained most from studying NDEs is that love is the driving force of all humanity. I have reevaluated my beliefs about God, reincarnation, and spirituality in that my belief in them is stronger. I felt that, with this course, I have grown as a person.

What I have gained from studying the NDE this semester: (1) more compassion for all people; (2) less fear of the ending of this life; (3) more openmindedness to learn as much as I can, while I still can.

I have found a spirituality that has been hiding within myself. I see how I affect others more, and I want to let this new spirituality grow over time.

I have felt a feeling of being set free from much of the negative aspects of life. I have gained some profound self-knowledge and an increased sense of self-worth. I have become more appreciative of life and love. I feel less negative—and I have less animosity toward others. I feel this course has been extremely helpful in my life.

A more spiritual view of myself and the world. The understanding of what is REALLY [her capitalization] important in life, and a break from some of the materialistic values that I had.

The very exposure to NDEs was interesting and enlightening. I feel this course has made me more open-minded and caring.... The NDE has given me a positive outlook on death and life.

This little survey of mine has since been repeated in two more NDE courses—one that I taught the following semester, the other, a similarly structured course at another university—with virtually identical results. This makes it clear that these findings do not depend in any way on the instructor involved, and makes it more likely they can be attributed solely to the content of the material presented in NDE courses.

Now that we have a general picture of the outcome of these studies, what is it reasonable to conclude in regard to the benign virus hypothesis?

Despite the small, self-selected nature of the samples and the ad hoc character of these surveys, one general finding shines forth from these studies that is undeniable: These students expressed sentiments, feelings, values, and beliefs that are indistinguishable from those commonly uttered by NDErs themselves. The same effects that NDErs tend to attribute to their experience, these students indicated derived from their exposure to their course on NDEs. What this suggests is certainly in accord with the benign virus hypothesis: It appears as if some of the benefits of the NDE can be transmitted vicariously, simply by presenting relevant information on the subject to individuals who are or become interested in NDEs. The implications are obviously profound. And specifically for readers of this book, there is now additional evidence not only to support the idea that what happened to my students can also happen to you, but, in all probability, it already has.

Still, before we wax too enthusiastically about the power of the NDE to act as a benign virus, we need, of course, to express a note of caution. Even taking these findings at face value, we must admit, for example, that at this stage we do not know how indicative of deep-lying changes they are or whether they proved to be long-lasting, as the effects of NDEs themselves seem to be. We could, indeed, raise a host of additional interpretative questions of this kind, which only future research itself can resolve. All the same, these new findings, combined with the results of the studies I have already cited, do offer us a reasonable basis for believing in the power of the NDE to affect not only those who have had this experience, but also even those who are prepared to open themselves up to its lessons.

## MORE EVIDENCE FOR THE BENIGN VIRUS HYPOTHESIS: SOME CASE HISTORIES

Of course, while systematic research on the benign virus hypothesis will settle some of the pending uncertainties I have just spoken of, we already have more evidence available to us that points to its validity. What I am referring to here is the wealth of anecdotal reports that many NDE researchers have gathered in the course of work concerning the effects of learning about NDEs on the part of those who have never had the experience themselves. Much of this information, not surprisingly, comes in the form of letters and other testimonies of a more evanescent kind, such as those shared orally at conferences, and some derive from interviews with nonexperiencers. In this section, I present just a small sampling of such material in order to illustrate how much some persons can come to emulate NDErs just by immersing themselves in the literature on NDEs. And in Chapter Eleven, there will be even more cases of this kind, to further buttress this point.

But here, let me begin with a man named James, who wrote me to share the impact of his reading the NDE literature for many years. As you will see, he is not only an exemplar of the benign virus effect, but, like me, an advocate of the hypothesis, which he derived independently.

> I don't have all of the NDE effects on me completely sorted out and properly organized, but I suspect that if this [his reading of this literature] has affected me so strongly, then there must be a lot of other nonexperiencers out there that have also been powerfully influenced.

James then goes on to list some of the changes he has observed in himself over the years:

> NDEs have greatly reduced any fear of death I had. In fact, they've eliminated it. I have a very positive view of death, and the beginning of a much clearer picture of life after death. NDEs have enriched my spiritual life by

helping to move it out of the mystical and into a more direct way of seeing things. They have also introduced and/or clarified many spiritual concepts that I hadn't been able to see clearly, such as reincarnation and the purgative effects of the life review. They have brought these out as something real, and not just something hoped for and presented to us as theological theories and myths. NDEs have greatly enhanced my awareness of the primacy of love as a Living Force, and as the meaning and goal of all of our actions and of all things. They have also enhanced my belief that what is truly spiritual goes far beyond the beliefs and restrictions of any and all religions (as the mystics all seemed to indicate).

Another similar instance of this effect of exposure to NDE literature came to my attention when a retired professor of languages and literature named Donald wrote to me a few years ago. Like James, though not for so long a time, Donald had taken the time to study and ponder the literature on NDEs, which brought about, he said, a "major life change." In this regard, he comments significantly: "I have found myself identifying so closely with these people that I have been experiencing vicariously much of what they experienced in fact." Then, like James, he continues by providing me with a brief itemized list of some of the changes this process had put him through:

1. A noticeably reduced fear of death, and with it, the attendant disappearance of all fear of living.
2. An absolutely positive attitude toward life, toward the world and everyone in it, in conjunction with an unprecedented zest for living and a marked increase in creative activity.
3. A genuine and seemingly permanent feeling of well-being, one noticeably beyond any expected levels.
4. A continual desire to get back to some sort of teaching and/or to find ways to go out and help other people.
5. Prior to my research, I characterized myself as a rip snortin' atheist.... Now, while my researches have not much improved my attitude toward organized religion, I am firmly convinced that human consciousness survives bodily death.

Finally, let me present a portion of an interview with a Swiss non-experiencer named Béatrice, which was kindly furnished to me by my colleague, Evelyn Elsaesser Valarino. This interview is particularly of value to us here because it helps us to see not just the outcome, but the very process by which an interested and curious person comes to appreciate and integrate the insights from NDEs into her life. Evelyn has pointed out to me, however, that one should bear in mind that in Switzerland, where this interview was conducted, the NDE phenomenon is not nearly so well known as it is in the United States. As to the interviewee herself, she is a forty-five-year-old woman with a university degree.

EV: When and how did you first hear about near-death experiences?

B: It was about ten years ago. I don't remember exactly how I first became aware of the NDE phenomenon. I only recall that I saw a publication in which there was a quote from Moody's book, *Life after Life*. At that time, the NDE phenomenon was not very well known in Europe, much less in Switzerland.

EV: What was it about this subject that captured your interest?

B: I have always been the kind of person who asks a lot of questions and isn't easily satisfied with the answers usually provided. In fact, when I first heard about NDEs, I had already been searching for some time for answers to existential questions. I read a lot—mostly scientific and philosophical books. They stimulated my intellect, widened my knowledge and opened my mind to the world, but they left my heart as unsatisfied as ever!

EV: What happened to you after you read *Life after Life*?

B: I don't want to sound pompous, but it was a revelation to me. Not Moody's comments or analysis, but the testimonies of experiencers. I read, cried a lot and knew it was true! I was profoundly touched at a level other than the intellectual, rational one. The experiencers' words went straight to my heart, my soul, the essence of my being—whatever you want to call it. I immediately knew it was true. It had nothing to do with the kind of knowledge you acquire when you evaluate a piece of information and say, yes, this is possible and makes sense, or, no, this is logically not possible. It was not that kind of intellectual knowledge, but rather a gut feeling. I had the impression that this was a truth I had always known, but had simply forgotten. Yes, it was a revelation—and a relief.

EV: What do you mean, "a relief"?:

B: When you feel like you are walking in the dark, trying to find your way, and then, all of a sudden, you see the light and the path. You feel relieved!

EV: Yes, I see what you mean. Now, can you give me a more specific indication as to how familiar you are with NDEs?

B: I have read books and articles about it, and have seen several TV shows.

EV: How many books have you read on the subject?

B: Somewhere between ten and fifteen. I'm not sure. I didn't count them.

EV: Have you ever met an experiencer?

B: Never, I've only seen them on television.

EV: Have you ever had an NDE yourself, or any other kind of spiritual or mystical experience? Or experienced a state of expanded consciousness?

B: No, I haven't.

EV: And how has your knowledge of NDEs changed your life?

B: It has changed everything.

EV: Can you be more specific?

B: Well, what I learned about NDEs confirmed my intuitions, and in some way my secret hopes about the survival of consciousness after bodily death.

EV: Did you believe in a life after death before coming aware of NDEs?

B: To be honest, I wished for it to be true, but I didn't know if it actually was. At that point, it was simply a matter of faith.... [but] I am a questioning kind of person and I don't easily take things for granted.

EV: If that's so, why do you believe the experiencers?

B: Because I don't think I know better than thirteen million Americans [the number estimated by some polls to have had an NDE], and who knows how many others in the rest of the world! Besides that—and what is more important to me—I just *feel* that it's true.

EV: How else does this affect your life?

B: It reinforces my belief in the survival of consciousness after death, and in the existence of an encounter with God or the Light or whatever you want to call it. It makes me believe that everything that happens to me, however painful, sad or unjust, has some meaning—that nothing happens by chance.

EV: How has the NDE changed your daily life?

B: It has changed my obsession with the passing of time. I have completely lost it. Before, it was a constant worry. When I was twenty, I was very much aware that I was no longer in the prime of my youth. At each of my daughter's birthdays, I felt myself getting older and was saddened at the idea. I looked at my face in the mirror, and scanned it for any new wrinkles. All this has completely disappeared now. I know that time doesn't exist in the realm of consciousness—so why should I worry about aging and the passing of time?

## BECOMING AN NDEr WITHOUT AN NDE

Through these testimonies, we can see how it is not only possible for persons open to NDEs to learn from them, but to *internalize their essential insights and make them their own.* In this way, such persons become like NDErs themselves and come to see the world with NDE-mediated vision. And in doing so, these individuals have clearly come to exemplify the proposition enunciated by Steve at the beginning of this chapter: "It is possible to gain all the knowledge a person learns when they die, without dying. You don't have to die to get there."

Others, then, have already done what you may choose to do in using this book to change your life. Of course, as I have previously pointed out, if the benign virus hypothesis is true, some of these changes should already have become seeded in you and may very well blossom in time without your doing more than reading and reflecting on the contents of this book. This is the principle of contagion that I mentioned at outset of this chapter, which much of the remainder serves to document. However, you may remember that early on, I also referred to a second principle of which we would need to make use. That one involved the deliberate emulation of the mind-set of an NDEr so as to practice what the NDE lives. Now, it is time to return to that strategy in order to fulfill the purpose of this chapter and the promise of this book: to learn to see and act in the world as NDErs do. This requires an effort on your part, but most things of value do. Here is one suggestion for how to begin making it.

First, set some time aside for an experiment. It will take at a minimum several hours, but, if it is possible, you might wish to set an entire day aside for it. Begin by immersing yourself again in some of the stories of this book (or any other on NDEs) that have particularly moved you, and allow yourself to reflect upon them and what they teach. Sit quietly and let your mind dwell on these lessons, and especially those of self-compassion and compassion for others. Take a while to let these thoughts and feelings radiate through you and, just as one might do in meditation, allow the process of absorption continue until it feels full.

At that point, go about your daily activities—trying as much as you can to be mindful of what the NDE teaches about how to be, how to see, and how to treat others. You are in effect role-playing an NDEr for the time you have set for this experiment, and, though it may seem artificial at first, with practice you will feel more at home with it. And, remember, we know from experiments such as Charles Flynn's "Love Project," that this is a technique that can be very successful in instilling the perspective of an NDEr into one's mind and heart. If you fall out of the NDEr mind-set (and you will, repeatedly), just re-mind yourself, gently, of your purpose. Let yourself experience the world with eyes tender with compassion—for yourself as well as for others. Cultivate this in yourself, and you will eventually come to acquire this gift of the NDE for yourself—and in that way, be able to give it, as NDErs do, to others.

Afterward, write in a journal about your experiences with this practice: how you felt, what insights came to you during its practice. Describe some of the encounters you had with others in which you felt you acted in a way that reflected what you have learned and absorbed from the lessons you were trying to actualize in your own life. Look at them from your own point of view, and then imagine what a being of light might communicate to you about them. Look at and analyze your failures, but do not judge them. Learn from them, and make a note of what you have learned. Let the writing flow, as it will, along these lines, for certainly other things will come to you.

If you can, make this a frequent, or even a daily, practice for a while. You may not always be able to devote several hours to it, but whatever time you spend on it will pay you abundant dividends. Eventually, you will find that you are becoming the kind of person you have been reading about.

Of course, your family and friends will probably notice some of these changes, and, just as NDErs themselves report, they may not always like what they see. Problems may arise. But life is not a problem-free state! And change does not come easily, either for those attempting to bring it about in their own lives or for those affected by it. Still, if your heart is set on this goal, you must be willing to face the consequences and deal with what comes up.

You have only to ask an NDEr if it has been worth it to let the Light be your guide in trying to learn how to live and how to die.

## Chapter Ten

# They Come by Light:
# Healing Gifts and the Near-Death Experience

One of the earliest of the now many motion pictures that have featured stories based on NDEs was called *Resurrection*, which enjoyed a measure of popularity when it was released in the early 1980s. Starring Ellen Burstyn, it depicted the life of a young woman who, after suffering a near-fatal automobile accident, during which she undergoes an NDE, eventually becomes an enormously talented healer with almost magical powers to restore damaged bodies to health. Because I had some very peripheral connection with this film when it first appeared and eventually met some of those involved in it, such as its screenwriter, Lou Carlino, I happen to know a little about the incidents on which this film was based. For example, some of the events in the life of the protagonist, after she becomes a public healer, are actually recreations of episodes that occurred to a well-known American healer, Rosalyn Bruyere, who served as a consultant to this movie. However, Rosalyn herself told me that she never had had an NDE as such, so she was not really the prototype for the NDEr the film portrays. When I asked Lou Carlino about this, he simply said that, in fact, there was no one NDEr who served as his model here, but rather his story reflected something of a composite of those he had met or read about.

But this was, of course, a movie churned out of Hollywood's dream factory, so you might well be excused if you were tempted to regard it mainly as an entertainment that perhaps plays a little fast and loose with the facts of NDE research. However, if you took that understandable view, you would turn out to be quite mistaken, because the data fully support Carlino's premise: A significant number of NDErs *do* seem to develop healing gifts of one sort or another following their experiences. And that being so, it will reward us to see if we can extract some lessons here from this specific, fairly common aftereffect of NDEs for our own lives. If, for example, we can understand what might be the basis of these healing gifts, we might be able to learn how we can access it and learn to use it to heal our own lives or those of others.

But before we are able to follow this more practical course, we need to take some time to consider some of the evidence that NDEs do indeed generate healing abilities afterward and how these might come about.

To begin with, let us consider a few specific studies to get an overall sense of how pervasive is the link between NDE and healing. For example, one of the earliest such investigations to touch on this topic was carried out by an English researcher, Margot Grey, who reported her findings in her 1984 book on NDEs, *Return from Death*. There, to begin a chapter entitled "Healing Manifestations," she writes as follows:

> There is another spectacular manifestation that appears to be spontaneously triggered by the near-death experience, which is the gift of healing. Like the faculty of clairvoyance, this ability also seems to be bestowed upon the individuals (in many instances) as a direct result of their having had a near-death encounter.[1]

Likewise, one American researcher, P. M. H. Atwater, has interviewed more than 3,000 NDErs over the course of twenty years and though she does not provide a precise figure, she states in her latest book that more than 50 percent of her NDErs develop "healing hands"[2] following their experience. And other research tends to bear out Atwater's claims. For instance, in my own most recent study of NDErs, I found that 42 percent of them reported an increase of healing abilities following their experience, compared to only 11 percent of my control group, and more than four times as many NDErs (47 percent) as controls specifically mentioned the presence either of unusual energy discharges in their hands or the "hot hands" syndrome itself as a part of this phenomenon.[3] And finally, there is the corroborative and even stronger research of the Australian sociologist, Cherie Sutherland, who found in her sample of NDErs that whereas only 8 percent of them had indicated any healing gifts whatever prior to their

NDEs, fully 65 percent claimed such talents flowered afterward. Accordingly, it seems safe to conclude from this set of representative findings that there is indeed something about an NDE that tends to unleash what is probably a latent potential in us all—the ability to mediate healing energies to others.

Over the years of my own involvement with NDEs, I have, of course, met quite a few of these persons who have discovered, sometimes seemingly by accident, that they have acquired some kind of healing or diagnostic gift that they then feel led to put at the service of others. One of my good friends, for instance, Barbara Harris Whitfield, who wrote one of the first of the popular autobiographical books about her NDE and life afterward,[4] can serve as an exemplar of this type of development among NDErs. Barbara, whom you have already heard about in connection with her life review (see pp. 178–179), had her NDE in 1975, when she was hospitalized for a spinal fusion operation. After recovering, she noticed that she had what she described as "healing energies" coursing through her. And she most definitely had the "hot hands" syndrome as well: One day, she told me, when she and her then husband were driving in their car, Barbara innocently touched her husband's thigh (he was wearing shorts at the time), and he cried out in pain because of the intense heat he felt emanating from her hand. In time, Barbara became a respiratory therapist, which helped to satisfy her desire to be of service to others, but because she continued to feel a strong need "to get her hands on people," she eventually became a massage therapist. As she explained it to me, part of her motivation was to find a legitimate means to touch people, because that way, she felt, she could actually transmit some of the healing energies that seemed to radiate through her after her own NDE. Her book gives many examples of how Barbara has worked with various healing modalities in helping others suffering from illness or other difficulties, and I can personally testify—from my own experience with her on more than on occasion—that her hands do indeed have a healing power.

And not just her hands, either, because, as I myself have had the opportunity to observe, Barbara's presence itself is a conduit of that energy. When she would speak to my classes at the university, for instance, it would not be uncommon for numbers of my students to crowd around Barbara following her talk and afterward to comment to me about the power she radiated, which was palpable. These days, Barbara continues to do her work largely within the Recovery movement, where she has joined forces with her second husband, the distinguished author and physician, Charles Whitfield.

Another woman I have known since the very beginning of my own work in the NDE field is Helen Nelson, and she, too, has developed along a similar path following her NDE from a cardiac arrest in the mid-1970s. In Helen's case, however, she seems to be able to perceive directly the energy field surrounding the human body as well as the energy vortices *within* the body, which in the esoteric psychospiritual traditions of the East are known as *chakras*. Her work involves an intuitive diagnostic assessment of the individual's energy field, as well as an attempt to clear energetic blockages and restore balance to the system as a whole. Although, in recent years, I have not seen Helen as frequently as I once did, from what she has told me over the phone and through correspondence, she has continued to have some remarkable successes in this work, particularly with cancer patients. When I last heard from her, several doctors had expressed interest in her abilities, and a book was in preparation about her life of service following her NDE.

Still another NDEr who has developed obvious abilities to heal, and who, like Barbara and Helen, exudes a tremendous personal charisma when she speaks to audiences, is a woman I will call Stella, whom I first met in the late 1980s. When we were first getting to know each other, she wrote me about the work she was then doing with terminally ill patients, especially those dying of AIDS:

> My compassion for these individuals has created a new "gift." I have learned how to "scan" a body for aberrant energy patterns. (I feel heat when I pass my hand over those areas.) I then focus and send energies through my hand to help balance their energies. Those I work with state they feel a relief of pain which lasts several hours. I know that I'm transferring some type of energy and that the amount is directly correlated to the amount of compassion I feel.

It is unfortunate but understandable, I suppose, that there has not yet been any rigorous and systematic study of the healing gifts that are claimed by so many NDErs like Barbara, Helen and Stella, as a result of which we are left with many testimonies like the last that hang solely on the word on the individual involved. In short, what you will find if you consult some of the books I have already referred to this chapter, or others on NDEs, is largely stories told by NDErs themselves, who recount instances where they feel or allege that they have been helpful in healing others or at least, as in Stella's case, in bringing about significant relief of pain. Furthermore, it is usually asserted or implied that these abilities developed or increased after their NDEs. The very frequency of these claims, as the statistics I cited earlier attest, is impressive and many of the anecdotes themselves are compelling, so it is hardly likely that these effects as a whole are suspect. On the contrary, it seems probable, even in the absence of solid research on the matter, that healing gifts do abound among NDErs, but we nevertheless must acknowledge that we do not yet know this for certain.

This is not, however, to say that we do not already have some fairly significant clues from other NDE research that help to make at least an indirect case for the linkage between NDEs and healing. For instance, as I have already indicated (see Chapter Five), several independent studies have now consistently shown that one of the frequent outgrowths of an NDE is a heightened electrical sensitivity[5]; that is, NDErs often report afterward an increased incidence of various electrical or electronic anomalies in their presence: Digital wristwatches fail to function, computers unaccountably short out, automobile electrical systems go haywire, tape recordings produce blank cassettes, and so on.

Now, as it happens, long before this connection between NDEs and electrical sensitivity was established through research, I had already noticed that all three of the individuals I just described—Barbara, Helen, and Stella—were remarkable for the degree to which they were susceptible to these anomalies. Each of them related to me, with some wry amusement and genuine bafflement, various incidents such as this, which at the time I could only note but not explain. But the following event, which I and a number of others witnessed, showed that these occurrences were on the level, and further inquiry suggests strongly that the factors responsible for them may be intimately involved in the putative healing ability of NDErs.

Come with me now to one of my NDE classes. Stella is there, one of three NDErs who have been invited to share with me and my students a little about their lives following their NDEs. In these classes, I would give no directives as to what I wanted my guests to talk about so long as it dealt with the aftereffects of their NDEs. At one point, Stella began to tell a curious and amusing story. It went like this: She and her husband were vacationing in Florida. One evening, strolling through a little town they were fond of, they found themselves alone on a street illuminated by a series of street lamps. As they walked up this road, Stella said, they noticed that as they passed each lamp it would go out. The husband, who was an engineer [I later met him], and who had observed other anomalies around his wife since her NDE, asked her to walk on ahead, and sure enough, she said, the lights continued to blow out as she moved alongside them.

Several years later, on another vacation, they found themselves in the same little town, and Stella said to her husband: "Do you remember the time we were here last and all the lights went out?"

"Yeah, sure. Of course, I remember."

"Let's go back there."

The husband demurred at this point, but Stella eventually prevailed and they again began their walk up this street. "And, believe it or not," Stella continued, "once again all the lights began to go out."

And, just as she was saying that, all the overhead lights in my classroom flickered briefly and then actually did go out! Right at that moment.

And then they came back on.

Stella paused. Titters and unbelief from the students and me. Everyone had noticed what had happened and when it had happened. The lights going out had startlingly punctuated the story about lights going out by virtue of interrupting it.

Did Stella cause the lights to flicker and lose power? Was it just the result of a temporary electrical outage at the university? Was it simply a fluke, a meaningless coincidence? Was it the Trickster having fun with us?

I do not know what it was, but I know it got everyone's attention and that, at the time, it seemed to have the kind of kinky weirdness that sticks with you regardless of whatever voices of dismissal your rational mind was already beginning to whisper in your ear.

In any event, since that incident took place, it has become more and more obvious to NDE researchers like me that it is hardly a matter of chance that all three of the NDE healers to whom I have introduced you in this chapter are persons with pronounced electrical sensitivities. Furthermore, you will also remember that all three of these persons themselves radiate a vibrant energy and have charismatic personalities. Figuratively, at least, they give off sparks. But maybe we are not just talking figuratively. Maybe something has happened to people like Barbara, Helen, and Stella—and seemingly countless other NDErs who emerge from their NDEs with healing gifts—when they find themselves caught up in the energy field of the Light. Maybe the Light is not something merely seen and felt. Maybe it is a lightning bolt.

## THE LIGHT AS A HEALING FORCE

By now, we are so familiar with the image of the Light in the context of the NDE that it may be time to try to look at it with new eyes. Of course, from all I have already said about this aspect of the experience, we know this radiantly beautiful, all-encompassing light is the very heart of the body of the NDE, its central shining core. But to divest it for a moment of all poetic imagery, what is this light in its essence?

To begin with, of course, we could say it is no mere metaphor. Light is at bottom an electromagnetic phenomenon. And it is worth noting that when NDErs talk about their experience in the Light, they will not uncommonly use phrases such as "being immersed in the Light" or "becoming absorbed in the Light" or even, as I have heard, "receiving a transmission from the Light." Now, we human beings are by nature "electrical beings" in the sense that we all possess energy or electrodynamic fields in and around us. Therefore, it is possible, perhaps even plausible, to suppose that when a person undergoes an NDE, there may actually be some kind of electrical or energetic transmission while in the light field that continues to perturb that individual's own electrical field after he or she returns to life. Of course, it is now possible to measure electrical fields in the laboratory, and with the rise of energy or vibrational medicine, which is rooted in the study and application of subtle energies, it is decidedly feasible that such studies could be undertaken with a sample of NDErs, especially those who claim to have acquired healing abilities, in order to see whether there are any distinguishing features in their electrical fields. If my own speculations here have any merit, there should indeed be some unusual properties of the electrical fields of these NDErs that set them apart from others and correlate with their healing gifts.

While this is still an untested hypothesis, there are already empirical grounds, as we have seen in Chapter Five, that support it. For instance, you may recall that I have previously discussed some of the research that indicates that following an NDE, there tends to be a distinctive pattern of physiological and neurological changes (including hyperaesthesia and electrical sensitivities) that collectively suggest that there is something about the NDE that fundamentally "rewires" the individual at a psychophysical level. If that is so, it is only a small but logical step to assume that this fundamental rewiring must also involve energetic shifts as well, which could provide the underlying basis for the healing talents claimed by so many NDErs.

In a nutshell, what I am suggesting is that it is *the Light itself that heals, and that the near-death experiencer who has received a direct transmission of this light is someone who in turn can mediate this healing force.* In that sense, these NDErs might be thought of as little "beings of light" who continue to transmit to others something of those healing energies they themselves encountered while in the Light.

This conception of the role of light in the NDE now leads us to an obvious implication. If the Light—that preeminent symbol of wholeness—is indeed the primary healing agent in life, it should follow that there will be cases in which the Light itself is perceived to be the sole cause of a seemingly otherwise inexplicable recovery from a fatal illness. Clearly, then, there should be instances of this sort among NDErs, too—and there are.

Other NDE researchers, too, have already been alert to this type of case. For example, the English writer, Margot Grey, to whose work I referred earlier in this chapter, pointed out as long ago as 1985 that in these NDEs, "respondents would usually assert that it was their guides or the being of light who healed them at that time."[6] I only wish that when I was actively interviewing my own NDE respondents I had done more to investigate these claims, but I have certainly heard them often enough from the lips of my interviewees. A generic statement of this kind would typically be along these lines: "I am a medical miracle. I never should have survived. My doctor didn't give me any reason for hope, and my recovery astonished him. But I knew when I was in the Light that I was being healed." Several years ago though, Massachusetts psychologist, Paul Roud, actually did investigate and document a number of these cases, including some involving NDEs, in his provocatively entitled book, *Making Miracles*,[7] and reached conclusions similar to mine. However, I can at least present a half-dozen summary examples of my own here or of those provided by other researchers to illustrate the way in which the Light seems to be the source of seemingly miraculous healing during NDEs.

One quite remarkable instance was shared with me by Howard Mickel, Professor Emeritus of Religious Studies at Wichita State University in Kansas, who investigated this case very thoroughly and can authenticate it. The story, in brief, involved a patient by the name of Ralph Duncan, who in the mid-1970s was dying of leukemia. He apparently was told that he had only a short time to live and was prepared to die. But while hospitalized, he had an NDE, and during it, he encountered a luminous being, whom he took to be Jesus (though Ralph observed that it did not look anything like traditional images of him), and whose eyes were "shooting fire." In any event, there was then a telepathic communication from this being in the form of three short phrases, which were "That's enough, it's dead, it's gone." These words, Ralph said, were still ringing in this ears as he returned to his body.

Afterward, puzzling about all this, he was mystified about the significance of the phrase, "that's enough." But, he continues, "I do know what he meant when he said, 'It's dead.' To me it meant that the germ was dead. I no longer have leukemia."[8] To my mind, however, the entire set of phrases coheres meaningfully in the context of this healing. For instance, when the being, his eyes "shooting fire," says, "That's enough," it means in effect, "I've zapped you with enough voltage for this to cure you." And then, "It's dead, it's gone."

The last I heard about this case, in 1989, Ralph was still hale and living near Boulder, Colorado.

A somewhat similar case was described by Margot Grey. Five days after abdominal surgery, an English patient underwent complications and his wife was told her husband was dying. At that time, however, he was having an NDE, and during it he saw

> an entity clothed in a colored cloak [of] indescribably beautiful colors, and a brightness most intense. This something stood at the right-hand side of my head, two hands were lightly placed on my body, slowly moved down to my feet, and up the left side, pausing at my head, and then was gone. I have no recollection of anything until next day. From then I made a very rapid recovery and was soon back with my family.[9]

Again, we seem to have a healing performed within the general context of a light-filled scene.

Not long ago, some further cases of this kind were shared with me by my friend, Steve, who you might remember was himself the recipient of an apparently otherworldly stabilizing treatment rendered by a female light being when Steve experienced a respiratory arrest during surgery (see pp. 37–38 for the full account). Significantly, Steve recently told me that, as in the case of Ralph Duncan, this being had "intense blue eyes that shined like they were on fire." And as he felt this energy radiating into him, she communicated telepathically to Steve these thoughts:

> You're not breathing regularly. There is some concern that your respiration might stop. I'm here to stabilize it, and make sure the problem doesn't go any further. You are very valuable, and no one is willing to take any chances with your life.

In some ways an even more dramatic case that Steve related to me involved a diabetic Mexican woman who speaks no English (Steve is fluent in Spanish) and who, Steve ascertained, was completely unfamiliar with NDEs before her own experience. Here is her story.

Prior to her experience, she had lost the ability to see. Diabetes had taken away her retina, and her heart wasn't supplying enough circulation to her brain to allow her to speak. She was in very poor shape. They prepared her for surgery.

Open-heart surgery on a diabetic woman of sixty-seven is full of risk. The doctors went outside to discuss their strategy. While they were conferring, she saw the wall open up and a brilliant light pour out. A bearded man in white stepped up beside her. He was made of white light.

"You're not ready to follow me yet ... you're not prepared. I'm going to give you back your eyesight. You'll need it to finish your life. And I'm going to heal the heart valve, so you can speak again. You still have a few more things to do. Your grandchildren need you to teach them."

According to the woman's account, he placed his hand on her chest, and her eyesight returned. [Later] she sat in a wheel chair, serene, full of confidence, and smiling. Her legs were gone, but her eyes were clear, and she was happy in a calm way.

[Her cardiologist later told her] "Something has happened to change your body. We don't have an explanation for it. I personally ascribe it to the will of God. You can go home now. We did nothing."[10]

Steve concluded this portion of his letter to me with this comment: "I tell you this to give you some idea of the immense, unequaled power that some of these beings of light have."

And there are, finally, a couple of cases of my own that I can briefly cite here, too. One of them, significantly enough, involves Stella, the woman who turned on my students by turning off their lights, so to speak, and to whose healing gifts I have already alluded. What she further told us the day she so memorably came to my class was that she had had a diagnosis of terminal cancer when her NDE took place, and in her opinion, it was her encounter with the Light during it that had provided her cure. In any event, she remains well to this day.

Another instructive example comes from the experience of a woman named Kathy Hayward, whom I met just once in Washington, D.C., in the mid-1980s, but whom I had actually seen many times before that because she was featured in a film on NDEs I used to show to my classes every semester. At one point in the early 1970s, Kathy was dying of Hodgkin's disease, which was then far more difficult to treat than it is these days. Entering the hospital, she collapsed and was expected to die that very night. She did (her heart monitor went flat, which she was able to see from an OBE vantage point) and had an NDE. During it, she, too, met a being of light and within the Light felt his healing energies permeate her as he told her he was sending her back. As a direct result of her experience, she feels, she was completely cured of her disease. In fact, when I finally met Kathy in person, years after first having seen her in that film, she was not only well, she looked radiant.

## FURTHER GIFTS OF THE LIGHT: HEALING FROM DESPAIR

Our discussion about the power of the Light and the role of beings of light in healing may easily have given the impression that these healing agencies pertain only to physical cures and organic illnesses. But this would be an erroneous inference, because it is also very clear that the Light heals spiritually as well. In other words, it does not just mend bodies, *it mends lives.* This is particularly obvious, I think, in the case of those persons who have had very difficult or troubled lives and find themselves, at the time of an NDE, in such an emotionally beleaguered state as to be almost at the end of their tether. Here, we can see plainly quite a different aspect of the Light's capacity to heal, and by healing, to make the person whole again. Whereas in cases involving a physical healing, it is as if we are seeing the Light in its role as Master Physician, here, it is more akin to Master Therapist. As such, the Light seems able not only to illuminate the way out of the deepening shadows of a dead-ended life, but can also provide such complete succor and love that we can finally feel the burdens of life lift from our shoulders and again enjoy the pure bliss of what the great Indian saint, Ramana Maharshi, called our true nature, happiness itself.

To appreciate this facet of the Light's power to confer this kind of blessing on distressed individuals, consider this observation from my an Australian friend, Andrea. During her recovery from serious surgery, while still in the hospital and very ill, Andrea underwent an NDE. At one point, she found herself in a tunnel, and recounts the following experience:

> While in the tunnel, I experienced a total change when touched by the Light. Up to that moment in time, I had traveled an extraordinarily long, hard and sometimes bitter road. I was quite exhausted emotionally and very scarred over with resentment over the difficult times I had to endure.
>
> When this overwhelming unconditional love flowed over me, and through me, every atom of my soul was bathed and altered in its light. All my scars, and bad memories, vanished instantly. None of it mattered except this love I was receiving. None of the bad times seemed real at that point. They were only learning experiences, and I could feel them flowing away,

all the pain gone; just this one wonderful timeless moment, where I was totally accepted for who I was, and where I had come from.

Later, I realized how transforming this encounter was, and could understand the biblical phrase, "of being reborn in spirit," as it would have come from that source of "Eternal Light." I felt brand new, and the world was a beautiful place to return to.

In my work in the NDE field, I have frequently had cause to be impressed with how often in seemingly an almost providential way the Light of the NDE comes into an individual's life at the very moment when that person was preparing to follow an obviously self-destructive course or, indeed, had already taken the first but still reversible steps in that direction. In such cases as these, we can see even better the other function of the Light as Master Therapist, whereby it guides the individual back on track.

One of the first instances of this kind came my way quite adventitiously when I was starting out in this field in 1977. Angela was a student of mine at the University, and, a couple of years before I met her, had been deeply suicidal. At that time, she told me, she was chronically depressed for a variety of reasons: She was not only fat but also obese; she was a drug addict and alcoholic; her grades were borderline; and she had been abused as a child and continued to have a poor relationship with her parents. As she put it, she was simply "a mess" and could not see much point in living. In fact, she had previously made several suicidal gestures but had never come seriously close to killing herself until one occasion around the time of final exams in late fall, as winter was fast approaching and her spirits were sinking ever lower than her grades.

Angela worked in the infirmary on campus and had already been secreting away a cache of some of its drugs in her dorm room, where she had also stored her supply of liquor. One day, while alone, she shallowed everything she could and waited to die. But for some odd reason, before she was overcome, she decided to go out on campus "to have one last look around." Providentially, it would seem, some of her friends then came upon her, and noticing how Angela's speech was slurred and how peculiarly she was behaving, immediately leapt to the correct conclusion and called an ambulance to rush her to a nearby hospital. Angela remembers "punching out" the attendant before lapsing into unconsciousness—and entering into the Light.

And while in the Light, she heard in her mind these words, "You will never again attempt suicide and you will be well." In that moment, she told me, it was as if she were already well. She just had to go through the formality of actually becoming whole, but she insisted that she *felt* whole the moment she heard those words and experienced the love emanating from the Light.

Nevertheless, her recovery was not immediate. It did take time. But soon enough, she had got off drugs and had joined Alcoholics Anonymous, giving up drinking as well. In that context and others, she actually counseled a number of suicidal people, telling them about her own NDE and recovery. She remained very fat, but even that was not the problem it had been for her beforehand, because she now understood that "she was not her body." "So, I'm fat," she laughed. "Big deal! That isn't who I am!"

Eventually, Angela graduated successfully and went on to work for the American Red Cross. She got married, and the last I heard of her (and we kept in touch for many years), she was planning to go to nursing school. In our many conversations, and in the talks she used to give to my classes, she made it clear that, as far as she was concerned, she was immediately healed in and by the Light, and her job in life now was to share with others what she had received when she was close to death because of her suicidal despair. And this, I can attest, she did with great good humor, a wonderful smile, and an abundance of love.

It is important to realize, however, that the healing balm of the Light is available not just to NDErs, of course, but *to anyone* who finds him- or herself in a deep spiritual crisis or on the verge of suicide. In my years of researching NDEs, I have in fact heard from many persons who, though they clearly were not physically near death, nevertheless had a kind of NDE, which in its properties *and* effects was indistinguishable from those that are triggered by an actual condition in which one's life is at risk. Thus, the Light seems to come to those who need it, *regardless* of the individual's physical state. Instead, it is the state of one's spiritual condition that appears to set the stage for the Light's salvational appearance in one's life.

Here, to illustrate the way in which the Light can come to those who have found themselves bereft of all hope, let me simply share three such instances with you, letting these three stand for the many such stories I have encountered in the past twenty years.

Here, first of all, are some excerpts from a letter written to me in 1985:

My experience happened at a time in my life when I *wanted* to die. I was in a miserable marriage. My husband was unemployed most of the time, into drugs, and was prone to violent outbursts. I was supporting us with freelance work and trying to care for our daughter, who was three at the time. The stresses and tensions of my environment were unbearable. I remember wanting to die and feeling that suicide was not an alternative due to my daughter. However, one evening I was so miserable I believe I *willed* myself to die. I was sitting alone on the sofa in the dark. I had not been able to sleep so I just got up and sat alone. Apparently, I fell [in]to another state of consciousness. For suddenly I was in the presence of a light so grand that it radiated perfect love, harmony, pure bliss—these words do not begin to describe what I experienced. There is nothing in this dimension that comes close in comparison.

Very gently, after I had bathed in this pure joy, a voice told me that I had to go back. At this point I became very upset; and I begged him not to send me back. I was told again that I had to go back; and then I was forced back into my body through my forehead. As I returned to consciousness, I was crying and very upset to be back.

The period that followed was one of many changes and difficulties. I had severe headaches for about a year. I began to search and thirst for knowledge. Finding the truths of our existence became very important to me; and I became a very spiritual person. Finding my purpose here also became paramount in my thoughts. My marriage dissolved. I spent two years in therapy, which accelerated my personal growth and awareness.

The process has not stopped. I am still searching, learning and growing. Life for me is exciting and joyous most of the time. Knowing that others are out there like me has helped a lot. It feels the cosmos has speeded up; and truth is rapidly shining through.

Another case about which I have a great deal more information is based on an encounter I had with an IANDS conference attendee in Washington, D.C., in 1990, where I had given a talk on the relationship between NDEs and child abuse. Although we first met at that time, Lorna is still someone I am in touch with and know very well. Therefore, I am in a position not only to vouch for the account that follows but also to assure you that she continues to live, as it were, in the Light and that her life has had many blessings, including a successful marriage, since the events she related to me shortly after we met, which I will now share with you.

Since the manner in which I first encountered Lorna is relevant to her story, I will give a little background first. At the conference, I had been asked to be the emcee for the Saturday night banquet, which featured a talk by Raymond Moody. At the end of the banquet, a number of persons from the audience gathered around the head table, hoping to speak to some of the presenters, and we all did our best to oblige them. However, time constraints and other postbanquet plans prevented us from talking to everyone afterward. One woman in particular had been very persistent in wanting to talk with me, and I especially took note of her and gave her my sincere regrets for having no more time that evening. "Maybe tomorrow," I mumbled apologetically, knowing in my heart that tomorrow's schedule for me was even more crammed than Saturday's had been.

We never did talk, though, and I returned to the University without seeing her again. Three days later, however, I received this letter:

Dear Dr. Ring,

My name is Lorna Stephens. I don't know if you'll remember me, but I was the "pest" at the IANDS conference last week. I wanted very much to speak with you, but there were so many, many people that needed to speak with you and I was heartfelt for them. I was kind of hoping that maybe someday you would be in Detroit and get in touch with me, but I can't wait for that, I guess. I need to tell you my NDE, but I also feel you need to hear it. I think it pertains to your research concerning NDEs and child abuse victims. I have been an experiencer in both. I need to begin at the very start, so this may run kind of long, but I think it is important for you to know all details.

When I was a little girl—the youngest in my family—my earliest memory is my father waking up my older brother at night and beating him. I was about three and I can still hear Stephen (my brother) screaming for help. When I was little, Stephen always watched me. He was more like my father than my brother. My father should never have had children. He can't take noise.

When I was six years old, Stephen started to abuse me sexually. It was to be a secret. And I never told anyone until years later. I, of course, couldn't understand why at times he loved me so much—and at the same time he would hurt me so bad. The sexual abuse continued until I was sixteen and finally strong enough to push him away from me. All during those years, though, I witnessed Stephen, my mother, and other members of my family being both physically and mentally abused. My father was a tyrant and seemed to want to abuse everyone but me. I had terrible feelings of guilt. And I grew up in what seems now as total fear and confusion.

When I was about six or so, I began to have the experience of *déjà vu*. But it was not so much that I felt I was here before. I knew that what I was doing, I had seen myself doing it before in my mind. I learned—well, I actually taught myself how to do this. I would just stare at an object and become deep in thought, [and] would have flashes of future events. But they never really had any significance, but they did seem to happen at turning points in my life.

Soon I learned that Stephen and I had a connection. It seemed we could tell what the other was thinking. I know this will sound very strange, but even though he was my abuser, as a young person I was very, very close to him. I just bottled the abuse part up inside of me and kept it there.

One day when I was about seven or eight years old, I was sitting in class and staring at a desk. I had flashes of a man in a studio with microphones and lots of buttons. All of a sudden, Stephen was yelling, "Lorna, Lorna, wake up." He had come to pick me up from my school class and walk me home.

As the years went by, Stephen and I became closer and closer. I loved him, I just hated the abuse. When we were teenagers we would go out together when neither of us had a date. We always had a lot of fun. He would always seem to forget birthdays and Christmas, so he would give you presents in between those times. He would take me shopping, just to look, and if I saw something that I liked, he would buy it for me. He really loved me. I don't think he ever wanted to hurt me.

When I was seventeen, my mom and I were talking about my father and all the terrible things he had done. I still remember the terrible guilt my mother showed in her face. I felt very sorry for her. Then she finally told me that my father had sexually abused my sister. It finally became clear why Stephen had done what he had done. It was what he had learned from my father.

A year later, when I was eighteen, I married a man who was very abusive as well. I was still too young to realize that I was marrying someone like my father. Stephen was very upset that I was marrying this man. All hell broke loose between us. We were no longer close. I got married and two years later had a little girl, and two years after that, I had a little boy. My marriage was falling apart. My husband was into drugs and was physically abusing me. He was also seeing many women on the side. I acted like nothing was wrong, but Stephen knew.

I had a part-time job as an aerobics instructor at the YMCA. I had hardly any money. My husband was spending everything we had on cocaine (crack), women, and booze. I dealt with the bill collectors and my phone, gas, and electricity being turned off, not to mention two small children, the worries of how to feed them, and all of the physical and mental abuse.

As time went on, I began to realize that Stephen was right. I also began to heal the wounds from my childhood even though I was still dealing with abuse. I had always had what I felt as a close relationship with God. I talked all the time to Him as a child, and always felt He was there for me. I began to forgive Stephen and had verbalized this to my best friend, Tina, who knew all about the abuse. She said she couldn't understand how I could forgive something like that and I couldn't explain it either, except that I had always loved Stephen and he was the only father I had ever had.

My mother and I were together one day talking and after a while, we both admitted that we had strange feelings someone close to us was going to die. I began to have strange dreams after that. I had a dream that I was running through a woods, and I felt like something was chasing me, or I was chasing something—I'm not sure which. All of a sudden, in the middle of the forest was a log cabin. I ran inside it and directly opposite the door, I ran in was another door. There was darkness all around me inside this log cabin, but outside the other door was this incredibly beautiful meadow with flowers like I had never seen before. It looked so inviting but I knew that if I went through that door, I could never go back. Then I woke up.

Stephen had gotten married and moved to Madison, Wisconsin. I knew he was having problems. His wife had been married before and they were in a battle with her ex-husband for custody of her children. Stephen had become a truck driver and was very happy, but he wanted to father those children. I didn't know how to feel about that, but it seemed he had grown as a person, so I hoped it would be all right. Stephen's wife's ex-husband hated Stephen, and had threatened to kill him. It turned out that Stephen's wife's ex-husband wanted to keep the children. He was sexually abusing the little girl. I think Stephen wanted that little girl so he could raise her with no abuse, to make up for me, his first little girl. (He really was more of a father to me than anything else.)

I only heard bits and pieces of this from my mom and small conversations I had with Stephen on the phone. I was back in Michigan with my own battles. My marriage was coming to an end and I knew it. Shortly after Christmas in January 1986, I had taken back Christmas presents that had been given to me—to have money for shoes my children needed. That night, when I came home and went to sleep, I had a dream that I was standing outside in the dark between what looked like trucks. It was a parking lot, I think. There were puddles on the ground and I looked up to see a figure standing in front of me, but in the distance. I saw the figure raise his arm and then I saw the barrel of a gun. I knew he was going to shoot me. He fired, and I felt the bullet hit me. I fell to the ground and then I was across the parking lot looking at my body and I saw a green—I'll be honest, I don't know how to describe it. It glowed and was shaped like a skeleton. It was rising out of my body. I woke up with a start and sat up in bed. I was in a cold sweat and very shaken.

The next day, I spoke to Stephen on the phone. He said he had the feeling I was in too deep with something and that he just had the feeling that something very wrong was happening in my life. I lied and said that everything was fine. I asked him how he was and he said, "If you only knew what was going on in my life." I wanted so much to forgive him, to say I loved him and tell him I missed him, because I did. I really missed him. I really felt at peace about all that happened between us and I wanted to make up, but somehow it just didn't seem appropriate over the phone. We said good-bye and hung up.

In February, my mom called me [and] said that Stephen had left with his truck but had been missing for four days. She was very upset. I didn't know what to tell her, but not to worry. I said he probably was just busy on his run and hadn't gotten the chance to call. She said no, that he always called his wife and [she] hadn't heard from him and the trucking company he was working for didn't know where he was. I tried to assure her that everything would be all right. I went to work that night at the YMCA, and I feel guilty to say this, but I wasn't worried about Stephen. The next morning, the phone rang. My husband answered it. I heard him saying, "You're kidding" and and "Oh, no." I thought Stephen had been hurt. My husband handed me the phone. He said it was my mother. I took the phone and said, "Hi, mom." She said, "Stephen is dead." I said, "What?" I couldn't believe my ears. She kept repeating, "Stephen is dead." We both began to sob. They found Stephen in the back of his cab. He had never left the truck stop in Wisconsin to his run down south.

They did an autopsy. I received a copy and it's full of contradictions. They never ruled out foul play and a lawyer told my mom to have a second autopsy done, but by that time it was too late—he had already been cremated.

We went through the funeral and I was devastated. Stephen's birthday was February 22, twenty days after his death (he would have been thirty-one). We, as a family, decided to get together at my sister's house in Ann Arbor for his birthday. It was very sad. I baked a cake, even, and covered it with jelly beans (they were his favorite thing to eat). When I got to my sister's, she had pulled out all those pictures from our childhood that my mother had sent her when she lived in England. (She lived in England for some years when I was a child to get away from my father.) I had never seen most of those pictures. And many of them were of Stephen and me. They brought back memories that I hadn't had in years. Happy memories of the good times he and I had shared, and there were so many. It was my life in review. I became so sad.

I drove home that evening. My husband was in bed asleep, and I wanted—I really wanted to die. Dr. Ring, I was dying inside—dying of a broken heart. I fell on my couch, and as I fell, I started to rise up. I was floating up to the ceiling and then it was like a broken TV screen, a bad signal. Suddenly I saw I was floating in space, but it wasn't like a night sky because the stars were colored and iridescent looking. In the middle of this was a loaf of bread. I know that sounds strange, but it wasn't like a loaf of bread you'd find in a grocery store. It was like homemade bread or a loaf of bread that they would use in church for communion.

All at once, I was inside this bread and it was filled with light. Bright, white light, yet soft and easy to look at. It was like the light was alive. And I felt like I was being embraced. Hugged.

Standing in front of me was Stephen. And between us was a window— well, really a hole that looked out to the iridescent stars. He had the same stars in his eyes. He was dressed just like he always had, in blue jeans and a plaid flannel shirt. He looked like Stephen always looked, except for the stars in his eyes. He spoke to me, but he didn't use words. I mean he didn't talk. I just heard him in my head. He said he knew all that I was feeling and that I forgave him and that he forgave me, too. He said he loved me and not to worry about him. Then he said some things I don't remember. But the last thing he said was that when the time came he would meet me there.

All of a sudden, I was falling back, not fast like falling off a cliff or something, but very gently. And then, and I know this sounds strange, I was in my living room looking at my body on the couch from across the room— and then, snap, I was back in my body. I got up from the couch, and even though all that had happened, I didn't feel shocked or surprised, but drained. And I went to bed. (This was not a dream. I would know if it was a dream. *I wasn't asleep.*)

After this, I still felt very sad and missed him very much. About six months later, I was supposed to be going to a meeting of instructors at the YMCA, but I was sad and missing Stephen. I just couldn't go. I found myself driving by an old graveyard we used to think was really neat when we were kids. It has old tombstones from 100 or 50 years ago. I got out of my car and started walking through this graveyard. It was a warm, sunny, summer day, but I felt like it should have been raining. Suddenly, a thought popped into my head–"John 6." I wasn't thinking about anything like that. I had gotten away from going to church, but "John 6" kept popping into my head.

For a week after this, it kept coming to me. Finally I thought, "Sit down and read this." I read it, and in it, it says, "I am the bread of Life and all who believe in me shall not die, but have eternal life." And then I thought: "So that's the bread!" That's what the bread meant.

About two months after this, I was at a friend's house who knew Stephen. We were talking about old times we all shared together. I had mentioned to her how my mom wished I would go back to church. She said, "Well, why don't you go and surprise her?" It was about 2 a.m. Sunday morning when we were talking. I said to her, "Yes, I should." So I went home and got a couple hours sleep and then went to the church. I got there before my mom. She was very surprised to see me. She went downstairs, where she teaches Sunday school. I went into the Sanctuary. As I went in, someone handed me a program, and on the cover was a picture of my loaf of bread! Just like I had seen it. And about it, it said, "That you may Live ..." I started to cry. I went in the church and sat down. It so happened that they were having communion that day. As the minister gave out the communion, he said, "I am the bread of Life, and all those who believe in me shall not die, but have eternal life." Well, you can imagine how astounded I was.

Since that time, I did nothing but search for something. At the time I didn't know what to look for. I went to the library and looked up a book on astral projection. On the cover of it was the green, glowing skeleton-shaped thing I saw in my dream. (I had never seen this book before.) I didn't find anything I wanted in that book, though. Then I found *Life after Life* by Raymond Moody. I loved it, but I only wanted to read more—and I kept reading anything I could on NDEs.

I divorced my husband. Went to school for broadcasting (something I had always wanted to do). Met my fiancé (he was one of my teachers). I kept looking for NDE books. After a few years, I got a job at a radio station. One day, when a basketball game was being broadcast and I didn't have to do any reports, I went to a nearby bookstore (this was last April). I saw a book called *Full Circle* by Barbara Harris. I loved it. At the end she mentioned IANDS. And also the conference in August. I knew I was going.

The next day, I was talking to a friend I work with about it and suddenly realized it was what I saw as a little girl—the man in the studio with microphones and all of our buttons. I know now my whole life has led to this.

I bought *Life at Death* and *Heading toward Omega*, and I'm still reading the latter. When I saw you at the conference, I recognized you at once. I hope I have given you something. I feel a Love for you, Dr. Ring, and hope someday you'll say, "Call me Ken." I've pestered you enough and hope maybe someday we'll be able to talk. I don't know where all this is taking me next, but I have never been happier. I'm getting married again next April thirteenth. He, the man that I'm marrying, knows this story, my story, and loves me unconditionally and supports me.

My name, again, is Lorna, but you can always call me "Pest." I Love you.

Lorna's story was long and intricate, but its pieces fit together so perfectly and with such an uncanny sense of articulated design that it is hard to imagine it without the Light's guiding hand in leading Lorna along the road that eventually brought her to her healing vision and ultimate peace.

Finally, we come to a third story, and, quite remarkably, this one, too, begins with that same IANDS conference. It was on that occasion that I met another woman who, like Lorna, has become very dear to me and with whom I have remained in frequent contact. In her case, I did have a chance to chat with her briefly, but only long enough to know that I was very intrigued to learn more about an experience that she had years before, which appeared to have been a very rich NDE that had somehow been *willed* into being by extreme circumstances. There not being time for me to get more than the barest account of this event, I asked her if she would write to me about it, and just around the same time I had received Lorna's moving letter, I found that I was holding another from this woman, Beverly Brodsky, that was just as powerful.

In presenting Beverly's story here, however, I am—for the moment—going to omit her account of some of the most profound insights her experience disclosed to her because this aspect of her encounter with the Light will be featured in a later chapter. My interest here is purely to provide one last instance of how a condition of the most desolate hopelessness can bring forth the love and healing power of the Light.

Beverly began her letter by giving me some information concerning her background, and the circumstances that led up to her experience in 1970:

I was raised in a nonobservant Conservative Jewish family in an overwhelmingly Jewish neighborhood in Philadelphia. The atmosphere was materialistic and, for me, claustrophobic. In high school girls were judged by their clothes and beauty. Bookish, shy, and serious, I went through my teens as an atheist. Since learning, in very muted terms, of the Holocaust at age eight, I had turned angrily against any early belief in God. How could God exist and permit such a thing to occur? The secularism of my public school education and the lack of any religious training added fuel to my beliefs.

I went through a period of depression growing up that was not treated, due to my parents' unfortunate adherence to the belief that psychological treatment was disgraceful, and that personal problems or family secrets should never be aired outside the home. I had reached a desperate phase upon graduating from high school. Too upset to go to college despite my brilliant academic performance, I had trouble facing the future. To make things worse, shortly after graduation, at age seventeen, my father died suddenly from a heart attack. He had been my rock, my strength, in this world.

My mother went through an emotional crisis of her own after this loss, simultaneously entering menopause. No longer able to bear this unhappy environment, I left home at age nineteen, living first in Philadelphia's center city, and later moving out to California, where people then wore flowers in their hair and spoke of peace and love for all mankind. I had learned to meditate and for the first time had some hope that I could start over. To me the journey out West was like Hesse's *Journey to the East*—a quest for a new world.

In July 1970, I suffered a fractured skull and numerous broken bones in my head due to a motorcycle accident that occurred in Los Angeles. I had just arrived in California the day before. The motorcycle ride, my first, was part of the celebration of arrival; we were returning from seeing the play *Hair*. I was a passenger on a small highway where helmets were not required, and was struck by a drunken driver. I was thrown to the ground headfirst. When the police arrived, they initially took one look at me and started to book the driver of the car on manslaughter charges since my head was so badly mangled.

I spent two weeks in the hospital, where my fracture was sutured and I was given morphine for the pain. Then I was sent home and told to take aspirin. Since my pain threshold has always been very low, and my self-image was shattered by the contusions which had torn off half the skin from my face, I went home to my temporary apartment with the firm intent that the first night home would be my last. I lay down on the bed and, becoming an agnostic in this moment of trial, as many atheists do, prayed fervently for God to take me; I could not live another day. At twenty I had no goals but to enjoy life and find someone to share it with. The pain was unbearable; no man would ever love me; there was, for me, no reason to continue living.

At this point, obviously, Beverly's only wish was to die, though it is important to note that physically, she was no longer in any danger of doing so from her injuries. But just here, all the same, she finds her wish being granted. Her letter continues:

> Somehow an unexpected peace descended upon me. I found myself floating on the ceiling over the bed looking down at my unconscious body. I barely had time to realize the glorious strangeness of the situation—that I was me but not in my body—when I was joined by a radiant being bathed in a shimmering white glow. Like myself, this being flew but had no wings. I felt a reverent awe when I turned to him; this was no ordinary angel or spirit, but he had been sent to deliver me. Such love and gentleness emanated from his being that I felt that I was in the presence of the messiah.
>
> Whoever he was, his presence deepened my serenity and awakened a feeling of joy as I recognized my companion. Gently he took my hand and we flew right through the window. I felt no surprise at my ability to do this. In this wondrous presence, everything was as it should be.

Now, in the company of her spiritual guide, Beverly went on to have one of the most extraordinary NDEs that I have ever come across in the course of my work, which is why I want to reserve this portion of her experience for a later chapter, where I can give it a proper context. For now, I will just ask you to take it on faith that it enabled her to enter into a region *beyond* any of the realms we have so far discussed in connection with NDEs, and that, incredibly, she was able to write about it with such an inspired eloquence that her overall narrative is possibly the most moving in my entire collection.

Here, however, I simply confine myself to its effects on Beverly's life. Let me pick up her account, then, with her coming back to herself in the room where she had yearned for death:

> Suddenly, not knowing how or why, I returned to my broken body. But miraculously, I brought back the love and the joy. I was filled with an ecstasy beyond my wildest dreams. Here, in my body, the pain had all been removed. I was still enthralled by a boundless delight. For the next two months, I remained in this state, oblivious to any pain....
>
> I felt now as if I had been made anew. I saw wondrous meanings everywhere; everything was alive and full of energy and intelligence....
>
> I don't remember too much of this period, except that I did some things that were, for me, incredible. In the past I had been painfully shy and had felt myself unworthy of being loved. I went out, my head swathed in bandages like a creature from a horror film, landed a job in one week, made many friends, and got involved in my first serious romantic relationship. After the earthquake in 1971, I moved back East, went home to my mother, with whom I became reconciled, and started college at twenty-three, another thing I never thought I could handle, and graduated Phi Beta Kappa. Since then I have married, become a mother, pursued a career, and have sipped deeply from the cup of life's blessings that I had never believed would come my way in those dark years before I found the Light. In that encounter with death, I was given joy and purpose to continue on with life.

Although it's been 20 years since my heavenly voyage, I have never forgotten it. Nor have I, in the face of ridicule and disbelief, ever doubted its reality. Nothing that intense and life-changing could possibly have been a dream or hallucination. To the contrary, I consider the rest of my life to be a passing fantasy, a brief dream, that will end when I again awaken in the permanent presence of that giver of life and bliss.

## THE HEALING GIFTS OF NDE STORIES

Reading such stories as Lorna's and Beverly's, as well as many of the others I have already related in this chapter, makes it clear that NDEs, whether associated with an actual near-death crisis or not, can often help to heal the individual of either a seemingly fatal illness or a conditional of spiritual despair. What is not so obvious is that even *reading* such stories can heal *us*. Let me give you just one simple illustration of this.

I have a good friend who lives in Bogotá, Colombia. We have only met once, fairly recently, when I was giving a lecture there, but we have corresponded for many years, and she has long taken an interest in my work. Several years ago, I sent her a copy of an article that began with a full account of Beverly's experience, and here is what she wrote to me about two weeks later in this connection:

> Due to stressful events in the clinic these days, I developed a throat infection with acute pain, which I had when I started to read your article. I read the Beverly Brodsky document during ten minutes, and when I finished reading it, many things had occurred: my acute pain had disappeared, my throat infection had disappeared, all objects around me vibrated with light, and I felt weightless.
>
> I have no words to describe the deep knowledge that Beverly's experience is the encounter with ultimate truth. The most intimate part of me recognizes the truth in her experience.

Although I have no hard evidence of this, I can scarcely persuade myself that my friend is unique in the world in her response to such stories. But I will present some evidence in later chapters that *just reading* such accounts as those I have shared with you here can indeed heal us of many things, including our fear of death. My friend's comment, though, suggests that there may be hitherto unsuspected power in these stories to bring about some measure of physical healing as well, and not merely (though this is, of course, no small thing) provide comfort and inspiration to those who may never have had an NDE. So one of our lessons from this chapter again point to the role of the NDE as a healing agent, both for the experiencer *and ourselves*. At any rate, the "benign virus" of the NDE may seemingly sometimes be transmitted directly through the reading of stories such as those that fill this chapter.

## NDERs AS LIGHT-MANIFESTING THERAPISTS

There is still another way in which we can derive healing benefits from our exposure to NDEs. Consider the following two observations we have already made in this chapter: (1) The Light sometimes seems to act as a Master Therapist; and (2) NDErs sometimes claim to have received a transmission from the Light during their experience. Putting these two ideas together leads to an obvious implication: NDErs should not only be able to function as Light-assisted healers of *physical illness*, but should also have the gift of manifesting the therapeutic power of the Light in their relations with others.

And, indeed, once again, there is an abundance of anecdotal material from my interviews with, and letters from, NDErs that attests to just how easily NDErs may find themselves in this role and how naturally effective they seem to be in it. Here, however, I will only offer two brief examples to show you what I mean.

You may remember my friend, Nel, whom I mentioned in earlier chapters. She is someone with whom I had a great deal of contact in the 1980s and I can certainly speak from my own experience of her that she is one of these therapeutically gifted NDErs. In a talk she gave in 1983, she indicated clearly what she thinks is the source of her talent and why she has felt moved to use it in this way:

> Over the last six weeks, on three different occasions, strangers have come to me and before long, they seem to be pouring their hearts out to me. All three believed all hope was lost. I was able, in some way, to give hope back to them. Unfortunately, I did not have my tape recorder with me and I don't remember what I said, but my words did make a difference. I was able to offer a different alternative, or option, to what they were thinking. I see this as one of the things that I will be doing. I would like to take the Light which is within me, and it is in everyone, and I would like to be able to give it back to those who have lost it. I was lucky to have this experience and have it still so vivid. It is something I want to share.

A second instance comes from a woman I will call Marilyn, who wrote me in 1990. Her NDE, like some of the others I have already described in this chapter, also came about as a result of a drug and alcohol overdose, though in her case, she claims it was accidental, not deliberate. Since returning to life, Marilyn has been deeply involved in Alcoholics Anonymous, where she functions as a counselor to adults and adolescents who still have drug- or alcohol-related dependencies. In her understanding, this work is a direct outgrowth of her experience in the Light and its greatest gift to her. In this regard, she writes,

> It would be difficult to fully describe the exact benefits I have derived from my NDE. The most extraordinary gift I gained from my NDE is complete intuitive understanding of others' feelings—when I choose to use it. Because of this gift, I am a skilled therapist. The only negative consequence of this ability is that it is often difficult for me to "veil" my ability in front of my colleagues, who sometimes wonder where I get my sense of conviction! I suppose I have a reputation of being "too perceptive" and not academic enough in my orientation—which is fine with me, as long as I continue to help my patients. Several of my patients—those deemed "hopeless" (*chronic* is the professional term)—are now free of chemical use and happy, I believe, directly through the influence of my higher power's gift to me. Because of the nature of my "special abilities," I am at times filled with sadness at the way many mental patients are treated within the system, and I can most certainly relate to their humiliation at the hands of practitioners who themselves do not feel comfortable with suffering. I believe the finest therapists are those who have suffered greatly—and who have been able to heal.

Through the ministrations of people like Nel and Marilyn, who bring to their therapeutic interventions the living power of the Light, we, too, can reap some of the benefits and blessings NDErs have received. As Nel said in so many words, her joy is to spread the Light to others in order to put them back in touch with the Light they carry within themselves. And contact with the Light, whether direct or mediated by others, is the source from which all true healing springs.

## MAKING THE CONNECTION: WHAT THE NDE TEACHES ABOUT HEALING

The stories in this chapter and the other data I have reviewed on the connection between NDEs and healing gifts make it plain that we who have not had NDEs can learn much from those who have about the healing energies that are available to us all. Indeed, the basic message of this chapter may well be summed up by the simple declaration: The Light—

the ultimate healing power itself—is omnipresent and ready to come to our assistance when we find ourselves derelict and without hope. And, as we have seen, even reading such stories as those provided in this chapter or having direct contact with NDErs can confer a healing gift upon us.

Nevertheless, apart from the sense of comfort or even inspiration we can derive from this material, it may still be difficult to see how we can make active use of it in our own lives. In other words, how can we begin to put these insights to *practical* use when confronted with illness or overwhelming psychological pain?

Here, to conclude this chapter by speaking about this issue, I would like to draw on some of the ideas of a man not previously introduced in this book, whom, after his preference for a pseudonym, I will call Gerald. This is a man I know only through correspondence, but it has been extensive and I have myself learned much from it, which is why I would like to share some of it with you. Gerald has had a life full of both acute psychological problems, mostly stemming from chronic alcoholism, *and* severe and debilitating illnesses, and by the age of sixty had long triumphed over his alcoholism and nearly overcome a succession of crippling diseases. His NDE, which was very extensive and complex,[11] played a significant part in his recovery, but more from what lessons he extracted from it than any curative effect as such. And he has continued to study the dynamics of healing for many years after his NDE, which occurred in 1979. It is the fruit of his inquiry, which only *began* with his NDE, that I would like to offer here for your consumption.

First, however, let Gerald tell you what his situation was like before his NDE.

In 1978, I found myself in what appeared to be a totally hopeless and untenable position. Primarily due to alcohol abuse, I had reached the stage where neither my body nor my employers could stand it any longer and I was given no choice in the matter: Stop it or be fired. I was forty-six years old and unemployable, and physically, emotionally, and mentally very ill— spiritually empty. I had used an alcohol crutch for twenty-five years and was terrified at the thought of being without, to the point of routinely contemplating suicide.

Though I had been given my ultimatum, I continued to drink to oblivion, and was so sick from forced periodic withdrawals that I could barely function. One dark morning, on my hands and knees crawling back from the bathroom and unable to get up from the floor, I groaned a desperate unbeliever's prayer: "If there's anybody out there, please...." Circumstances began to change relatively quickly then, though only in retrospect is it possible to see this clearly. I was soon admitted at an excellent alcohol treatment center where, though I was frightened, defensive, angry and resentful, I was fascinated to learn something about the reasons behind self-destructive behavior. A year later I was still very ill, but had managed to avoid drinking. I had certainly changed, however reluctantly, and though I had succeeded in stopping the behavior, I was still depressed beyond rationality. My career and private life were a shambles, and most of my friends were either dead or out of my life. I had been under the care of a psychiatrist before, and after clinical treatment he had diagnosed me as manic-depressive and was recommending lithium treatments. I refused, frightened of yet another addiction.

Out of this seeming impasse, however, Gerald receives help from an unanticipated source, whose nature you can guess.

As part of my rehabilitation, I decided to undergo remedial surgery to a knee, which had been the cause of intense physical pain. It had been shattered in an alcohol-related automobile wreck some years earlier. I had a strong premonition I would die on the operating table but went ahead anyway, probably hoping I would be spared the responsibility of doing away with myself. Instead, I was the recipient of a truly amazing near-death experience. I awakened from the anesthetic mystified by what felt like a whole new perspective on life, though the circumstances I faced were exactly the same. I knew what had occurred was enormously important no matter how incredible it seemed, but I had no idea what it meant. Later, others perceived the change too. The psychiatrist was one of the first, suggesting I no longer required his services. Fourteen years later, I might well find it easier to write about how this event has *not* affected my life than how it *has*. Indeed, there is little resemblance to the old personality in the new, yet the same "I" gazes out through these eyes.

From this observation, you might be forgiven for thinking that we have here still another case where a shipwrecked man was rescued from spiritual death by the Light of an NDE and went on to live out his remaining years in the sunshine of health and well-being. But in Gerald's case, other and quite unsettling challenges still lay ahead. His story continues:

Several years after beginning my investigation into why the most important event of my life had happened while I was unconscious—perhaps even dead—my wife and I left careers in the city behind to follow the Light full time. This was not without its trauma. Despite my newfound philosophy and holistic lifestyle, I soon contracted Guillain–Barré syndrome, a near-fatal dysfunction of the central nervous system, resulting in almost total paralysis and agonizing pain. It would have been easy to give up, because I knew for certain there was a life of peace and joy after this one. Instead, and because I really had no alternative but to try or suffer agony, I determined to find out why I had again succumbed to disease.

I had plenty of time for insight, for my days were, of necessity, spent doing nothing but thinking. I had not the strength to read a book and it was too painful to watch TV for long. At first I made a conscious effort to stop resisting the pain, to accept it, and this helped considerably. Subsequently, as life became more bearable, this evolved into a process of "feeling into" the pain and dysfunction as deeply as possible to discover what it was trying to tell me, why it was there. I know there are no accidents in life, so there had to be a very good reason for the disease.

And here is where Gerald begins to go beyond what we have so far discussed in this chapter—the healing gifts of the NDE—and into the very roots of illness itself. Not just his own illness, but illness in general, for it seems to have been the function of Gerald's NDE to teach him more about the causes of illness than to furnish him with a cure. For that, he had to work with all his strength. But meanwhile, these insights came:

Each part of the human body has its esoteric counterpart on the higher plane, and if there is physical dysfunction, there is a lesson for the soul to learn from the physical symptoms. In my case these were, in general, crippling and painful, and I deduced initially that I must feel imprisoned by and extremely uncomfortable with life (though I certainly didn't think so!); and that I had "arranged" to avoid the responsibility of it by creating circumstances in which I might escape. Day by day, through spiritual and mental insight, a greater perspective emerged, and I discovered I actually *feared* life incarnate and many of its ordinary circumstances, yet was *addicted* to the thrill, the risk and ongoing excitement of it.

By the way, this is not the type of fear I could have discovered readily in any other way; nor is it easy to describe or recognize, for it is not the sort that makes us run away or fight. Indeed, it is so much an habitual part of our character as to be virtually undetectable to subjective observation without spiritual help. We have, of course, lived with our personalities all our lives and the way we perceive ourselves seems just the normal way to "be." I had read that certain types of prayer and contemplation would help clarify these matters, and I set out to look within at greater depth by applying them. This was no easy task, for one's personality goes to much trouble to hide the truth from itself, and wasn't about to give up its secrets easily.

And as Gerald improved physically, his insights into the formative causes of disease and how they could be removed continued to deepen.

After a year or two of this inner search, I began to regain some strength, and the symptoms [began] to abate. From being almost totally helpless in a wheelchair, I found myself living a more or less "normal" life. As I became more proficient at insight, I found many other sensitive areas to explore, deeply ingrained but almost invisible dysfunctional attitudes concealed by me in this lifetime and no doubt left over from others. With daily application, I've been able to reduce these thought forms to acceptable levels, and eventually will remove them altogether. As this process continues, my physical health improves daily to parallel my growing peace of mind. I believe that when a person is totally free from inner stress and judgment—the fears that prevent us from loving ourselves unconditionally as God loves us—there will be no further need to experience disease, and the body will reflect the perfect health of the soul. The techniques I used made it possible to withdraw medication for pain and stress, and despite a certain amount of residual discomfort and physical weakness, I now have a greater sense of freedom, peace, and love for life than at any other time I can remember.

Now, the point of this is to say that my recovery has not been accomplished by means of physical therapy, diet, or drugs, but exclusively by mental techniques. In short, I believe (indeed personally I KNOW) that the reversal of my disease has come about through application of affirmation, prayer, and contemplation: the utilization of focused positive thinking. I believe, and have established completely to my own satisfaction, that disease stems from mental dysfunction causing stress and imbalance, which allows the existing viruses and bacteria and so on to proliferate and produce weakness and deterioration of the body. There is, of course, much more to it than this, but in simplest terms, mental attitudes, which are-founded-in-fear and are therefore out of alignment with the energy we in the West call God, are the root cause of all illness.

If my posit is correct, and I assure you that for me it is, then the area of your specialty is a major source of hope for the future of mankind. When doctors of psychiatry and medicine, and those who practice alternate forms of healing, begin to collaborate, first to identify the stressors and eliminate them, and in the interim to help the patient survive while he begins to understand the source of his problems, the lessons of disease will eventually no longer be necessary.

What Gerald is saying here brings into relief (no pun intended!) the special contribution the NDE has to make to our understanding of disease and its healing, and at the same time his remarks sum up the most important lesson the NDE has to teach us about what keeps us locked in the prison house of disease in the first place. *It is at bottom the fear to love ourselves unconditionally as the Light does.* If the Light does not blast away these fears, we need to do it! The Light may in some cases, as we have seen, suffice to lift us out of despair or heal us of disease, but when disease remains or recurs, it is well to inquire into its meaning deeply, as Gerald did, because it, too, however unwelcome, may be still another offering from the Light, which is meant to show us the very blockages that keep us from realizing fully the Light not only in ourselves, but *as* ourselves.

Gerald's final comments give an even fuller scope to these ideas as he shows that the failure to learn the lessons of the Light is not merely an individual loss but the continuing sorrow of the world, while their realization is our salvation:

> I believe anyone who chooses to explore these issues—by first embracing their own spiritual reality—can find a cure, or at least a degree of freedom from their disease, right now. It is neither simple nor easy, but it is possible, and I stand as a living example.
>
> I know now that disease is simply part of life's ongoing process of discovery, caused by our fear of aligning with the Universal Love we call God. It is my impression that the majority of the human family shares many of the hidden dysfunctions I discovered in myself. These are the errant thought forms which cause not only disease, but are at the root of all the world's pain and suffering, greed and aggression, violence and war. In the future, I believe that disease and the troubled life we know today will no longer be a necessary part of our experience. Instead, as we return to an understanding of who we are spiritually, apply preventive and vibrational modalities combining spiritual with emotional counseling, holistic and allopathic medicine, disease—and perhaps even death as we presently perceive it—will become an archaic relic of our ignorance.

## Chapter Eleven

# New Light on Death, Dying, and Bereavement

In his celebrated novel, *Moby Dick*, the great nineteenth-century American author, Herman Melville, presciently remarked, "And death, which alike levels all, alike impresses all with a last revelation, which only an author from the dead could adequately tell." Those "authors from the dead," who in Melville's time, could scarcely be said to exist, are in our own time today's NDErs of course, and their collective testimony is giving us a new view of death.

There is little doubt that in the Western World, at least from the time of the devastating plagues that caused the death of millions of Europeans in the thirteenth century, the dominant symbol of death has been "the grim reaper," that hooded and faceless figure who comes to take us away, we know not when, we know not where. This forbidding specter, who haunted Europe for centuries before Mr. Marx suggested we should be frightened of another kind altogether, has thus long been a part of our collective psyche, and its image is still powerful enough to conjure up in us feelings of dread concerning the inexorability of our own deaths. And yet, in just the last quarter of a century, ever since the advent of modern research into the NDE, this frightening scythe-bearing harbinger of death has finally begun to be eclipsed by another image—the Light of the NDE itself, or to personify it, perhaps we should say by the oft-mentioned radiant figure that Raymond Moody called "the being of light." Can there be any doubt that in the light (no pun intended) of all the publicity that has been given to this aspect of the NDE ever since the phenomenon itself became an object of worldwide fascination, we in the West have come to see death with new eyes, now filled with hope rather than glazed over with fear?

In one of Joseph Campbell's books—I have forgotten which one, frankly—there is a phrase to the effect (and I am paraphrasing here, even though I know it is risky and bad form to paraphrase an aphorism) that seen from afar, death is an horrific specter, but seen up close, it has the face of the beloved. With our familiarity with the NDE, it is obvious that those who have had this experience have indeed seen the face of death "up close," and their narratives serve to assure us that Campbell is right on target here. As we move from the external perspective of death—that where the grim reaper has sway—to an internal one, where we *experience* the moment of death itself, all fear dissolves and we know a love that is as overwhelming and welcoming as it is incomparable. In Betty Eadie's memorable phrase, we find ourselves "embraced by the light." And having felt the absolute love of this embrace, we can never forget it. Moreover, it extinguishes, usually forever, the fear of death, for, as we know, "perfect love casts out fear."

This is in a nutshell what the collective testimony of NDErs has to tell us about what awaits us at the moment of death, and because their testimony is, by and large, so consistent and compelling, and because literally thousands of persons who have approached the threshold of death and returned have similar stories to tell, those of us who listen to such tales cannot help but be affected by them. Thus, we who have only heard these NDE stories begin perhaps by marveling at them, but after a while, we find that they have silently entered into our psyches and have caused us to have a view of death that no longer has any place for the grim reaper. Instead, when we think of death, images of a loving light pervade.

Now, we know that this kind of testimony, as it has been fanned through the media throughout the past twenty years, and most recently, of course, over the Internet, is indeed beginning to have an impact on people's thinking about the nature of death.

Just to take one example, those studies I introduced in Chapter Nine, by myself and other college professors who have taught courses on the NDE, show that between 80–90 percent of students enrolled in these courses emerge from them with a much more positive view of death.[1] Moreover, 60–70 percent of these students report a decreased fear of death after being exposed to a semester-long course on NDEs, a figure that increases to more than 80 percent for persons, not necessarily students, who are known to have developed a strong interest in NDEs.[2]

Of course, it has been known for a long time that one of the most consistent and powerful effects of having an NDE is the loss or at least the drastic reduction of one's fear of death. NDErs typically tell us that while they retain a fear of the pain associated with the *process* of dying, their NDE has stripped them of all fear of the moment of death itself and has assured them that no pain will follow them where they are going.

Consider, for example, some of the following comments from a representative panel of NDErs on these points.

My friend Tom Sawyer, to whom we paid such close attention in Chapter Seven in connection with his life review, expressed himself very succinctly on what his NDE had taught him about death:

> As a result of that [experience], I have very little apprehension about dying my natural death ... because if death is anything, anything at all like what I experienced, it's gotta be the most wonderful thing to look forward to, absolutely the most wonderful thing.[3]

Likewise, Nel virtually echoes some of Tom's sentiments on the basis of her own NDE:

> The most profound thing which has happened to me is that I no longer fear death. This is probably the most common result of having an NDE. I had a great fear before. Pain, severe pain, used to trigger the response of "this is my entrance into Hell." The pain which I experienced a few hours before I had my NDE gave me that impression very clearly. I was going down and I probably was not going to come up again. Since the NDE I do not fear it at all. I have been there, I know what to look for, I have felt it, and I actually find myself looking forward [to it]. When the time is right for my physical body to die, I will go on to something so absolutely out of this world that it defies comparison.

My Australian friend, Andrea, the healing effects of whose NDE I discussed in the last chapter, also emphasizes the loss of the fear of death and the certain knowledge that, at death, all pain will cease.

> I now have no fear of death. Let me reassure you from personal experience, no matter how bad the pain gets, it does end, and you will find yourself out of the body, in another dimension, still very much alive, and in no pain.

Another man, whom I know only from correspondence, speaks to another insight about death that the NDE confers: For the dying, it doesn't exist!

As a result of going through this experience ... I knew that as ordinarily perceived, what is called death is only experienced by the survivors.... There is no such thing as death per se. Death in our three dimensional space/time view of things is simply a biological event that has nothing to do with consciousness, which is continuous both before what we call birth and after death.

Finally, a now deceased woman named Minette, with whom I enjoyed a warm correspondence for several years, spoke with great enthusiasm about what her NDE had taught her and of how much she wanted others to know what she had learned. Perhaps her posthumous words will speak to you, as well as honor her ambition to reach others with her message:

I decided I had to tell what I had learned about this magnificent domain. At the time, I had not heard of anyone who had gone beyond death. Millions upon millions feared death. Wouldn't they be glad to know that only the body dies, but not their inner person? I wanted to shout what I'd learned from the housetops, share it with all people in the world.

When you put together these two sets of findings—the latter pertaining to NDErs alone and the former to those who have not had NDEs but who have become familiar with them—what they seem to suggest, once again, is that here, too, mere knowledge of the NDE may act like a benign virus. Persons who are exposed to the stories and views of NDErs—as long as they are open to such matters—become influenced by them and begin to express beliefs and attitudes about death that are very similar to NDErs themselves. We might well call such persons, "near-death experiencers, once removed." They have not had the experience, but "they get the message," and it, in turn, becomes theirs. If fear of death is contagious, so, too, is its loss when one keeps the company of NDErs. Perhaps you have already noticed a similar shift within yourself.

What I have offered so far, however, by way of evidence for the contagious effect of NDEs on nonexperiencers' views of death is admittedly little more than some suggestive statistical data. Unfortunately, in the absence of any large-scale and systematic surveys on this point, we are forced to rely mainly on these promising but clearly preliminary investigations. However, we *do* have other sources of information here—indeed, an abundance of it—once we move away from the realm of formal studies and into the capacious archives of personal testimony based on those who those who have written to me (or other NDE researchers) or whom I have interviewed in the course of my work. And since stories teach better than statistics, anyway, it will behoove us to sample this material for further and even more compelling evidence of the way in which the NDEr's view of death has already affected in a most beneficial manner many individuals who have had to deal with their own imminent death or that of others.

## WHAT NDEs HAVE TO TEACH US ABOUT DYING AND DEATH

One of the great practical gifts—perhaps the greatest—of the NDE is what it can teach the living about dying. Here, I would like to focus on just three specific applications where information about the NDE has proved useful to those either facing or contemplating death, or coping with the grief that comes from bereavement.

### Facing Death

As we have said, there is little doubt that the testimony of NDErs has had an effect on how people think about their own prospective deaths, even when they are not imminent. Evelyn's interview with Béatrice, whom we introduced in Chapter Nine, furnishes a good example of how these stories can strengthen one's belief in the possibility of survival of bodily death. At the same time, it is apparent in her case that her convictions are still a bit theoretical, since her life circumstances have not yet tested her NDE-based beliefs.

EV: How did your knowledge about the NDE phenomenon influence your attitude toward death?

B: I had always secretly wished that consciousness would survive after bodily death. I wanted it to be true, but maybe my faith was not strong enough to make this true for me. Through the experiences, I now have empirical corroboration of this—but I don't go so far as to call it proof. The question is, will this be strong enough to withstand panic if, say, tomorrow, I learn that I am terminally ill? I don't know. Will this console me if I lose a person I love? I think—I even believe—it will, but I can't be sure since it hasn't happened to me yet. But I am convinced that we should think about these issues before something sad happens to us, before we confront death or mourning, in order to be prepared as much as possible.

Here Béatrice can only wonder what she will think and feel when the time comes for her to face death firsthand. But others have already had to deal with death, not just in the abstract, but as a matter of personal, quickly impending, and inescapable fate. The issue of the value of NDE testimony is obviously much more immediate in such instances. Now, Béatrice's question is squarely put to the test: When the chips are down, does knowledge of NDEs help to insulate one from the terror of death? Does it in fact make any difference at all?

If you, along with Béatrice, find yourself having a lingering doubt about the actual worth of NDEs should you have to stare imminent death in the face, perhaps the following case history will be reassuring.

In 1991, Deborah Drumm, a nurse living in Nashville, Tennessee, learned that she had developed breast cancer. Her condition was serious and required a modified radical mastectomy as well as intensive chemotherapy, and she was understandably very frightened. Within a relatively short time, a friend of hers had called her attention to some articles and books about NDEs (which, previously, she had never taken seriously), and she began to read them—with increasing avidity. She soon had exhausted the materials she had been given and then sought out additional references and even contact with some NDErs directly. As she indicates, she found all this information tremendously reassuring, and her fear of death began to recede.

Within months of her exposure to the world of NDEs, she was doing very well physically. Her CAT scans and mammograms were clear, and her cell counts were again normal. She continued to have checkups every two months and in this regard wrote:

> If cancer should be found [again], I would still be initially shaken; but I think my adjustment would be much easier. That paralyzing fear that haunted me the first six months of this year I do not believe will ever come again. Death to me now is not what it was a year ago. Now when I imagine that last moment, I see light. I feel peace, love and tranquility.[4]

Significantly for us in this context, she then goes on to describe her own experiences of the contagious effects that NDE accounts kindle in others:

> And the hope offered by the NDE is infectious. When these stories are shared with others who are afraid or grieving, it seems to provide them peace also. For instance, I recently met a woman whose 23-year-old daughter had committed suicide one month before our conversation. This woman was tormented because some persons in her church had told her that her daughter would go to hell. I showed her an article … in which the NDEs of suicide attempts were described as being beautiful and tranquil, like any other

NDE. After reading the article, she told me that she felt greatly relieved, and added, "God bless you."

I hope ... psychiatrists, physicians, nurses and other health-care professionals ... will seriously consider exploring the use of NDE accounts with the seriously ill and grieving, as well as, certainly, dying patients and their families. I can attest to the inspiring, invigorating power of this "therapy." I *am* stronger and more confident than I was before my illness, because I have finally dealt with my fear of death.... Near-death accounts give peace of mind and renewed purpose, and allow life to move ahead. I am no longer plagued by fear, but I still enjoy reading NDE accounts. They always make it joyous![5]

Unfortunately, this is not the end of Deborah Drumm's story. Writing a few months later to the editor of the *Journal of Near-Death Studies*, she revealed that subsequent tests had shown that her malignancy had spread and become incurable and that, as a result, death was now staring her in the eye as quite possibly an imminent event. In view of that prospect, she was moved to remember the lines she had written in her first letter: "If cancer should be found [again], I would still be initially shaken, but I think my adjustment would be much easier. That paralyzing fear that haunted me the first six months of the year I do not believe will ever come again." In this connection, she now attests:

I am writing to tell you that my previous statement does hold true.... The most important factor in my psychological recovery, once again, has been the regular reading of near-death experiences.... I keep these books by my bed. For the six weeks after news of my recurrence, not a single day went by that I did not read or re-read some of the accounts. Still, when I begin to feel fear or sink into depression, reviewing these accounts is my first line of defense....

In short, believing in the content of NDEs has kept me functional. It has allowed me to feel that there is purpose in everything, including my illness, and that I can somehow find and profit from the meaning in that illness. After all, if NDEs are to be believed, there is value to every experience and a loving God or Presence watches and guides us through every experience.

I wish that all seriously ill persons could have the chance to study NDEs. For various reasons, some might not want to continue their study very long. But I am convinced that many would be greatly comforted.[6]

Although Deborah Drumm is only one case, surely she speaks for many who, like herself, in having to confront the looming specter of physical death, have found sources of deep solace and hope in the plenitude of NDE accounts that are now available to us. And we can only echo her advice that health care professionals as well as the lay public should be directed to these materials so that they, too, can benefit from the lessons that NDErs have to offer us about what tender blessings we can expect when the moment of death finally comes to liberate us from the bondage of pain and decrepitude.

In addition to the way in which NDE accounts (in written form or from direct oral testimony) can be useful to individuals who are facing death, there are as well *certain groups or categories of persons* that seem to be especially open to the lessons and implications of these experiences.

For instance, there appears to be a special place for NDE accounts for persons who are facing death from AIDS. An example of this comes from the work of Ganga Stone, who for many years in New York ran an organization called God's Love We Deliver, which ministered to the need of such persons. Ganga, whom I have met several times over the years, managed to cadge food for her clients from some of New York City's finest restaurants, and she and her volunteers would then deliver it, along with God's Love—*and* the NDE. In short, what Ganga told me was that she would make a point of bringing information about the NDE to her clients and she couldn't say enough about how much these accounts meant to the persons she was working with. Indeed, she was so inspired by the use of this kind of information with her clients that she eventually wrote a book, *The Start of Conversation*, that is concerned in large part with the uses of the NDE in enabling others come to terms with death. Ganga's book—an in-your-face approach to dealing with death by a fast-talking, wise-cracking New Yorker—is based on a six-week course she taught for New Yorkers, many of them suffering from AIDS. She helps them confront and overcome the fear of death and the need for grief by teaching them to see that "There is no death" and that "You are not your body"—and for all this, the research on the NDE plays a pivotal role in her argument. Thus, Ganga is a good example of someone who has used NDE stories as an antidote to the fear of death in persons who were facing imminent death, as well as for persons, whether they were suffering from AIDS or not, who took her course. The book itself is filled with humor, anecdotes, and many moving stories, and is written in peppy, zingy language with drill-sergeant-like exhortations to "get with it." Her style may not be for every-one, but the message is salutary and will lighten the hearts of many who read it, as well as cause a few belly laughs in the process.

Another instance of how this material can be helpful to persons suffering from AIDS, as well as their loved ones, came to me quite fortu-itously one day when I happened by a local yogurt shop close to my university. A young man behind the counter, whom I did not recognize, identified himself as a former student of mine who had taken my NDE course a few years previously. Since there were no other customers in the store at the moment, he then turned from the cheerful, breezy clerk he had first appeared to be into someone with a much more serious expression and proceeded to confide to me the following information in a sort of *sotto voce*.

He was gay, he said, and in the last year or so had been with his lover, who had eventually succumbed to AIDS. He wanted me to know how useful my course had been to him and his friend because, as the latter was dying, my ex-student found that he was drawing on the NDE material he remembered from my class in order to comfort his lover. My ex-student said he had always meant to come into my office to tell me all this, but he never had. However, since I had just popped into his store and briefly back into his life on this occasion, he knew now was the time.

Another obvious "target group" for such information are hospice patients. While I would, of course, never urge that NDE material be foisted indiscriminately upon dying patients, those who are open to it appear to benefit greatly from exposure to it, especially with respect to the reduction in their fear of death. Certainly, in my twenty years of working in the field of near-death studies, I have met with or heard from many hospice workers—volunteers, nurses, chaplains, and even administrators—who have told me some very moving stories concerning how they have been able to make highly effective use of these materials in their encounters with dying patients.

And other investigators have reported further evidence of the ubiquity of NDEs in hospice settings, too. For example, critical care nurse Linda Barnett found that in a sample of sixty hospice nurses, 63 percent had worked with at least one NDEr patient.[7] Similarly, a hospice physician I know, Dr. Pamela Kircher, conducted a survey at a meeting of the National Hospice Organization that revealed that 73 percent of her sample of hospice-based health care professionals had heard descriptions of NDEs from their terminally ill patients.[8] As a result of the very frequency of such experiences in dying patients, the author of a highly regarded volume on dying and death in America has recently stated that in the 1990s, a working knowledge of NDEs has been "officially incorporated into hospice work, into hospice philosophy, and into work with the dying even in mainstream medical institutions."[9] "These stories are bringing a new kind of hope to the terminally ill," she concludes.[10]

In this regard, many NDE researchers have had cause to notice that quite a few NDErs themselves are drawn to work in this kind of setting, usually as volunteers, because they have come to feel such an affinity with the dying and know they can help such persons more easily make their transitions and with less fear. Although you might think that NDErs might naturally be tempted to share their own near-death encounters with the dying patients they care for, this is not necessarily the case. Among the many NDErs of my acquaintance who have found themselves involved with hospice care, I especially remember one named Pat, whom I met in the early 1980s in southern California. At that time, she had had her own NDE nineteen years earlier and since then had worked almost continuously in caring for the dying. When I specifically inquired how she had made use of her experience in her work, she surprised me by saying that she could only recall mentioning it on four occasions! So what NDErs share with the dying is not always their personal stories—though, of course, they often do—but just their being itself, which in some tacit but undeniable way helps to communicate their own lack of fear about death to their patients. What NDErs have become, not necessarily what they have gone through, is the final gift they have to offer those who are about to enter into the Light of death.

One prominent NDEr, Dannion Brinkley, who is the author of two popular books about his own NDE and his life afterward[11] has, however, given a great deal of his own personal life over to his hospice work (he has, by his own estimate, been with more than 150 patients, including his mother, who have died in his local hospice). Moreover, in his lectures and books, he has exhorted his listeners and readers to become involved in this work and, because he has become such an influential figure on the NDE scene during this decade, has doubtless been responsible for creating a flood of volunteers for these institutions and programs. All of this, of course, stems directly from the lessons he himself learned from his NDEs, which, through his personal charisma, he has succeeded in bringing to a mass audience.

Still another target group that invites special consideration here are the elderly—that category of persons that, while not exactly facing imminent death, as were those we have been referring to in the foregoing passages, nevertheless have to confront the prospect that their own deaths may not be that far off.

Not that much specific attention has been given to this group of persons as such from the standpoint of NDE applications, but recently a modest beginning was made by some of my students and me at the University of Connecticut. What we did, in brief, was to develop an educational program based on the NDE for senior citizens, which we were then able to present at selected senior citizen centers in Connecticut. The program itself was offered over three successive days and consisted of the following segments: (1) an introductory lecture on NDEs; (2) a presentation of videotapes featuring NDEs; and (3) a personal account of an NDE by a senior citizen, followed by questions and answers.

Our findings are only preliminary and our samples too small to support any firm generalizations, but questionnaires given both before and after these presentations revealed the following effects:

1. A decrease in fear of death.
2. An increase in belief that the moment of death will be peaceful.
3. An increase in belief in life after death.
4. A decrease in belief that life after death will be unpleasant.
5. An increase in belief that one will be reunited with deceased loved ones.
6. An increased belief in God.

Moreover, there was a very strong qualitative response to these programs, with many of the attendees expressing appreciation for the information and a desire to learn more about NDEs.

We did not have a chance to develop these programs further, but in lectures I have given on NDEs, especially in the United States, to audiences made up primarily of health care professionals, a number of persons later expressed interest to me in developing similar programs for the elderly in their localities. Perhaps, then, we shall be seeing more of these offerings in the years ahead, which will also permit us to evaluate these effects of these presentations, particularly over the long term.

## Contemplating Suicide

A second general domain in which NDE material has proved useful and has even, quite literally, saved lives has to do with suicide prevention. Here, of course, persons are not merely facing death but are impelled to seek it prematurely by their own hand. Fortunately, a number of suicidal persons have apparently been led to abandon their suicidal intent through either deliberate or inadvertent exposure to information about NDEs.

As an example of the first approach, I mention the role that the NDE has played in psychotherapy with suicidal patients. As far as I know, the first clinician to make use of NDE material in this context was a New York psychologist named John McDonagh. In 1979, he presented a paper at a psychological convention that described his success with several suicidal patients using a device he called "NDE bibliotherapy."[12] His "technique" was actually little more than having his patients read some relevant passages from Raymond Moody's book, *Reflections on Life after Life*, after which the therapist and his patient would discuss its implications for the latter's own situation. McDonagh reports that such an approach was generally quite successful not only in reducing suicidal thoughts but also in preventing the deed altogether.

The effectiveness of this approach seems to have stemmed largely from the patient's having acquired a sense from NDE accounts that suicide would be useless because after death, one would not only have to continue to deal with the besetting problems, but would no longer have the opportunity to solve them. As one of McDonagh's suicidal patients, who, while breaking into tears upon hearing some of the passages in Moody's book, exclaimed: "There's no way out!" McDonagh adds: "She became convinced that she would have to work through her problem in this life, as difficult as that might be."[13]

In addition, one would now have to suffer the further consequences of an irrevocable action, with a knowledge of the pain that would have brought to others. In short, coming to realize that, in effect, committing suicide would—if the implications of NDEs are to be credited—not succeed in bringing about an obliteration of consciousness itself forced suicidal patients to find other means to cope with their problems. Suicide was no longer an option because, in a certain sense, it was now seen to be impossible: One could kill only the body but never the self.

Since McDonagh's pioneering efforts, other clinicians knowledgeable about the NDE who have had the opportunity to counsel suicidal patients have also reported similar success. Perhaps the most notable of these therapists is Bruce Greyson, a psychiatrist now at the University of Virginia, whose specialty as a clinician has been suicidology. He is also the author of a classic paper on NDEs and suicide, which the specialist may wish to consult for its therapeutic implications.[14]

Quite apart from the clinicians who have developed this form of what we might call "NDE-assisted therapy," I can draw upon my own personal experience here to provide additional evidence of how the NDE has helped to deter suicide. The following case would be an example of the way NDE information may come to play an adventitious role in a person's life.

Several years ago, I heard from (and later met) a woman in New York who had attended one of my lectures. In the course of a series of letters, she informed me that she had suffered permanent neurological damage and had come close to death as a result of chemical poisoning. Her illness was prolonged and, although she had had no previous knowledge of such states, she found herself drifting in and out of what we might call near-death realms. While in these realms, she was provided with many spiritual revelations that were later to serve as the basis for an entirely different way of life that came to be organized about living in harmony with nature and with the arts of healing.

However, during the first phases of her illness, these insights were greatly overshadowed by the physical and psychological suffering she was undergoing, which seemed to be unrelenting, and she fell into a dark depression so severe that she was on the verge of suicide. "Illness," she wrote to me, "had shredded the fabric of my life and the urge to let go of its remaining threads was frequently both tempting and terrifying." Also, since she had never heard of NDEs, she was very confused about the inner experiences she was having and feared that in addition to her other problems, she might be becoming mentally unhinged as well.

> One day, while browsing through a bookstore in search of information that might help to explain the mystifying spiritual changes in my life, books on the near-death experience caught my eye, the first being Raymond Moody's *Life after Life*. Several hours elapsed in front of the same bookshelf as I scanned the chapters of this classic work and other books on the subject, eventually purchasing a number of them. On many profoundly moving pages I found words which seemed to unlock the doors of mystery and fear behind which I had hidden for more than three years. References to experiences similar to my own ... all affirming the ineffability and ecstasy of the near-death experience instantly dispersed the clouds of fear and doubt about the validity of my perceptions.

From then on, she was a different woman and began following a spiritual path in her life. As she later confessed to me, however, had she had not discovered this information about the NDE at this crucial and apparently hopeless time in her life, she feels quite certain that she would have probably have chosen to end it forthwith.

Here, we have a case with an clear parallel to that of Deborah Drumm, except in this instance the menace was suicide rather than death by cancer. Nevertheless, the psychological outcome was precisely the same: In each example, information about the NDE rescued these women from despair and gave new spiritual meaning to their lives. And just as Deborah Drumm could hardly be unique in her response to her discovery of NDEs, so, too, we must suppose that there have been other suicidally inclined individuals who, like the woman from New York, find that the accidental discovery of the NDE itself provides a life-saving deliverance.

## DEALING WITH THE GRIEF OF BEREAVEMENT

From my many years of involvement with the NDE, it will not surprise you to learn that my files are filled with many letters attesting to how much comfort and hope NDE accounts have brought to bereaved persons, especially those who have had to cope with the death of a child. Here, I will only present a relatively small sampling of these testimonies, beginning with and emphasizing those where a parent has been forced to confront the loss of a beloved child.

I will start with a case that is particularly dear to me and one that, more than any other, elicited the strongest response from readers of my book, *Heading toward Omega*, where it was originally published. Though I will be able to give only the briefest summary of it here, this story is of special value because it shows the way in which having an NDE in itself can virtually *eliminate* all grief about the death of a child and—though you may be incredulous—even replace it with joy. How this could possibly be, I will now attempt to tell, but for the complete story, you may wish to consult the relevant pages in *Heading toward Omega*.[15]

The woman I there called Ann had her NDE at twenty-two when delivering her second child, Tari. In her NDE, she found herself drawn by a great force toward a bright light, and eventually, emerging from it, was a radiant figure. Of him, Ann said,

> When he took hold of my hand, I immediately knew him to be the greatest friend I had. I also knew that I was a very special person to him. The thrill of this touch of hands exceeds anything I have ever experienced on earth.

But then, Ann learns from this being some news that would be expected to cause any new mother the worst dread possible:

> Without vocal communication he "told me" he had come for my child. "My child?" I asked, scarcely able to contain my joy and happiness over the news that one of my own children would be going back with *him*! It was, I knew, a very high honor to be selected for this. I had the honor of being a mother of

a very extra special child, and I was so proud that he had picked *my* child ...
and it never occurred to me to refuse to give my child to this man.

The light being told Ann that he would be back for Tari in four days,
and although Tari seemed to be fine when born, she soon sickened, and
exactly four days after her birth, as Ann had been forewarned, her baby
died. Ann's nurse, feeling compelled to tell her this news, was devastated.

"Oh, God!" she wailed. "Your doctor should have been here by now! I'm
not supposed to tell you, but I can't let you go on believing Tari is alive.
She died this morning."
"Are you okay?" she asked.
"Yes," I told her much too calmly under the circumstances.
"This is the fourth day!" (I felt *joy!*)
In the weeks following, I felt no grief of my own loss, but I felt sorry for
my friends and relatives who didn't know where Tari was, and couldn't
believe—really believe—that my "experience" was anything more than a
vivid dream.

Ann concluded her letter to me with these comments:

It would have been easier, I think, to try to forget my own name, than to
forget that wonderful feeling, that surge of sheer joy I had felt when he
took my hand, and told me he had come for *my* child. That was the greatest
moment I've ever known....
Well, I soon realized that my acceptance back into this world depended
upon pretending to forget, and "pretending" to grieve the loss of my baby. So
I did this for everybody else's sake—except my husband, who believed me,
and gained some comfort from it, secondhand....
I had three more children after Tari's birth. My beloved husband died in
my arms at home sixteen years later. My firstborn son lived to be twenty-five
and was killed in a car accident (instantly—no time for pain or suffering)
seven years after the death of my husband. My grief was softened and
shortened each time. People said, "She's in shock now, she'll grieve more
later." Later they said, "She must be a very strong person to live through
what she's had to live through so calmly." Neither statement was true....
They aren't dead. They are all alive, busy and waiting for me. Our separation
is only temporary and very short, compared to all of eternity.

The inner knowledge experiencers like Ann have that "there is no
death" not only enables them to release, sometimes even with joy, their
beloved ones, but sometimes to help others grieve, as Ann was able to
console her husband. Another instance where an NDEr was able to play
this role, in this case, for her entire family, involved Stella, one of the trio
of NDEr/healers we met in the preceding chapter. Here, Stella was confronted with the tragic accidental death of her three-year-old grand-

daughter, Marissa, one of a set of twins. Her son was doing some construction work in the yard and had asked the twins' brother to hold their hands. Just as he was backing up the dump truck, however, Marissa broke free and was caught under the back wheel. She died instantly. About this incident, Stella later wrote me:

> Having experienced the NDE I was able to *know*, not just "hope" that Marissa's spirit continues. I believe that silent, strong "knowing" helped our family through. I didn't speak about it, I didn't have to. Yet, I felt that each family member, as they spoke to me, was reaffirming their own beliefs in life after death. Within three weeks after the tragedy, our pastor friend stated that he had never seen a family come back so quickly from such devastation.

Of course, it is not just NDErs who are helped to deal with otherwise devastating loss by their NDEs. *Many persons* who have become familiar with these experiences have also benefited greatly from the knowledge and comfort they provide, as they have often attested to me and other NDE researchers. Recently, in the course of reviewing a book by a colleague, I came across a very poignant and instructive example of this very effect for a nonexperiencer, which I would like to share you with next. First, however, let me give you just a little background on the book itself, which is called *Children of the Light* and was written by Cherie Sutherland, the Australian NDE researcher I have mentioned previously.

In the course of giving lectures on NDEs, Sutherland found herself meeting or hearing from a substantial number of grieving parents, who expressed to her how much stories of NDEs had helped to succor them in their own loss, and, eventually, she was led to persons, some of them still children themselves, who had had NDEs as kids—and *their* stories were even more helpful to those dealing with the desolating anguish that the death of a child often unleashes. Sutherland came to write *Children of Light* out of a desire to bring these stories to a larger audience, particularly to parents and siblings of a deceased child, in order to spread a blanket of comfort over those who are still grieving and to accelerate the process of healing from one of life's most unbearable ruptures.

And Sutherland herself presents some compelling testimony throughout her book to show just how healing it can be to such parents when they learn about the NDEs of children. Her book, in fact, begins with one very touching account of this kind of discovery. A mother named Maria had lost her five-year-old son in a tragic drowning incident, and was in despair over it. In addition to all her natural grief, she was tormented by questions concerning whether her son had been frightened as he was drowning, or whether he had cried out desperately and in vain for his parents to save him. As she testifies, she was obsessed with the question, "Was it terrible to die?"

In time, and quite unexpectedly, she came across a story of a childhood NDE based on a *near-drowning* incident that had much in common with the actual drowning of her son. Reading it was a revelation and immediately provided a powerful anodyne that relieved years of protracted suffering, guilt, and doubt. In Maria's own words,

> I felt exhilarated after I had finished. I was so astonished by the almost identical conditions at the two scenes of accident, and the two little boys of virtually the same age, that I had no trouble believing that this "coincidence" was, indeed, the answer I had been searching for. From that day on, my thirst for more and more information about the NDE was unquenchable. I read everything I could find about it, and with each new account, the bottomless, black despair I had felt for so long receded, and a wonderful new hope was born somewhere deep within me.[16]

Now, through the instrumentality of Sutherland's book, Maria's own experience of healing can itself be a source of solace and hope for bereaved parents and others who have suffered a similar loss. And from reading stories like Maria's and the many moving accounts of childhood NDEs that Sutherland provides in this book, there are even more benefits to be derived, as Maria's own narrative suggests:

> Not long afterwards ... I realized that the devastating grief and suffering I had been through had produced after-effects similar to those following a near-death experience: I was no longer afraid of death; I felt more genuine compassion for others; I wanted to help others; I was more aware of others' pain. In a sense, I too had died and been brought back to life ... [And] I now believe that death is truly a transition from our limited existence into a splendid new life, an adventure beyond our wildest dreams.[17]

Of course, my own files are replete with similar stories of the consoling power that NDE visions bring to the bereaved who have not had NDEs themselves. Although the following case highlights one of my own books, I only cite it to illustrate what is true for NDE literature in general, and will let this one example serve to stand for the many such testimonies I myself have received.

> I just had to write after reading your book, *Heading toward Omega*. My life has been a living nightmare for the last two years, but after reading your book I have found the strength needed to go on and to live. I think that a parent's worst fear is that something will happen to their child, and my worst fear

came true two years ago when my 18-year-old son was killed instantly in a car wreck. After the shock wore off, my fear turned to what happened to him. Where is he now? Is there really a life after death? The religion I was raised in wasn't any help as they taught of a "God" of wrath and unforgiveness to a child dying in "sin." As a result I turned away from religion and "God."

But after reading your book I think I understand a little better now that "the light" is not the God I was taught but one of peace and love. I have read many books in the past two years … but none has affected me the way your book did. I can now accept the fact that I'll never see my son again in this life, but I know he is at peace and I'll see him again when it's my time to go. For now he is with "the light" and has found and peace and love of family and friends (also killed in the same wreck) in a life after death. Maybe he was trying to tell me this in repeated dreams when he would come to me and say, "Mom, see I'm not hurt, everything is all right." But I just wasn't ready to listen.

Finally, let me present one further case, which, though it has echoes of all of those I have offered in this section on bereavement and the NDE, has some special features that make it particularly instructive for us. First of all, it involves not the death of a child, but one that is much more common and that many of us will have to confront in our own lifetime—that of a spouse. Second, it shows the way in which being present at the death of a beloved person can sometimes instill some of the qualities of NDEs themselves. Third, it indicates how subsequent familiarity with the literature on NDEs can transform grief and ultimately lead to a life of service toward others. In this instance, therefore, we will be able to discern still another and impressive contagious effect of the NDE.

Peter had loved his wife very much, and when she died from cancer after ten years of marriage, hard times awaited him. As he wrote to me:

> She died from an inoperable brain tumor and lung cancer, and I was privi-
> leged to help nurse her and care for her at home during the final weeks of her
> illness. I had absolutely no idea that any change would come about in me
> after her death, at which I was present. She died peacefully, surrounded by
> love, and I held her hand as she left, and asked God to take good care of
> her. After that I went through hell. I did not want to live. She had been my
> life. Everything in my world collapsed.

He then went on to describe how his transformation took place, slowly and painfully. It began with doing volunteer work at the hospital where his wife had been treated. He felt the need to be close to persons who suffered—"the way she suffered," he said. Gradually, he returned to life and saw that "there was a small part of me that was alive and growing—like a new green shoot growing out of a fallen tree trunk." He began attending church but stopped after one year because "I could not accept the dogma and because the churches could not answer the deepest questions that were troubling my heart and mind."

Finally, he was led to the literature on NDEs, life after death, and related subjects, and these, he said, brought him what he had been searching for.

> As a result, and with my own overpowering conviction that Gloria had not gone into oblivion, but somewhere, somehow, was still alive and even close at hand as an intact soul with memory and personality, I began to fashion—or maybe it was fashioned for me—a philosophy of life and death that was unlike anything I had thought or dreamed about in my life up to that point.

Peter then underwent a change of vision similar to those of experiencers: He began to see the unity in all forms of life, found himself reflecting on the nature of consciousness and on nature itself during long walks, opened himself to the simple everyday natural beauty of life—"birds, trees, clouds, water"—which aroused in him a long-dead feeling of hope. And he noted other changes, too:

> Since that night of June 18, 1985 [when his wife had died], I have had no fear of death. That was an immediate transformation, and two and a half years later, it has not changed one whit. I have a hunger for knowledge on spiritual matters, and I feel it in the sense of preparing myself for something greater. I seem to have lost all interest in, and desire for, material things. My interest now is in BEING, not HAVING.

He wondered about the meaning of his life and asked himself what his mission could be, for he now knew he had a mission—like everyone else. Volunteer work with suffering and dying persons is the way he has chosen.

> The most powerful driving-force in my life is my belief in life after death. And that what we do in this physical world has a direct bearing upon what we will face in the next stage. I have had no illuminating experience such as many of the NDErs had, no personal message, no experience with the Light, but I have arrived at this point in my life for some reason, and what it tells me is that I am supposed to help others. As Albert Schweitzer said: "Whoever is spared personal pain must feel himself called to help in diminishing the pain of others."

Peter's journey and his life of service continue, but his story is primarily of interest here because it shows how grief, when aided by the kind of knowledge that NDEs provide, can actually sometimes lead to a transformation of worldview and personal values that is virtually identical to that of NDErs themselves. Granted, Peter himself did much to bring about this transformation born of his grief for his wife, but his example may well inspire others to follow a similar path when confronted with an otherwise inconsolable loss.

In light of this raft of personal testimony on the value of the NDE for bereavement, it occurred to me that just as we might develop educational programs for senior citizens, we could also tailor-make some for the needs of bereaved persons. Several years ago, therefore, some students and I once again began putting together such presentations to be offered to preexisting bereavement groups. They were generally along the same lines as those for our senior citizens, only more compact in form, and our preliminary testing showed them to produce similar, though somewhat lesser effects. Nevertheless, we were encouraged by the response and feel that this is yet another area where further work using NDE materials would certainly be warranted.

## FROM NDEs to ADCs

In addition to the role of NDEs in helping bereaved persons, it has recently been suggested that other similar experiences might also be used to serve the same purpose. Of these, perhaps the single most relevant variety of death-related experience—which represents a direct and obvious extension of the NDE itself—would be what have been called "after-death communications," or ADCs for short.

This term has been now been used by several writers, but the principal proponents of the utility of ADCs for bereavement are Bill and Judy Guggenheim, who several years ago wrote a massive book on the subject with the regrettably treacly title of *Hello from Heaven!* The tabloidal title, however, should not blind us to the value of the book itself, which, in my opinion, represents a major contribution to bereavement studies.

For this book, the Guggenheims personally amassed more than 3,300 accounts of cases indicative of *real*—not hallucinatory—contact with deceased loved ones, of which they have chosen to present about 10 percent, some 350 stories. And, as one reads through this extensive collection of testimonies, the implications of their findings become increasingly hard to deny. In summary, they seem strongly to suggest that *those dear to us who have died continue to exist after death, and that they can communicate to us in ways that help to heal us of our grief and enable us to let go.* Furthermore, many of the vignettes the Guggenheims recount have strong evidentiality; that is, they appear to be authentic instances of postmortem contact, and not just psychological fantasies rooted in understandable grief.

To illustrate some of these ADCs, and to make it clear how they can help in bereavement, consider—and ponder—the following cases.

Leslie, thirty-nine, is a volunteer worker in Virginia. She had this happy reunion with her father four months after he died of cancer:

> I had just gone to bed and turned the light off when I saw my father standing in the doorway! All the lights were out in the house, yet I could see him very clearly because there was a glow around him. I kept thinking, "This is really Daddy! This is really him!" I was so excited that I sat up and said, "Daddy!" I wanted to go over and touch him, and I started to get out of bed. He smiled and said, "No, you cannot touch me now." I began to cry and kept saying, "Let me come to you." He said, "No, you can't do that. But I want you to know that I am all right. Everything is fine. I am always with you."
>
> Then he paused and said, "I have to go look in on your mother and Curtis now." Curtis is my son, and he and my mother were in the next room. I got up and followed my father to the hallway. But he disappeared—he just faded away. So I went back to bed and kept saying to myself, "This is just your grief. Daddy wasn't really here." Then I finally fell asleep after tossing and turning for quite some time.
>
> The next morning I got up, and Curtis, who was three, almost four at the time, came out in the hallway. He said, "Mommy, I saw Granddaddy last night!" My mouth fell open and I said, "You did?" He said, "Yes! He came in my room. He was standing by my bed." How could a three-year-old come up with that? I questioned him, "Were you dreaming?" He said, "No, Mommy. I had my eyes open. I was awake. I saw him!"
>
> So then I knew that Daddy had to have actually been there. There was no way to refute what had happened. It was a wonderful experience for me because I learned that love continues on.[18]

A second case provides an example of a *simultaneously shared* ADC: Benjamin, age twenty-one, works in the publishing business in Iowa. He and his wife, Mollie, age twenty, reported having virtually identical ADC experiences with his mother just a few days after she died of cancer.

Here is Mollie's account:

> The night of his mother's funeral, my husband, Ben, and I went to her house and visited with his family. We were there quite late. As we got back in the car, I looked at the front door. I saw his mother standing in the open doorway waving good-bye to us! She looked like she normally did—it was definitely her! She looked very peaceful, very healthy, and younger. In times past, when we would visit her, she always stood by that door and waved good-bye. So this was just like she had done many times before.
>
> I looked over to Ben and said, "Did you ...?" and he started crying

real hard. I realized we had both seen his mother at the same time, but Ben wasn't able to speak. As soon as I looked over to him, she was gone. I think the reason I was allowed to see his mother was for confirmation for Ben so he would know she was not a figment of his imagination.

And this is Benjamin's account:

The day of my mother's funeral, my wife, Mollie, and I visited my cousin and her husband at Mother's house. We stayed well into the night, and then Mollie and I got into the car. I put the key in the ignition, and as I did I looked up. About ten yards away, I saw my mother standing in the doorway behind the clear glass storm door! She would always stand in the doorway out of kindness and courtesy to make sure we had gotten safely to the car. This was a common practice of hers—I had seen it a thousand times. The inside door was open so the light from the house was illuminating Mother from the back and the porch light was illuminating her from the front. She appeared to be in good health and was very solid. She was there waving good-bye. She seemed relieved—less tired, less stressful. I got the definite impression that this was a "don't worry" type of message.

Instantly, I had a tremendous physical feeling, almost like being pinned to the ground. It was like a wave came over me and went completely through me from head to toe. It seemed like an eternity yet it seemed like a split second. I tried to speak but I couldn't. At the same time, Mollie said, "Ben, I just saw your mother in the doorway!" I bowed my head and said, "So did I," and I began to cry. That was the first time I had shed any tears over my mother's death. I have never wept so hard in my entire life. And I felt a sense of relief, like "good-bye for now."[19]

And, finally, from the Guggenheim's collection, this corker of a story:

Adele is a television producer in the Northwest. Fortunately, she followed the guidance of her nine-year-old son, Jeremy, after he died of leukemia:

My son, Jeremy, died the day after Mother's Day. Three weeks later, just before I woke up, I heard him ask, "What are you going to do with my money?" I said, "What money?" And he said, "All the money that you saved for me." I had totally forgotten about Jeremy's savings account, and I didn't even know where he had hidden his savings book. I asked what he wanted me to do with it because obviously it must have been very important to him. Jeremy said, "I want you to go see Malcolm." Malcolm is a friend of mine who is a diamond wholesaler. I said, "Well, whatever is in that account isn't enough to go see Malcolm!" And Jeremy replied, "Yes it is! Just go see Malcolm, and you'll understand what I'm talking about. When you see it, you will know. You will think of me." Then he was gone and I woke up.

Although I thought this was kind of crazy, I looked around the house for my son's savings book but couldn't find it. Several days later, I happened to be in the same building as Malcolm's wholesale jewelry store. So I popped in there and started looking around. I saw a beautiful butterfly necklace with a diamond in it. It suddenly clicked what Jeremy had said. "You'll know it when you see it. It will remind you of me." My heart started pounding and I got kind of nervous. I asked Malcolm how much the necklace would cost. After some figuring and some bantering back and forth, he told me $200. I told him I would come back later.

My heart was still pounding when I went back to my office and called the bank. I explained that I couldn't find my son's savings book and wanted to know how much money was in his account. In a few minutes, I was told the amount was $200.47! I went back to Malcolm's store after work and bought the butterfly necklace with Jeremy's money. Now I don't go anywhere without it. I can touch it and say, "My son gave me this for my last Mother's Day with him!"[20]

These very poignant and moving stories touch our hearts and give us added confidence that the testimony of so many NDErs throughout this book that there is no death is a truth that we can accept and live by. Thus, we might say that NDEs + ADCs = immense hope for all those who are burdened with grief and tormenting questions about the continued existence of their loved ones.

Although the Guggenheims' book is a rich treasury of contemporary accounts of ADCs and an extremely significant contribution to the literature on bereavement, the stories it tells are astonishingly common, even if, until recently, not commonly talked about. I have also encountered them in my work, and would like to conclude this section by telling you about one that had special meaning for me.

It had to do with the death of Ann, Tari's mother.

A few years ago, I received a letter from Ann's son, from whom I had never before heard, informing me that his mother had died of cancer shortly after Christmas. As he went on to explain to me,

On the day she died, my family was to have celebrated Christmas with my dad and Ann at the nursing home. But she crossed over a half hour before our arrival. At the house my eyes were drawn to the bookshelf where I saw your book, Heading toward Omega. I was very curious about this because I had recently read The Omega Project, and also because I had never noticed that book on her shelf before. Inside the front cover were your letters to Ann. I asked my dad about the book and he said I could take it.

So I browsed through the book quickly after discovering from your letters that Ann had written you about her experience. I was astounded reading her story that the topic had never come up between us. But I took it as a message (the "coincidence" that I saw the book that day) from Ann even after her death, that we should be assured she was well and happy.

As the son's letter continued, the rest of Ann's surprising farewell message was quickly unfolded to me:

> Her story does not end there, however. On December 31, we attended her funeral, a sad but inspirational service at which her godson, the son of her best friend, called her "a saint."
>
> That evening, as I was putting my three young daughters (ages six, four, and three) to bed, I went downstairs to my oldest daughter Mallory's room. I was surprised to see her head buried in the pillow, as she usually waits for me to rub her neck and back. As I entered the room she lifted her head and said, "I'm not sleeping."
>
> I said, "What were you doing?"
>
> "I was crying," was her reply.
>
> "Why were you crying?"
>
> "Because I saw Grandma Ann up by the ceiling."
>
> When I asked her about it further, she said Ann "was dressed in a white suit and she looked like an angel."
>
> I asked what Ann did. "She told me she loved me a lot, and that this was the last time I would see her."
>
> Later, when I asked Mallory why that made her cry, she said, "Because I was so happy, and sometimes when you're happy, you cry."
>
> Of course, it is common for recently passed people to appear to their spouse or child, and I pondered the fact that because my dad would not be open to belief, Ann had chosen Mallory to send her message back from the other side. I have long suspected at least two of my daughters have abilities I long ago forgot, but they have "humored" me by not telling me they have superior senses to mine. I asked Mallory why she decided to tell me this time.
>
> "Ann convinced me to tell you," was her answer.

I remember that after reading this letter, while still holding it in my hands, I could not help wondering—but my wondering was really more a knowing—whether my dear friend, Ann, was now finally reunited, not only with that radiant being she called her greatest friend, but with her beloved Tari, whom she had so joyfully surrendered so many years before.

What do you think?

## CONCLUSIONS: THE REVISIONING OF DEATH IN THE LIGHT OF NDEs

The many stories I have related to you in this chapter, combined with the statistics quoted at its outset, together serve to illustrate the thesis I advanced to begin with, namely, that there is a new view of death that is now emerging from two decades of research into NDEs and allied phenomena. One cannot read the testimonies of this chapter without feeling a sense that we are finally beginning to see, in our own time, the dark curtain of death to which we have so long become accustomed parting to reveal it standing in its true light—Light itself. Where once we had seen death as a final, terrible, and irrevocable separation, we now understand that it only represents the continuity of life in realms that are normally, but not always, closed to our ordinary sense perception. There is, after all, a kind of commerce between these realms, between the living-here and the living-elsewhere, and nowhere is there death as we have known and believed it to be. In the light of the NDE, death is nothing more than *the illusion of separateness and finality,* and those who can believe in this vision of death, like NDErs themselves, lose all fear of it, for how can you fear that which does not exist?

Moreover, we have seen just how healing this new understanding of death is. Those facing death do not fear it; they know the Light awaits them. Those who wish to take their own life learn that it is impossible to do so; there is *only* life. Those who grieve are comforted and sometimes even transformed. And those blessed with a vision of a loved one who has left them know with certitude that their beloved still lives and that the connection has not been broken. In the face of all of this, the grim reaper skulks away, exposed as the fraud he always was. Light, the great liberator, has freed us by showing itself to us in a thousand ways.

And this view of death is by no means confined mainly to those interested in NDEs and like subjects or, even more broadly, to individuals associated with the death and dying movement. Rather, as the kind of applied work, based on the NDE, has gained momentum, particularly in the past decade, more and more persons who are a part of the mainstream culture have begun to take note of it. We have already remarked, for example, about how this work and perspective have already begun to permeate the hospice movement here in America, and are even coming to influence the treatment of the dying and care for the bereaved in more traditional institutions.

And more and more books are beginning to appear, not just on NDEs, but on the very theme of this chapter—how to use the knowledge about NDEs to deal with death, dying, and bereavement. We have already mentioned in passing some of these, such as Marilyn Webb's monumental study of the art of dying in modern American life, *The Good Death,* and Ganga Stone's irreverent but effective treatment of this new view of death, *The Start of Conversation.* But there are others, too, such as Sogyal Rinpoche's *The Tibetan Book of Living and Dying* and Christine Longaker's *Facing Death and Finding Hope*, that are finding large and responsive audiences. All of these books have extensive discussions of the uses of NDEs in the context of death and bereavement work. Furthermore, a number of textbooks on death and dying also have begun to include sections describing research and applications of NDEs.[21] The Light of the NDE seems to be shining everywhere these days to banish death to its own underworld of shadows and phantasms to haunt us no longer.

I hope what I have been able to share with you in this chapter—especially the stories that I have narrated—will help to instill this new understanding of death in you and begin even more to erode whatever lingering fears and doubts you may have about what it holds for you and those close to you. Certainly, this would be the universal wish of NDErs themselves—that their brief glimpse of the transcendental field of Light, at once our true home and our true nature, could somehow be of direct benefit to all of us living and dying on planet earth.

## Chapter Twelve

# Crossing over into the Light

The concerns of the previous chapter—how the NDE can help us deal with death—naturally raise the perennially speculative issue of what happens following the cessation of all biological function. Although no living person, however sapient, can bestow on us absolute knowledge concerning life after death, many NDErs nevertheless speak with great certitude on this point and as a group are convinced, almost unconditionally, that some kind of postmortem existence awaits us all. Indeed, even a casual perusal of the NDE literature would be sufficient to demonstrate just how prevalent these beliefs are among those still living who have doubtless come the closest to crossing the bourne from which Shakespeare taught— wrongly, as it turns out—no traveler returns.

Having now read so many narratives of NDEs, you may already have a deep grasp of just why those who have returned from death's brink to tell us their stories testify with such assurance about the self-evidentiality of an afterlife. But before we begin to examine the virtually universal belief structure of NDErs on this point, it pays to take a few moments here at the outset to focus in closely and dilate upon the very moment that seems to presage the transition from physical life to another kind of life altogether. It is just here that we can see most clearly how the individual is confronted with such a powerful vision and feelings so overwhelming that it is simply impossible not to recognize with one's whole being that one has crossed over into Greater Life.

To illustrate this point of transition and awakening in the NDE, let me draw on the account of a good friend of mine, Jayne Smith, who now lives in South Carolina, but whom I met about 1980, when she was still a resident of Philadelphia. I originally presented Jayne's story in full in my book, *Heading toward Omega*, but here, I want to zero in on just that portion of it in which she comes to realize that she has died:

> The next thing I knew … I was standing in a mist and I knew *immediately* that I had died and I was so happy that I had died but I was still alive. And I cannot tell you how I *felt*. It was, "Oh, God, I'm dead, but I'm here! I'm me!" And I started pouring out these enormous feelings of gratitude because I still existed and yet I knew perfectly well that I had died.
>
> While I was pouring out these feelings … the mist started being infiltrated with enormous light and the light just got brighter and brighter and brighter and, it is so bright but it doesn't hurt your eyes, but it's brighter than anything you've ever experienced in your life.… And this enormously bright light seemed almost to cradle me. I just seemed to exist in it and be nurtured by it and the feeling just became more and more and more ecstatic and glorious and perfect. And everything about it was—if you took the one thousand best things that ever happened to you in your life and multiplied by a million, maybe you could get close to this feeling, I don't know. But you're engulfed by it and you begin to know a lot of things.
>
> I remember I knew that everything, everywhere in the universe was OK, that the plan was perfect. That whatever was happening—the wars, famine, whatever—was OK. Everything was perfect. Somehow it was all a part of the perfection, that we didn't have to be concerned about it at all. And the whole time I was in this state, it seemed infinite. It was timeless. I was just an infinite being in perfection. And love and safety and security and knowing that nothing could happen to you and you're home forever. That you're safe forever. And that everybody else was.[1]

For Jayne, this was indisputably not only a world of perfection, but it was also eternity itself ("It was timeless") into which she, and everyone, returns following physical life. Here, one enters into a state of exhaustless bliss, unceasing preternatural light, and total knowledge—a perfection so complete that one is enabled to see the perfection in all things.

This is the dazzling vision of the gateway into the afterlife that is so frequently, if rarely so eloquently, recounted by those NDErs whose journeys carry them this far.

If Jayne's epiphany had been yours—if you could, for example, even begin to imagine what it would feel like if the thousand best things in your life could be multiplied by a million—could you possibly doubt that you were experiencing a true vision of the world beyond death?

NDEs cannot, and many of them, of course, tell the same story of this transitional moment and of the realizations that come with it. In these accounts, one finds repeatedly the same elements that Jayne mentions—the heralding light, the sense of returning home, the feeling of absolute safety, the knowledge that no one is excluded from this domain, and even, in some cases, an insight that Jayne does not express here: that we ourselves, in *our essence*, are made of same light that we glimpse there. Here is just a small seasoning of these revelations that come from NDErs who have found themselves where Jayne did.

An experiencer named Bill wrote me the following:

> I looked further down the tunnel and saw the light. I realized immediately where I was. The light was home. I knew that I could only return here. There was no question of losing this place. It was home, and I, and everyone else, came here and there was no possible way to avoid it or miss it. It was the only thing that was guaranteed, returning here.

Nel told me the following:

> My experience was not deep enough to go further than the Light and the presence, but I know that when the time is right and my physical body dies, I will go on living in the Light and in the life, and I will find the entire world up there.

And, finally, my friend Steve, in one of his letters, observed what the essential teaching of the NDE is in this respect:

> It's about a life that has no end point.... We have this light within us. Inside, we are all like him. We are all made to become like the person composed of the intense and loving Light who meets us at the end of the tunnel.

With such experiences as these to inform their views, it is little wonder, then, that NDErs as a whole have beliefs about an afterlife that are stated with rock-solid conviction. To appreciate this, we have only to sample briefly a few typical opinions from some other NDErs I have met and worked with over the years. Here, after having peered into these once obscure and shadowy realms with Light-aided eyes, is what they have come to believe afterward about an afterlife:

> I *know* there is life after death! Nobody can shake my belief. I have no doubt—it's peaceful and nothing to be feared. I don't know what's beyond what I experienced, but it's plenty for me.... I only know that death is not to be feared, only dying.
> Upon entering that light ... the atmosphere, the energy, it's total pure energy, it's total knowledge, it's total love—everything about it is definitely the afterlife, if you will.... As a result of that [experience], I have very little apprehension about dying my natural death ... because if death is anything, anything at all like what I experienced, it's gotta be the most wonderful thing to look forward to, absolutely the most wonderful thing.

> I have a message to others living an ordinary earth life.... "There is more." Our identity will continue to be—in a greater way. Friends will not be lost to you. You will know a beauty and peace and love [and] that loving light that encompasses and fills you is God.
>
> This experience was a blessing to me because now I know with certainty that there is a separation of body and soul, and there is life after death.
>
> It gave me an answer to what I think everyone must really wonder about at one time or another in this life. Yes, there is an afterlife! More beautiful than anything we can begin to imagine. Once you know it, there is nothing that can equal it. You just know!

What is striking about these quotes—and, as I will show, they are representative of the views of most NDErs—is not merely their unanimity of opinion but the tone of absolute certitude that pervades them. In these statements, we find not just a conventional expression of belief in an afterlife but an unshakable assertion of a spiritual truth that has apparently been unmistakably apprehended in and through the Light. Thus, we begin to see here the power of the NDE, not just to compel belief in an afterlife, but seemingly to confer a kind of *knowledge* that from a subjective point of view is incontrovertible. In short, the typical NDEr knows without question that life is not a dead end but continues in an exalted form after the physical body has finally ceased to function.

That these quotations are not merely highly selected examples of these convictions can likewise be easily shown by reference to various statistical surveys of NDErs that have been conducted by a number of researchers since the early 1980s. One of the earliest of these studies, for example, was carried out by the cardiologist, Michael Sabom, and published in his book, *Recollections of Death*, in 1982. There, he reported that of his sample of sixty-one NDErs, forty-seven, or 77 percent, said that their NDE had led to an increase in their belief in life after death. In my own most recent large-scale research study of NDEs, *The Omega Project*, I found that 86 percent of my seventy-four NDErs likewise professed an increase in belief in life after death following their experience. Similarly, in a recent study of fifty-one NDErs, Cassandra Musgrave stated that whereas only 22 percent of her sample "definitely believed" in life after death before their NDE, fully 92 percent of her sample asserted that they "definitely believed" afterward.[2] And, along these same lines, perhaps the most compelling set of findings was provided several years ago by the Australian NDE researcher, Cherie Sutherland. In her study,[3] based on fifty Australian NDErs, she found that prior to their NDE, belief in life after death was essentially a "fifty–fifty" proposition; in other words, about half of her sample were believers, whereas the others either were not, or, in a few cases, had formed no opinion on the question. Afterward, there was not a single NDEr who did not believe in some form of life after death! In short, following an NDE, there was complete unanimity of belief on this matter. Regardless of what her respondents had believed before and why, the NDE was manifestly sufficient to override all doubt—in everyone.

The ubiquity of these statements and the tone of certainty with which they are averred have plainly not been lost on those of us who have come to take an interest in the NDE. Used to the skepticism of scientists and philosophers, or even the sometimes wishy-washy equivocations of to-day's religious leaders, we could easily justify, if we cared to, a fashionable agnosticism about life after death or simply relegate the belief to history's dustbin of discarded fancies. But when hoards of NDErs from all over the world—*including* scientists, physicians, and philosophers, as well as religious persons—begin speaking, as in a single voice, of their certainty concerning a postmortem life, *based on their own experience with death*, an embarrassing fracture in the wall of received opinion begins to show itself. To paraphrase an old advertising slogan in America, "When NDErs begin to talk, people listen." And in listening, they come, if not always to believe, at least to be open to belief again. And, of course, for those who were already given to belief on this matter, the nondenominational testimony of so many NDErs can only reinforce their preexisting faith.

In short, here, too, we can already discern still another facet of the NDE as a benign virus. Increasing familiarity on the part of a large public with the effects of these experiences on belief in life after death is forcing a contemporary reconsideration of the issue, and, for many, it seems, the collective surety of NDErs on this point has been persuasive. As a result, the attention given to NDEs these days is not only bringing about a new view of death, as I argued in the last chapter, but is currently *renewing* a traditional belief in an afterlife that appeared to be heading toward extinction in the modern secular world.

## THE IMPACT OF NDE TESTIMONY ON BELIEF IN LIFE AFTER DEATH

Anyone who becomes familiar with NDEs must, of course, inevitably think about life after death. No matter how much skeptics may contend against drawing premature conclusions about the *afterdeath* from reports of near-death experiences, the implied promise of the NDE continues to exert a persuasive and powerful appeal. Indeed, everyone, critics included, understands that many moderns have become fascinated with NDEs not simply because they suggest that the moment of death is one of stupendous splendor and joy beyond reckoning. No—it is rather the unmistakable implication that this kind of experience *continues*, that there really is a life after death and that, furthermore, it will be wonderful.

Surely, this is one potent reason why the NDE, as soon as it was publicized through the work of Elisabeth Kübler-Ross and Raymond Moody nearly a quarter of a century ago, stirred the public imagination throughout the Western World and why the NDE has *persisted* as a topic of widespread interest to the present day. It is the precisely the picture of death and what lies beyond that I have painted in the first part of this chapter, using the narrative brush strokes of NDErs, that has proved as irresistible as it is glorious. Clearly, despite the prevalence and currency of postmodern skepticism, there is still something in most of us that yearns for this vision of the afterlife to be true and that thrills at the possibility that NDEs finally provide some creditable evidence that it is.

And so it is natural to ask, after so many years of familiarity with NDEs, what has been the effect of all this testimony on the public's belief in life after death? Has the NDE made a difference here?

Again, it is surprising that, to the best of my knowledge, we do not have any large-scale survey data to draw on here to demonstrate that people who become either familiar with or interested in NDEs increase in their belief in life after death. I personally have little doubt that once such a survey is undertaken, the results will be clear-cut on this point, but until we have such data in hand, we will have to content ourselves with what findings we do have from other studies. Here, I can refer briefly to two investigations of my own that are relevant.

The first is the little survey that I first mentioned in Chapter Nine, in connection with the benign virus hypothesis. As you may remember, I twice surveyed the students in my NDE course at the end of the semester (and, actually, a colleague of mine did likewise for an NDE course she was teaching at another university) concerning possible changes in some of their beliefs and attitudes. One of the questions on the survey pertained to belief in life after death. Overall, an average of 82 percent of the students in these three surveys reported that their exposure to NDE information in these courses had increased their belief in life after death. In other words, here, too, their responses mimic the actual effect of NDEs and therefore support the benign virus hypothesis.

These findings are impressive for three other reasons as well, which will not necessarily be obvious to you. The first is that, according to an initial survey I had taken at the beginning of the course, the overwhelming majority of my students had come into this course already believing in life after death. Despite that, more than four out of five of these students increased in that belief as a result of learning about NDEs. Second, not a single student in any of these three surveys afterward showed a lessening of belief in life after death. Finally, the personal comments that students had written on the questionnaires, as well as their course journals, made it evident how deeply many of them had been affected by the NDE testimony they had heard throughout the semester, and not just in regard to the matter of life after death, either.

The second study that bears on this matter is my work for *The Omega Project*. You will remember, I hope, that part of that investigation compared a sample of seventy-four NDErs with a control group of fifty-four persons who had never had an NDE themselves but were known to be interested in the phenomenon. It is the latter group that is relevant here. Again, on the single question pertaining to life after death, more than 80 percent of this sample, too, stated that *since* becoming interested in NDEs, they had increased in their conviction that there was a life after death.

Of course, as I have already indicated in this book, I have an abundance of additional documents, mostly letters, in my own archives that suggest this same effect, although I will spare you a string of further quotes to illustrate this proposition. The point is that although we cannot say from the foregoing studies and my own anecdotal sources that mere familiarity with NDEs *necessarily* increases belief in life after death, it seems pretty clear that so long as one is open to and interested in NDEs, one is likely to find that one has undergone a shift toward the beliefs of NDErs with respect to life after death. The testimony of the latter once more appears to have swayed those who have come to listen.

But to bring this issue to the fore for you, I must remind you that at the moment, you—a sample of one—are the only person who really matters. Obviously, if you have been reading this book to this juncture, you are one of those who has become, if you were not already to begin with, interested in NDEs. And like a student in one of my classes, you, too, have been exposed to a great deal of information about NDEs, including, of course, the material in this chapter on visions of a putative afterlife. Therefore, it might be worthwhile for you to take a few minutes now to reflect on just how all this information has affected your own belief about life after death. If you can think back to how you felt about this issue before reading this book, you will be able to determine whether and to what extent it has influenced you in this regard. Naturally, like many of my students, you may have come to this book already predisposed to believe in some form of an afterlife, yet like them, you may, on considering the issue more closely, find that there have been some important qualitative shifts in your conception of an afterlife as well as an overall change in your conviction that you will have one. In any case, I would ask you to take some time now to consider how the material in this book, especially that presented in the last two chapters, has influenced, if it has, your own attitudes toward death and beliefs about an afterlife. When you envisage yourself at the portals of death, what do you see now, and what do you imagine will follow your entrance there?

## VISUALIZING THE AFTERLIFE

The distinguished psychiatrist Carl Jung, who himself had a profound NDE when he was nearly seventy years old, was an ardent proponent of precisely this kind of imaginative exercise. In his celebrated memoir, *Memories, Dreams, Reflections*, he exhorts his readers as follows: "A man should be able to say he has done his best to form a conception of life after death, or to create some image of it—even if he must confess his failure. Not to have done so is a vital loss."[4] Yet at the risk of disagreeing with a great man, I find that I demur a bit at taking this exercise too far. I think, for our purposes, it may be enough to be convinced that something, and something truly inconceivably splendid, may await us when we cross that threshold into the Light, but I personally am loath to begin to try to imagine what follows in very specific terms.[5] In this respect, I am in my attitude rather like one of the NDErs I quoted earlier in this chapter, who said, after stating his absolute certainty in an afterlife, "I don't know what's beyond what I experienced, but it's plenty for me."

I have several reasons for this reluctance to follow Jung's admonition too closely. First, I think that the details of the afterdeath journey must ultimately be so variable that it would be a form of gross arrogance to imagine what course it would take in any individual case. Certainly, the individual's journey after death must eventually depart from the common story line we now know so well from our NDE narratives. That story, begins, as we have seen, with the pure light of the soul's unconditioned divine splendor, and then, presumably after the life review and other standard features of the NDE, must of necessity devolve into the further particularities of each person's own afterdeath journey, which the NDE alone is insufficient to predict.

Second, as much as we may have become accustomed to the language of NDErs, I would still contend that the *essence* of these experiences transcends all linguistic or imagistic representation that might be available to us in states of ordinary waking consciousness. Therefore, in trying to conceive of the afterdeath state too finely, we not only risk a certain *hubris*, but we also court the danger of transforming an experience full of symbolic shadings and redolent with flashes of higher consciousness into something that is too literal, banal, or otherwise full of conventional stereotyped imagery. Surely, despite our knowledge of NDEs, our own afterdeath journey will be like what J. S. Haldane said about the universe. To paraphrase his famous *bon mot*: Our death will not only be stranger than we suppose, it will also be stranger than we *can* suppose. Of course, I do not mean to imply that our afterdeath experience will be *strange*, but only that it is likely to be so different from what we might have imagined that we may as well not expend too much energy in persuading ourselves that we actually know more than we do.

And the third reason is I believe that focusing too much on the afterlife as such is often a distraction, a kind of siren that can draw us away from the lessons we have come into a body to learn and practice here. This is a point that I want to return to and elaborate upon later.

Before doing so, however, I certainly need to qualify what I have just written in order to prevent a very serious misunderstanding from arising. I definitely do *not* mean to suggest here that it is profitless to study and ponder the vast literature now available that treats an enormous variety of evidence for an afterlife as well as those voluminous writings that purport to describe the nature of afterlife existence. My own library, for example, contains many volumes in both categories, and I am glad to have them there. There are many books, for example, that are filled with accounts of afterdeath communications or deathbed visions, or apparent reincarnational episodes or regressions into possible states of consciousness between lives whose findings are highly congruent with the implications of NDEs and with the hypothesis of survival following bodily death. And had I chosen to, I could have cited many such cases, or provided a few of my own, in this chapter that would have added even more evidence in support of an afterlife, as well as helping us to conceive of it in the manner that Jung advocated. Likewise, it would certainly have been possible to extend the NDE trail that leaves off at the entrance hall of the Light, as it were, by availing myself of writings of various spiritual adepts who claim to have explored the entire mansion that awaits us in the afterdeath realms. And if you feel yourself drawn to explore this body of literature, you will not have any difficulty in locating an abundance of it.

But, as you see, I have resisted taking that path here for the reasons I gave earlier. My purpose in this chapter is much more specific and focused. I want only to make you even more aware than you might have been of a single fact: *NDEs conduce toward a belief in an afterlife*. Period. That is why I presented those cases at the beginning of the chapter to show you again just what it was about the NDE that makes experiencers so convinced that we live after we die and how common this belief is among NDErs as a whole.

Now, why I eschewed further particulars here has a lot to do with the last reason I gave, to which I now return. That was, in effect, that to dwell on the nature of the afterlife may divert us from paying attention to *this* life, where the lessons from the Light need to be practiced. For me, and for us in this book, the true promise of the NDE is not so much what it suggests about an afterlife—as inspiring and comforting as those glimpses are—but what it says about how to live *now*. After all, we are not dead! You may read this book in order to be reassured about death, and I certainly hope and trust you have been, but my aim in writing it has been to allow you to learn from NDErs about how to live, or how to live better, with greater self-awareness, self-compassion, and concern for others. Live well, and death will take care of itself.

There is another even more subtle danger here, too, that, though I doubt that any attentive reader of this book will succumb to it, I think may stem from too great a preoccupation with the intimations of immortality of the NDE. In a word, it is this: The extensive publicity that NDEs have received and the hope they inspire about a life to come may well seduce many persons into an attitude of comfortable complacency. The Light, after all, appears to shine on all with its unconditionally accepting radiance, and everyone, as we have seen, seems to enter eternity in an atmosphere of all-pervasive, pure love that reveals the soul in its blessed immanent divinity. However, to emphasize *only* the Light, or to suppose that it will, in itself, make all things well after death, regardless of how we have lived, is in my judgment a naive and fallacious reading of the implications of NDE research. That is why I have made such a point in this book to highlight the importance of the lessons of the life review and at other places have insisted that the unconditional and nonjudgmental love of the Light does not mean that all behavior is equally acceptable or, certainly, that "anything is permitted."

On the contrary, what the NDE really teaches about the afterdeath is that we are at this very moment and throughout our lives writing the script that will govern our soul's posthumous journey—that no one other than we ourselves is the shaper of our soul's destiny after death. The Light may indeed reflect our true nature and dissolve our personal sense of sin, but it can never absolve us of the responsibility for our own lives. Not just what we are in our essence, but how we have in fact lived will be evident— perhaps painfully so—after death.

So even the lesson of this chapter, as much as it has, until now, been about the implications of the NDE for an afterlife, is to force our attention back to what NDEs have to teach us about how to live in *this* world. And here, who is better than the great Indian poet, Kabir, to remind us of the uses we should make of our knowledge of the NDE and what it has taught us:

> Friend, hope for the Guest while you are alive.
> Jump into experience while you are alive!
> Think ... and think ... while you are alive.
> What you call "salvation" belongs to the time before death.
>
> If you don't break your ropes while you're alive,
> do you think
> ghost will do it after? ...
> What is found now is found then.
> If you find nothing now,
> you will simply end up with an apartment
> in the City of Death.[7]

All this, nevertheless, is not to say that we are quite ready to turn our gaze fully back to this world. Before we can do that, there is still one more set of lessons we need to derive from NDEs, which are, truly, the most important lessons of all, and which have the most far-reaching consequences for how we choose to live our daily lives. These lessons, however, are not, in a sense, simply more lessons from the Light but are its *ultimate* lessons. And they come to us in their most articulated and complete form chiefly from those who have actually journeyed *beyond* the Light and have thus gone further than any of the NDErs whose accounts you have yet read. In fact, without dying, they have gone all the way.

## Chapter Thirteen

# *Journeys to the Source: The Ultimate Lessons from the Light*

Our excursion into the afterdeath realms brings us close to the heart of the mystery of creation itself, though, of course, we who only hear the tales that near-death survivors return to tell of these realms can at best be filled with wonder but never with certainty concerning this ultimate mystery. Nevertheless, there have been a few NDErs who have seemingly penetrated well past the common zones of experience where almost all NDEs end, and their accounts of their journeys *beyond* the Light, as it were, give us a heretofore unrevealed glimpse of a radiant universe that truly appears to be something akin to the ultimate source of creation itself. From the standpoint of these extraordinary experiences, the NDEs we have been considering to this point, however glorious their splendor, seem incomplete and tell only a portion of the story we all long to know. Indeed, the journeys beyond the Light, some of which I would like to share with you next, almost always speak of or imply the existence of a *second* light, which is at once, a kind of ultimate Light, the source of everything, a place where we come from and to which we will inevitably return. And those who are blessed enough to travel there are the persons who are perhaps best equipped to express for us what might fairly be called "the ultimate lessons of the Light," from which, using a phrase associated with the world's great spiritual traditions, the essential "wisdom teachings" of the NDE can be extracted.

In this chapter, then, which will effectively bring to a close our long meditation on the mystery and meaning of the NDE, I would like to present some of the most profound and eloquent narrations concerning encounters of this kind, whose words, as much as words can do, can unveil for us all these deepest and most sublime revelations. As you read these stories, you will also be able to take away with you some of the most beautiful and inspiring articulations of the teachings of the NDE: not simply more lessons, but the treasures of the Light that these exceptional NDErs have been privileged to bring back for the benefit of us all.

## Mellen-Thomas Benedict

Without question, one of the most remarkable NDErs I have ever met is my friend, Mellen-Thomas Benedict, who is currently living in California, where he is very successfully developing some light-based healing technologies stemming in part from information he was given during his NDE. I first encountered Mellen in Baltimore, in 1992. Deeply impressed with the man and the very partial account of his NDE I heard at that time, I later traveled with some friends of mine to spend some time with Mellen where he was then living, in Fayetteville, North Carolina. During that visit in November 1992, I was able to tape-record an informal and spontaneous conversation we had in which Mellen described some portions of his unusually complex and extended NDE for my friends and me. In what follows, I present an edited version of a segment of this conversation in which he specifically relates his own journey to what he himself calls a "second light." From this excerpt alone, you will easily be able to see why I found Mellen's story to be one of the most memorable and significant of any I have heard in the course of my work on NDEs. It also shows what is possible when one has, as Mellen does, an unquenchable curiosity to learn everything one can about the nature of reality itself, and the presence of mind to ask the right questions when encountering the Light.[1]

The background of Mellen's of NDE in short was this: In 1982, he found himself very ill with an undiagnosed brain condition and was given six to eight months to live. During this time, he did, in fact, "die" for a period he estimates to have been over an hour and a half, and sometime in that interval, he underwent his very profound NDE. I will begin this extract from our conversation with Mellen's account of the opening stages of his journey:

> And the next thing I know is that I am standing in this dark room and there is my body on the bed and sort of a darkness, and I look down and see myself, and I said, "Oh." It is sort of surprising because you still feel real. It's like I am here but I am also over there. And about that time, one whole side of the wall in the room became like a scene of a dark forest with the sun rising behind it, and there was this path going out through the woods. And I looked at that path and I thought, "Boy, I really want to go up there. I really want to go up that path." And I started moving and then I suddenly realized, "Oh, I know what's happening, I've died. I know if I go up that path and go to the edge of the woods and into that light, I'll be dead."
>
> But it was *so*, so peaceful and felt so good. I had never felt that way on the planet. So I started moving up the path and the light got bigger and bigger. It got very big and I started seeing what you call now sort of past memories, a life review kind of a thing. And I could see stuff that made me unhappy, and how unhappy I had been, and things like that, and so at that point I said, "Stop!" and just everything stopped! And I was surprised; it stopped. And suddenly I realized that this must be an interactive experience because I am able to talk to it.

This discovery on Mellen's part that he could actually interact with the Light and was not constrained merely to react passively to it was a key insight on his part, and it was to set him on a trajectory far different from that which most NDEs tend to follow. He continues:

> And so, then next thing I know is I am heading up into this Light. It is sort of like a tunnel. And I go to this light and again I say, "Stop!" and it stopped. And I said—I don't remember the exact words but it was to the effect of—"I think I understand what you are but I really want to know what you *really* are. Like, reveal yourself, what is this Light? I have heard it's Jesus, I have heard it's this, I have heard it's that.
>
> And at that time, the Light revealed itself to me on a level that I had never been to before. I can't say it's words; it was a telepathic understanding more than anything else, very vivid. I could feel it, I could feel this light. And the Light just reacted and revealed itself on another level, and the message was "Yes, [for] most people, depending on where you are coming from, it could be Jesus, it could be Buddha, it could be Krishna, whatever."
>
> But I said, "But what it is *really*?" And the Light then changed into—the only thing I can tell you [is that] it turned into a matrix, a mandala of human souls, and what I saw was that what we call our higher self in each of us is a matrix. It's also a conduit to the source; each one of us comes directly, as a direct experience [from] the source. And it became very clear to me that all the higher selves are connected as one being, all humans are connected as

one being, we are actually the same being, different aspects of the same being. And I saw this mandala of human souls. It was the most beautiful thing I have ever seen, just [voice trembles], I just went into it and [voice falters], it was just overwhelming [he chokes], it was like all the love you've ever wanted, and it was the kind of love that cures, heals, regenerates.

But however overcome Mellen was by his experience at this point, he continues to persevere in his quest for ultimate answers:

M:   And the more I went into it, the more I just said, "I want to know, I really want to know what's going on." I just kept saying that "I want to know, I want to know." And I was taken *into* the Light and, to my surprise, *through* it, poom! Like some kind of sound barrier, so that I went *through* it. And if you can imagine the higher self being—it looks more like a conduit than a being, a navel cord, or something like that. At the time, it seemed like I was being propelled somewhere. I don't know if I was moving anywhere in space, but suddenly I could see the world fly away. I could see the solar system fly away. I could then see galaxies and—it went on.

Eventually I got the feeling that I was going through everything that had ever been. I was seeing it all—galaxies became little stars, and super-clusters of galaxies, and worlds upon worlds, and energy realms—it was just an amazing sight to behold. And it felt like I was zooming somewhere but I really think it was my consciousness just expanding at such a rapid rate. And it happened so quickly but it was in such detail that there came another light right at me and when I hit *this* light, it was like [pause] I dissolved or something. And I understood at that moment that I passed the big bang. That was the first light ever and I went *through* the big bang. That's what happened. I went through that membrane into this—what I guess the ancients have called the Void. Suddenly I was in this void and I was aware of everything that had ever been created. It was like I was looking out of God's eyes. I had become God.

K:   You had gotten back to the source of all.

M:   Yes. Suddenly I wasn't me anymore. The only thing I can say, I was looking out of God's eyes. And suddenly I knew why every atom was, and I could see *everything*. And I stayed in that space, I don't know how long. And I know something very deep happened there.

And then the experience reversed. I went back through the big bang and I understood at that point that everything since the big bang, since what they call the first word, is actually the first vibration. There was a place before any vibration at all.

As he is beginning his return, Mellen experiences a succession of further revelations about the nature of reality and of spirit, but I will resume his narrative here with just a few of his remarks about what he discovered concerning the immanence of God from this segment of his journey:

> The interesting point was that I went into the Void, I came back with this understanding that God is not there. God is here [laughs]. That's what it is all about. So this constant search of the human race to go out and find God.... God gave *everything* to us, *everything* is here—this is where it's at. And what we are into now is God's exploration of God through us. People are so busy trying to become God that they ought to realize that we are already God and God is becoming us. That's what it is really about.

Finally, Mellen returns to what he calls "the first light" through whose gateway he was able, through his unceasing questioning, to penetrate seemingly to the ultimate source of creation itself. But his vision, on coming back, is not what it was to begin with:

M: When I came back to the first light again—and there was a whole thing that happened between the second light and the first light [which I have only summarized portions of here]—it was like a reversal, but this time I could see everything in its energy form, its pure essence, as if I could see you as an atomic form. And it was quite a sight to see the entire universe as we know it as an energy form, and all of it interacting, and all of it having its place and reactions and resonances. It was just an unbelievable dance that was going on. So then there was the second light, the matrix I came through again and at that point ...

K (interrupting): Did it still appear as a matrix of human souls?

M: Oh yes, oh yes. But more than human souls. Human souls were a part of it. What I saw as I came back through was that whole Gaia thing, and this is before I even knew what Gaia was. I saw that the solar system we live in is our larger, local body. This is our local body and we are much bigger than we imagine. I saw that the solar system is our body. I am a part of this, and the earth is this great created being that we are, and we are the part of it that knows that it is. But we are only that part of it. We are not everything, but we are that part of it that knows that it is.

At the end of our conversation, I tried to clarify and distill the essence of what Mellen had been trying to convey to us about his journey to the second light and beyond.

K:  When you were talking about the first part of your experience, it seemed to me you were saying that, in a sense, your consciousness went back through time, went back fifteen billion years to the big bang, which is what you mean by the second light?

M:  Yes.

K:  Essentially what you experienced as the second light, then, was the return to the beginning fireball that created all of physical life. After that, you went, in a sense, through the big bang itself, back before time, into the Void and then had the revelations that you described. And then it was as though you were taking a return journey seeing it from God's perspective, as it were, with God's eyes, seeing the pure energy form of the universe, eventually coming down to our own particular neighborhood but seeing it in its cosmic context.

M:  Yes, I should have clarified that, because I spent quite a bit of time with the Light on the way back. And when I was in the Void, the feeling I had was that I was aware of [things] before I had been created.

As I indicated at the outset, what I have quoted here from our conversation describes only a portion of Mellen's NDE, but it is enough, I think, to make clear that his vision is one of absolute wholeness in which all things are connected in a living cosmic web of organic unity. The visible universe is a universe of vibrating fields within fields, a dance of exquisite harmony, where, as Blake said, "Energy is eternal delight," and everything sings of God's immanent presence. At its core, exfoliating from the Void, is that radiant Light, which some have called the Central Sun, and which metaphorically may have its physical representation in the Big Bang, the genesis of it all, including the star-stuff we call ourselves. Because all things are truly one within this vision of life, we human beings—indeed, all living creatures—are one body indivisible and, as such, not separate from God either, but His very manifestation.

Such is the view of the universe, at least, according to the vision Mellen was given. But the journey he took that disclosed it to him has not been his uniquely, and therefore its reality does not hang on his experience alone. Other NDErs appear to have traveled to the same source as Mellen did, and the insights they bring back from their journeys largely coincide with his. In short, like the NDE itself, these voyages to the primordial Light, though taken by only a relative handful of individuals, seem to constitute a shared vision of the ultimate nature of reality. But everyone tells the story somewhat differently, though with similar metaphors. Let us now sample a few more of these narratives so that we can discern even more clearly the treasured truths these gifted sojourners are so keen to share with us.

## Howard Storm

Howard Storm had been an atheistic art professor before his NDE. Afterward, he became a minister of God. Obviously, something ontologically shattering must have happened to Howard to bring about this conversion, and, if you were to read about his NDE in detail, your curiosity would be fully satisfied.[2] His NDE, however, was extremely complex, having both hellish and heavenly aspects, by turn, and it cannot even be easily summarized, much less told here. Instead, I will restrict myself to a single segment of it, which is highly pertinent to the notion of a radiant central source of all-pervading Intelligence, such as Mellen described.

Before relating this aspect of his NDE, however, I need to give you a little background on Howard, whom I know by virtue of correspondence and telephone conversations only, including a forty-five-minute interview I conducted with him over the phone on January 21, 1993. To begin with the circumstances that led up to his experience, I can tell you that it came at the end of a three-week-long European art tour that Howard had been conducting for a group of art students. On June 1, 1985, he was in Paris, and while in his hotel room, he collapsed in horrific pain, as if he had been shot. A doctor's examination showed that Howard had suffered a perforated duodenum, a condition, he was told, that if not immediately corrected by surgery would lead to his death. He was then taken to a large Paris hospital, where some hours later, still waiting for his life-saving operation, he underwent his NDE.

At one point, following some extremely frightening episodes, Howard, despite his many years of atheism, began to pray and, seemingly in response to his heartfelt entreaty, a radiant being of light, emanating "more love than one can imagine," rescued him. Here, we will listen to Howard's own words, taken from an interview he gave to Judith Cressy[3] as he describes what happened next:

> It was loving me with overwhelming power. After what I had been through, to be completely known, accepted, and intensely loved by this being of light surpassed anything I had known or could have imagined. I began to cry, and the tears kept coming and coming.
>
> I rose upward, enveloped in that luminous being. Gradually at first, and then like a rocket traveling at great speed, we shot out of that dark and detestable place. I sensed that we traversed an enormous distance, although very little time seemed to elapse. Then, off in the distance, I saw a vast area of illumination that looked like a galaxy. In the center, there was an enormously bright concentration. Outside the center, countless millions of spheres of light were flying about, entering and leaving what was a great Beingness at the center.
>
> The radiance emanating from the luminous spheres contained exquisite colors of a range and intensity that far exceeded anything I as an artist had ever experienced. It was similar to looking at the opalescence one experiences looking into a white pearl or the brilliance of a diamond.
>
> As we approached the great luminous center I was permeated with palpable radiation, which I experienced as intense feelings and thoughts. People who have had near-death experiences, I have since learned, have described encounters with the light as being exposed to complete knowledge. Yet when they are asked what they remember, they recall few if any specifics. That's the way it was for me. At the time, I felt that I was in touch with everything, but subsequently, I couldn't recall the knowledge. And there was a period of time, during my presence in the great light, when I was beyond any thoughts. It is not possible to articulate the exchange that occurred. Simply stated, I knew God loved me.

Again, we have the same basic constellation of motifs: a journey (and Howard agreed in his interview with me that the term, *journey*, was apt) toward a central point of enormous light (in his interview with me, he said it was a huge "congregation" of lights with an overwhelmingly brilliant core, which he could perceive as though at a distance), from which emanations of intense love and total knowledge radiated.

## Norman Paulsen

Although experiences of traveling to a central source of creation in which all love and all knowledge are contained are rare in NDEs, they are not limited, of course, to persons who are threatened with bodily mortality. In some cases, for example, similar journeys seem to occur to persons in deep meditation. One such person, with whom I had the pleasure of spending several days during the summer of 1987, is the author, Norman Paulsen, a spiritual teacher in his own right and longtime student of the celebrated Indian yogi, Parahamansa Yogananda. Paulsen has written the story of his own extraordinary life and spiritual experiences (which include, by the way, *several* NDEs, though they are not immediately at issue here) in a fascinating book called *Christ Consciousness*,[4] from which the following account is taken.

The experience I want to narrate took place during a seven-hour (!) meditation that Paulsen undertook on February 4, 1952. He was practicing a form of Kriya yoga at the time, which he had learned from his guru, Yogananda. It is most notable in the present context that Paulsen himself refers to this experience as a "journey to the center of the Great Central Sun" (p. 194). I now present a brief summary of some of the principal features of this journey, along with selected quotes from Paulsen himself.

As he sank into his meditative state, he first became aware of "tremendous and intense energy" at the base of his spine, rising up like flames. [Presumably, he had activated here the mechanism of *kundalini*.] His head now flung back, he saw before him a

> colossal sphere of brilliance.... It's hurtling toward me! There is [an] incredible voice coming as if from everywhere, *"My son, are you ready to die today and be with me?"* ... "Yes, my Lord, I am ready to die and leave with you." I feel no fear within. I am going to die and go with him whom I love more than anything else. That shimmering, pulsating orb, it's exploding all around me with a brilliance beyond anything I have ever seen. I am now whirling within this incredible light. (p.197)

> (Howard Storm also said he was *within* the light.)

> I am expanding as a sphere, moving outward in all directions at an incredible rate.... Now there are all around me, creation's light abounding. Yes, your images are floating right through me—star systems, galaxies, universes. I exist in them and they in me.... Ecstasy, I feel beyond the limits of all that I have ever conceived. (p. 198)
>
> The voice ... speaks again, but from where does it proceed? It is mine and yet not mine. What does it say? *"My son, my son, now you have seen: now I must put you back ..."* Now there within me, the image of the great Sphere of Creation appears, floating like an iridescent bubble in the infinite sea of life and consciousness of which I am a part. (p. 199)

Paulsen eventually returns to his body, of course, but comments that as does so, he is aware of universes, galaxies, familiar star systems, and "the bright blue sphere" of earth before sighting the California coastline (where his physical body was at the time)—in short, the outward journey in reverse.

Here, we have an experience that has some obvious points of commonality with the NDEs I cited earlier in this section, and particularly with that of Mellen-Thomas, who also felt as if he was not so much making a journey through physical space as that his consciousness was expanding so as to encompass everything in the manifested universe until he reached its all-luminous source and, finally, the Void itself. It is this kind of journey that Paulsen also seems to speak of, and it is worth pointing out that it appears to have been triggered by Paulsen's inner assent that he was *willing* to die, so in a sense it, too, might actually be regarded as a type of NDE in its own right.

## Virginia Rivers

Ginny Rivers, a resident of Florida, is someone I have known—albeit only through telephone conversations and correspondence—since 1994, when she first wrote to me and sent me an account of her NDE. When I read it, I nearly wept at its beauty, and I made contact with her immediately to express my gratitude for what I felt was one of the most sublime renderings I had ever encountered in the literature on NDEs of the complete journey to the Ultimate Place of Total Realization. Indeed, the only comparable narrative, in scope and spiritual eloquence, was that of Beverly Brodsky, whose entire story, you will recall, we have yet to learn. In Ginny's description of her journey, we can see, perhaps even more clearly than before, that the *full experience* into the very heart of the Light confers every answer to life to the individual and leaves him or her with unshakable knowledge concerning the ultimate lessons we are to learn and practice while living here in a physical body. Furthermore—and this may be as shocking to some traditionalists as it is self-evident to others—I think it is time to be entirely candid about the nature of this encounter: It is, in my view simply, undeniably, and incredibly one with God himself. The persons whose stories we are telling in this section have had a direct experience of and a personal revelation from God, and their inspired eloquence leaves us in no doubt that in returning to life, they have become his messengers, speaking in words of Light the Truth of the Light for all of us to hear and marvel at, so that we, too, can remember what already lies inscribed deep in the soul of each and every one of us.

Ginny's story, which was brought into being by a near-fatal bout with pneumonia, took place while she was hospitalized in 1986. At this time, she was extremely weak with a high fever, felt intense pressure in her ears, and had difficulty breathing. She remembers crying out inwardly, "Please, where is everybody? I must be dying." At that point, she lost consciousness, and her journey to the center of the universe and to the Source of All began.

There was total peace; I was surrounded on all sides by a black void. I was no longer frightened. I was comfortable and content to be where I was. No fear … no pain … just peace and comfort and amazingly undaunted curiosity. [All ellipses in this account are Ginny's. Nothing has been left out.] Immediately the blackness began to erupt into a myriad of stars and I felt as if I were at the center of the Universe with a complete panoramic view in all directions. The next instant I began to feel a forward surge of movement. The stars seemed to fly past me so rapidly that they formed a tunnel around me. I began to sense awareness, knowledge. The farther forward I was propelled the more knowledge I received. My mind felt like a sponge, growing and expanding in size with each addition. The knowledge came in single words and in whole idea blocks. I just seemed to be able to understand everything as it was being soaked up or absorbed. I could feel my mind expanding and absorbing and each new piece of information somehow seemed to belong. It was as if I had known already but forgotten or mislaid it, as if it were waiting here for me to pick it up on my way by. I kept growing with knowledge, evolving, expanding and thirsting for more. It was amazing, like being a child again and experiencing something brand new and beautiful, a wonderful new playground. As each second passed, there was more to learn, answers to questions, meanings and definitions, philosophies and reasons, histories, mysteries, and so much more, all pouring into my mind. I remember thinking, "I knew that, I know I did. Where has it all been?"

The stars began to change shapes before my eyes. They began to dance and deliberately draw themselves into intricate designs and colors which I had never seen before. They moved and swayed to a kind of rhythm or music with a quality and beauty I had never heard and yet … remembered. A melody man could not possibly have composed, yet so totally familiar and in complete harmony with the very core of my being. As if it were the rhythm of my existence, the reason for my being. The extravagance of imagery and coloration pulsed in splendid unison with the magnificent ensemble.

I felt completely at peace, tranquilized by the vision and the melodic drone. I could have stayed in this place for eternity with this pulse of love and beauty beating throughout my soul. The love poured into me from all corners of the universe. I was still being propelled forward at what seemed great speed. Yet I was able to observe all that I passed as if I were standing still. Each passing second I was absorbing more and more knowledge. No one spoke to me, nor did I hear voices in my head. The knowledge just seemed to "BE" and with each new awareness came a familiarity. A tiny pin point of light appeared far in front of me at the other end of my kaleidoscopic tunnel. The light grew larger and larger as I was soaring closer and closer to it, until finally I had arrived at my destination.

At once there was total and absolute awareness. There was not a question I could ask for which I did not already have the answer. I looked over to the presence I knew would be there and thought, "God, it was so simple, why didn't I know that?" I could not see God as I can see you. Yet I knew it was Him. A Light, a beauty emitting from within, infinitely in all directions to touch every atom of being. The harmony of coloration, design and melody originated here with the Light. It was God, his love, his light, his very essence, the force of creation emanating to the ends of all eternity … reaching out as a pulsing beacon of love to bring me "Home."

There was a time of exchange, in one moment or one eon, complete and absolute knowing and approval of me and what I had become. In that instant or millennium, I knew he had seen my entire life and he loved me still. Pure unadulterated, unselfish, ever-flowing, unconditional Love. God had seen my life and still loved me endlessly, eternally for myself, for my existence. He never spoke to me in words that I could hear with my ears, yet I heard his thoughts as clearly as words. The quality of his word, his thought, his voice in my head, was magnificent, enchanting, compelling without demand, gentle and kind and filled with more love than is possible to describe. To be in his presence was more inspiring, more inviting, than any kind of love or harmony ever discovered in this reality. No experience, no closeness has ever been so complete.

I was on what appeared to be a ledge of a huge mountain. The front side where we stood was flattened, possibly like a half butte. I stood, floated, maybe hovered by his side and I vaguely remember an altar built of golden shining light in front of me and slightly to the right. I was not aware or unaware of having a body. I was there and that was the most important thing I could imagine. He told me many things of which I have little or no recollection. I only remember that we spoke, or rather, he inspired and I learned. It seemed then that the exchange lasted for hours or eons and now it seems that eons passed in only moments. I remember only two things from that exchange. First, God told me there were only two things that we could bring back with us when we died … LOVE and KNOWLEDGE…. So I was to learn as much about both as possible. Second, God told me that I had to return, I could not stay, there was something I had yet to accomplish. I remember knowing at that moment what it was, I have no recollection now.

I remember pain. Great emotional sorrow, not physical pain. I think my soul cried. I begged not to leave. I pled. I told him how no one would miss me. My children would be better off without me. My mother and father and brother would take better care of them than I. My heart ached as if it were physically crushed. Again he told me there was something I must accomplish and his love began to soothe my tears and sorrow. I understood and he knew from the bottom of my soul that I wanted to be with him as soon as I did what was to be done.

Since she returned to physical life, which has been full of difficulties and challenges for her, Ginny has often expressed puzzlement to me and even deep frustration about what her task in life is. Though I could never presume to have the answer to that enigma, I personally cannot help thinking that in some way it must certainly be intimately related to her telling her story, and I feel privileged to be able to share a portion of it with you here.

## Beverly Brodsky

And, finally, we come back to Beverly Brodsky, whom you met in Chapter Ten, where I gave you a partial account, but not the heart, of her NDE. To remind you here of the pertinent details, Beverly had been involved in a serious motorcycle crash in Los Angeles, and though she sustained some dreadful injuries as a result, she was not actually physically near death when her journey beyond the Light began. She was, however, in such a state of despair that she wished *only* to die, and in a sense, she got her wish—and much more. You will also remember that Beverly is Jewish and that as a child, she had become an atheist because of her discovery of the Holocaust; this, too, figures into the experience she relates in the narrative that follows.

Now, to set the stage for this part of her narrative, you will need to recall that as her experience begins, Beverly is overcome by a sense of peace and well being, floats out of her body, and finds herself in the presence of a luminous and loving being, who gently guides her out of the room. It is at this point, where her journey really commences, that I pick up Beverly's story and allow her, once again, to tell it in her own words:

> Beneath us lay the beautiful Pacific Ocean, over which I had excitedly watched the sun set when I had first arrived. But my attention was now directed upward, where there was a large opening leading to a circular path. Although it seemed to be deep and far to the end, a white light shone through and poured out into the gloom to the other side where the opening beckoned. It was the most brilliant light I had ever seen, although I didn't realize how much of its glory was veiled from the outside. The path was angled upward, obliquely, to the right. Now, still hand in hand with the angel, I was led into the opening of the small, dark passageway.

I then remember traveling a long distance upward toward the light. I believe that I was moving very fast, but this entire realm seemed to be outside of time. Finally, I reached my destination. It was only when I emerged from the other end that I realized that I was no longer accompanied by the being who had brought me there. But I wasn't alone. There, before me, was the living presence of the Light. Within it I sensed an all-pervading intelligence, wisdom, compassion, love, and truth. There was neither form nor sex to this perfect Being. It, which I shall in the future call He, in keeping with our commonly accepted syntax, contained everything, as white light contains all the colors of a rainbow when penetrating a prism. And deep within me came an instant and wondrous recognition: I, even I, was facing God.

I immediately lashed out at Him with all the questions I had ever wondered about; all the injustices I had seen in the physical world. I don't know if I did this deliberately, but I discovered that God knows all your thoughts immediately and responds telepathically. My mind was naked; in fact, I became pure mind. The ethereal body which I had traveled in through the tunnel seemed to be no more; it was just my personal intelligence confronting that Universal Mind, which clothed itself in a glorious, living light that was more felt than seen, since no eye could absorb its splendor.

I don't recall the exact content of our discussion; in the process of return, the insights that came so clearly and fully in Heaven were not brought back with me to Earth. I'm sure that I asked the question that had been plaguing me since childhood about the sufferings of my people. I do remember this: There was a reason for *everything* that happened, no matter how awful it appeared in the physical realm. And within myself, as I was given the answer, my own awakening mind now responded in the same manner: "Of course," I would think, "I already know that. How could I ever have forgotten!" Indeed, it appears that all that happens is for a purpose, and that purpose is already known to our eternal self.

In time the questions ceased, because I suddenly was filled with all the Being's wisdom. I was given more than just the answers to my questions; all knowledge unfolded to me, like the instant blossoming of an infinite number of flowers all at once. I was filled with God's knowledge, and in that precious aspect of his Beingness, I was one with him. But my journey of discovery was just beginning.

Now I was treated to an extraordinary voyage through the universe. Instantly we traveled to the center of stars being born, supernovas exploding, and many other glorious celestial events for which I have no name. The impression I have now of this trip is that it felt like the universe is all one grand object woven from the same fabric. Space and time are illusions that hold us to our plane; out there all is present simultaneously. I was a passenger on a Divine spaceship in which the Creator showed me the fullness and beauty of all of his Creation.

The last thing that I saw before all external vision ended was a glorious fire—the core and center of a marvelous star. Perhaps this was a symbol for the blessing that was now to come to me. Everything faded except for a richly full void in which That and I encompassed All that is. Here, I experienced, in ineffable magnificence, communion with the Light Being. Now I was filled with not just all knowledge, but also with all love. It was as if the Light were poured in and through me. I was God's object of adoration; and from His/ our love I drew life and joy beyond imagining. My being was transformed; my delusions, sins, and guilt were forgiven and purged without asking; and now I was Love, primal Being, and bliss. And, in some sense, I remain there, for Eternity. Such a union cannot be broken. It always was, is, and shall be.

Suddenly, not knowing how or why, I returned to my broken body. But miraculously, I brought back the love and the joy. I was filled with an ecstasy beyond my wildest dreams. Here, in my body, the pain had all been re-moved. I was still enthralled by a boundless delight. For the next two months, I remained in this state, oblivious to any pain …

I felt now as if I had been made anew. I saw wondrous meanings everywhere; everything was alive and full of energy and intelligence.

At this point, you may remember, her narrative continues with some moving observations concerning the immediate aftermath of her NDE and an account of some of the momentous changes it eventually brought about in her life. Here, I simply reproduce her penultimate paragraph, previously quoted, wherein she reflects on the reality of what she calls her "heavenly voyage," and then conclude with her final statement in which, in one pithy paragraph, she beautifully sums up the Ultimate Lessons from the Light.

Although it's been twenty years since my heavenly voyage, I have never forgotten it. Nor have I, in the face of ridicule and disbelief, ever doubted its reality. Nothing that intense and life-changing could possibly have been a dream or hallucination. To the contrary, I consider the rest of my life to be a passing fantasy, a brief dream, that will end when I again awaken in the permanent presence of that giver of life and bliss.

For those who grieve or fear, I assure you of this: There is no death, nor does love ever end. And remember also that we are aspects of the one perfect whole, and as such are part of God, and of each other. Someday you who are reading this and I will be together in light, love, and unending bliss.

Can there be any doubt that Ginny Rivers and Beverly Brodsky both went to the same place—the Ultimate Source, the Great Central Sun, the Second Light, the Bosom of God (whatever term you may prefer)—where they both received and brought back essentially the same divine revelation to share with the rest of us? And reading their words, after reading so many similar words throughout this book from other NDErs, can you have any doubt that the voices you have listened to in this chapter attest to the highest teachings NDEs have to offer us?

We can ask no more of these people, make no further inquiries, or insist on additional proofs. Hearing what we have heard in these testimonies, we can only try, if we are open to them, for one last time, to take them into ourselves, to make them our own, and to practice the lessons from the Light in our own lives and thereby spread the Light to all the world.

## Chapter Fourteen

# Lighting up the Earth

In the tradition of Zen Buddhism, there is a famous series of drawings called the Oxherding Pictures, which are meant to depict the various stages leading to enlightenment. In the original set of these paintings, the last one simply shows a white and empty circle symbolizing the realization of Oneness and the essential emptiness of all things. But a later Zen master extended the progression to those states beyond the experience of awakening, and chose to end the series with a drawing of a realized person coming down from the mountaintop and entering the village with "bliss-bestowing hands," to mix freely with ordinary people, inspiring them with his presence and radiating compassion to all persons regardless of their station in life.

In the same way, having at least vicariously attained a glimpse through the narratives of the last chapter of the sublime splendors of the NDE empyrean, we must find a way to bring that divine vision back into the world of everyday reality, where the real test of this NDE-based knowledge is to be found. Certainly, the journeys we have described to the Source of All Light have the power to enthrall us, but if they succeed only in uplifting us for a few moments, they will have failed to achieve the real goal of this book. And that is, of course, not just to inspire us, but to *inspire us to action*. We need to take the vision and insights that NDErs have brought back to share with us *into ourselves* and, if we are so disposed, use them as mortar in building our own spiritual life in our familiar daily round and in our relations to others.

This is not, of course, to suggest that the knowledge that stems from the NDE is meant to substitute for one's own faith or spiritual tradition. No, it is rather that the lessons from the Light are more akin to Type O blood in transfusions: They are the "universal donor" to spirituality and religion in that they fit easily and well into a great variety of well-established spiritual traditions and world religions. And, more than that, as Carol Zaleksi, a theologian who has written extensively on NDEs, has shown, the modern NDE has served not to undermine but to *revitalize* religious faith by providing fresh and compelling stories from ordinary people that ultimately coincide with perennial spiritual teachings from around the world.[1] In this sense, the NDE generally serves to reinforce one's preexisting faith by *adding* something compatible to it, not by competing with it. On the other hand, while the spiritual teachings of the NDE are obviously not meant to provide the basis of a new religion, much less a cult (!), it is certainly possible that they can offer to those who are not themselves religious, or even to antireligious persons, a point of view that furnishes a credible experiential basis governing moral conduct in the world. In the end, one might say there is only the magnificence and incomparable radiance of the Light. But what one *makes of* this Light is an individual matter.

The issue we are concerned with here, however, is not so much how to *interpret* the Light, or whether or to what extent it may (or may not) accord with other spiritual or religious teachings, but *how to make use of the knowledge it affords.* I want to urge here a criterion of *utility* for the Light's offerings and not dissipate its value in fruitless discussions over just what it represents, which brings us back to the fundamental theme of this chapter: How to engage with the lessons of the Light so as to put them to practical use in your daily life.

If you have read this book to this point, you have already meditated much on NDEs, savored their stories, made mental applications of their teachings to your own life, and carried out certain exercises that have been strewn throughout its pages. This, certainly, is a good beginning, but now that the book is ending, you will be left on your own to continue these practices. So the obvious questions are: *What now?* and *Where do I go from here?*

Rather than listing, reviewing, and rehashing the various insights that we have already covered in this book, which would be little more than a sterile academic exercise at this point, I want to provide additional resources for you for deepening and internalizing the lessons that were

meant to be gleaned from the previous chapters. Therefore, I have prepared a special Appendix in which I have listed a variety of these
resources—further readings, audiocassettes and videotapes, organizations oriented to NDEs and their implications, NDE support groups, relevant conferences, and the names and addresses of NDErs willing to be
contacted. Wherever possible, I have also provided Internet information so
as to facilitate your access to these materials, organizations, groups, or
persons. By availing yourself of these opportunities, it is not only possible for you to go well beyond this book, but also to continue to search for
ways to implement into your own life what you have learned by reading it.
At the same time, I want to advise you of one caution before you venture in
this direction, should you choose to do so.

While I personally disavow any effort to make a cult out of the NDE,
I think it is fair to say that there is in a sense an emerging "culture of the
NDE," which is represented by the collectivity of persons that has either
had these experiences or has become interested in them, and this culture is
available to anyone who wishes to seek it out, learn further from it, and
even immerse him- or herself in it. As always, discrimination and discern-
ment must be exercised, because even in "the near-death world," if I may
use that expression here, there are persons, including some NDErs, who
are not always what they seem, or who suffer from obvious self-inflation
or other grandiose tendencies that any prudent person would do well to
eschew immediately. In this context, one might use an old but still apt
cliché, "Light casts shadows, too," and in your forays into the NDE culture, you should not be so focused on the Light that you fail to observe the
shadows. Please remember something that should be obvious: NDErs,
though they may have seen the Light, are still human and have human
failings. Not they, but only the Light should be exalted. So do not let your
enthusiasm for these teachings and for what the Light represents blind you
to possible excesses in its name.

That caveat aside, it must also be said that in many ways, the emerging
NDE community represents something approaching what in Buddhism—
just to stick with that tradition since we began with it (though, do not
worry, I am not myself any kind of crypto-Buddhist and do not have any
affiliation with any spiritual tradition or religious organization)—is called
a *sangha*. This means, in effect, a spiritual community of its own that is
drawn together out of its respect for and dedication to a particular set of
teachings. It would be an exaggeration to say that the NDE community—
as diverse and geographically separate as it is, and as dependent on cyber-

spatial communication as it will surely increasingly become—constitutes a *sangha* in any strict sense, but nevertheless, something like that has already developed in the last quarter of the twentieth century, and it is there for you, too, should you wish to make contact with it. The traditional aim of a *sangha*, of course, is to provide a setting in which the company of like-minded others can stimulate and deepen one's own spiritual practice. And this, quite apart from the specific resources listed in the Appendix, to which you may soon turn, it can do for you, too.

In fact, again in the Zen tradition, there is a saying that "after *satori* (or a first awakening to one's true nature), then practice can really begin." Likewise, in the context of this book, we could say that after so many exposures to the lessons of the Light and visions of the Light itself, we now understand why we practice and the necessity of practice, where practice here means *putting into practice what we have learned*. Not to do so is to have wasted a precious gift, which can only be realized by using it.

May the Light guide your every step and lead you to enlightened action in the world.

# Notes

## INTRODUCTION

1. One widely cited survey carried out by the Gallup organization in the early 1980s, for example, suggests that among the adult population of the United States alone, as many as *eight million* persons may have had this experience. For a discussion of these findings, see the book by George Gallup, Jr., *Adventures in immortality*.
2. In the United States, the best known of these investigations are to be found in my own books, *Heading toward Omega* and *The Omega Project*, and in such works as Charles Flynn's *After the beyond*, Phyllis Atwater's *Coming back to life*, and Melvin Morse's *Transformed by the light*. In England, Margot Grey was the first to examine this issue in her book, *Return from death*. In Australia, there are the books by Cherie Sutherland, *Transformed by the light* and *Within the light*. Finally, there is a recent report of these effects in Italy in the *Journal of Near-Death Studies*, "Extrasomatic emotions" by Emilio Tiberi.

## CHAPTER ONE

1. Laurelynn has since written a book about her NDE and the lessons it taught her: *Searching for home* (St. Joseph, MI: Cosmic Concepts, 1996.)

2. Laurelynn later clarified this passage for me, saying that this was her brother's message for her alone, and should not, in her opinion, necessarily be taken as a generalized proscription.
3. Morse is a well-known NDE researcher who has pioneered the study of NDEs in children.

## CHAPTER TWO

1. Richard Squires, "The meaning of ecstasy," *Gnosis Magazine, 33* (Fall, 1994), p. 69.
2. Ibid., p. 70.
3. Janice Miner Holden, "Visual perception during naturalistic near-death out-of-body experiences," *Journal of Near-Death Studies, 7* (Winter, 1988), pp. 107–120.
4. This interviewee later told me that after she recovered, she was able to go into the emergency room in order to confirm that the numbers she had seen on the machine were correct. She informed me that, indeed, they were, and that she told her anesthesiologist so shortly thereafter. However, at the time of her interview, I could only take her word for it, since it was no longer possible independently to check on this claim.
5. Kenneth Ring, *Heading toward Omega* (New York: Morrow, 1984), p. 42.
6. Ibid., p. 43.
7. Kenneth Odin Merager, "220 volts to my near-death experience." *Seattle IANDS Newsletter*, March–April, 1991.
8. Kimberly Clark, "Clinical interventions with near-death experiencers." In B. Greyson and C. P. Flynn (Eds.), *The near-death experience: Problems, prospects, perspectives* (Springfield, IL: Charles C. Thomas, 1984), pp. 242–255.
9. Ibid., p. 243.
10. Kenneth Ring and Madelaine Lawrence, "Further studies of veridical perception during near-death experiences." *Journal of Near-Death Studies, 11* (Summer 1993), pp. 223–229.
11. Kathy Milne, personal communication, October 19, 1992.
12. Joyce Harmon, personal communication, August 28, 1992.
13. Sue Saunders, personal communication, December 31, 1992.
14. See, especially, his book, *Recollections of death: A medical investigation* (New York: Harper and Row, 1982), Chapter 7. Also relevant is Sabom's first article on the subject, "The near-death experience: Myth or reality? A methodological approach," *Anabiosis, 1* (July, 1981), pp. 44–56.

## CHAPTER THREE

1. For example, Susan Blackmore has conducted an extensive search for such cases and finds the claims for them baseless. In my work with Madelaine Lawrence, we came to the same conclusion.

2. This hypothetical case appears at the beginning of Larry Dossey's book, *Recovering the soul: A scientific and spiritual search* (New York: Bantam, 1989), pp. 17–19. Dossey later confessed with some embarrassment to both Susan Blackmore and me, in separate correspondence, that he fabricated this case, but nevertheless believed at the time that such persons had in fact been interviewed by NDE researchers.

3. A brief popular account of our work has, however, already been published in an American periodical, *The Anomalist*. See Kenneth Ring and Sharon Cooper, "Mindsight: How the blind can 'see' during near-death experiences," *The Anomalist*, 5 (1997), pp. 28–40. A longer, more technical presentation of our findings has also recently been published in the professional literature. See Kenneth Ring and Sharon Cooper, "Near-death and out-of-body experiences in the blind: A study of apparent eyeless vision," *Journal of Near-Death Studies*, 16 (1997), No. 2, pp. 101–147.

4. Vicki's comment here is consistent with reports of persons who, having been blind all their life, undergo operations to restore their vision. Such suddenly sighted persons often find that the process of seeing is initially confusing and disturbing. Indeed, some of these individuals never adapt to the visual world and come to regret having had the new unwanted "gift" of sight thrust upon them.

5. Berström, personal communication, November 3, 1994.

## CHAPTER FOUR

1. In addition to *Closer to the light* (New York: Villard, 1990), Morse has also recently published a follow-up volume, *Transformed by the light* (New York: Villard, 1992), dealing mainly with the aftereffects of NDEs in children. Beyond these books, Morse, sometimes with colleagues, has published several seminal papers on this topic in the medical literature. Among them are M. Morse, "A near-death-experience in a seven-year-old child," *American Journal of Diseases in Children*, 137(1983), pp. 959–961; M. Morse, P. Castillo, D. Venecia, J. Milstein, and D. C. Tyler, "Childhood near-death experiences," *American Journal of Diseases in Children*, 140 (1986), pp. 1110–1114; M. Morse et al., "Near-death experiences in a pediatric population," *American Journal of Diseases in Children*, 139 (1985), pp. 595–600; and M. Morse, "Near-death experiences and death-related visions in children: Implications for the clinician," *Current Problems in Pediatrics*, 24 (1994), pp. 55–83.

2. I have based this account on Morse's book, *Closer to the light*, pp. 3–8, as well as additional information he has provided about his case in his article, "A near-death experience in a seven-year-old child."

3. R. Moody, *The light beyond* (New York: Bantam, 1988), Chapter 3, pp. 45–60.

4. Ibid., pp. 48–49.

5. William J. Serdahely, "A comparison of retrospective accounts of childhood NDEs with contemporary pediatric accounts," *Journal of Near-Death Studies*, IB, pp. 219–224.

6. Roxanne Sumners, *The wave of light* (Corvallis, Oregon: Agadir Press, 1994).
7. G. O. Gabbard and S. W. Twemlow, *With the eyes of the mind* (New York: Praeger, 1984), Chapter 9, pp. 154–166.
8. Ibid., pp. 154–156.
9. I have taken much of this account directly from a video made of this conference called *Transcending the limits, Seattle IANDS Newsletter*, 1993.
10. Morse himself gives a brief account of it in his book, *Closer to the light*, pp. 35–37.
11. The account of this case will be found in an article by Dr. Herzog and John T. Herrin, "Near-death experiences in the very young," *Critical Care Medicine*, 13 (1985), pp. 1074–1075.
12. Ibid., p. 1074.
13. A good introduction to this understanding of brain function is provided in Richard Restak's book, *The modular brain* (New York: Macmillan, 1994).
14. Grof is a Czech-born psychiatrist and psychoanalyst who was one of the founders of the field of transpersonal psychology in the late 1960s. He is best known for his research on the effects of psychedelic agents on human consciousness and for a form of nondrug experiential therapy called holotropic integration. He has written about his findings concerning perinatal experiences in his many books, including *Realms of the human unconscious* (New York: Viking, 1975), (with Joan Halifax) *The human encounter with death* (New York: Dutton, 1977), *Beyond the brain* (Albany, NY: SUNY Press, 1985), and *The adventure of self-discovery* (Albany, NY: SUNY Press, 1988).
15. David Chamberlain, *The mind of your newborn baby* (3rd ed.). Berkeley, CA: North Atlantic Books, 1998.
16. Ibid., p. 103.
17. Ibid., p. 104.
18. David Chamberlain, *Consciousness at birth: A review of the empirical evidence* (San Diego, CA: Chamberlain Publications, 1983), p. 34.
19. See his article, "The expanding boundaries of memory," *ReVision*, 12 (1990), pp. 11–20.
20. Chamberlain, *Consciousness at birth*, p. 35.
21. Chamberlain, "The expanding boundaries of memory," p. 18.
22. Chamberlain, *Consciousness at birth*, p. 43.

## CHAPTER FIVE

1. For bibliographic references to the major investigations of NDE aftereffects, please see note 2 in Chapter One.
2. I have presented some of my own findings along these lines in my last book, *The Omega Project* (New York: William Morrow, 1992). However, there is no dearth of them in the NDE literature. For intriguing accounts of this phenomenon by researchers, for example, see Melvin Morse's *Transformed by the light* (New York: Villard, 1992) and P. M. H. Atwater's *Beyond the light* (New York: Birch Lane, 1994). For a good autobiographical instance, see Dannion Brinkley's *Saved by the light* (New York: HarperCollins, 1994).

3. See, for example, my book, *The Omega Project*, Morse's *Transformed by the light*, Atwater's *Beyond the light*, and Cherie Sutherland's *Transformed by the light* (Sydney, Australia, 1992), for representative studies.
4. See *The Omega Project*, p. 278.
5. See Cherie Sutherland's *Transformed by the light*, pp. 128–129.
6. See, for example, the works previously cited by myself, Morse, and Atwater, in addition to the entire issue of the *Journal of Near-Death Studies*, 12(1), 1994, which is devoted to various neurological theories and speculations about the NDE, especially in connection with *kundalini*. Also, the article by Bruce Greyson, "Near-death experiences and the physio-kundalini syndrome," *Journal of Religion and Health*, 32(4), 1993, pp. 277–290, is most relevant here.
7. I first reported this effect in *The Omega Project*. Shortly afterward, Melvin Morse described virtually identical findings in his book, *Transformed by the light*. Most recently, P. M. H. Atwater has investigated this matter more carefully and has confirmed and extended the findings previously published by Morse and myself.
8. See, for example, the following sources: Michael Shallis, *The electric connection* (New York: New Amsterdam, 1988); Hilary Evans, *The SLI effect* (London: Association for the Scientific Study of Anomalous Phenomena, 1993); Albert Budden, *Allergies and aliens* (London: Discovery Times Press, 1994).
9. The most relevant studies here are mine and Atwater's, both previously cited.
10. Ring, *The Omega Project*, op cit., p. 277.
11. These studies are found in *The Omega Project*, Greyson (see note 6), and in Yvonne Kason's article, "Near-death experiences and kundalini awakening: Exploring the link," *Journal of Near-Death Studies*, 12(3), 1994, pp. 143–157.
12. There is already a small body of informed neurological opinion that holds that these subjective claims may well be justified or, at the very least, offers some degree of theoretical support for them. See, for example, Michael Persinger's paper, "Near-death experience: Determining the neuroanatomical pathways by experiential patterns and simulation in experimental setting," in Luc Besette (Ed.), *Healing: Beyond suffering or death* (Chabanel, Beauport, Quebec, Canada: MNH Publications, 1993), pp. 277–286. Also relevant is the article by Jean-Pierre Jourdan, "Near-death and transcendental experiences: Neurophysiological correlates of mystical traditions," *Journal of Near-Death Studies*, 12(3), 1994, pp. 177–200.
13. Indeed, at the end of her document, Mia recounted about twenty such specific examples for me, though I will omit mention of any of them here since they are not immediately relevant to our present concerns.

## CHAPTER SIX

1. Kenneth Ring: *Life at death* (New York: Coward, McCann and Geoghegan, 1980), p. 117.
2. Such episodes were described by 43 percent of their near-drowning victims, which is substantially higher than the figure of about 25 percent that is

generally cited as an across-the-board incidence level of the life review for NDEs in general. Noyes and Kletti's work will be found in "Panoramic memory: A response to the threat of death," *Omega, 8*(3), 1977, pp. 181–194. For a representative survey of the incidence of the life review generally, see the article by Bruce Greyson, "Near-death encounters with and without near-death experiences: Comparative NDE scale profiles," *Journal of Near-Death Studies, 8* (Spring, 1990), pp. 151–161.

3. Ring, *Life at death*, p. 116.
4. P. M. H. Atwater, *Coming back to life* (New York: Dodd-Mead, 1988), p. 36.
5. Noyes and Kletti, op. cit., p. 188.
6. For examples of some especially compelling cases, see Ring, *Heading toward Omega*, Chapter 7.
7. Ring, *Heading toward Omega*, p. 70.
8. Ibid., p. 67.
9. Ibid., p. 69.
10. Myra Ka Lange, "To the top of the universe," *Venture Inward* (May/June, 1988), pp. 40–45. (Myra Ka Lange was Minette Crow's *nom de plume* for this article.)
11. Ring, *Life at death*, p. 73.
12. Arvin S. Gibson, *Glimpses of eternity* (Bountiful, UT: Horizon, 1992), p. 281.
13. Ring, *Heading toward Omega*, p. 70.
14. Bruce Elder, *And when I die, will I be dead?* (Crows Nest, NSW, Australia: Australian Broadcasting Corporation, 1987), p. 24.

## CHAPTER SEVEN

1. I have taken this account from Sidney Saylor Farr's book, *What Tom Sawyer learned from dying* (Norfolk, VA: Hampton Roads, 1993), pp. 29–31. In adapting it for this book, I have made some minor alterations in content and punctuation and eliminated some redundancies, but have used Tom's words as much as possible. This book is unusually valuable, however, for its detailed descriptions of various episodes from Tom's life review, and I highly recommend it for this purpose, among others. For his life review material, see especially pp. 29–37.
2. This account is taken from my interview with Neevon Spring, May 20, 1994. At some points, I have altered his wording just slightly in order to eliminate a few of my clarifying questions.
3. Farr, op. cit., p. 33.
4. Ibid., p. 35.
5. P. M. H. Atwater, *Coming back to life*, p. 36.
6. Raymond A. Moody, *The light beyond* (New York: Bantam, 1988), p. 34.
7. The English writer, David Lorimer, has based one of his books, *Whole in one*, on precisely this point and argues that the NDE is helping to fashion a postmodern ethics of interconnectedness. Anyone interested in exploring the

ethical dimensions of this issue should certainly read Lorimer's thoughtful and impassioned work. Other writers have also dealt with this theme when discussing NDEs and the life review. The most probing discussions I have seen will be found in the late Darryl Reanny's *Music of the mind* (Melbourne, Australia: Hill of Content, 1994), Sogyal Rinpoche's *The Tibetan book of living and dying* (San Francisco: HarperCollins, 1992), and the late Michael Talbot's *The holographic universe* (New York: HarperCollins, 1991).

8. See her books, *Full circle* (New York: Pocket Books, 1990), with Lionel Bascom, and *Spiritual awakenings* (Deerfield Beach, FL: Health Publications, 1995).
9. Ring, *Heading toward Omega*, pp. 106–107.
10. Ibid., p. 106.
11. Farr, op. cit., p. 35.
12. Emily L. VanLaeys, "Life review revealed in near-death experience." *Venture Inward* (July/August, 1994), p. 51.

## CHAPTER EIGHT

1. See Chapter 4, especially pp. 100–103.
2. All these quotes are from *Heading toward Omega*, pp. 100–101.
3. Sutherland's findings are reported in *Transformed by the light*, pp. 134–135. And, incidentally, almost all of those who fail to report an increased level of self-esteem or self-worth state that there was no change in this regard for them.
4. I have actually taken these cases from another of Sutherland's books, *Within the light*, where she presents much more case history material on her interviewees for *Transformed for the light*. The comments I have cited come from her respondents, Moira, p. 192, and Patrick, p. 207.

## CHAPTER NINE

1. See, for example, D. Royse, "The near-death experience: A survey of clergy's attitudes and knowledge," *Journal of Pastoral Care*, 1985; Roberta Orne, "Nurses' views of NDEs," *American Journal of Nursing*, 1986; B. A. Walker and R. D. Russell, "Assessing psychologists' knowledge and attitudes toward near-death phenomena," *Journal of Near-Death Studies*, 1989; E. R. Hayes and L. D. Waters, "Interdisciplinary perception of the near-death experience: Implications for professional education and practice," 1989; Linda Barnett, "Hospice nurses' knowledge and attitudes toward the near-death experience," *Journal of Near-Death Studies*, 1991; L. J. Bechtel, A. Chen, R. A. Pierce, and B. A. Walker, "Assessment of clergy knowledge and attitudes toward the near-death experience," *Journal of Near-Death Studies*, 1992; L. H. Moore, "An assessment of physicians' knowledge of and attitudes toward the near-death experience," *Journal of Near-Death Studies*, 1994; Allan Kellehear and P. Heaven, "Commu-

nity attitudes towards near-death experiences: An Australian study," *Journal of Near-Death Studies*, 1989; and Allan Kellehear, P. Heaven, and J. Gao, "Community attitudes toward near-death experiences: A Chinese study," *Journal of Near-Death Studies*, 1990.

2. Charles Flynn, *After the beyond* (Englewood Cliffs, NJ: Prentice-Hall, 1986), p. 7.
3. Leo Buscaglia, *Love* (New York: Fawcett, 1982).
4. Flynn, op. cit., p. 7.
5. Kenneth Ring, *The Omega Project* (New York: Morrow, 1992).
6. This quarterly scholarly journal is published by Human Sciences Press, Inc., whose address is 233 Spring Street, New York, NY 10013-1578.
7. Bruce Greyson, "Near-death experiences and personal values," *American Journal of Psychiatry*, 140(5), 1983, pp. 618–620.

## CHAPTER TEN

1. Margot Grey, *Return from death* (London: Arcana, 1985), p. 134.
2. P. M. H. Atwater, *Beyond the light* (New York: Birch Lane, 1994), p. 132.
3. Kenneth Ring, *The Omega Project*, p. 278, and previously unpublished data.
4. Barbara Harris and Lionel C. Bascom, *Full circle: The near-death experience and beyond* (New York: Pocket Books, 1990).
5. See, for example, Kenneth Ring, *The Omega Project*; Melvin Morse and Paul Perry, *Transformed by the Light*; and P. H. M. Atwater, *Beyond the Light*.
6. Grey, op. cit., p. 136.
7. Paul Roud, *Making miracles* (New York: Warner Books, 1990).
8. Quotes are from a private tape of an interview conducted by Howard Mickel that he sent to me.
9. Grey, op. cit., p. 138.
10. Quotes are from a letter to me dated February 27, 1995.
11. I have written an account of it elsewhere, but respecting Gerald's wish for anonymity, I will not cite the reference here.

## CHAPTER ELEVEN

1. See my study, "The impact of near-death-experiences on persons who have not had them: A report of a preliminary study and two replications," *Journal of Near-Death Studies*, 13(4), pp. 223–235.
2. This figure comes from unpublished data from *The Omega Project*.
3. Ring, *Heading toward Omega*, p. 59.
4. Drumm, "Near-death experiences as therapy," *Journal of Near-Death Studies*, 11(2), 1992, p. 68.
5. Ibid., p. 69.
6. Drumm, "Near-death experiences as therapy: Part II," *Journal of Near-Death Studies*, 11(3), 1993, pp. 189–190.

7. Linda Barnett, "Hospice nurses' knowledge and attitudes toward the near-death experience," *Journal of Near-Death Studies*, 9(4), 1991, pp. 225–232.
8. Pamela Kircher, "Near-death experiences and hospice work," paper presented at the annual conference of the IANDS, 1993.
9. Marilyn Webb, *The good death* (New York: Bantam, 1997), p. 248.
10. Ibid., p. 248.
11. Dannion Brinkley, *Saved by the light* (New York: Villard, 1994) and *At peace in the light* (New York: HarperCollins, 1995).
12. John McDonagh, *Bibliotherapy with suicidal patients*, paper presented at the American Psychological Association, New York, 1979.
13. Ibid., p. 2.
14. See B. Greyson, "Near-death experiences and attempted suicide," which is also reprinted in the anthology edited by Greyson and Charles Flynn, *The near-death experience: Problems, prospects, perspectives*, pp. 259–266. Also relevant is his paper, "Near-death experiences precipitated by suicide attempts," *Journal of Near-Death Studies*, 9(3), 1991, pp. 183–188.
15. See Ring, *Heading toward Omega*, pp. 76–82.
16. Sutherland, *Children of light*, p. 6.
17. Ibid., pp. 6–7.
18. Guggenheim and Guggenheim, *Hello from Heaven!* (Longwood, FL: ADC Project, 1995), p. 292. I have changed the paragraphing for this and subsequent excerpts, but the content is unaltered, of course.
19. Ibid., pp. 299–300.
20. Ibid., p. 325.
21. See, for example, Lynne Ann DeSpelder and Albert Strickland, *The last dance* (Mountain View, CA: Mayfield, 1996), and Michael R. Leming and George E. Dickinson, *Understanding dying, death and bereavement* (New York: Holt, Rinehart and Winston, 1985), for some representative treatments in the literature on thanatology.

## CHAPTER TWELVE

1. Ring, *Heading toward Omega*, pp. 61–62.
2. Cassandra Musgrave, "The near-death experience: A study of transformation," *Journal of Near-Death Studies*, 15(3), 1997, p. 194.
3. Cherie Sutherland, *Transformed by the light* (New York: Bantam, 1992).
4. Carl Jung, *Memories, dreams, reflections* (New York: Vintage, 1961), p. 302.
5. For an alternative approach to the afterlife, see my essay, "Shamanic initiation, imaginal worlds and light after death," in G. Doore (Ed.), *What survives?* (Los Angeles: Tarcher, 1990).
6. For a recent attempt to do exactly this, see Leon Rhodes's recent book, *Tunnel to eternity: Beyond near-death* (West Chester, PA: Chrysalis, 1997), which uses the writings of the great Swedish sage and seer, Emanuel Swedenborg, to extend the insights of the NDE to the afterdeath realms, as depicted by Swedenborg.
7. From Robert Bly's, *The Kabir book* (Boston: Beacon, 1977), pp. 24–25.

## CHAPTER THIRTEEN

1. A fuller account of Mellen's NDE, in his own words, will be found in Lee W. Bailey and Jenny Yates's anthology, *The near-death experience: A reader* (New York: Routledge, 1996), pp. 39–52.
2. The most complete version of Howard Storm's NDE, in his own words, that I have seen is to be found in Judith Cressy, *The near-death experience: Mysticism or madness* (Hanover, MA: Christopher, 1994), pp. 19–34.
3. Ibid., p. 28. I prefer Cressy's interview to mine because in it, Howard speaks more directly to the issues I am concerned with here.
4. Norman Paulsen, *Christ consciousness* (Salt Lake City, UT: Builders, 1984).

## CHAPTER FOURTEEN

1. See Zaleski's book, *Otherworld journeys: Accounts of near-death experience in medieval and modern times* (New York: Oxford University Press, 1987).

# References

Atwater, P. M. H. *Coming back to life: The after-effects of near-death experience.* New York: Dodd and Mead, 1988.

Atwater, P. M. H. *Beyond the light: What isn't being said about the near-death experience.* New York: Birch Lane Press, 1994.

Bailey, Lee W., and Yates, Jenny (Eds.). *The near-death experience: A reader.* New York: Routledge, 1996.

Barnett, Linda. Hospice nurses' knowledge and attitudes toward the near-death experience. *Journal of Near-Death Studies, 9*(4), 1991, 225–232.

Bechtel, Lori J., Chen, Alex, Pierce, Richard A., and Walker, Barbara A. Assessment of clergy knowledge and attitudes toward the near-death experience. *Journal of Near-Death Studies, 10*(3), 1992, 161–170.

Bergström, Ingegard. Personal communication, November 3, 1994.

Blackmore, Susan. *Dying to live: Science and the near-death experience.* Buffalo, NY: Prometheus, 1993.

Bly, Robert. *The Kabir book.* Boston: Beacon, 1977.

Brinkley, Dannion. *Saved by the light.* New York: Villard, 1994.

Brinkley, Dannion. *At peace in the light.* New York: HarperCollins, 1995.

Budden, Albert. *Allergies and aliens.* London, England: Discovery Times Press, 1994.

Buscaglia, Leo. *Love.* New York: Fawcett, 1982.

Chamberlain, David B. *Consciousness at birth: A review of the empirical evidence.* San Diego, CA: Chamberlain Publications, 1983.

Chamberlain, David B. *The mind of your newborn baby* (3rd ed.). Berkeley, CA: North Atlantic Books, 1998.

Chamberlain, David B. The expanding boundaries of memory. *ReVision, 12,* 1990, 11–20.

Clark, Kimberly. Clinical interventions with near-death experiencers. In B. Greyson and Charles P. Flynn (Eds.), *The near-death experience: Problems, prospects, perspectives.* Springfield, IL: Charles C Thomas, 1984, 243–255.

Cressy, Judith. *The near-death experience: Mysticism or madness.* Hanover, MA: Christopher Publishing, 1994.

DeSpelder, Lynne Ann, and Strickland, Albert. *The last dance.* Mountain View, CA: Mayfield, 1996.

Dossey, Larry. *Recovering the soul: A scientific and spiritual search.* New York: Bantam, 1989.

Drumm, Deborah L. Near-death experiences as therapy. *Journal of Near-Death Studies, 11*(2), 1992, 67–70.

Drumm, Deborah L. Near-death experiences as therapy: Part II. *Journal of Near-Death Studies, 11*(3), 1993, 189–191.

Eadie, Betty. *Embraced by the light.* Placerville, CA: Gold Leaf Press, 1992.

Elder, Bruce. *And when I die, will I be dead?* Crows Nest, New South Wales, Australia: Australian Broadcasting Corporation, 1987.

Elsaesser Valarino, Evelyn. *On the other side of life: Exploring the phenomenon of the near-death experience.* New York: Plenum Press, Insight Books, 1997.

Evans, Hilary. *The SLI effect.* London: Association for the Scientific Study of Anomalous Phenomena, 1993.

Farr, Sydney Saylor. *What Tom Sawyer learned from dying.* Norfolk, VA: Hampton Roads, 1993.

Flynn, Charles P. *After the beyond: Human transformation and the near-death experience.* Englewood Cliffs, NJ: Prentice-Hall, 1986.

Gabbard, Glen O., and Twemlow, Stuart W. *With the eyes of the mind.* New York: Praeger, 1984.

Gallup, George, Jr. *Adventures in immortality: A look beyond the threshold of death.* New York: McGraw-Hill, 1982.

Gibson, Arvin. *Glimpses of eternity: Near-death experiences examined.* Bountiful, UT: Horizon, 1992.

Grey, Margot. *Return from death: An exploration of the near-death experience.* London: Arcana, 1985.

Greyson, Bruce. Near-death experiences and attempted suicide. *Suicide and Life-Threatening Behavior, 11*, 1981, 10–16.

Greyson, Bruce. Near-death experiences and personal values. *American Journal of Psychiatry, 140*(5), 1983, 618–620.

Greyson, Bruce. Near-death encounters with and without near-death experiences: Comparative NDE scale profiles. *Journal of Near-Death Studies, 8*(3), 1990, 151–161.

Greyson, Bruce. Near-death experiences precipitated by suicide. *Journal of Near-Death Studies, 9*(3), 1991, 183–188.

Greyson, Bruce. Near-death experiences and the physio-kundalini syndrome. *Journal of Religion and Health, 32*(4), 1993, 277–290.

Grof, Stanislav. *Realms of the human unconscious: Observations from LSD research.* New York: Viking, 1975.

Grof, Stanislav. *Beyond the brain: Birth, death and transcendence in psychotherapry.* Ithaca, NY: State University of New York Press, 1985.

Grof, Stanislav. *The adventure of self-discovery.* Ithaca, NY: State University of New York Press, 1988.

Grof, Stanislav, and Halifax, John. *The human encounter with death.* New York: E. P. Dutton, 1977.

Guggenheim, Bill, and Guggenheim, Judy. *Hello from heaven!* Longwood, FL: ADC Project, 1995.

Harris, Barbara, and Bascom, Lionel C.: *Full circle: The near-death experience and beyond.* New York: Pocket Books, 1990.

Hayes, E. R., and Waters, L. D. Interdisciplinary perception of the near-death experience: Implications for professional education and practice. *Death Studies, 13,* 1989, 443–483.

Herzog, David B., and Herrin, John T. Near-death experiences in the very young. *Critical Care Medicine, 13,* 1985, 1074–1075.

Holden, Janice Miner. Visual perception during naturalistic near-death out-of-body experiences. *Journal of Near-Death Studies, 7*(3) 1988, 107–120.

Jourdan, Jean-Pierre. Near-death and transcendental experiences: Neurophysiological correlates of mystical traditions. *Journal of Near-Death Studies, 12*(3), 1994, 177–200.

Jung, Carl G. *Memories, dreams, reflections.* New York; Vintage, 1961.

Kason, Yvonne. Near-death experiences and kundalini awakening: Exploring the link. *Journal of Near-Death Studies, 12*(3), 143–157.

Kellehear, Allan, and Heaven, Patrick. Community attitudes towards near-death experiences: An Australian study. *Journal of Near-Death Studies, 7*(3), 1989, 165–177.

Kellehear, Allan, Heaven, Patrick, and Gao, Jia. Community attitudes toward near-death experiences: A Chinese study. *Journal of Near-Death Studies, 8*(3), 1990, 163–173.

Kircher, Pamela. *Near-death experience and hospice work.* Paper presented at the annual conference of the International Association for Near-Death Studies, St. Louis, Missouri, June 27, 1993.

Lange, Myra Ka. To the top of the universe. *Venture Inward,* May/June, 1988, 40–45.

Leming, Michael R., and Dickinson, George E. *Understanding dying, death and bereavement.* New York: Holt, Rinehart and Winston, 1985.

Longaker, Christine. *Facing death and finding hope.* New York: Doubleday, 1997.

Lorimer, David. *Whole in one: The near-death experience and the ethic of interconnectedness.* London, Arcana, 1990.

McDonagh, John. *Bibliotherapy with suicidal patients.* Paper presented at the American Psychological Association, New York, 1979.

Merager, Kenneth Odin. 220 volts to my near-death experience. *Seattle IANDS Newsletter,* March–April, 1991.

Moody, Raymond A., Jr. *Life after life.* Covington, GA: Mockingbird Books, 1975 (now distributed by Bantam, New York).

Moody, Raymond A., Jr. *Reflections on life after life.* New York, NY: Bantam, 1977.

Moody, Raymond A., Jr. *The light beyond.* New York: Bantam, 1988.

Moore, Linda Hutton. An assessment of physicians' knowledge of and attitudes toward the near-death experience. *Journal of Near-Death Studies, 13*(2), 1994, 91–102.

Morse, Melvin. A near-death experience in a seven-year-old child. *American Journal of Diseases in Children*, 137, 1983, 959–961.

Morse, Melvin. *Closer to the light: Learning from children's near-death experiences.* New York: Villard, 1990.

Morse, Melvin. *Transformed by the light: The powerful effect of near-death experiences on people's lives.* New York: Villard, 1992.

Morse, Melvin. Near-death experiences and death-related visions in children: Implications for the clinician. *Current Problems in Pediatrics*, 24, 1994, 55–83.

Morse, Melvin et al. Near-death experiences in a pediatric population. *American Journal of Diseases in Children*, 139, 1985, 595–600.

Morse, Melvin et al. Childhood near-death experiences. *American Journal of Diseases in Children*, 140, 1986, 1110–1114.

Musgrave, Cassandra. The near-death experience: A study of spiritual transformation. *Journal of Near-Death Studies*, 15(3), 1997, 187–201.

Noyes, Russell, and Kletti, Roy. Panoramic memory: A response to the threat of death. *Omega*, 8(3), 1977, 181–194.

Oliver, Mary. *Dream work.* New York: Atlantic Monthly Press, 1986.

Orne, Roberta. Nurses' views of NDEs. *American Journal of Nursing*, 86, 1986, 419–420.

Paulsen, Norman. *Christ consciousness.* Salt Lake City, UT: Builders Publishing, 1984.

Persinger, Michael. Near-death experience: Determining the neuroanatomical pathways by experiential patterns and simulation in experimental settings. In Luc Bessette (Ed.), *Healing: Beyond suffering or death.* Chabanel, Beauport, Quebec, Canada: MNH Publications, 1993, 277–286.

Reanny, Darryl. *Music of the mind.* Melbourne, Australia: Hill of Content, 1994.

Restak, Richard. *The modular brain.* New York: Macmillan, 1994.

Rhodes, Leon. *Tunnel to eternity: Beyond near-death.* West Chester, PA: Chrysalis, 1997.

Ring, Kenneth. *Life at death: A scientific investigation of the near-death experience.* New York: Coward, McCann and Geoghegan, 1980.

Ring, Kenneth. *Heading toward Omega: In search of the meaning of the near-death experience.* New York: Morrow, 1984.

Ring, Kenneth. Shamanic initiation, imaginal worlds, and light after death. In Gary Doore (Ed.), *What survives? Contemporary explorations of life after death.* Los Angeles: Tarcher, 1990, 204–215.

Ring, Kenneth. Amazing grace: The near-death experience as a compensatory gift. *Journal of Near-Death Studies*, 10(1), 1991, 11–39.

Ring, Kenneth. *The Omega project: Near-death experiences, UFO encounters and mind at large.* New York: Morrow, 1992.

Ring, Kenneth. The impact of near-death experiences on persons who have not had them: A report of a preliminary study and two replications. *Journal of Near-Death Studies*, 13(4), 1995, 223–235.

Ring, Kenneth, and Cooper, Sharon. Mindsight: How the blind can "See" during near-death experiences. *The Anomalist*, 5, 1997, 28–40.

Ring, Kenneth, and Cooper, Sharon. Near-death and out-of-body experiences in the blind: A study of apparent eyeless vision. *Journal of Near-Death Studies*, *16*(2), 1997, 101–147.

Ring, Kenneth, and Lawrence, Madelaine. Further studies of veridical out-of-body perception during near-death experiences. *Journal of Near-Death Studies*, 11, 1993, 223–229.

Rinpoche, Sogyal. *The Tibetan book of living and dying*. San Francisco, CA: Harper-Collins, 1992.

Rogo, D. Scott. *Life after death: The case for survival of bodily death*. Wellinborough, Northampshire, UK: Aquarian Press, 1986.

Roud, Paul C. *Making miracles*. New York: Warner Books, 1990.

Royse, D. The near-death experience: A survey of clergy's attitudes and knowledge. *Journal of Pastoral Care*, *39*, 1985, 31–42.

Sabom, Michael B. The near-death experience: Myth or reality? A methodological approach. *Anabiosis*, *1*(1), 1981, 44–56.

Sabom, Michael B. *Recollections of death: A medical investigation*. New York: Harper and Row, 1982.

Serdahely, William J. A comparison of retrospective accounts of childhood NDEs with contemporary pediatric accounts. *Journal of Near-Death Studies*, 1991, 219–224.

Shallis, Michael. *The electric connection*. New York: Amsterdam, 1988.

Squires, Richard. The meaning of ecstasy. *Gnosis*, *33* (Fall), 1994, 68–71.

Stone, Ganga. *Start the conversation: The book about death you were hoping to find*. New York: Warner Books, 1996.

Sumners, Roxanne. *The wave of light: A quantum near-death experience*. Corvallis, OR: Agadir Press, 1994.

Sutherland, Cherie. *Transformed by the light: Life after near-death experiences*. New York: Bantam, 1992.

Sutherland, Cherie. *Within the light*. New York: Bantam, 1993.

Sutherland, Cherie. *Children of the light*. New York; Bantam, 1995.

Talbot, Michael. *The holographic universe*. New York: HarperCollins, 1991.

Tiberi, Emilio. Extrasomatic emotions. *Journal of Near-Death Studies*, *11*(3), 1993, 149–170.

VanLaeys, Emily L. Life review revealed in near-death experiences. *Venture Inward*, July/August, 1994, 51.

Walker, Barbara A., and Russell, Robert D. Assessing psychologists' knowledge and attitudes toward near-death phenomena. *Journal of Near-Death Studies*, *8*(2), 1989, 103–110.

Webb, Marilyn. *The good death: The new American search to reshape the end of life*. New York: Bantam. 1997.

Whitfield, Barbara Harris. *Spiritual awakenings: Insights of the near-death experience and other doorways to our soul*. Deerfield Beach, FL: Health Communications, 1995.

Zaleski, Carol. *Otherworld journeys: Accounts of near-death experience in medieval and modern times*. New York: Oxford University Press, 1987.

# Appendix A:
## Bibliography on NDE Literature

We give here a list of many of the books, and all of the best-known ones, that have been written in English about the NDE. In all but a few cases, Evelyn and I are familiar with these books, though that does not imply that we necessarily personally endorse them; however, you will find that many of these books are also included in the reference section for this volume. In offering this bibliography, we believed it would be helpful if we distinguished general treatments of NDEs from those books that are primarily testimonial or autobiographical in nature. Therefore, you may wish to consult each section separately for the type of reading material you are most interested to explore. In any case, we hope that you find our list a useful guide to what is available in NDE literature.

## GENERAL TREATMENT OF NDEs

Atwater, P. M. H. *Coming back to life: The after-effects of the near-death experience.* New York: Dodd and Mead, 1988.

Atwater, P.M.H. *Beyond the light: What isn't being said about the near-death experience.* New York: Birch Lane Press, 1994.

Bailey, Lee W., and Yates, Jenny L. (Eds.). *The near-death experience: A reader.* New York: Routledge, 1996.

Basford, Terry. *Near-death experiences: An annotated bibliography.* New York: Garland, 1990.

Becker, Carl B. *Paranormal experience and survival of death*. New York: State University of New York Press, 1993.

Berman, Phillip L. *The journey home: What near-death experiences and mysticism teach about the gift of life*. New York: Pocket Books, 1996.

Blackmore, Susan. *Dying to live: Science and the near-death experience*. Buffalo, NY: Prometheus, 1993 and London: Grafton/HarperCollins, 1993.

Cox-Chapman, Mally. *The case for heaven: Near-death experiences as evidence for the afterlife*. New York: G. P. Putnam's Sons, 1995.

Cressy, Judith. *The near-death experience: Mysticism or madness*. Hanover, MA: Christopher Publishing, 1994.

Elsaesser Valarino, Evelyn. *On the other side of life: Exploring the phenomenon of the near-death experience*. New York: Insight Books, Plenum Press, 1997.

Fenwick, Peter, and Fenwick, Elizabeth. *The truth in the light: An investigation of over 300 near-death experiences*. New York: Berkeley Books, 1997.

Flynn, Charles P. *After the beyond: Human transformation and the near-death experience*. Englewood Cliffs, NJ: Prentice-Hall, 1986.

Gallup, George, Jr. *Adventures in immortality: A look beyond the threshold of death*. New York: McGraw-Hill, 1982.

Gibson, Arvin S. *Echoes from eternity: New near-death experiences examined*. Bountiful, UT: Horizon, 1993.

Gibson, Arvin S. *Glimpses of eternity: Near-death experiences examined*. Bountiful, UT: Horizon, 1992 (4th ed., 1994).

Gibson, Arvin S. *Journey beyond life*. Bountiful, UT: Horizon, 1994.

Grey, Margot. *Return from death: An exploration of the near-death experience*. London: Arkana, 1985.

Greyson, Bruce, and Flynn, Charles P. (Eds.). *The near-death experience: Problems, prospects, perspectives*. Springfield, IL: Charles C. Thomas, 1984.

Hampe, Joann Christoph. *To die is gain: The experience of one's own death*. Atlanta, GA: John Knox, 1978.

Harpur, Tom. *Life after death*. Toronto: McClelland and Stewart, 1992.

Hill, Brennan (Ed.). *Near-death experience: A Christian approach*. Dubuque, IA: William C. Brown, 1980.

Kastenbaum, Robert J. (Ed.). *Between life and death*. New York: Springer, 1979.

Kastenbaum, Robert J. *Is there life after death?* New York: Prentice-Hall, 1984.

Kellehear, Allan. *Experiences near death: Beyond medicine and religion*. New York: Oxford University Press, 1996.

Kircher, Pamela M. *Love is the link: A hospice doctor shares her experience of near-death and dying*. Burdett, NY: Larson, 1995.

Kübler-Ross, Elisabeth. *Death is of vital importance: On life, death and life after death*. Barrytown, NY: Station Hill Press, 1995.

Lorimer, David. *Whole in one: The near-death experience and the ethic of interconnectedness*. London: Arkana, 1990.

Lundahl, Craig R. (Ed.). *A collection of near-death research readings: Scientific inquiries into the experiences of persons near physical death*. Chicago, IL: Nelson-Hall, 1982.

Lundahl, Craig R., and Widdison, Harold A. *The eternal journey: How near-death experiences illuminate our earthly lives*. New York: Warner Books, 1997.

Moody, Raymond A. *Life after life: The investigation of a phenomenon—survival of bodily death.* New York: Bantam, 1975.

Moody, Raymond A. *Reflections on life after life.* New York: Bantam, 1977.

Moody, Raymond A., and Perry, Paul. *The light beyond.* New York: Bantam, 1988.

Morse, Melvin, and Perry, Paul. *Closer to the light: Learning from children's near-death experiences.* New York: Villard, 1990.

Morse, Melvin, and Perry, Paul. *Transformed by the light: A study of the powerful effect of near-death experiences on people's lives.* New York: Villard, 1992.

Morse, Melvin, and Perry, Paul. *Parting visions: Uses and meanings of pre-death, psychic, and spiritual experiences.* New York: Villard, 1994.

Nelson, Lee. *Beyond the veil.* Orem, UT: Cedar Fort, 1988–1990, 3 vols.

Nelson, Lee. *NDE: Near-death experience.* Springville, UT: Cedar Fort, 1995.

Rhodes, Leon S. *Tunnel to eternity: Beyond near-death.* West Chester, PA: Chrysalis Books, 1997.

Ring, Kenneth. *Life at death: A scientific investigation of the near-death experience.* New York: Coward, McCann and Geoghegan, 1980 and Quill, 1982.

Ring, Kenneth. *Heading toward Omega: In search of the meaning of the near-death experience.* New York: William Morrow, 1984 and Quill, 1985.

Ring, Kenneth. *The Omega project: Near-death experiences, UFO encounters and mind at large.* New York: William Morrow, 1992.

Rogo, D. Scott. *The return from silence: A study of near-death experiences.* New York: Harper and Row, 1990.

Roszell, Calvert. *The near-death experience: In the light of scientific research and the spiritual science of Rudolf Steiner.* Hudson, NY: Anthroposophic Press, 1992.

Sabom, Michael B. *Recollections of death: A medical investigation.* New York: Harper and Row, 1982.

Sorensen, M. R., and Willmore, D. R. *The journey beyond life.* Orem, UT: Family Affair Books, 1988.

Steiger, Brad. *One with the light.* New York: Penguin Books, 1994.

Sutherland, Cherie. *Within the light.* New York: Bantam, 1993.

Sutherland, Cherie. *Children of the light: Near-death experiences of children.* New York: Bantam, 1995.

Sutherland, Cherie. *Reborn in the light: Life after near-death experiences.* New York: Bantam, 1995.

Top, Brent, and Top, Wendy. *Beyond death's door.* Salt Lake City, UT: Bookcraft, 1993.

Vincent, Ken R. *Visions of God from the near-death experience.* Burdett, NY: Larson, 1994.

Wheeler, David R. *Journey to the other side.* New York: Grosset and Dunlap, 1976.

Whitfield, Barbara Harris. *Spiritual awakenings: Insights of the near-death experience and other doorways to our soul.* Deerfield Beach, FL: Health Communications, 1995.

Whitfield, Barbara Harris. *Final passage: Sharing the journey as this life ends.* Deerfield Beach, FL: Health Communications, 1998.

Wilkerson, Ralph. *Beyond and back: Those who died and lived to tell it.* Anaheim: Melody Land Productions, 1977.

Wilson, Ian. *The after death experience.* New York: Quill, 1990.

Zaleski, Carol. *Otherworld journeys: Accounts of near-death experience in medieval and modern times*. New York: Oxford University Press, 1987.
Zaleski, Carol. *The life of the world to come: Near-death experience and Christian hope*. New York: Oxford University Press, 1996.

## TESTIMONIES AND AUTOBIOGRAPHICAL ACCOUNTS

Ajamila, Swami Prabhupada. *Second chance: The story of a near-death experience*. Los Angeles, CA: Bhaktivedanta Book Trust, 1992.
Brinkley, Dannion. *Saved by the light: The true story of a man who died twice and the profound revelations he received*. New York: Villard, 1994.
Brinkley, Dannion. *At peace in the light*. New York: HarperCollins, 1995.
Bubulka, G. *Beyond reality: A personal account of the near-death experience*. Fresno, CA: Grace Bubulka, 1992.
Chimes, Julie. *A stranger in paradise*. London: Bloomsbury, 1995.
Dennis, Lynnclaire. *The pattern*. Lower Lake, CA: Integral Publishing, 1997.
Duran, Laurel. *The blue cord*. Santa Fe, NM: DuirSoul Books, 1995.
Eadie, Betty J. *The awakening heart: My continuing journey to love*. New York: Pocket Books, 1996.
Eadie, Betty J., and Taylor, Curtis. *Embraced by the light* (Reprinted ed.). New York: Bantam Books, 1994.
Eby, Richard E. *Caught up into paradise*. Tarrytown, NY: Fleming H. Revell, 1978.
Eby, Richard E. *Tell them I am coming*. Tarrytown, NY: Fleming H. Revell, 1980.
Farr, Sidney. *What Tom Sawyer learned from dying*. Norfolk, VA: Hampton Roads Publishers, 1993.
Ford, Marvin. *On the other side*. Plainfield, NJ: Logos International, 1978.
Harris, Barbara, and Bascom, Lionel C. *Full circle: The near-death experience and beyond*. New York: Pocket Books, 1990.
Malz, Betty. *My glimpse of eternity*. Old Tappan, NJ: Spire Books, 1977.
Martin, Laurelynn G. *Searching for home: A personal journey of transformation and healing after a near-death experience*. Saint Joseph, MI: Cosmic Concepts Press, 1996.
McMurray, Mary V. *I died to remember*. Traverse City, MI: Mallard, 1991.
Preston, Betty. *Fear not*. Seattle, WA: Ibby Books, 1991.
Price, Jan. *The other side of death*. New York: Fawcett Columbine, 1996.
Ritchie, George, and Sherrill, E. *Return from tomorrow*. Waco, TX: Chosen Books, 1978.
Ritchie, George. *My life after dying*. Norfolk, VA: Hampton Roads Publishers, 1991.
Scarinci, Tom. *After the last heartbeat*. Chappaqua, NY: Christian Herald Books, 1980.
Sharp, Kimberly Clark. *After the light*. New York: William Morrow, 1995.
Sumners, Roxanne. *The wave of light: A quantum near-death experience*. Corvallis, OR: Agadir Press, 1994.
Yensen, Arthur E. *I saw heaven*. Pittsburgh, PA: There Is Light, 1974.

# Appendix B: Resource Suggestions

The following list of NDE-related audiocassettes and videos is by no means complete, but consists simply of the ones about which we have some information. Our listing here does not necessarily imply our endorsement, nor should it be inferred that those we do not include are not worthwhile.

## AUDIOCASSETTES

*Coming back to life*, by P. M. H. Atwater. Mithra Corporation, P.O. Box 447, Organ, NM 88052-0447; Fax (505) 382-9821.

*Embraced by the light*, by Betty J. Eadie. Simon and Schuster Audio, 1993.

*The awakening heart: My continuing journey to love*, by Betty J. Eadie. Simon and Schuster Audio, 1996.

*Finding the light*, by Raymond A. Moody. CD Audio Edition, 1994. (NB Publisher not known)

*The door to the secret city*, by Kathleen J. Forti. Contact: Kids Want Answers Too! 1544 Bay Point Drive, Virginia Beach, VA 23454 (NDEs explained for children).

Many audio cassettes of talks given at IANDS conferences may be obtained by writing to the following address: IANDS International Association for Near-Death Studies Inc., P.O. Box 502, East Windsor Hill, CT 06028-0502 (or E-mail at services@iands.org)

## VIDEOS

*A glimpse of forever*, by Nancy Maier. Contact Nancy Maier, P.O. Box 9373, Marina del Rey, CA 90295; (310) 822-6767.

*A message of hope.* Contact Counseling Institute, 40 Grand Avenue, Suite 304, Ft. Thomas, KY 41075; (606) 781-1344.

*Life after life*, featuring Raymond A. Moody. Contact Victor Rumore, President, Cascom Inc., 806 Fourth Avenue South, Nashville, TN 37210.

*Life after life*, by Reinee Pasarow. Contact New Age Industries, 9 Cupania Circle, Monterey Park, CA 91754; (213) 888-6938.

*Moment of truth.* This video can be ordered by sending a check for $19.95 to Jayne Smith, 71 Skull Creek Drive, 303B Indian Springs, Hilton Head Island, South Carolina 29926.

*Prophetic visions.* Contact Andrew Silver, 260 Beacon Street, Boston, MA 02116; (617) 266-6482.

*Round trip.* Contact Tim O'Reilly Productions, P.O. Box 1701, Branford, NJ 07016-1701.

*Shadows: Perceptions of near-death experiencers.* Contact Norman Van Rooy, 23632 Highway 99, Box 343, Edmonds, WA 98026; (206) 776-0152.

*The aftereffects of the near-death experience*, by P. M. H. Atwater. Contact P. M. H. Atwater, P.O. Box 7691, Charlottesville, VA 22906-7691. http://www.cinemid.com/atwater

*The near-death experience teaching unit.* Contact Theta Project, P.O. Box 618, La Jolla, CA 92038; (619) 456-0523. Text of basic introductory NDE material and video of Raymond A. Moody lecturing on the near-death experience.

*Transcending the limits: The near-death experience.* Produced by Joan Peter. Contact Seattle IANDS, Video Resource Center, IANDS, P.O. Box 84333, Seattle, WA 98124; (206) 525-5489. Recorded at the Pacific Northwest Conference on near-death experiences, produced for Seattle IANDS.

## MUSIC TO EVOKE NDE MOTIFS

The following list of music evocative of NDE themes has been compiled and furnished to us by a Canadian NDEr named Gilles Bédard, who is currently head of the Québec branch of IANDS. In making a tape of some of the selections, Gilles tells us that he "played the tape for many people who had had an NDE, and most of them were overwhelmed by the music, some even returning into the Light they encountered during their NDE." We ourselves can make no claims for these selections, but we are happy to pass Gilles's recommendations along to you for your possible interest.

David Darling: *Eight string religion* (Hearts of Space HS 11037-2)
Constance Demby: *Aeterna* (Hearts of Space HS 11051-2)
Constance Demby: *Novus magnificat* (Hearts of Space HS 11003-2)
Constance Demby: *Set free* (cut 4/11) (Hearts of Space HS 11016-2)
Robert Haig Coxon: *The inner voyage* (R.H.C. Productions CD-4401-2)
Robert Haig Coxon: *The silent path* (R.H.C. Productions CD-5501-2)
Jon Mark: *The land of Merlin* (Kuckuck 11094-2)
Jon Mark: *The standing stones of Callanish* (Kuckuck 11082-2)
Vidna Obmana: *The spiritual bonding* (Extreme XCD 027)
Vidna Obmana: *The Trilogy '90–'92* (Relic 14/Projekt/3 CD)
Steve Roach: *Dreamtime return* (Fortuna 18055-2/2 CD)
Steve Roach: *The magnificent void* (Fathom/Hearts of Space HS 11062-2)
Steve Roach: *Quiet music* (Fortuna 18043-2/2 CD)
Steve Roach: *Structures from silence* (Fortuna 17024-2)
Steve Roach and Vidna Obmana: *Well of souls* (Projekt 60/2 CD)
Therese Schoroeder-Sheker: *Rosa mystica* (Celestial Harmonies 13034-2)
Michael Stearns: *Encounter* (Hearts of Space HS 11008-2)

## INTERNET INFORMATION

Here, we list only a few selected sites relevant to NDEs. We might have listed many more but for two reasons: (1) We have not been able to check out many of these sites ourselves, and (2) because of the rapidity of change on the Internet, many Web sites might well no longer be located at the same address by the time this book comes to your attention. Accordingly, if you have Internet access, we simply suggest that you do your own surfing of the Web to check out the multitude of NDE-related sites for yourself, using such search engines as *Alta Vista, Excite, Webcrawler, Yahoo, Magellan,* and so on. Search using the key words *near-death experience* or *NDE.*

Specific Web sites of NDE relevance:

The International Association for Near-Death Studies (IANDS)
http://www.iands.org   This organization is discussed in the next section, but we recommend it as the place to start your search.

IANDS Seattle
http://www.serv.net/~seande/   This is a particularly active branch of IANDS and features an annotated NDE bibliography under the following address: http://www.serv.net/~seande/biblio.html

The Journal of Scientific Exploration
http://www.spiritweb.org/Spirit/nde-scientific.html   A collection of articles that appeared in the Journal of Scientific Exploration (SSE), presenting a review of near-death experiences.

P. M. H. Atwater
http://www.cinemid.com/atwater   Atwater is a well-known NDE researcher; some of her books are listed in our bibliography.

Bill and Judy Guggenheim, The ADC Project
http://www.after-death.com   This site provides further information about ADCs (afterdeath communications) as discussed in Chapter Eleven.

## THE INTERNATIONAL ASSOCIATION FOR NEAR-DEATH STUDIES (IANDS)

This association was established in 1981 by Kenneth Ring, Bruce Greyson, and John Audette, and since its founding has served as the principal organization in the world for disseminating information about and furthering the study of NDEs. It is a membership organization, open to anyone with an interest in NDEs, and publishes both a quarterly scholarly journal, *The Journal of Near-Death Studies*, and a quarterly newsletter, *Vital Signs*, for its members. It also sponsors regional, national, and international conferences on NDEs. It now has many local chapters in the United States as well as a number of branches in other countries of the world.

Below, we tell you how to reach its main headquarters in the United States, as well as provide the latest information on its branches worldwide. Be aware, however, that some of the specific information about the branches may have changed by the time you read this. If you would like to

determine whether there is an IANDS chapter near you in the United States or get a complete list of them, please write or call the main headquarters.
Head Office:
IANDS
PO Box 502
East Windsor Hill, CT 06028-0502
Tel: (860) 528-5144 Fax: (860) 528-9169
E-mail: Services@iands.org
Web: http://www.iands.org

## IANDS CANADA

*British Columbia*

Vancouver: Christopher Lovelidge, (604) 543-7446
Victoria: Christopher Kunz, 1269 Queensbury Avenue, Victoria, BC V8P 2E1; (250) 386-9208

*Ontario*

Ottawa: Marion Tapp, (613) 728-9199

*Québec*

Gilles Bédard a/s Inerson, CP 1370, Succ, Desjardins, Montréal, Québec, Canada H5B 1H3
Telephone/Fax: (514) 727-3827
E-mail: inerson@microtec.net
Web: http://www.microtec.net/~inerson/iandsqc.html

## IANDS INTERNATIONAL

*Australia*

Cherie Sutherland, School of Sociology, University of New South Wales, P.O. Box 1, Kensington, NSW, Australia
Linda Opolion, 123 Aquariuv Drive, Frankston, Victoria 3199; Telephone: (61) 03 977 66121
Fler Beaumont, P.O. Box 772, Brunswick Lower, Victoria 3057

## France

Marc-Alain Descamps, 18 rue Berthollet, 75005 Paris
Telephone: (33) 1 45 35 41 95
E-mail: IANDS-France@cao-vlsi.ibp.fr
Web: http://www.europsy.org/iands-france

## Belgium

Marie Haumont-Coolens
Place Van Meenen 2     Van Meenenplein 2
B-1060 Bruxelles         B-1060 Brussel
Telephone: (32) 253 73 531

## Germany

Michael Schroeter-Kunhardt
Professional address: Zentrum für Psychiatrie Weinsberg, D-74184 Weinsberg
Telephone: (49) 7134 750 Fax: (49) 7134 75334
Private address: Goerrestrasse 81, D-69126 Heidelberg, Telephone/Fax: (49) 6221 336 240

In 1997, the Nordic branch of IANDS decided to cease its activities temporarily. Nevertheless, the persons listed below, formerly involved with IANDS in this region, are still willing to be contacted by our readers in that part of the world.

## Sweden

Göran Grip Torbjörnsgatan 10, S-753 35 Uppsala
Telephone: (46) 18 24 23 23 or (46) 70 605 78 87 (cellphone)
Fax: (46) 18 24 23 24
E-mail: goran.grip@uppsala.mail.telia.com

## Finland

Sture Enberg, Skagbackvagen 18, SF65 870 Bjorkoby
Telephone: (358) 6 352 41 63
E-mail: sture.enberg@multi.fi

*Norway*

Rune Amundsen, Friheten, 6900 Flora
Telephone: (47) 57 74 01 07

## NDEr CONTACT LIST

In connection with this book, we asked some of the NDErs who appear in the preceding pages—and a few that do not—if they would be willing to be available for written contact with our readers. The following list consists of those persons who were amenable to this request. Whenever possible, we suggest you use a self-addressed, stamped envelope when writing to any of these persons listed.

Fler or Andrea Beaumont
P.O. Box 772
Brunswick Lower Victoria 3056
Australia
Telephone: (61) 03 9387 1634

Mellen-Thomas Benedict
P.O. Box 1848
Soquel, CA 95073
Telephone: (408) 427-5554

Nancy Clark is the founder and president of the Columbus, Ohio, IANDS Organization and is currently writing a book about her experiential encounter with the Light, and the insights she gained as a result of that experience. She can be reached at:

P.O. Box 835, Dublin, Ohio 43017

Patricia Coomes
1197 Ashover Drive
Bloomfield Hills, MI 48304

Elaine Durham
P.O. Box 17616
Holladay, UT 84117

Peggy Holladay
P.O. Box 5412
Shreveport, LA 71135-5412

Bonnie Long
6601 210th Avenue SW
Apt. 202-A
Lynnwood, WA 98036

Laurelynn Glass Martin
Light Endeavors
P.O. Box 366
Danielson, CT 06239

Helen Nelson
33 Barton Street
Torrington, CT 06790

Judy Poehler
318 West 105th Street
New York, NY 10025

Virginia Rivers
801 Wildabon Avenue
Lake Worth, FL 33853
E-mail: ginnyl@gate.net or
    trivers@gate.net

Jayne Smith
P.O. Box 21005
Hilton Head Island, SC
    29905-1005

Carolyn Talmadge
Continuing Education Department
College of Marin
835 College Avenue
Kentfield, CA 94904

Steve Tomsik
2000 Montego Avenue
Apt. 150
Escondido, CA 92026
E-mail:stomisk@connectnet.com

Cullen Wheelock
1855 Coyote Point Drive
Colorado Springs, CO 80904
E-mail: Cullen@poisys.net

# Index